POLAND
A HISTORICAL ATLAS

by
Iwo Cyprian Pogonowski

REVISED EDITION

DORSET PRESS
New York

Acknowledgments

I am grateful to my wife Magdalena for her help and patience during the period in which I have dedicated 3300 hours of work for the actual preparation of *Poland, a Historical Atlas*. I owe a debt of gratitude to all those who were willing to review the texts, maps and graphs of this atlas.

In particular I thank Dr. Richard Pipes, professor of history at Harvard University and former director of East European and Soviet Affairs in the National Security Council, for donating long hours to review the texts and give frequent consultations; Dr. Joseph Wieczynski, professor of history at Virginia Polytechnic Institute and State University, editor-in-chief of the 50-volume *Modern Encyclopedia of Russian and Soviet History,* for making readily available the necessary data and giving consultations; Dr. Z. Anthony Kruszewski, professor and chairman of political science at the University of Texas in El Paso, for giving many consultations, providing important data and for preparing the multilingual glossary of geographic names used in this atlas; Dr. Aleksander Gella, professor of sociology at the University of New York in Buffalo, for generously giving consultations on sociological history of Poland and providing important materials and references; Dr. Jacek Jedruch, author the *Constitutions, Elections and Legislatures of Poland, 1493–1977,* for consultations and important materials; Dr. Jan Karski, professor of government at Georgetown University, School of Foreign Service, for consultations on the format and organization of the Atlas; Dr. Konstantin Kolenda, Professor and Chairman of Philosophy at the Rice University, Houston, Texas for checking the accuracy of the text as related to Copernicus, Polish rationalists, Locke and Jefferson; Dr. Norman Davies, Chairman of the History Department, at the School of Slavonic and East European Studies, University of London, for consultations and help; Dr. Richard Lukas, professor of history at Tennessee Technological University and author of a number of books on Poland, for consultation on English terminology for Polish constitutional acts; the Rev. Ronald Modras, associate professor, Dept. of Theological Studies, Saint Louis University, for evaluation of texts and suggestions; Dr. Robert B. Frary, professor and assistant director of the Learning Resources Center at Virginia Polytechnic Institute and State University, for reviewing of texts and consultations on organization of the atlas; Dr. Mieczyslaw Maneli, professor of Political Science at Queens College, for consultations and materials. Mr. Dan H. Pletta, University Distinguished Professor Emeritus, Virginia Polytechnic Institute and State University, for reviewing and proofreading texts; Mr. Emil Skibinski, of Medicus Educational Foundation, for extensive proofreading of texts; the Kosciuszko Foundation and Jozef Pilsudski Institute of America, for promptly making available materials on the modern history of Poland; the office of Polish American Congress in Washington D.C., for help in contacting prominent Polish scientists in the United States; Mr. Henry Brzezanski of the Library of Congress, for a generous help in obtaining important data; Mr. Wojciech Zalewski, curator for Slavic and East European collections of the Stanford University libraries, for help in evaluating sources and materials on modern Polish history; Ms. Dina Abramowicz, librarian of YIVO Institute for Jewish Research, for supplying me with reprints of "Statut Kaliski of 1264" and other important materials on Jews in Poland; Ms. Krystyna M. Olszer, associate editor of "The Polish Review" of the Polish Institute of Arts and Sciences of America, for her help; Ms. Anna H. Bobak of the Ford Foundation for consultation on philology and history of Polish literature; Mr. Boleslaw T. Laszewski, national commander of the Association Veterans of Polish Armed Forces and vice-president of the Bicentennial Publishing Corporation of New York for his help in collecting coats-of-arms of Polish towns in full heraldic colors; the Rev. Lenard F. Chrobot, president of St. Mary's College in Orchard Lake, for providing materials on Polish Catholics in the United States; Dr. Zbigniew Brzezinski, National Security advisor under President Carter, professor of government, Columbia University, counselor, Center of Strategic and International Studies, Georgetown University; and Mr. Jan Nowak, national director of Polish American Congress and former director of the Polish section of Radio-Free Europe for supplying the original text of the secret Soviet-German pact on friendship and cooperation forming Hitler-Stalin partnership and the original map on partition of Poland in 1939, which includes signatures of Stalin, Molotov and Ribbentrop.

This edition published by Dorset Press,
a division of Marboro Books Corporation,
by arrangement with Hippocrene Books, Inc.
1989 Dorset Press

ISBN 0-88029-394-2
(formerly ISBN 0-87052-282-5)

Printed in the United States of America
M 9 8 7 6 5 4 3 2 1

To my late father Jerzy Pogonowski who inspired my interest in languages and history and was the author of many works. In 1941 Gestapo men came to arrest him. They called him the "Jewish Ambassador in Warsaw" because of his protests against Nazi treatment of the Jews. He was one of many Christians arrested for helping the Jews in Warsaw.

CONTENTS

HOW TO USE "POLAND: A HISTORICAL ATLAS"

Readers interested in Poland's history, can use this atlas as an introductory textbook. For readers who wish to discuss published views on Poland, this atlas can serve as a source for appropriate quotations. This atlas can also serve as an orientation book to follow and evaluate reading material dealing with Poland such as James Michener's epic "Poland," for example, or even the current reportage.

Readers who want to know Poland's past in terms of a long perspective, can use the following summaries:

Readers who want to know, in more detail, the course of Poland's history, please turn to page 269 for the:

Readers, who wish to follow in detail the important developments of Poland's past, will find them in the sequence of the maps and graphs of this atlas starting on page 47 as well as in the:

FOREWORD

THE KNOWLEDGE OF POLAND'S HISTORY in the English-speaking world is fragmentary, vague, and often distorted. Textbooks used in secondary schools mention the partitions of Poland in the 18th century but fail to present Poland's contributions to the development of European civilization. This subject of great importance and interest has been neglected and misunderstood. Few people realize how many times Poland has determined the course of European history and civilization. Recently Poland single-handedly—with more hindrance than help from the West—delayed for a quarter of a century the expansion of Soviet Communism into eastern and central Europe. Only rare individuals are familiar with Poland's quest for democracy and representative government that marked the 1,000 years of Polish history.

In recent years several excellent works have been published such as Norman Davies' *God's Playground, A History of Poland*, Jacek Jedruch's *Constitutions, Elections, and Legislatures of Poland, 1493–1977*, Norman Davies' *White Eagle, Red Star, the Polish-Soviet War, 1919–1920*, Richard M. Watt's *Bitter Glory, Poland and Its Fate, 1918–1939*, Jan Karski's *The Great Powers and Poland, 1919–1945*, Richard C. Lukas' *Forgotten Holocaust, 1939–1944*, Steven Zaloga and Victor Madej's *The Polish Campaign, 1939*, and Wladyslaw Kozaczuk's *Enigma, How the German Machine Cipher Was Broken, and How It Was Read by the Allies in World War Two*. The last book, published by University Publications of America, Inc., documents Poland's most important contribution to the Allied victory over Nazi Germany.

Iwo Pogonowski contributes to these most valuable efforts a pictorial perspective which should prove very helpful to familiarize the English-speaking readers with the history of Poland.

Poland, a Historical Atlas illustrates Poland's millennium within Western Christianity. In a condensed and graphic form it presents the sequence of historic events which shaped the Polish national character and set of values, such as the love of liberty and individualism, devotion to democratic legality, toleration, and, above all, self-determination and national independence. The atlas shows the setting in which these values were formulated in the middle ground of Europe during the period when Poland was ruled by the largest political leadership community of free citizens anywhere and later during the relentless struggle for independence and liberty.

Pogonowski's historical atlas includes 180 maps and 14 diagrams preceded by a comprehensive essay entitled "Poland the Middle Ground," which is followed by a 1,000 year "Chronology of Polish Constitutional and Political Development"—a unique compilation in the English language. The chronology also includes details of 19th and 20th century Polish history. Next the text on "Poland's Indigenous Democratic Process" documents the uniqueness of the early modern Polish civilization. A short summary of the evolution of Polish identity concludes the introductory texts.

The Atlas begins with eight maps that show Poland in the context of Western civilization during the last 1,000 years. It covers the building of the nation under the hereditary monarchy (c.840–1370), the rise of east-central Europe under the leadership of Poland—first during the era of the multinational commonwealth (1370–1569) and then during the first century of the Polish Nobles' Republic (1569–1795). The atlas shows the vulnerability of Poland's open parliamentary government during the Republic as she faced a deluge of invasions and the rise of the political machines of her large landholders. It describes the degradation of the Republic in the face of foreign subversion. It leads the reader through the struggles for national independence during the period of partitions (1795–1918), the era of the Second Polish Republic (1918–1945), ending with betrayal by the West and the creation in 1944 of the Third Polish Republic, the People's Poland in the Soviet Bloc.

An appendix on "Prehistory and Language Evolution" provides a comparative study of prehistory with linguistic evidence. Illustrated with 28 maps and four diagrams, it describes the roots of the Poles and, indeed, of all the other Slavs.

Graphs, diagrams, and tables provide information on the first and second Polish dynasty including marital alliances and a table of ten general elections to the Polish throne and thereby to the office of the chief executive of the Republic of Poland-Lithuania. Graphic presentations give convenient summaries of such studies as the number of Polish-speaking people within the population of Europe during the last millennium, or the Vistula grain trade as an index of Poland's economic and political fortunes during the last medieval and the early modern periods.

Extensive consultations with a number of authorities on Poland and Slavic Europe conducted by the author helped to design and update Pogonowski's atlas. These consultations were generously given by such prominent specialists as Richard Pipes, Jan Karski, Richard Lukas, Aleksander Gella, Jacek Jedruch, Z. Anthony Kruszewski, Mieczyslaw Maneli and many others.

The atlas constitutes a convenient reference book on Polish roots and history. In just a few pages and with unusual economy of words this book presents a huge amount of information about Poland's history in a logical and concrete way. It places Poland within the panorama of the European continent. A complete index of names and events together with a multilingual glossary of geographic locations provide for convenience in the use of this atlas. It will be a great addition to our libraries and bring greater recognition to the Poles.

Aloysius A. Mazewski
President
Polish American Congress

POLAND THE MIDDLE GROUND

THE HISTORY OF POLAND, and of other countries, has followed a pathway which was only one of many possible. History, as it has occurred, has resulted from the interplay of political forces and human choices within particular geographic, cultural, and socio-economic realities. Thus, the history of nations is not only a sum of long-range historical processes which make up successive epochs or eras, but it is also an intricate and intriguing chain of unpredictable events.

The historical processes are often suggested by hindsight analyses which also serve to justify them. Such justification of recorded events makes them appear as if they "had" to happen—as if they were preordained by inevitable "laws of history." Contrary to this notion, each of the past events was no more than just one of countless alternatives which were realistically possible. For this reason and because of accidental events and the capricious will of individuals, the history of all nations can not be repeated and therefore is unique.

The fortunes and misfortunes of Poland and other nations are also shaped by such critical factors as the ability of a central government to govern and to maintain a sufficient military strength in order to protect the well-being and way of life of the people it is supposed to serve.

The history of Poland is the history of the middle ground of Europe, not only in a geographical sense, but also culturally and spiritually. Therefore, a survey of the history of Poland must include an analysis of important cultural and geopolitical facts that influenced the fate of the Polish nation.

The root of Polish self-perception and patriotism, which is the unifying force that forms Poles into a nation, is steeped in the remote past, when the Polish ethnic character and culture started to evolve. This unifying love, so essential to the very existence of any national identity, acquired a unique character throughout Poland's history, beginning with the maturity of the Polish monarchy by the end of the 10th century through the next one thousand years of the quest for a representative government, democracy, and freedom for all.

The two most important elements that shaped the course of Polish history are the geopolitical location on the open plain in the middle ground of Europe and the fundamental set of values which directed the decisions of the men who led the Polish state. They made decisions based on their understanding of the Polish national past as it impacted on the everchanging reality of the present. Each critical time, at more than a dozen turning points ranging from the 966 A.D. conversion to western Christianity through the 1385 founding of the great multinational Commonwealth, to the 1980 founding of Solidarity, their decisions could have been different.

Like leaders of men the world over, Polish leaders were subject to limitations resulting from what could be called "the evolutionary law of history," namely, that men never are equal to the task of leadership as they tend to overreach themselves. Thus, men never fully achieve their intended results because they are fallible. Men are handicapped by not knowing exactly their own and their country's situations. This condition makes men basically irrational. Men act out their fears and emotions because at the time they make their decisions, their factual information is rarely complete and, what is worse, their decisions taken with the best of intentions often contribute to calamities for their people.

The geographic location of Poland's ethnic area is half-way between the Urals and Portugal, just west of the central meridian of Europe. This central geographic area became the linguistic and cultural middle ground when speakers of Western and Eastern Indo-European language groups met there. Today the Polish language is the northwesternmost of the Eastern Indo-European languages in Europe.

Archaeological studies suggest that during the early medieval period, Polish ethnic-area settlements acquired a more self-sufficient and independent character than those settlements to the east and west of Poland. The transition from east to west produced a unique settlement pattern in the middle ground of the continent. This settlement pattern led to an early tribal democracy.

For the last thousand years, Poland has been the easternmost member of western Christianity. Conversion to Christianity made Poland a religious and cultural middle ground between the Slavs and Germans, western and eastern Slavs, western and eastern Christianity, Christians and Moslems, and also between Roman and Greek alphabets.

As early as the 14th century Poland rejected forever the idea that the political power of a hereditary monarch comes from God. The turning point of the evolution of Poland's representative form of government came in 1370 at the end of the 530-year reign of the hereditary Piast (pyast) dynasty, when throughout Europe the kings were threatened by the power of feudal aristocracy.

West of the Elbe River, the dilemma of royal power was solved by the growth of towns which became junior partners of the king in political struggle against aristocracy. This partnership laid the foundation for western European absolutism while the prosperous towns became a thirsty market for the Polish wheat.

Poland had the most numerous lower and middle nobility in Europe and the king allied himself with them in order to limit the power of aristocracy. Poland was becoming a unique democracy of the nobility and the most militarized society of the European continent. Thus, the democratic process in Poland encompassed Europe's largest political nation of free citizens. It was located in the wide open middle ground of Europe and it was geopolitically much more exposed than was the Alpine home of the Swiss or the island home of the British, both of which also were to develop their own experiments in democratic government.

The voluntary unions of Poland and Lithuania, established first in 1385 and concluded for peaceful cooperation and mutual security, created the most tolerant nation of its time in all of Europe. Among the great powers of Europe, Poland became the leader in 16th century science, philosophy and moderate political theory, establishing Europe's only true representative form of government based on the democratic process. From 1374 to 1795 Poland was governed by the world's largest political nation of free citizens. A 500-year process, begun in 1385, started Polonization of the leadership community and middle class of Lithuania, Byelorussia, and Ukraine. In 1569 the Union of Lublin transformed the Polish-Lithuanian Commonwealth into a formal republic.

By the end of the 15th century, national and regional parliaments became catalysts of social and cultural life in Poland, a role played in the rest of Europe by the royal court and the town. The Polish law, *Neminem Captivabimus*, of 1425 was equivalent to the English Act of Habeas Corpus of 1679 and preceded it by 250 years. In 1493 the Polish parliament became bicameral. The first Polish constitution of 1505 gave parliament the supreme power and kings, elected for life, became successive chiefs of the executive branch of the Polish government.

Poland became a sanctuary for Jews in medieval Europe during the mass murders and almost total eviction of the Jews from Western Europe. The European Jews were saved from extinction in Poland. There the Jewish people were given, for four hundred years ending in 1795, unique self government and legislative institutions during the entire period between the Sanhedrin of antiquity and Knesset of the State of Israel. For nearly 500 years Poland was the home of the world's largest Jewish community, which constituted an autonomous Yiddish-speaking nation within the Polish state—a nation within a nation.

Among the native leaders of the Polish Renaissance, the Golden Age of Poland, was Nicolas Copernicus (1472–1543), in Polish Mikolaj Kopernik (mee-ko-way ko-per-neek). His alma mater, the University of Krakow, had an excellent college of astronomy, then the best in all of Europe and located in the most tolerant and free society on the European continent. There Copernicus discovered the structure of the solar system. The Copernican calendar was proven to be accurate within two minutes of the correct year's length—an amazing accuracy considering the condition of European science in early 16th century.

Copernican heliocentric theory was circulated in his *Commentariolus* in 1510 and published in 1543 in *De Revolutionibus Orbium Coelestium*. Copernicus published in 1526 *Monetae Cudende Ratio* on stabilization of currency, in which he discovered the law of currency, later named in England after Thomas Gresham (1519–1579).

Copernicus served as administrator of Warmia in northern Poland, military commander and finance minister; he was a trained astronomer, mathematician, economist, lawyer and medical doctor. He made important contributions in each of these fields including the inception of bread buttering, which improved European diet.

Copernicus moved the leadership of philosophical thought of Western civilization from the Mediterranean basin into the northern middle ground of Europe. The philosophical implications of the great Copernican discovery were fundamental. The idea that the Earth is a stationary and flat central area in the universe, on which the human drama of personal salvation goes on without privacy under the eyes of God and his angels, was shaken irreparably. Eventually it became apparent that life on earth is a thin surface-effect on a minor celestial body traveling through cosmic space at a high speed.

The age-old human yearning for safety and stability was destroyed by the realization that the Earth is not immovable or the largest celestial body, central in the cosmos. The Copernican universe brought home, as no other idea in the history of the human thought, the frightening realization that all existence is in a permanent flux of ever-changing and ever-becoming.

Twenty years after the Copernican revolution the rationalist philosophy was founded in Poland in 1562. It was published in 1661 in Amsterdam in the monumental *Biblioteca Fratrum Polonorum*. Polish rationalist philosophy formed the basis of the world view of such philosophers as John Locke (1632–1704) whose thinking was fundamental in formulation of the American Declaration of Independence.

Poland created a unique civilization which was in many respects in advance of medieval and early modern Europe and which became a major center of development of civil liberties and a pioneer of the representative form of government. The Polish Republic, called in Polish *Rzeczpospolita* (zhech-pospo-lee-ta) which means "a republic," was by far more republican both in structure and in spirit than the constitutional monarchies of England and Sweden. She was the very opposite of the absolutist systems of Russia, France, Austria, and Spain.

The Polish Ministry of Public Education was established in 1773. It was the first in Europe. The second Polish constitution was passed on May 3, 1791. It was modern and it was the first formal constitution in Europe. The Constitution of May 3, 1791, was the first in Europe that voluntarily granted extension of civil rights held by the political nation of the noble class to townspeople and in a more diluted form to the peasantry. Polish politicians had much in common with their contemporaries in America such as Thomas Jefferson, George Washington and the other founding fathers of the United States. Poland was the only major country which was a republic (1569–1795) until the founding of the United States of America.

The new ideas introduced in the middle ground of Europe in the 16th century by the Polish Republic were modern even by the standards of the 20th century. They are fundamental to contemporary political theory: general elections, the social contract between government and the citizens, the principle of government by consent, personal freedom and civil rights of the individual, freedom of religion, the value of self-reliance, and prevention of the growth of authoritarian power of the state.

Erosion of the Republic began when a deluge of invasions in the 17th century ruined the economy and shifted the political power from the lower and middle gentry to the owners of rapidly expanding huge estates. This paralyzed the progress of reforms necessary for updating the constitution of 1505. Instead of broadening the democratic process, reverse trends were set in motion. The condition of the peasant serfs worsened. A number of rebellions broke out for diverse reasons, ranging from the civil rights of the Ukrainian Cossacks to opposition to constitutional reforms.

Poland, with the largest number of citizen-soldiers in Europe produced for centuries brilliant military victories on her western and eastern frontiers. These victories were won over the German invaders in the 10th, 11th, 15th, and 16th centuries and over the Moslem Ottoman Empire and its vassals in the 15th, 16th, and 17th centuries. Thus, Poland gained a reputation as the bulwark of Christianity. However, the wars with the Turkish Empire exhausted the military might of Poland. Shortly afterwards the Polish military establishment was critically and irreparably subverted during the years 1697–1717.

The central government of Poland was weakened while foreign interference and subversion, aimed at fostering anarchy in the Republic, grew in strength, especially after the Russians were able to seize control of the eastern Ukraine. The Polish national catastrophy of partition came by the end of the 18th century paradoxically at the time of national rebirth and constitutional reforms. In 1795 Poland disappeared from the map of Europe and the Polish state ceased to exist.

The abrupt fall of this unique Polish civilization threw the Poles into a dark age of tyranny and a century of struggle as they sought to preserve their national identity under the onslaught of the new Prussian and Russian empires. Both Prussia and Russia deprived the Poles of their proud tradition of freedom and civil rights. Until this time, Poland had government-from-below, controlled by provincial legislatures. This form of government was brutally replaced by an oppressive rule-from-above by foreign governments.

Polish people preserved the memory of moral and cultural values from the past great-power status during the Commonwealth (1385–1569) and Republic (1569–1648). The tradition of Poland's high spiritual values, freedoms, and basic vitality encouraged the Poles to fight for a rebuilding of the Polish State despite partitioning. However, the Poles were aware that the annexations of one million square kilometers of the old Republic cemented the anti-Polish alliance of the partitioning powers in 1795.

The history of Poland, the middle ground of Europe, witnessed periods of great political power and even greater cultural and social progress. These achievements provided Poland with a rich heritage in freedom that later became the cultural and moral means to defend herself against the two new European powers that did not have this tradition. Both Russia and Prussia considered subversive the very nature of the democratic process and the republican institutions which became Polish national tradition.

In order to preserve Poland's culture, and even the nation itself, an independent education in her history and language became essential as Prussia and Russia proceeded systematically to purge all knowledge of Poland from the cultural and political history of Europe and to suppress the Polish language. Knowledge of the past strengthened Polish national consciousness and helped to preserve such social values as human dignity, patriotism, freedom, democracy, toleration, and striving for truth. Polish literature achieved great artistic heights while preserving the glorious and tragic periods in Poland's history.

Christianity, the very foundation of European civilization, became a fortress which replaced the obliterated Polish state. Christianity became a refuge of the Eternal Poland, as the church-state relations changed to one between Church and the Polish people. The Poles turned to the Church like victims of an assault who, facing mortal danger, enter a temple in the hope of saving their lives. The Catholic Church acquired a new role, as the tormentors of Poland were Prussian Lutherans and Russian Orthodox (first Byzantine and now Communist). The Catholic Church was strengthened as Catholics became the core of the Polish nation, and a popular notion developed that "Polish" meant "Catholic." This did not change the fact that Polish patriotism, like patriotism everywhere else, is a freely chosen obligation of loyalty towards one's people, and therefore includes persons of different religious and world views.

When the Polish middle ground was lost between anarchy and tyranny, the spiritual survival of Poland, in spite of the physical destruction of the old Republic, was seen by the Poles as a victory in defeat. The very preservation of a Polish national identity and culture, in confrontation with brutal policies under the Prussian and Russian occupation during the 19th century, was also a victory.

The prototype of the Polish state left by the old Republic was difficult to restore in the 20th century. Poland, reborn in 1918, once again lived up to her best military traditions when her armies defeated the Bolsheviks in 1919 and 1920 and prevented them from joining the German communists. Despite the lack of support from Western democracies, Poland prevented the spread of communism into Western Europe. Located in the middle ground between Hitler's Germany and Stalin's Russia, Poland lasted as a sovereign state for only 20 years, until 1939.

Failure to revive the old Polish federation with the Lithuanians, Byelorussians, and Ukrainians created a territory that neither coincided with the original Polish ethnic lands nor those of the old Republic of 1569–1795. The population of the Second Polish Republic between the wars included 35 percent minorities who were difficult to integrate.

The rebirth of the Polish Republic brought a flourishing of literature, innovative theater and fine arts. Polish scientists were among the world leaders in mathematics, early computer science, chemistry, physics, biology, archaeology, anthropology, sociology and political history. Cultural and economic integration of the Poles in the three areas of former partitions was accomplished. A central industrial region was added to the existing industries. Polish engineers were among the pioneers of aircraft design and production. The new and modern port of Gdynia was built. And these were but a few of the outstanding achievements of the twenty short years of Poland's independence, which included the consequences of the Great Depression on the 30s.

In 1939, when the British were pressing Poland to cooperate as an underling with the Soviets, the Poles answered: "The Soviets plan to subvert the very soul of Poland while the Germans intend to destroy the Polish people." The Poles refused to be subjugated by one of their totalitarian neighbors in return for a worthless protection from the other. In this sense the answer by the Polish foreign minister to the British turned out to be prophetic.

The partnership of Hitler and Stalin against Poland started World War II. This world war brought to Poland the worst catastrophy of her 1000-year history and the Poles were faced with extinction. The Germans perpetrated the holocaust on the prostrated Polish territory. This time, in spite of the bravery of Polish soldiers, Poland could not save her people, Jews and Christians alike. The Germans destroyed three million Polish Jews and inflicted huge and irreparable losses on the Polish nation itself. Over six million Polish citizens perished in World War II, approximately five million were killed by the Germans and one million lost their lives as a result of the Soviet invasion.

After the Nazi terror, which was by far fiercer and lasted longer in Poland than anywhere else in Europe, postwar Poland emerged as a people's republic with an incomplete sovereignty and a feeling of defeat, in spite of the allied victory over Germany. Poland was reorganized in 1945 on the original lands of the Piasts, but this time on the basis of Yalta agreements between the Soviet Union, the United States and England; she became part of the postwar Soviet Bloc.

Massive resettlements after World War II created in Poland the most homogenous population anywhere in Europe. Polish people resisted the Sovietization program imposed upon them. After all armed resistance to Soviet supremacy was suppressed from 1944 to 1947, major strikes and riots caused minor and temporary changes in the Polish government. Since 1976 growth of organized political opposition to the pro-Soviet regime in Poland led to the founding of the massive labor and social movement called Solidarity. It was founded in 1980 and sixteen months later crushed in December of 1981.

The Solidarity movement was nonviolent. Solidarity represented an ideological middle ground of moderation. It was based on the patriotism and courage of the Polish people and their loyalty to Poland's democratic ideals. Solidarity intended to ease the totalitarian grip of the regime controlled by the Soviets and tried to bring to Poland freedom and human dignity. Solidarity was a phenomenal mass movement that spread with unusual speed and eventually included some 14 million people from the industrial and rural areas.

Solidarity was born when an economic and ecologic crisis was imminent. Post-war reconstruction and industrial expansion reached a peak in 1972–1973. Poland became the world's tenth largest industrial economy. The Soviets coerced the Poles to invest in heavy industry, rather than in high technology, much more suitable for Poland. The Soviets also coerced the Poles to use Soviet style over-centralization. This resulted in an ecological catastrophy and a massive squandering of national resources such as raw material, industrial equipment and production, and more importantly the labor force—which includes in Poland a large number of engineers (equal to that in West Germany).

The ground water table fell to catastrophically low levels in the areas of heavy industry. Water shortages became widespread. Only five percent of water in Poland's rivers and streams is not toxic. The southern Baltic, of which Polish coastal waters are a part, is one of the most polluted seas on earth. Acid rain and industrial dusts ruined the forests. Seventy percent of *Puszcza Jodlowa* (poosh-cha yod-wo-va), the central national park, is already destroyed. Loss of forests causes violent and uncontrollable floods. Soviet plans put the protection of environment at the bottom of their priorities. The result has been declining health of the Polish population, as is clearly shown by recent government statistics.

Rebuilding from the ecological and economic crisis of 1980–1985 in the presence of a foreign debt of about thirty billion dollars requires lessening of the power monopoly of the communist regime by accepting the basic socio-economic demands made by Solidarity. Then the Polish nation could work with self-reliance, self-management of enterprises and, what is very important, generate maximum possible self-financing. Had it been done in 1980, the tremendous enthusiasm generated by the rise of Solidarity would not have been wasted. Brutal humiliation of the Polish people in the name of Soviet Union would have been avoided. The enthusiasm and accomplishments that the Poles have shown in rebuilding devastated post-war Poland gives an idea of the wasted potential.

Solidarity demonstrated the scope and maturity of the Polish national consciousness. It broke for good the forty-year-long continuity of official Communist distortions of Polish history, both past and present. It enhanced the political identity and national aspirations of Poland. Solidarity established an international awareness of the problems and issues which face the Polish people today. The very existence of Solidarity and the short-lived atmosphere of freedom it brought constitutes an important spiritual and moral victory in the Polish quest for national independence and democracy. Thus, Poland was not only the political and military middle ground between Russia and Germany through the 19th century, World War I and World War II; more recently the Polish nation became the middle ground between the ideologies of the East and West.

Poland is here to stay, judging by the permanence of Polish culture, which is one of the important cultures of Europe, located in the middle of the continent. The cultural history of Poland constitutes an uninterrupted and original achievement which, unfortunately, has not been reflected in her political history. However, the spirit of the Polish nation lives on with the knowledge that the Poles have done great things together and have the will to do them again.

CHRONOLOGY OF POLAND'S CONSTITUTIONAL AND POLITICAL DEVELOPMENT

POLISH CONSTITUTIONAL ACTS PRIOR TO YEAR 1569

Hereditary Monarchy (c.840–1370)—First Acts Limiting the Power of the Throne

c.840 Founding of the Piast (pyast) Dynasty by Chrosciszko (khrosh-cheesh-ko), Prince of the Polanians.

966 Conversion to Latin Christianity of the court of Mieszko I (c.921–992), the ruling Monarch of Poland, by his own free will.

1000 Establishing of Polish Metropolitan See of Gniezno—a formal church hierarchy during pilgrimage to Poland of the Holy Roman Emperor Otto III. He recognized political equality of Italy, France, Germany and Poland and brought with him the papal decision to crown Boleslaus I as King of Poland.

1018 Peace of Bautzen (Budziszyn) ending 14-year war with Germany, leaving Lusatia and Milzenland in Poland.

1025 Coronation of Boleslaus I (967–1025) as King of Poland followed by coronation of Mieszko II (990–1034).

1031 First German-East Slavic alliance against Poland of the Holy Roman Emperor and Grand Duke of Kievian Rutheno-Russian State.

1076 Coronation of Boleslaus II (c.1040–1081) who for a short time achieved imperial status in Central and Eastern Europe.

1116 Writing of the Chronicle by Gallus Anonimus.

1138 Testament Act of Boleslaus III (1085–1138), initiation of the "principate" period of fragmentation of Piast realm 1138–1295.

1180 Act of Leczyca, Kazimierz II Sprawiedliwy—Casimir II (1138–1194), giving up the right to inherit property of church dignitaries and exempting peasants of the church-owned villages from the duty of giving transportation to state officials; act given in return for church's political support.

1215 Founding of the Apostolic See of Prussia by Konrad I of Mazovia (1138–1247), for conversion of the Prussian pagans and bringing them under his political influence.

1220 Chronicle of Wincenty Kadlubek (veen-tsen-ti kad-woo-bek).

1228 Act of Cienia, Wladyslaw III Laskonogi—Ladislas III (1161–1231), promising to preserve "just and noble laws according to the council of the bishops and barons" in return for succession to the throne of Krakow.

1228 Act of Kruszwica, Konrad I founding of temporary fief of Chelmno of the German Brethren known as Teutonic Knights in return for conversion of the Prussians to Christianity. Polish temporary grant falsified in 1234 by the German Brethren to read as "permanent" thus becoming the "legal" foundation of the German Monastic State in Prussia independent of both the Roman Empire of the German Nation and of Poland. (In 1701 Brandenburg renamed itself Kingdom of Prussia to become a new and independent political entity in Germany).

1241 First Mongol Invasion (battles of Tursk, Chmielnik, and Legnica).

1242 Act of Incorporation of the first Polish municipality in Wroclaw.

1264 Act of Kalisz, Boleslaw Pobozny—Boleslaus the Pious (1221–1279), guaranteeing a General Charter of Jewish Liberties which became the basis of development of a Jewish sanctuary in Poland and creation of Yiddish-speaking autonomous Jewish nation based on the Talmudic Law (until 1795); establishing Jewish courts for the Jews and one tribunal for matters involving Christians and Jews; exemption from slavery and serfdom; no Jewish obligation for defense of Poland or to speak Polish.

1291 Act of Lutomysl, Waclaw II (1271–1305), guaranteeing civil rights of the nobles of Krakow and Sandomierz region during the struggle for the Polish throne, to strengthen his claim through female succession to the Piast dynasty.

1295 Restoration of Polish Kingdom, coronation of Przemyslaw II (1257–96).

1343 Treaty of Kalish, the Order of German Brethren in Prussia, known as the Order of Teutonic Knights, recognizing the King of Poland as its founder.

1346–1347 Codification of the Polish Common Law by Kazimierz Wielki, Casimir the Great (1310–1370), in Wislica for Lesser Poland and in Piotrkow for Greater Poland; uniformly extending Jewish liberties throughout Poland as a distinct legal, national, religious, and cultural Judeo-Germanic language group; arrival of waves of Jewish refugees from Germany creating in Poland and later in Polish lands within the Russian Empire the world's largest Jewish community (until World War I); establishing punitive assessments for towns in case of anti-Jewish activities—half of the money to pay for damages to the Jews and half to the state treasury; banning of ritual murder accusations against Jews (brought to Poland by German immigrants). Polish economy becoming capable of supporting a rapidly growing population and providing a steady surplus for trade (a situation not reached in central Russia until the middle of the 19th century).

1348 Treaty of Namyslow—ceding of Silesia to Bohemia—Bohemian renunciation of claims to the Polish throne (German immigrants in Silesian towns supported Bohemian claim because Bohemia was the Czech part of the German Empire).

1355 Act of Buda, Ludwik I, Louis I (1326–1382), confirming all previous acts and privileges in order to secure his succession to the Polish throne and to overcome the weakness of his female succession to the Piast dynasty.

1356 Founding of the Supreme Court for Urban Affairs in Krakow by King Casimir the Great.

1364 Founding of the University of Cracow by King Casimir the Great after long negotiations with Pope Urban (Charter of Foundation providing at first for one chair in the liberal arts, two chairs in Medicine, three in Canon Law, and five in Roman Law); Wieliczka salt mines were to provide a quarterly income of the new university.

Negotiated Royal Succession—Electoral Monarchy (1370–1572) and the Evolution of the Constitutional Monarchy (1370–1493)

1374 Act of Koszyce, Ludwik I bestowing taxing authority on regional legislatures, reducing taxes, promising to nominate local people to territorial offices, limiting obligation of military service to national territory, promising payment for military service and injuries outside of the national territory, guaranteeing inviolability of the territory of Corona Regni Poloniae, or the Kingdom of Poland, in return for the right of succession to the Polish throne. Strengthening of the power of regional legislatures called "Sejmiki" (sey-mee-kee) and defining the noble estate of about 10 percent of population and crystalizing the estates system in Poland. Reconfirmation of the indigenous parliament in form of regional legislatures based on democratic process. Noble immunities granted.

1381 Act of Cracow, Ludwik I reducing Church land taxes in return for acceptance of succession of his daughter to the Polish throne.

1385 Union Act of Krewo, Jogaila, Jagiello, the Grand Duke of Lithuania, committing himself to convert Lithuania to Latin Christianity and unite with Poland all Lithuanian and Ruthenian lands and to recover Polish territories lost to the Germans in exchange for marriage to Polish Queen Jadwiga and coronation as a Catholic King of Poland.

1386 Act of Cracow, Wladyslaw Jagiello, Ladislas Jogaila (c.1350–1434), before coronation confirming the 1374 Act of Koszyce.

1387 Act of Wilno, King Wladyslaw Jagiello bestowing hereditary ownership of land and freedom from taxation by the local princes on newly-converted Catholic Lithuanian nobles, the boyars.

1388 Act of Piotrkow, King Wladyslaw Jagiello increasing the civil rights of nobility and clergy further limiting royal power in Poland.

1413 Union Act of Horodlo, King Wladyslaw Jagiello, following Polish-Lithuanian victory over German Monastic State of the Teutonic Knights in 1410, uniting by personal union Poland and Lithuania, establishing territorial office of wojewoda (vo-ye-vo-da) or provincial governor, initiating a new administrative and defensive organizational model for central and eastern Europe while Polish families extended the use and privileges of their coats of arms to Lithuanian and Ruthenian clans.

1414–1418 Council of Constance, Pawel Wlodkowicz, Polish ambassador, president of the University of Cracow, proposing seventeen basic theses of international law: Licence to convert is not a licence to kill or expropriate.

1422 Act of Czerwinsk, King Wladyslaw Jagiello issuing a ban on confiscation of private property, *Nec bona recipiantur,* by promising not to allow the confiscation of privately held property without court sentence based on written law and by excluding officials of the crown from judgeships. Refusal to answer a call to arms to be punished by confiscation of property.

1423 Statute of Warka, King Wladyslaw Jagiello enlarging the Act of Czerwinsk of 1422 by inclusion of burghers and free peasants; also abrogating the hereditary rights of bailiffs or *soltys* (sow-tis) (*Schultheiss* in German).

1425 Act of Brzesc of Kujawy, King Wladyslaw Jagiello spreading to all provinces uniform civil rights in return for recognition of succession right of his sons to the Polish Crown.

1430 Act of Jedlno, King Wladyslaw Jagiello strengthening the civil rights of nobility and clergy in return for a promise to elect one of his sons as King of Poland and incorporation of the Grand Duchy of Lithuania into the Polish Commonwealth; organizing of provincial government of Podolia at Kamieniec.

1433 Act of Cracow, equivalent to the English act of Habeas corpus of 1679 and preceding it by 246 years, King Wladyslaw Jagiello guaranteeing personal freedom of the citizens under protection of the courts of law; it is known as the law *Neminem captivabimus nisi iure victim.* The 1422–33 Acts constituted the first in Europe formulation of the due legal process guaranteeing inviolability of citizen's person who was not caught in the act of committing a crime. This due process was the basis of the legal system in Poland all the way through the period of European absolutism. The middle nobility allied with the royal court winning the power struggle against huge land owners—democracy of the nobility (10 percent of population) led by the middle nobility acting as the middle class of the political nation of free citizens.

1434 Act of Troki, Zygmunt, Grand Duke of Lithuania (?–1440), including in the Polish civil rights the gentry of Halicia (Galicia) and Podolia.

1440 Act of Confederation of Prussian nobility and towns aginst the yoke of the German Monastic State of the Teutonic Knights and for incorporation in freedom into the Polish Commonwealth.

1440 Act of Wilno, abrogation of the Polish-Lithuanian Union.

1446 Act of Wilno, King Kazimierz IV Jagiellonczyk (1427–1492), agreeing to reign in Poland and Lithuania as two equal countries in a "brotherly union" and confirming the existing civil rights in both countries.

1447 Act of Grodno, King Kazimierz Jagiellonczyk spreading Polish type civil rights to the Lithuanian and Ruthenian nobility.

1453 Act of confirmation of Jewish liberties specified first in 1264.

1454 Act of Incorporation of Prussia into the Polish Crown by King Kazimierz Jagiellonczyk after a revolution against the yoke of the German Monastic State of the Teutonic Knights by the Prussian Union of Polish and German speaking population of Prussia.

Formation of the National Bicameral Parliament (1454–1493), an Indigenous Polish Development and the Maturing of an Original Polish Civilization in Early Modern Europe

1454 Act of Nieszawa, King Kazimierz IV Jagiellonczyk officially confirming the existence of Seymik (sey-meek) or regional legislature in each district with jurisdiction to approve every military mobilization and the right to name four candidates for local judiciary of which one would be nominated by the King to a vacant post. This limited the power of aristocracy in favor of the middle nobility. Beginning of transformation of unicameral regional legislature with an open attendance into an orderly system of representation in a bicameral national parliament—maturity of representative form of government in Poland. Indigenous Polish democratic process based Seymiks or regional legislatures where ordinary citizens had a dominant voice as long as the lower and middle nobility were winning the power struggle against landed aristocracy. Seymiks became platforms for political emancipation and a source of information about the affairs of state for the ordinary citizen. Seymiks created the means for mutual consultations through duly elected representatives equipped with a real and clear mandate. It was the beginning of reshaping of Polish monarchy into a republic of the nobility which represented about 10 percent of population (in some regions up to 20 percent and eventually numbering one million citizens).

1457 Act of Gdansk, King Kazimierz Jagiellonczyk bestowing self government and trading and defense fleet privileges on Gdansk, Elblag (Elbing), and Torun recently freed from domination by the German Monastic State of the Teutonic Knights or German Armed Brethren.

1463 Co-sponsorship by Poland, Hungary, and Bohemia of the earliest in Europe international charter for peace, similar to the United Nations. The full text surviving in the Polish state records (*Metryka Koronna* of 1463).

1475 *Pro Republicae Ordinatione* political program of Jan Ostrorog, Wojewoda of Poznan, against papal power, for right to appeal from local Church courts, for taxing of the Church for national defense, for improvement of the civil rights of the burghers and peasants, and for limitation of power of aristocracy.

1479 Founding of the Obrona Potoczna (ob-ro-na po-toch-na)—Current Defense of 2000 to 4000 men mobile force against Crimean Tartars, acting as a terrorist vanguard of the Turkish Moslem Empire since 1475, called the "hornets nest," raiding yearly Ukraine and Red Ruthenia and turning southern Ukraine into Wild Plains.

1480 Twelve-volume Polish history by Jan Dlugosz (dwoo-gosh), (1415–1480).

1485 Act of Cracow regulating the standing of Jewish craftsmen in the guilds (organized Jewish communities, the Kahals attacking separate Jewish guilds trying to enforce its own rigid control).

1488 Printing of the first Digest of Polish law.

POLAND A CONSTITUTIONAL MONARCHY (1493–1569)

1493 Maturity of Polish Constitutional Monarchy—Bicameral National Parliament the *Seym Walny* (seym val-ni), composed of *Izba Poselska* (eez-ba po-sel-ska) or Chamber of Deputies, presided over by speaker or marshal, and Senate presided over by the King.

An important step in the indigenous Polish development of the representative form of government which lasted uninterrupted until 1795. The beginning of Polish Constitutional Monarchy (1493–1569) followed by the First Polish Republic (1569–1795). The year 1493 marked the beginning of 160 years of successful parliamentary activity of the Seym lasting until a crisis caused by the first use of a veto power *(liberum veto)* of an individual deputy in 1652.

1494 Act of Seym ratifying incorporation of the Duchy of Zator and Oswiecim and confirming local laws of Prussia.

1497 Act of Piotrkow, King Jan Olbracht enlarging the rights of nobility at the expense of burghers and peasants; appropriation of funds for construction of multi-story artillery bastion (the largest in Europe) called *barbican* in front of St. Florian Gate in Cracow.

1499 Union Act of Wilno further uniting Poland and Lithuania at the request of Lithuania faced with war against Russia.

1501 Union Act of Mielnik, King Aleksander Jegiellonczyk yielding to aristocracy assigning to the Senate the exclusive right to elect and control the king who would be disobeyed if he tried to establish a "tyrannical rule" violating the will of the Senate; establishing of election ordinance.

1504 Seym of Piotrkow abrogating the Union Act of Mielnik, placing crown estates and properties under partial control of the Chamber of Deputies, prohibiting one person from holding more than one office; establishing of the office of grand hetman, or defense minister, administrator of the armed forces and head of the military court.

1505 Constitution Seym of Radom, passing of the first Polish constitution *Nihil novi* "nothing new about us, without us" meaning that nothing new will be decided in Poland without concurrence of the Senate and Chamber of Deputies composed of the representatives of the basic units of legislature—the regional or county diets: the Seymiks. The new constitution prohibited the political nation of free citizens to occupy themselves with commerce and crafts under the penalty of loss of civil rights. General Charter on Jewish Liberties confirmed. The Seym gradually becoming the supreme political power in the Polish Commonwealth. Seym's approval of new laws required; however, in practice the King alone or in cooperation with the Senate could still decree many new regulations which then increased the area of existing laws under the jurisdiction of the Seym. Growth of its parliamentary experience made the Seym all powerful.

1506 Act of Seym codifying the Articles of War.

1508 Codex of Cracowian City Legislation by Baltazar Behem (1460–1508).

1509 Act of Seym replacing internal tolls by border custom duty; first bestowing of nobility on a Jewish convert, Abraham Ezofowicz, Treasurer of Lithuania, first of hundreds of Jewish converts admitted to the ranks of nobility and given Polish names.

1510 Act of the Seym prohibiting bequests of property to the Church in the last wills and testaments in order to limit the political and economic power of the clergy.

1517 Act of Seym ratifying the Statute on Mining; report to legislative committee for reform of currency by Nicolas Copernicus defining measures to counteract fraudulent minting of Polish currency by the Hohenzollerns of Brandenburg; first stating that "bad money chases good money out of circulation" (before Thomas Gresham was born in England in 1519).

1519 Chronicle of the Poles by Maciej Miechowita (c. 1457–1523).

1520 Statutes of Torun and Bydgoszcz, obligating the peasants to work one day a week without pay as a form of rent for the use of land. Codification of electoral functions of the regional legislatures, the Seymiks; establishing of joint artillery and military engineering command; European price revolution reaching Poland, bringing towns to the peak of their importance while inflation grew to 300 percent and wages doubled over the next 100 years; Jewish immigrants from the west permitted to settle in all parts of Poland, elect elders and administer affairs themselves.

1521 Act of Seym—Prussian Code of Law confirmed.

1523 Act of Seym, *Formula Processus*, code of courts of law standardizing legal procedures throughout the Polish Commonwealth, the earliest in Europe. In France, for example, such a code was first instituted some 270 years later during the French Revolution, Roman letters replacing Gothic, making printing more readable.

1524 Act of Seym revising instructions for tax collection.

1525 Act of Seym establishing courts for the mining industry; secularization of the Monastic State of the Teutonic Order; missed opportunity to evict from Prussia the remnants of the

Teutonic Order; Albrecht of Hohenzollern (1490–1568) paying an act of homage in the market of Cracow and recognizing the suzerainty of the Polish king over Prussia; first pact in Europe between a Catholic king and a Protestant vassal duke.

1526 Act of Monetary Reform in Poland introducing system based on the Polish unit *zloty* (zwo-ti) meaning golden coin; *red zloty* or dukat equals 3.5 grams of gold; regular Polish zloty equals 30 grosz, each grosz equals .77 grams of silver; also each zloty equals 5 szostaks equals 10 trojaks; each grosz equals two half grosz equals 3 szelag equals 6 ternars equals 18 denars. Polish monetary system adopted in Prussia in 1528 and in Lithuania in 1569 (at the time of the founding of the Republic of Poland-Lithuania at the Seym of Lublin).

1526 Act of Seym ratifying incorporation of Mazovia.

1527 Decree on subordination of hetman polny or field commander to the grand hetman or defense minister; separate appropriations for artillery; mass production of gun barrels in foundries of Cracow, Lwow, and, after 1540, Wilno.

1530 Establishing of a Jewish Supreme Tribunal at Lublin.

1532 Formation of a committee of the Seym for codification of all Polish common and written laws—the earliest such legislative project in Europe; introduction of codification procedure based on a public debate based on a printed proposal made by the National Seym and sent to every one of the regional legislatures for examination and evaluation. Written report from each Seymik was to be sent back to the Seym to be processed by the law codification committee. Seym Act prohibiting peasants from moving without consent of their landlord; prohibition to employ runaway serfs and to give them citizenship in towns; penalties for runaway serfs specified.

1535–1538 Respect of the Law Political Program for strict execution of the laws for reform and modernization of the government; return of illegally held crown lands by the lords; prohibition from holding more than one office by one person; for a closer union with Lithuania; for establishing of a national church, etc.

1537 Protest Seym during mobilization for war with Moldavia; demands for adoption of Respect of the Law Program by the King's government.

1538 Seym Act ordering sale of farming properties by the burghers.

1540 Seym Act revising electoral apportionment.

1543 Seym Act attaching serf to the land and denying the right of serfs to free themselves from servitude by cash payments. Proscribing serfs to the land of their origin as *glebae adscriptus*.

1544 Seym Act codifying the ordinance for courts.

1549 Decree on the Jewish autonomy to assess and to collect their poll tax which was determined in bargaining sessions with officials of Polish treasury; maturity of autonomous Jewish legislative institutions in Poland, unique between Sanhedrin of antiquity and the Knesset of the State of Israel. Jewish population exceeding 200,000.

1550 Seym Act strengthening the prohibition to perform bughers' occupations by the gentry under the penalty of losing their civil rights.

1551 Publication of political program *De Republica Emendada* by Andrzej Frycz Modrzewski (1503–72) for legal equality of all, against oppression of the peasants and inadequate laws to protect them, against wars of aggression, etc. (reprinted throughout Europe).

1552 Seym Act suspending for a year execution of church court sentences by the county chiefs, the starostas; passing resolutions against heresy.

1553 Seym Act establishing ordinance for impeachment tribunals of the Seym.

1556 Seym Act constraining ecclesiastical jurisdiction.

1558 Seym Act establishing of Post Office.

1560 Act of Gdansk founding a privateer navy for blockade of Russian Narva River trade (in 1571 the Danes destroyed this fleet).

1561 Act of Wilno ratifying treaty with Livonia making Kurland Poland's fief; secularization of the German Brethren of the Sword—formerly a part of the Monastic State of the Teutonic Brethren (or Knights); incorporation of Livonia south of the Dvina River into Poland-Lithuania; earmarking for defense the income from royal demesnes.

1562 Seym Act making Respect for the Law Program a law; return of all the lands illegally held since 1504 to the state. Exemption of the gentry from the jurisdiction of the Church courts; prohibition to execute the sentences of the bishops' court by the territorial officers, the starostas.

1563 Seym Act on control of town administration and prices by territorial officers of the king's government; separation of defense treasury from the royal government's treasury; Seym compelling the Church and peasantry to pay the land tax and to contribute to the costs of the national defenses; granting by an executive decision the right of succession in Prussia to the Brandenburgian branch of Hohenzollerns in return for promises of support in the war against Muscovy.

1565 Seym Act on codification of commerce regulation; exemption of gentry from custom duties; abrogation of towns' storage of goods privileges; prohibition to export from Poland by local merchants; no limitation of imports.

1568 Act of Gdansk, founding of the Maritime Commission, central government's authority and courts for control of maritime commerce, shipbuilding, coastal defenses and enforcement of maritime blockade of Russia.

1568 Publication *De Optimo Senatore* by Wawrzyniec Goslicki (1530–1607), political program for the Polish political system based on a pluralistic society with perfect equilibrium between power and liberty; defining the responsibility of the King as a head of state; three times translated and published in England, to be banned and confiscated; 150 years later highly praised by Sir Robert Walpole (1676–1745).

1569 Seym Act of Lublin resulting in royal decree on incorporation of Ukraine (formerly part of Lithuania) into Poland.

1569 Seym Act of Lublin, admission of Prussian senators and deputies into Polish parliament and offer of emancipation to the Moslem and Jewish minorities without obligation to convert to Christianity; offer accepted by the Moslems and rejected by the Jews, satisfied with their autonomy governed by the Talmudic Law. The 16th century brought the final Polonization of the urban population of the Polish Commonwealth including immigrants from Germany. Jewish population, however, allowed to continue speaking Yiddish and thus preserving its separate Judeo-Germanic subculture based on a Germanic language and Jewish ethnic and religious tradition.

RZECZPOSPOLITA (ZHECH-POS-PO-LEE-TA) OR RES PUBLICA— THE FIRST POLISH REPUBLIC (1569–1795)

1569 Union Act by the Seym of Lublin, founding of the First Polish Republic; Poland and Lithuania formally becoming one country and electing one head of state and chief executive with the title of King crowned in Krakow; one national parliament, the Seym Walny in Warsaw; one currency; one foreign policy; freedom of Poles, Ruthenians, and Lithuanians to settle anywhere in the Republic; identical but separate territorial offices, treasury, and army. July 1, 1569, the senators and deputies ratify the Union Act. July 4, 1569, formal proclamation of the Union Act by the King Zygmunt August Jagiellonczyk (1520–1572). Formation of the First Polish Republic, the most militarized society in Europe. A unique act on the European scene of peaceful and voluntary federation making one out of two separate states. Maturity of the Seym's role as a "guardian of freedom" supervising the actions of the King, elected chief executive of the Republic. Warsaw becoming the permanent seat of national parliament, the Seym Walny.

1569 Act of Seym extending to the burghers of Wilno the representation in the national parliament and the rights to own land.

1572 Founding of emergency (hooded) courts, to maintain law and order during preparation of the elections. Senate's call for Convocation Seym to conduct the elections.

1573 Toleration Act of Warsaw, proclamation by the Seym of the law guaranteeing religious freedom (civil rights of the political nation of free citizens lay at the root of the religious toleration in Poland; the health of democracy of the masses of Polish nobility continued as long as the middle nobility was strong enough to lead the Republic); Postulata Polonica, concessions in favor of Protestants in France secured by Polish envoys. Spreading of Calvinism among gentry and Lutheranism among burghers; forming of a unifying "low brow" Sarmatian myth that all the people of the Republic allegedy descended from the Sarmatians of antiquity.

1573 Election Seym, election of Henry de Valois (1551–1589) as King, head of state and chief executive of the Republic upon an oath on preservation of the Social Contract composed of the *Pacta Conventa* and *Henrician Articles* guaranteeing preservation and enforcement of the Polish Bill of Rights and Constitution, the first formal conclusion of a comprehensive social contract in Europe. The terms of the Social Contract included calling parliament into session every two years; a continuous supervisory council of sixteen senators as a "watchdog" commission over government activities; declaration of war only after approval by the Senate; new taxation and mobilization for war only after approval by the Chamber of Deputies. In case of a breach of the Social Contract by the King, a release from civil obedience (de non prestanda obediencia) of the political nation of free citizens (nearly one million people). The part of the Social Contract called *Pacta conventa* also included specific agreements with each king elect; in case of Henry de Valois an "eternal alliance with France," construction of the Polish navy on the Baltic, payment of the debts of the previous administration. The article on religious toleration represented an important element in the Polish political culture of the period which was based on the belief that an honest agreement and mutual respect were fundamental for successful political action. The Seym continuing to be the main forum for political dialogue in the Polish Republic including confrontation of views between Catholics and Protestants.

1573 Convocation of Seym in Warsaw passing constitutional amendment establishing the first in Europe general elections (viritim) for the King acting as the head of state and chief executive of the Polish Nobles' Republic. Appointing of the Primate Bishop of Poland as the head of state for the period after death of an elective king and until the election of the next. The Primate Bishop of Poland was to call for the new session of the parliament, to preside over the Senate, to establish who were the candidates approved by the Seym for the next royal election, to name the king elect and to perform the act of coronation. The formal public statement naming the king elect was made by the Grand Marshal of the Crown. Warsaw was to be the election site where each member of the gentry could cast his vote. Elections were to be decided by a simple majority. Formulation of the Social Contract between the royal candidates and the electorate in the Articles of Agreement. Watchdog senatorial committee confirmed.

1575 General Election (the first in Europe) of King Stefan Batory (1522–1586) as the head of state and chief executive of the Polish Republic. Ratification of royal election.

1576 Seym Act on protection of the rights and laws of the Jews.

1577 Seym Act on creation of peasant elite infantry, one man selected per 823 acres, known as *Piechota Wybraniecka* (pye-kho-ta vi-bra-nets-ka). It soon became known for its patriotism.

1577 Seym Act founding the Supreme Court of Appeals, independent from the executive branch of the government; freely elected judges pronouncing final decision in civil and criminal cases previously tried in lower courts; a unique development in generally absolutist Europe where a king was the supreme judge whose authority could not be challenged; an important step in the division of power in Poland into legislative, executive, and an independent judiciary. (This preceded similar proposals in France and in the United States by 200 years.) Supreme Court sittings: Piotrkow for Great Poland and Lublin for Lesser Poland. The Seym reserved its right to act as the highest court above the Supreme Court of Appeals.

1581 Seym Act founding the Supreme Court of Appeals for Lithuania with sittings, at first, in Nowogrodek and Minsk, and then in Wilno and Grodno.

1585 Seym Act founding the Supreme Court of Appeals for Prussia known as the Supreme Tribunal of Civil Law of Prussia. Convening of the supreme parliamentary court of the Seym for dealing with high treason which was punishable by deprivation of civil rights and honor as well as eviction from Poland.

1587 General Election in Warsaw of King Zygmunt III Vasa (1566–1632) as the head of state and chief executive of the Polish Republic on the platform of *Pax Baltica*, sponsored by Chancellor Jan Zamoyski, who at first advocated election of a native Pole, but then supported the nephew of the last Jagiellonian king with hopes for union with Sweden on the basis of the Polish constitution in the Jagiellonian tradition of a voluntary union for peaceful cooperation and security.

1589 Pacification Seym, rehabilitation of the losers of the election of 1587 who backed Maximilian Habsburg, the Holy Roman Emperor and King of Germany. Chancellor Jan Zamoyski sponsoring plans for elimination of Habsburgs as future candidates for the Polish throne in favor of native Poles or Slavs; the Church, giving secret support to the Habsburgs, successfully opposing these plans. Zamoyski foresaw that unrestricted access of foreign candidates could turn the general elections into a vehicle of foreign interference in the internal affairs of Polish Nobles' Republic. The Seym voting to prevent disintegration of large estates in form of *maioratus* or ordination inherited in full by *ordinatus* or the senior male; this Law of Entail was to preserve economic strength and military potential of the holdings of huge land owners against the effects of Polish law of succession according to which the family property was divided by all sons and daughters alike. Fortress repair, the upkeep of garrisons, the winter quartering of troops, and maintaining of a fixed quota of regiments in time of war were among the legal obligations of an *ordinatus*. Dynamic growth of new land potentates accompanied by transformation of all former knights who owned land into gentlemen-farmers prospering on the grain trade.

1590 Seym Act establishing State Treasury and a separate Royal Treasury for upkeep of the court.

1595/96 Union of Brest, the Orthodox Church accepting control of Catholic Rome; a tie to the western civilization of the Ukrainian people, a third element shared with the Polish tradition besides government from below and opposition to all forms of autocracy; roots of Ukrainian nationalism led by Uniate clergy (tsarist and Soviet Russia later treating the Ukrainian nationalism as a "Polish invention").

1596 Act of Warsaw, Zygmunt III, Sigismundus Vasa, formally transferring the capital of Poland from Cracow to Warsaw.

1609 Seym Act of General Amnesty for those who rose to protest the violation of the Social Contract when in 1606 the government reform project included an increase and reorganization of the armed forces in an abandonment of the principle of unanimity in favor of a majority rule; also a general confirmation of the civil rights of the citizens and inviolability of the general elections.

1611 Seym Act specifying refusal of obedience to the King's government; banning of purchases of landed estates by the burghers; in spite of the protest by the Prussian population, an agreement to the succession rights of the Berlin line of Hohenzollerns in the Polish fief of Prussia (in return for Brandenburgian neutrality in the Polish conflict with Sweden and Russia).

1613 Seym establishing the Tax Court of the Treasury.

1619 Seym authorizing an agreement with the Cossacks.

1621 Seym reiterating military duties of the citizens of the Republic.

1623 Seym promulgating the Ordinance for Commerce.

1629 Seym approving instructions for the Custom Service.

1632 Seym passage of the Law on Taxation

1633 Seym control of the mint established; serfs' labor rent for land increased; penalties for runaway serfs specified; banning of import, printing, and distribution of anti-Semitic literature in Poland.

1637 Seym enactment of the "severe" Cossack constitution making into serfs the Cossacks not registered in the territorial defense; abolishing of an elective Cossack command (the atamans); replacing it with a commissioner nominated by the Seym and serving under the grand hetman.

1638 Seym banning the use of titles other than knighthood (with the exception of six Lithuano-Ruthenian princes' families who could use their traditional titles stripped of all legal privileges). The golden decade of peace (1638–1648) and economic expansion of landed estates in Ukraine, founding of numerous new towns and villages based on serf labor and mostly financed with arenda-type leases; (pre-paid short time leases with built-in incentive for severe exploitation; concluded between noble estate owners and Jewish financiers); an important factor in drawing Poland to the east at the expense of regaining ethnic Polish provinces of Silesia and Stettin Pomerania.

1641 Seym enlarging the Senatorial watchdog committee; regulating issue of coinage. The last homage paid out of Polish fief of Prussia by Elector of Brandenburg Frederick William of Hohenzollern (1620–1688) at the castle of Warsaw.

1643 Seym specifying maximum rates of interest on loans.

1648 Seym rejection of Cossack demands for eviction of Jesuits and Jews from southern Ukraine and a guarantee to nominate there only orthodox officials; establishing of Taxation Register of Prussia. Cossack uprising under Bohdan Khmielnitsky during growing political strength of huge land owners and widening of pauperization of lower and middle nobility; beginning of the deluge of invasions which ended the great power status of Poland; growing of masses of landless nobles *szlachta golota* (shlakh-ta go-wo-ta) or *holota* (kho-wo-ta) soon meaning "mob" or "rubble," corruptible by bribery and easily manipulated. 1648

Cossack rebellion marking the beginning of military and political disintegration of the Polish Nobles' Republic during the next 147 years; mass murders of Catholics and Jews by revolted Cossacks and Ruthenians in Ukraine with simultaneous reconversion of the Uniates to Orthodoxy. Jews of Lwow saved by Polish inhabitants.

1649 Seym agreement with the Cossacks giving to Khmyelnitsky the title of hetman; increasing to 40,000 the number of Cossacks registered in the territorial defense; eviction of Jesuits and Jews from southern Ukraine; a guarantee to nominate there only orthodox officials; confirming Mining Laws.

1650 Seym establishing of the Mint Commission.

1652 Seym session declared null and void by precedent setting admission of a single vote of protest, the Liberum Veto as legal and valid. Polish parliamentary principle of agreement deteriorating into a rigid and formal requirement of unanimity (which often paralyzed the Seym in 1652–1764). The first veto cast by Jan Sicinski (?–1664) was formally registered before he left the Seym. The fact of his early departure could have been used to disqualify his veto, but it was not. Sicinski acted on orders of Janusz Radziwill (1612–55), one of the wealthiest magnates in Lithuania and a leader of dissidents, who later (in 1655) committed a high treason and signed allegiance to the King of Sweden. Liberum Veto together with the misconceived "Golden Freedom" and general elections admitting foreign candidates became a tool of subversion by neighboring absolutist regimes of the political nation of Noble Citizens of the Republic. The magnates, whose political machines were to promote their oligarchic control over the Republic, were often becoming mere tools of foreign subversion, especially of the Russian autocracy. Contradictory trends: rationalism of Polish Brethren vs. Sarmatian irrationalism; reshaping of the "Sarmatian Myth" by exclusion of the lower classes from the ancient Sarmatian links as a justification of social injustices.

1654 Seym authorizing devaluation of coinage; Khmyelnitsky signing transfer of Eastern Ukraine to Muscovy at Pereyeslav; Tsar Alexis Mikhailovich (1629–76) obtaining the support of the Zemsky Sobor, representing Russian nobility, to incorporate Ukraine into Russia.

1656 Seym notified that Frederick Wilhelm Hohenzollern of Berlin offered himself as a vassal of Sweden out of the Polish fief of Prussia.

1657 Seym passing the Excise Tax Law and ratifying the Treaty of Bydgoszcz and Welawa relinquishing the fief of Prussia in exchange for termination of the Hohenzollerns' association with Sweden.

1658 Seym admitting permanent representation of the burghers of Lwow; expelling of the Arian Sect of the Polish Unitarians (an act of intoleration breaking with the tradition of toleration as a result of political victory of counter-reformation and loss of political power by the middle gentry in favor of the magnates).

1659 Seym ratifying the Treaty of Hadziacz with the Cossacks; recognition of Kievian Ukraine as an equal partner of Poland and Lithuania in an effort to make Poland a Republic of Three Nations; authorization of copper coinage (Warsaw population dropping to 6,000, from 18,000 in 1655, as a result of wars).

1662 Seym prohibiting royal elections *vivente rege* (while the King is still alive); facing rebellion of the soldiers, unpaid for years, and forming unions, the "Holy Alliance" and the "Pious Alliance," to get the back pay.

1665–6 Seym facing of the rebellion to uphold the Social Contract and the Constitution of the Republic by the Grand Marshall and Army Commander Jerzy Lubomirski (1616–1667). The rebellion degenerating into high treason weakening the Republic and making impossible necessary political and social reforms and preventing the armed forces from recovery of Eastern Ukraine lost to Russia after the Cossack rebellion of 1648 and obstructing the effective defense against Muscovites. In 1666 battle of Matwy won by Lubomirski against loyal troops of Hetman John Sobieski; perishing of some 2000 elite cavalry and weakening of the Republic's armed forces needed on the Russian frontier.

1667 Seym ratification of Truce with Russia at Andruszow and loss of eastern Ukraine to Russia and of Kiev for two years and payment of a ransom (which never was paid and Kiev was lost permanently). The ceded territories gave Muscovites the critical advantage of resources over Poland. They represented the most important element in transformation of Muscovy into the great Russian Empire, which could then proceed to fill and consolidate the power vacuum created in northern and central Asia by the earlier disintergration of the Mongol Empire.

1667 Seym authorizing war with Turkey because Cossack Hetman

Pyotr Doroshenko (1627–1698) made Southern Ukraine a Turkish fief.

1668 Seym ratifying the abdication of King John Casimir Vasa (1609–1672).

1670 Seym recognizing a permanent representation of burghers of Kamieniec Podolski. Publication of *The War of Khochim* (Wojna Chocimska) by Waclaw Potocki (1621–96), one of many "literary" chronicles and memoirs which also included writings of Jan Chrisostom Pasek (1636–1701) in style of a historical novel.

1672 Treaty of Buczacz (boo-chach) ceding to Doroshenko southern Ukraine as a Turkish fief, including Podolia and Kamieniec Podolski; agreement to pay Turkey 22,000 ducats yearly ransom, considered a disgrace throughout the Republic; Seym passing new appropriations for the defense.

1674 Coronation of John III Sobieski (1629–1696) after his victory over the Turks in 1673 at Chocim (kho-cheem).

1675 Treaty of Jaworow (ya-vo-roof) between Poland and France against Brandenburg and Austria to re-establish Polish suzerainty over Prussia and to recover all of Silesia (treaty thwarted in 1681 Seym by pro-Austrian magnates lobbying against growth of executive powers of the King, also influenced by the Pope worried about collapse of Austria and Turkish threat to Italy); Polish victory over Turkey at Lwow.

1676 Seym ratifying the Treaty of Zurawno, Turkey returning two-thirds of Ukraine; leaving one-third of Ukraine under Doroszenko as a Turkish fief; the matter of Podolia left for further negotiations; revising Treasury operations.

1677 Seym setting the rates of Church taxes paid to Treasury.

1681–3 Seym ratifying the anti-Turkish treaty with Austria to prevent Turkish advance along southern border of Poland into Austria and threatening the Papal State in Italy. Preparation for life-and-death struggle with the Turks who were at the zenith of their territorial expansion in Europe. King John III Sobieski to be the Supreme Commander of the Allied Christian Armies (in this capacity he won the crucial battle of Vienna on Sept. 12, 1683, which ended Turkish expansion in Europe).

1684 Founding of the "Holy League" of Poland, Austria, Venice, and the Papal State against Turkey; Poland and Austria continuing war against Turkey; Poland and Turkey exhausting each other, gradually becoming the "sick men" of Europe.

1687 Seym not ratifying Krzysztof Grzymultowski (1620–1687) peace Treaty with Moscow, giving up eastern Ukraine, Kiev, and Smolensk, a turning point giving Russia for the first time an upper hand over Poland; recognizing Russia's interest in preservation of the Orthodox Church in Ukraine, thereby giving to the Tsar an opening for subversive activities against the Republic in her eastern borderlands.

1697 Coronation in Cracow of Augustus II Wettin (1670–1733), a minority candidate, thanks to Russian and Saxon military occupation of the coronation site, a scheme of Peter I the Great (1672–1725) to subvert the Polish Nobles' Republic by illegal imposition of a unstable administration of a Saxon king.

1698 Private treaty between Tsar Peter the Great and King Augustus II at Rawa Ruska embroiling Poland in war against Sweden; Russia's aim to break the sea power of Sweden on the Baltic, while Augustus II tries to make Polish fief of southern Livonia (then occupied by Sweden) into a fief of Saxony.

1699 Seym ratifying the Treaty of Karlowice of Poland and Austria with Turkey, recovery of southern Ukraine with Kamieniec Podolski.

1701 Proclamation of a new Kingdom of Prussia in Brandenburg with capital in Berlin; a new location and a new use for the name of "Prussia" introduced to exploit the difficulties of the Polish Republic with the Russian Empire.

1702 Occupation of Warsaw by Charles XII (1682–1718), King of Sweden, followed by defeat of Augustus II at Kliszow.

1703 Seym recognizing a permanent representation and land purchase rights of the burghers of Lublin.

1704 Confederation Seym in Warsaw impeaching King Augustus II and holding general elections; ally of France and Sweden, Stanislaw Leszczynski (1677–1766), elected King of Poland.

1706 Abdication of King Augustus II.

1710 Seym ratifying of Augustus II of Saxony as King of Poland (despite irregularities in his coronation in 1697) as a result of defeat of Charles XII at Poltava in 1709.

1713 Seym protest against bringing of the Saxon Army to Poland by Augustus II.

1715–1717 Confederation Seym of Tarnogrod protesting an attempt to abolish the Constitution and Social Contract of the Republic by Augustus II's using Saxon troops to establish himself as an absolute ruler in Poland; "mediation" between Polish Seym and the Saxon administration by Peter the Great.

1717 Dumb Seym (Sejm Niemy), no deputy or senator was permitted to speak, by the Russian army of Peter the Great whose arbitration was accepted by the Saxon administration; Seymiks' taxing and armed forces control restricted; tax to support 24,000 troops passed; first budget formulated and accepted; Russian guarantee of status quo accepted; Saxon army evicted except 1200 bodyguards of Augustus II and six officers of the Saxon Chancery. (Beginning of 50 years of Russian and Brandenburgian terrorism and subversion in the Republic of Poland; secret pact of Russia with Brandenburg-Prussia concluded in 1720 at Potsdam, formulating detailed plans for further fostering of anarchy in Poland; interferring in general elections by military force and bribery, utilizing of the liberum Veto and "Golden Freedoms" against reforms; preventing the passage of defense appropriations); Russia acquiring a free hand in Poland after peace treaties with Turkey and Sweden.

1726 Seym establishing improvements in procedures of the Supreme Court.

1732 Seym mandate for new issue of currency; publication of *Volumina Legum* or volumes of Polish laws.

1733 Seym banning elections for deputies and senators of non-Catholics. Double royal election bringing war for the Polish throne; majority electing Stanislaw Leszczynski while Russia and Austria support politically and militarily the minority candidate Augustus III (1696–1763) of Saxony; Stanislaw Leszczynski writing *A Free Voice Insuring Freedom* for personal freedom of the peasants, cash payments for land use by peasants, limits on the use of Liberum Veto, reform of Seym sessions, reform of taxation, and a permanent Army of the Republic of 100,000 men.

1734 Seym passing Ordinance for the Post Office. Flight of King Stanislaw Leszczynski to France (where his son-in-law King Louis XV gave him for life the duchy of Lorraine in 1735) and his formal abdication in 1736.

1736 Seym passing an amnesty for confederates of Dzikow (supporters of King Stanislaw Leszczynski and an alliance with France) who were defeated by the joint efforts of Russian and Saxon armies; passing of the voting ordinance of Kurland (Latvia).

1740 Collegium Nobilium founded in Warsaw by Stanislaw Konarski (1700–1773), reformed seven-year high school with teaching of foreign languages, mathematical and physical sciences, geography, history, and civic virtues.

1740–48 Austro-Prussian war for Silesia; Brandenburg-Prussia nearly broke while acquiring Silesia, flooding Poland with bogus money, continuing to act as an international parasite (so far on three occasions in 1656, 1720, and 1733 proposing dismembering of the Polish Republic).

1744 Seym disrupted by Liberum Veto and project of treasury-army reform killed.

1747 The 400,000-volume library and 10,000 manuscript collection founded by Zaluski (za-woo-ski) brothers opened to the public; former King Stanislaw Leszczynski publishing *A Free Voice Insuring Freedom*.

1751 Publishing of economical program for raising standard of living of the peasants *Anatomy of the Polish Republic* by Stefan Garczynski (1690–1755), wojewoda (governor) of Kalisz and later of Poznan.

1760 Publishing of *On Effective Counsels* program by Stanislaw Konarski on removal of anarchy by abolition of Liberal Veto and royal elections, and on reform of the Seym

1761 Seym issuing a universal proclamation on coinage; (perennial problems of fraud by the Berlin government's issuing fake Polish money to fill its coffers).

1763 Attempted coup d'etat led by Czartoryski family to form a confederation for reform and reconsolidation of the Republic.

1764 Convocation Seym creating treasury and army reform in Poland and Lithuania; abolition of private tolls; establishing of customs duties on the borders of the Republic; improving of the parliamentary procedures and establishing of majority rule in the matters of treasury revenues; National Treasury Commissions established; mint transferred to executive control; forming a proposal for emancipation of the 750,000 Jews in Poland (without conversion to Christianity), abolition of the Jewish Seym of the Four Lands; Jewish congregations, the Kahals, acting as little republics governed with Tolmudic Laws by elective presidents. Election of Stanislaw August Poniatowski (1732–98) as King of Poland, signing the Social Contract and promising political and educational reforms.

1765 Founding in Warsaw of the *szkola rycerska,* or military academy, including general education and promoting civic virtues; publishing of the journal *Monitor* until 1785.

1766 Seym voting reform of coinage; revising the Tax Law.

1767 Kidnapping of senators opposing Russian subversion and their deportation by the Russians to Kaluga, inside Russia.

1768–1772 Bar Confederacy, war with Russia for freedom and national independence led by conservatives; among its military leaders the "eagle of Bar Confederacy" Kazimierz Pulaski (1747–79), later "father of the American Cavalry." The Confederacy defeated by the Russian army developed national consciousness in the masses of Polish nobility and started shaping modern Polish national identity; fall of Bar Confederacy leading to the First Partition of Poland. *Koliszczyzna* Cossack rebellion in Ukraine; repetition of mass murders of Catholics and Jews on a scale equal to or exceeding the massacres of 1648.

1768 Seym restoring candidacy rights to non-Catholics; modifying voting rules.

1770 Bar Confederacy proclaiming impeachment of the King Stanislaw Augustus.

1772 Russo-Prussian agreement on partition of Poland with Austria; the government of King Stanislaw August protesting against the illegality of the partition throughout Europe; struggling against hostile statements of Voltaire (1694–1778) and other exponents of enlightment who, paradoxically, became apologists for the partitioning powers while ignorant of Polish history and values; beginning of unending process of slandering of everything Polish on the international scene by propagandists of the despotic governments of Russia and Prussia (including their 20th century successors).

1773 Seym voting hearth tax and equalizing custom duties.

1773 Seym establishing ministry of public education (the first in Europe) and reorganization of the school system, financed with the funds available from the liquidation of the Jesuit Order by the Pope Clemens XIV.

1773–1775 Seym Extraordinary called by a General Confederation led by Adam Poninski, a paid traitor, leading men corrupted by Saxons and Russians and selected in the Seymiks under guns of Russian, Prussian, and Austrian amies. The form of confederation in which majority ruled was used to avoid a possible veto by a patriotic deputy. In fact several deputies led by Tadeusz Reytan (1742–1780) raised a strong protest. The Seym setting the army of the Polish Republic at 30,000; 24,000 for Poland and 6,000 for Lithuania; ratified Treaties of the First Partition; establishing the government by the Permanent Council of 18 senators and 18 deputies (departments: foreign, interior, war, justice, and treasury) and Army and Education Commissions; land-buying rights extended to Lithuanian burghers. The illegality of the partition was publicized throughout Europe by the government of King Stanislaw August Poniatowski (1732–1798); Russia, Prussia, and Austria responding to all resistance with threats of immediately extending their annexations. This moment of truth strengthened the voices calling for reforms and consolidation of the Polish Nobles' Republic.

1776 Founding of Department of Defense; limiting the power of grand hetman.

1778 Reform proposal by Jozef Wybicki (1747–1822) for abolition of serfdom and a new Code of Law by Chancellor Andrzej Zamoyski (1716–1792), improving the condition of the serfs, personal freedom and protection under the law of the peasants, duty of the state to provide rural elementary education.

1780 *History of Polish Nation* by Adam Naruszewicz (1733–1796).

1782 Seym reorganizing the Treasury Commission. Publishing of the *Scientific Record of History, Politics, and Economics* by Piotr Switkowski (1744–1793).

1783–1794 Tsarist decrees limiting the Jewish Pale of Settlement to the provinces annexed from Poland.

1784 Completion of canals connecting Baltic with the Black Sea through Niemen and Vistula River basins to Dnieper.

1785 Seym reforming the Permanent Council.

1786 Publication of the *Commercial Daily* in Warsaw by Tadeusz Podlecki.

1787 Publication by Stanislaw Staszic of a program for political, economic, and social reforms and improvement of Poland's defenses; and in 1788 program by Hugo Kollataj (1750–1812) for abolition of serfdom, introduction of free hiring, complete equality of townspeople and nobility, strong executive under a modern constitution, and efficient legislative procedures.

1788–1792 Seym (The Four Year Seym or The Great Seym) included projects for emancipation of the 900,000 Jews in Poland whose number was growing due to deportation into Poland of poverty-stricken Jews (called *betteljudgen* in German) from Brandenburg-Prussia and Austria; flight of the Jews from Russian held Ukraine into Poland. Progressive Jews supporting the emancipation project while Jewish Orthodox oligarchy in control of the Kahals opposing it and in 1791 calling a General Synod to collect money to lobby against full emancipation.

1788 Seym setting the Army complement at 100,000.

1789 Seym setting the tax rate 10 percent for nobility, 20 percent for clergy.

1790 Seym ratifying the Treaty of Alliance with Prussia while desperately trying to strengthen Poland's position vis-a-vis Russia; falling for the provocation of the Kingdom of Prussia (Brandenburg-Prussia) which intended to stiffen the hopeless Polish resistance against the Russian Empire in order to stab Poland in the back and participate in further land grab in the following partition. Seym establishing City Commissions of Good Order.

1791 Seym revising the electoral Ordinance for the Seymiks (regional legislatures); voting Seym representation of the burghers; voting a New Constitution (of May 3) for the purpose of regaining a full sovereignty; extending civil rights to all burghers and in a more diluted form to peasants; abolishing the political machines of the huge land owners in regional legislatures; conversion of the Republic into a constitutional monarchy in order to prevent foreign powers from interfering in Poland's internal affairs through general elections, which no longer could be safeguarded by Polish defense forces and kept immune against corruption. The new constitution was of an evolutionary character and in this differed from the French constitution which followed it. Constitution of May 3, 1791, created conditions for rebirth of Poland, and it was perceived as a "death blow" to the Prussian monarchy by E. F. Hertzberg (1726–1795), the Prussian minister, who wrote that it was better than the English and would permit Poland to regain the lands lost in the first partition and to dominate again the area from east Baltic to the Moravian Gate. When in Jan. 1792, Russia concluded her war with Turkey and turned her attention to Poland, Prussia was able to return safely to her parasitic activities against Poland and plans of further partitions.

Apr. 27, 1792 Signing in St. Petersburg of an act of Confederation and dated on May 14, 1792, at Targowica and condemning the "monarchial and democratic revolution of May 3" by a group of huge land owners and Russia's henchmen.

May 22, 1792 Seym increasing the army to 100,000; Poland unable to buy arms abroad because of a new Prussian blockade. Poland able to put 37,000 man army to face 97,000 Russian veterans of the Turkish campaign. War in defense of the Constitution of May 3, 1791. Battles of Zielence, Dubienka, Krzemien, and Brzesc.

1793 Seym (dominated by Russia) repealing the Constitution of 1791; ratifying Treaties of the Second Partition; voting a Conservative Constitution; re-establishing general elections for the King as the head of state and chief executive of the Republic; (Russia and Prussia considering the general elections as a vehicle for their interference in the internal affairs of the Republic).

1794 Act of insurrection in Cracow by Gen. Tadeusz Kosciuszko (1746–1817) as Commander-in-Chief (an American general, architect of West Point and other river fortifications to block British barge movements, saved the American Revolution by engineering the victory at Saratoga, an event without which the French refused to join the war against Great Britain.)

1794 Act of Polaniec, the first thorough reform of the status of the serfs, in the First Polish Republic; freeing from serfdom the peasants who joined the national uprising; protesting against violation of the Constitution of May 3, 1791 and of the Social Contract; for regaining independence from Austria, Prussia, and Russia; (for peasants, not participating in the uprising, a reduction of payments for land leasing by 25 to 50 percent). Formation of the first Jewish regiment (all-volunteer) by Berek Joselewicz (1764–1809) to help in the struggle for Polish independence and with it preservation of the unique Jewish liberties in Poland against anti-Semitic policies of Austria, Prussia, and Russia.

1794 Act of Cracow, proclamation of Supreme National Council; land grants to the soldiers fighting in the uprising and their families.

1795 Abdication of King Stanislaw August Poniatowski, the last head of state and chief executive of the First Polish Republic elected in a general election. Third Partition of Poland and commitment of Austria, Prussia, and Russia to eradicate the name of

Poland and the Polish presence from the history of Europe. Final obliteration of the First Polish Republic. Austria renaming southern Poland (including Cracow) with the names of Ukrainian provinces of Galicia and Lodomeria.

CENTURY OF PARTITIONS (1795–1918)

Grand Duchy of Warsaw (1807–1813): A French Protectorate

1807 Napoleonic Constitution for the Grand Duchy of Warsaw; strong central executive; chief executive office assigned to the Saxon house of Wettin; King of Saxony, the Grand Duke of Warsaw; in practice, the executive functions in hands of a prime minister; the Seym a bicameral legislature in charge of budget and judiciary only; abolition of privileged classes, legal equality of all; Seymiks retained as electoral assemblies for the gentry; communal assemblies added for burghers and peasants. Senate composed of eighteen appointed senators; Chamber of 100 deputies; 60 nobles and 40 professionals, burghers and peasants.
The territory of the Grand Duchy of Warsaw was 104,000 sq.km. with population of 2,600,000 in six departments, Warsaw, Poznan, Kalisz, Bydgoszcz, Plock, and Lomza; each department contained ten districts. This territory was made up of the annexations by Brandenburg-Prussia in the second and third partitions of Poland minus Bialystok region which was ceded by Napoleon to Russia at the Treaty of Tylza.
1807–14 Publication in six volumes of the first complete dictionary of recent Polish by Samuel Bogumil Linde (1771–1847), member of a Polonized Swedish family and a lexicographer who worked at the Zaluski Library; at that point Polish language was equally developed as German and more advanced than Russian; it was one of major European languages possessing rich literature and vocabulary of arts and sciences; the character of the dictionary was historical and not normative, it included 60,000 entries; Linde also prepared a huge material for comparative Slavic dictionary (especially Russian texts).
1808 Decree on founding of the Law School of Warsaw; Izba Edukacyjna or the Department of Education adding 500 new elementary schools; Jewish population choosing to continue their education in Judeo-Germanic tradition in Talmudic schools (unchanged for three hundred years); agreement to purchase in Bayonne, France, Polish long term mortgages held by the Berlin Bank for 20 million Francs and pay them in three years, French economic exploitation, the proverbial "sumy bajonskie."
1809 Treaty of Vienna, territory of the Grand Duchy of Warsaw increased by four departments of Krakow, Radom, Lublin, and Siedlce to 142,000 sq.km with 4,300,000 in total of 72 districts; the Chamber of Deputies added 66 deputies. Tarnopol region ceded by Napoleon to Russia.
1812 Seym constituting itself into a General Confederation of Poland for reviving the Polish-Lithuanian Commonwealth (on the eve of Napoleonic invasion of Russia).
1814–1815 Congress of Vienna, a new partition of Polish lands of the Grand Duchy of Warsaw; "free, independent, and strictly neutral" City Republic of Cracow created as a joint protectorate of Austria, Prussia, and Russia; Prussia annexing Torun and departments of Bydgoszcz and Poznan as the Grand Duchy of Poznan; Austria annexing Tarnopol region, highlands south of Cracow including Wieliczka.

Kingdom of Poland within Russian Empire (1815–1916)

1815 Act by Tsar Alexander I, Constitution of the Kingdom of Poland (the only constitutional experiment within the Russian Empire); government by the Administrative Council; Tsar's decisions on war and peace with all executive and many legislative powers; guarantee of basic civil rights; bicameral Seym without right to initiate new laws and a subject to the royal veto; independent courts. Kingdom of Poland on 127,500 sq. km. with population of 3,300,000
1819 Appropriation of funds for the first 1,000 km of paved roads completed by 1830.
1829 *Poland's Past* (History) by Joachim Lelewel (1786–1861).
1830 Act of Seym proclaiming national uprising for independence (after outbreak of revolution of Warsaw and assumption of

dictatorship by Gen. Jozef Chlopicki [1771–1845]) in protest against the planned use of Polish army against revolutionary movements in Western Europe and for independence of Poland. Polish forces included besides the regular well-trained army of 40,000, also National Guard (Gwardia Narodowa) in which served a separate battalion of 850 Jewish volunteers. A Russian army of 115,000 marched into Poland.
1831 Seym passing the law on duties of a Supreme Commander after collapse of Chlopicki's dictatorship.
1831 Seym issuing a Proclamation of Independence and Dethronement of the Tsar of Russia as a King of Poland invoking the Polish Social Contract of the First Polish Republic (1569–1795); passing a law to compensate wounded soldiers and their families.
1831 Seym deciding to go into exile rather than submit to the Tsar. Beginning of the Great Emigration of some 9,000 members of the insurrection, two-thirds to France and the rest to England, Switzerland, Belgium, United States, and Canada. Forming of the Polish National Committee in Paris; then in 1832 the Polish Democratic Society for an independent and reformed Poland free of serfdom. Adam Czartoryski (1770–1861) attempting to solve the Polish question by diplomacy, in 1834 supported by Association for National Unity; publishing of *History of the Uprising of the Polish Nation* in 1830–1831 by Maurycy Mochnacki (1804–1834) and of the epic poem *Pan Tadeusz* by Adam Mickiewicz (1798–1855) and drama *Kordian* by Juliusz Slowacki (1809–1849) in Paris; 1836 the *Great Manifesto of the Democratic Society* for struggle for independence based on a democratic program of equality of all, freedom from serfdom, and conversion of the land held in tenure into ownership by the peasants.
1832 Act by Tsar Nicolas I abolishing constitution in the Polish Kingdom; incorporation of the Kingdom into the Russian Empire without removal of customs; imposition of martial law; (conspiratorial activities for independence throughout the former lands of the First Polish Republic).
1858 Lifting of the martial law; easing of censorship; amnesty for emigrants.
1861 Imposition of martial law in Warsaw; Agrarian Association proposing cash rent for land use instead of peasant labor; proposal of Land Reform and Jewish Emancipation by Aleksander Wielopolski (1803–87); banning of political demonstrations; mass arrests; deportation of activists including Catholic and Jewish clergymen; the high point of the trend towards Jewish assimilation.
1862–63 Decrees prepared by Aleksander Wielopolski, the head of civil government in Polish Kingdom, on individual land use contracts with peasants and on reforming Polish language school system including Szkola Glowna, the University of Warsaw; decree on complete emancipation of the Jews; it benefited primarily educated professionals who assimilated into Polish culture; Yiddish-speaking Jewish masses remaining within their traditional subculture based on Jewish religious and ethnic tradition and the use of Germanic language, Yiddish.
1863 Proclamation of the Provisional Government of Poland in Warsaw; abolition of serfdom; land to become property of the tenants; all declared free and equal citizens of Poland; request for help from Poles in Austria and Prussia, without armed insurrection there, in order not to unite against Poland Austria, Germany and Russia. Insurrection spreading from Poland to Lithuania, Byelorussia and Ukraine; English, French, and Austrian demand for revival of the constitution of Kingdom of Poland of 1815; Romuald Traugutt (1826–64), acting dictator after Ludwik Mieroslawski (1814–78) and Marian Langiewicz (1827–87). Mass reprisals by "hangman" of Wilno, Governor General Michail Muraviev (1796–1866), who coersed the Kahals to cooperate against the insurrection, which in sixteen months fought in 1229 engagements against the Russian Army (956 in the Polish Kingdom, 237 in Lithuania, and 36 in Ukraine and Byelorussia).
1864 Imposition of martial law in Galicia; cooperation of Austrian, Prussian and Russian governments against the insurrection; execution of Romuald Traugutt and other Polish leaders; abolition of serfdom by the Tsar; prohibition of Poles to buy land, build and repair Catholic churches in Lithuania, Byelorussia, and Ukraine; beginning of an intense Russification program. Beginning of modern Jewish nationalism after collapse of the uprising; growing interest in colonization of Palestine. Warsaw population 223,000; beginning of rapid growth due to industrialization. Publishing of *Monumenta Poloniae Historica* by August Bielowski (1806–1876).
1874 Placing the Kingdom of Poland under Russian military rule with a general and governor in command of the garrison and in charge of administration.

1876 Decree replacing Polish language in courts of law by Russian.

1879 Russia military courts acquiring jurisdiction over civilian Poles.

1880 *Poland's Internal History* by Tadeusz Kurzon of the "optimist" school.

1881 Killing of Tsar Alexander II in a suicidal bombing by Ignacy Hryniecki (1855–1881), Polish engineering student associated with Russian revolutionary conspiracy the Narodna Vola, followed by police terror. Mass evictions of Jews from Russia and Lithuania (the *Litwaks*) mainly to Warsaw and Lodz, where they competed with local Jews and Poles in commerce and industry; the Litwaks opposed assimilation trends among Jewish professionals and cooperated with tsarist programs of Russification of Polish Kingdom.

1882 Anti-Jewish May Laws of strict enforcement of the regulation of the Pale or restriction of the Jews to the lands annexed from Poland-Lithuania, limiting Jewish education, reduction in the jurisdiction of the Kahals; beginning of pogroms organized by Russian provocateurs who led the Black Hundreds; political and cultural disintegration of the Jews.

1887 Exile to Siberia of Jozef Klemens Pilsudski (1867–1935) for conspiracy with his brother Bronislaw (1866–1918) and Lenin's older brother Alexander Ulyanov (1866–87) to kill Tsar Alexander III (1845–1894).

1894 Clandestine socialist publication of Robotnik ("The Worker") by Jozef Pilsudski; his arrest and imprisonment in the Warsaw Citadel in 1900.

1903 Pogrom of the Jews of Kishinev in Moldavia by the Black Hundreds.

1904 Attempt by Pilsudski to enlist support in Japan (thwarted by Dmowski).

1905 Increased security measures in response to widespread strikes.

1905 Creation of Russian Parliament, the Duma, based on general elections with legislative powers; first recognition of civil rights of the population, followed by imposition of marshal law in the Kingdom of Poland; formation of a Polish Circle of Deputies led by Roman Dmowski.

1906 Decree on temporary labor unions; military tribunals to execute within 24 hours after sentencing; staging of a pogrom against the Jews of Bialystok by Tsarist army garrison.

1907 Decree on Polish language in private schools only.

1908 Kazimierz Sosnkowski (1885–1967) founding in Lwow of Union for Active Resistance with funds obtained in "expropriation" of Russian treasury shipment at Bezdany, Lithuania, by *Bojowka* (bo-yoov-ka) or a "fighting team," led by Pilsudski; co-organizer of the new military union Wladyslaw Sikorski (1881–1943)

1912 Roman Dmowski, leader of the National Democratic Party, predicting outbreak of World War I and proclaiming the need to assist Russia to prevent any additional annexation and brutal Germanization of Polish lands by Germany.

1913 Decree on the takeover of the Warsaw-Vienna Railroad through purchase by Tsarist government.

1914 Conversion of the Riflemen's Association into Polish Legions entering Kingdom of Poland with the Austrian Army; Pilsudski founding Polish Military Organization in Kingdom of Poland (*Polska Organizacja Wojskowa*, POW) as a nucleus of an independent Polish armed force; Dmowski forming in Warsaw a pro-Russian Polish National Committee and the Pulawski Legion, a division of Polish Riflemen, which became in 1917 a part of the First Polish Corps under Gen. Jozef Dowbor-Musnicki (1867–1937).

1916 Tsarist government protesting proclamation in Warsaw of the Kingdom of Poland in the lands of former Russian partition by Germany and Austria.

1916 Formation of Regency Council in Warsaw by Germany and Austria as a Provisional Council of State (Tymczasowa Rada Stanu) including J. Pilsudski.

1917 Attempt to subordinate Polish legions by Germany to create a *Polnische Wehrmacht* opposed by Pilsudski; issuing of Polish marks as currency.

1917 Declaration by President Woodrow Wilson of support for an independent Poland, reunited and with a free access to the Baltic Sea.

1917 Pilsudski resigning in protest from the Provisional Council of State; arrest and deportation of General Pilsudski and Colonel Sosnkowski to German fortress of Madgeburg.

1917 Provisional government of Russia establishing a commission to liquidate Russian presence in the Kingdom of Poland and

recognize independence of Poland in a military union with Russia.

1917 Act of Versailles proclaiming reunited independent Poland by the Western Allies; decree of the president of France, Poincare, on formation of the Polish Army in France.

1917 Supreme Polish Military Committee formed in Petersburg.

1917 Formation of Polish Army units in Brazil.

1917 German and Austrian proclamation of the Regency Council in Warsaw as the supreme authority in the Kingdom of Poland replacing German military rule.

1917 France recognizing the Polish National Committee as representing Polish nation; the rest of the Western Allies follow.

1917 School system in the Kingdom of Poland under Polish administration.

1917 American government permitting recruitment of volunteers to Polish Army on United States territory.

1917 Formation of government in Warsaw by the Regency Council.

1918 Elections for the Polish Council of State on the lands occupied by Germany and Austria.

1918 Great Britain, France and Italy declare support for independent Poland.

1918 Annulment of the treaties of partition of Poland by the Bosheviks.

1918 Jurisprudence taken over by Poles in the Kingdom of Poland from German occupational authorities.

1918 Declaration of independence of Poland and rejection by the Regency Council in Warsaw of the German-Austrian protectorate; dissolution of the Council of State and Cabinet of Ministers.

Nov. 11, 1918 the Regency Council in Warsaw, upon collapse of Germany, dissolving itself and transferring its powers to Jozef Pilsudski (the commander of Polish Legions released from internment in Germany at Magdeburg fortress) as the Commander-in-Chief and on Nov. 14, 1918 as the Head of State.

Note: *Total of two million Poles were mobilized by Russia, Prussia, and Austria in 1914–1918; of these 220,000 were killed while serving in Austrian Army, 110,000 in German, and 55,000 in Russian Army. Polish losses represented equivalent of ten billion dollars (of 1918), including half of all bridges, two-thirds of railroad yards and stations, and two million buildings (mostly rural).*

Grand Duchy of Poznan and Polish Provinces within Kingdom of Prussia (1815–1918)

1816 Decree by Berlin government to divide the Jews in territories annexed from Poland into *Schutzjuden* or "protected" (wealthy) and *Betteljuden* or "tolerated" (poor) who were to be deported to the Polish Kingdom under Russia where by 1910 Yiddish speaking Jewish population represented nearly 15 percent of population; while in Austrian Galicia 11 percent, and in Prussian Poland 1.3 percent, down from the original pre-partition uniform distribution of the Jews numbering about 10 percent of population throughout the Polish Republic. The first anti-Jewish laws for the former Polish provinces were already enforced by the Berlin government in 1797.

1824 Act by King Fredrick Wilhelm III von Hohenzollern: Constitution of the Grand Duchy of Poznan; an executive branch headed by the King; actual administration by provincial president; unicameral Seym; two-thirds majority rule; elective rights of Christian males only; appointed judges to enforce the laws decreed by the king; right to demand protection of person and property.

1824 Act of incorporation of Gdansk, Pomerania, into Prussian province with its capital in Koenigsberg (Krolewiec), while the rest of Pomerania was formed into a province with its capital in Stettin (Szczecin), for the purpose of enforcing Germanization program of the Berlin government; imposition of German language in church services in Silesia; protest led by Jerzy Terski, arrested in Breslau (Wroclaw) in 1826; massive expropriations of Polish landholders, Germanization pressure on the 416 Polish elementary schools in the Grand Duchy of Poznan.

1827 Seym included successful petitioning to extend political rights and obligations to the Jews; this created favorable conditions for upper class Jews and led to their eventual assimilation in Germany, after eviction of Jewish proletariat to the Polish Kingdom; the successful assimilation of the wealthy Jews remaining in Germany was facilitated by their subculture based on Yiddish, a Germanic language (success of assimilation was evident during World War I when the Jews represented the highest percentage of decorated German officers of any ethnic group in Germany. For a short few years in recent times being an assimilated Jew in Germany was a touchstone of respectability as nowhere else in Europe. Jews were among patriotic supporters of policies of Berlin government and made an important contribution to the German culture); Seym of Poznan protesting political discrimination against the Poles.

1834 Ordinance prohibiting the use of Polish language in the schools of Pomerania (1842–46, growth of conspiratorial activities for Polish independence in the Grand Duchy of Poznan).

1847 Political trials in Berlin, sentencing to death of Ludwik Mieroslawski (1814–1878), Karol Libelt (1807–1875), and others—protested by German liberals including Karl Marks (1818–1883); set free in the revolution of 1848.

1848 Act of installation of Polish Administration in Poznan; insurgents fighting against German army; Polish victories at Miloslaw and Sokolow under the commander-in-chief of the forces of insurrection Ludwik Mieroslawski; Church and owners of manorial estates demand cessation of hostilities; brutal pacification of Poznania by Prussian Army followed by amnesty; restoration of Polish language in elementary schools of Upper Silesia; admission of Polish deputies to the parliament in Berlin; formation of Polish parliamentary circle in Berlin; Poles obstructing full German unification under Prussia; German radicals including Friedrich Engels (1820–95) supporting the anti-Polish policies; Poles perceived as a threat to German security and prosperity.

1849 Grand Duchy of Poznan denied autonomy (promised earlier).

1850 Polish deputies to Berlin Parliament refusing to swear allegiance to the new Prussian constitution and resigning in protest against making the Grand Duchy of Poznan a part of the Prussian State.

1852 Decree banning Polish associations and newspapers; new rules designed to hamper Polish press.

1858 Eighteen Polish deputies elected to the Prussian Parliament.

1871 Declaration of German Empire by Prussia in conquered Paris, Prussians "the best of the Germans,"; Germanity becoming the touchstone of respectability; growth of German ethnocentricity; increasing intensity of anti-Polish policies.

1871–78 *Kulturkampf*, anti-Catholic policies of the Berlin government for imposition of the "blood and iron" hegemony of Prussia over the rest of Germany; in Polish areas *Kulturkamph* lasted past 1878 and it was connected with politics of forced Germanization of Poles; it resulted in unification of Catholic clergy with intellectuals, nobles, townspeople and peasants in Polish resistance.

1872 Berlin Congress of Emperors of Austria, Prussia, and Russia, commemorating the first partition of Poland and recommitting their governments to eradicate Poland "forever."

1877 German lanaguage imposed on the Seym of the Grand Duchy of Poznan packed with Germans.

1886 Decree founding German Colonization Commission with initial capital of 100,000,000 marks for purchases of land held by Poles and for resale of it to Germans; Berlin government's response to the economic success of Polish banks in Poznan and mass migration of the German settlers away from Polish provinces; founding in 1886 of Polish cultural and educational newspaper in Warmia, the *Olsztyn Gazette* (published until 1939).

1887 Decree on removal of Polish language from all schools in Poznania, Pomerania, Warmia, and Mazuria.

1889 Polish Miners' Union of Self-Help in Upper Silesia conducting ten day general strike in protest against German exploitation and Germanization.

1893 Founding of Polish Socialist Party of Greater Poland in Poznania with the purpose to rebuild an independent Polish state; program proclamation in 1897.

1894 Anti-Polish extremist lobby formed as the *Deutscher Ostmarkenverein*, or *Hakata* with political slogans similar to Hitler's *Lebensraum;* glorification of German Brethren known as Teutonic Knights, perpetrators of medieval mass murders including genocide of the Balto-Slavic Prussians committed in the name of the gospel of charity (and leading to extinction of the Prussian language); further intensification of anti-Polish measures; widespread Polish response; "No Kashubia without Poland," massive Polish national revival.

1895 Founding of Polish People's Bank in Bytom, Silesia, followed by forming similar savings and loans banks throughout Upper Silesia in Opole (1897), in Siemianowice (1898), in Katowice (1898), and in Raciborz (1900).

1896 Founding of Peoples' Party of Mazuria and newspaper *Peo-*

ple's Gazette.

1898 Anti-Polish Emergency Laws in Prussia. An increase of funds of the German Colonization Commission in Polish provinces to 200,000,000 marks; growth of German sense of insecurity in the East. Prohibition to settle in new Polish villages without a special permit. Growth of membership in the Polish National League for self-defense.

1901 School strike in Wrzesnia against changing school prayer from Polish to German; public flogging of children; jailing of protesting parents (up to two years).

1903 Election victory in the race for Berlin parliament by Wojciech Korfanty (1873–1939) in Katowice-Zabrze against government backed German political machine.

1904 Anti-Polish law on land settlements.

1904–1906 Wave of strikes protesting persecution of the Poles in Silesia, especially Rybnik and Katowice region, in all of Poznania, in Pomerania (in Gdansk, Torun, Sopot, and Elblag), in Warmia, and in Mazuria.

1906 Strike of 100,000 school children in Pomerania and Poznania demanding education in the Polish language.

1907 Election victory in Upper Silesia of five Polish deputies to the Berlin Parliament, where they joined Polish Circle of Deputies.

1908 Prussian government's Law of Compulsory Expropriation of lands of Polish owners for sale to Germans; decree on elimination of Polish language from public meetings leading to creation in 1909 of the National Democratic Party in Greater Poland.

1910 Founding of the Mazurian Peoples' Bank in Szczytno by the Mazurian Peoples' Party; founding of Polish Christian Democratic Party of Silesia and its newspaper the *Goniec Wielkopolski (Greater Poland's Messenger)*.

1912 Founding of the Polish-Catholic Peoples' Party in Grudziadz.

1913 Act of Abolition of the Grand Duchy of Poznan and its incorporation into Germany; raising the funds of German Colonization Commission in Polish provinces to 995,000,000 marks to stem German flight from the East which in the last twenty years included three million Germans.

1918 Mass meetings in the Polish lands occupied by Germany (Poznania, Silesia, Pomerania, Kashubia, Ermland-Warmia, and Mazuria), and by the Poles in the German army and in coal mines of Westphalia to elect deputies to the Seym of Poznan for the purpose of joining an independent Poland.

City Republic of Cracow (1815–1846)—"A Free City," a Joint Protectorate of Austria, Prussia and Russia

1818 Constitution prepared by Adam Czartoryski (1770–1861), approved by Austria, Prussia, and Russia; bicameral parliament: House of Representatives (the Seym) of 42 members and the Senate of 13 members.

1831 Russian occupation of Cracow.

1833 Revision of the constitution; rule by representatives of Austria, Prussia, and Russia; suspension of the freedom of the press and autonomy of the University of Cracow; population under strict police control.

1831–41 Austrian occupation of Cracow.

1846 Act of Cracow: Proclamation of the National Government of the Polish Commonwealth; Revolution of Cracow; armed forces under Ludwik Mieroslawski planning an offensive on Warsaw; lack of peasant support; support by miners and steel mill workers; pacification by Austrian, Prussian, and Russian armies; defeat of the insurrectionists in battles in Cracow and vicinity; obliteration of the Republic of Cracow; annexation by Austria; peasants continuing to refuse to do serf work.

Kingdom of Galicia and Lodomeria (Southern Poland) under Austria (1772/95–1918)

Renaming of Southern or Lesser Poland with names of Ruthenian-Ukrainian provinces consistent with Austrian policy to eradicate everything Polish and to extend Ukrainian ethnic claims all the way to Cracow; steep rise in taxation; police terror; close cooperation with police forces of Prussia and Russia; strict censorship; numerous imperial bureaucracy staffed by Germans pestering the population with intricate formalities.

1817 Revival of provincial Seym of Estates in Lwow (after functioning in 1782–88 and to function in 1817–1845) by a decree of Francis

I of Austria including wealthy landowners with aristocratic Austrian titles, two deputies from Lwow and the Chancellor of the University of Lwow, not a representative body, entitled to petitions only and allowed cultural activities such as the Ossolinski Foundation.

1845 Proposal by the Seym of Estates to convert peasant serfs into rent paying tenants not approved by Austrian government which was about to use the peasant grievances to thwart an imminent uprising for independence of Poland.

1846 Cracow Revolution thwarted by Austrian Army; Peasant uprising in Galicia inspired by Austria's Klemens Metternich (1773–1859) to counteract Polish national uprising led by nobles and intellectuals; killing of 2,000 Polish nobles; pogrom of 470 manorial estates; pacification of Galicia by the Austrian army.

1848 National Council of Lwow demanding a representative Seym and an abolition of serfdom; Austrians creating a mass of tiny peasant holdings unable to support the former serfs. Creation of the Central Ruthenian Council in Lwow under leadership of Uniat clergy.

1848 Seym of Lwow acting in tradition of General Seymiks of Lesser Poland and Ruthenia with limited but well-defined legislative powers and elective deputies. Building of Cracow-Vienna railraod with earnings of Wieliczka salt mines.

1852 Distillation of crude oil and (in 1853) invention of oil lamp by Ignacy Lukasiewicz (1822–1882), who in 1862 built the first oil refinery in Europe and used American oil drilling techniques.

1861 Act of Vienna by Franz Joseph of Austria: Constitution of the Kingdom of Galicia and Lodomeria, the speaker of the Seym of Lwow and the viceroy appointed by the Austrian emperor (liberalization after Austrian defeat in Italy in 1859, Austria falling into German sphere of influence).

1861–1875 Seym of Lwow reverting to the function of Provincial General Seymik, electing 38 deputies to the parliament in Vienna.

1864 Marshal law in Galicia; prohibition of helping the insurrection in the Polish Kingdom under Russia.

1866 Agenor Goluchowski, viceroy of Galicia, establishing Polish language in the provincial administration (after the defeat of Austria by Prussia).

1867 Autonomy of Galicia while Austria becoming Austro-Hungary; Polish and Ukrainian language in public schools; legalization of labor unions.

1869 Decree of replacing German with Polish in all state offices and courts of Galicia; publication of conservative program of cooperation with Vienna government for expansion of Polish autonomy and against radical conspiracies.

1872 Polish autonomous administration of Galicia and Lodomeria; re-introduction of Polish and Ukrainian official languages. Polish restored as the language of instruction at the universities of Lwow and Cracow and in the newly created Politechnic Institute of Lwow; reforming of the Scientific Society into Academy of Sciences in Cracow.

1874 Opening of the first national fair and exhibition in Lwow showing Galicia as the least industrialized and poorest province of Europe with the highest birthrate and deathrate; ridiculing of the "Austrian program" which set 3 percent of Germans to oppress 45 percent of Poles, who were to oppress 41 percent of Ruthenians, who were to oppress 11 percent of Yiddish-speaking Jews, who, in turn by virtue of their "stranglehold" on economy, were to oppress everybody. The 200,000 public officials ruling over 180,000 Jewish merchants and 220,000 Jewish innkeepers and a mass of undersized Jewish businesses and equally undersized Polish and Ukrainian farms supporting 81 percent of the population; only 400 families had enough land to be considered wealthy; Galicia, the largest province of the Austrian Empire paid the highest rate of income taxes in Europe (by 1914 two million people emigrated from Galicia, mostly to the United States).

1877 *Poland's Past in Outline* by Michal Bobrzynski (1849–1935), of the "Stanczyk Group" or the "Pessimist" school of Polish history in Cracow.

1877–1913 Seym of Lwow controlled by a Polish majority; friction with the Ukrainian minority.

1890–1911 Galician crude oil production rising from 92 to 1,488,000 tons.

1890–1913 Cieszyn, Silesia, coal mining increasing from 3,400,000 to 7,600,000 tons or about half of the entire Austro-Hungarian production.

1892 Founding of Social-Democratic Party of Galicia with own newspapers; demands for 10 or 8 hour work day, better working conditions, and cheap housing.

1895 Founding in Lwow of *All-Polish Review (Przeglad Wszechpolski)* by Roman Dmowski (1864–1939) of the National League, which in 1897 became National Democratic Party.

1903 Proclamation of political program of National League or National Democracy in Dmowski's book *Thoughts of a Modern Pole* including the idea that Germany is the main enemy of Polish people and that Poland may be rebuilt only in alliance with Russia; Dmowski believing that there is no hope to assimilate Yiddish-speaking Jewish masses and formulating anti-Semitic political programs.

1905 *History of Polish Government in Outline* by Stanislaw Kutrzeba (1876–1946), first of the many well documented 20th century works.

1908 Founding in Lwow of Union for Active Resistance by Pilsudski's associates Kazimierz Sosnkowski (1865–1967) and Wladyslaw Sikorski (1881–1943).

1910 **Founding of Rifleman Association for conventional military training in Lwow, Galicia; upgrading of guerrilla training of the Union for Active Resistance under the guise of training Austrian Army reservists; developing a small part-time army by 1911; branches in France, Belgium, Switzerland and the United States contributing money. A separate drive for a public subscription and erection in Cracow of a monument in commemoration of the Polish victory in 1410 over the Order of Teutonic Knights, a response to persecution of Poles in the German Empire under Prussia.**

1914 Conversion of the Riflemen's Association into a small army of Polish legions composed of Polish patriots, including a number of Jewish Poles. The percentage of college graduates and students among them was relatively high.

1916 A promise by the Emperor Franz Joseph of Austria to give political autonomy to Galicia and Lodomeria; proclamation of a constitutional Kingdom of Poland in the areas of the Russian partition by Germany and Austria, protested by the Tsar of Russia.

1917 Austrian project of a Kingdom of Austria-Hungary-Poland rejected by Polish representatives who demanded a reunited and independent Poland with a free access to the Baltic Sea.

1918 Polish Auxiliary Corps breaking through the Austrian lines at Rarancza under Col. Jozef Haller (1873–1960), to join Polish forces formed out of the disintegrating Russian Army; a protest against German-Austrian treaty concluded at Brest Litovsk with the Central Ukrainian Council providing for inclusion in Ukraine of Chelm region and eastern Galicia (German and Austrian need for Ukrainian grain prompted these terms); after breaking through German encirclement at Kaniow, Haller traveling through Murmansk to Paris to take over the command of the Polish Army created in France out of Poles from former German and Austrian armies.

1918 Polish deputies to the Austrian parliament declaring themselves citizens of an independent Poland.

1918 Proclamation of independence of the Duchy of Cieszyn (the Moravian Gate in the Carpathian Mountains) and intention to reunite Silesia with the reconstituted Polish Republic.

1918 Formation in Cracow of the Liquidation Commission to replace Austrian authorities.

1918 Austria transferring of political control and weapons in Lwow to the Ukrainian Committee fomenting (Nov. 3) a war between Poles and Ukrainians.

CONSTITUTIONAL ACTS IN THE SECOND POLISH REPUBLIC (1918–1945): SELF-DECLARED INDEPENDENCE SECURED BY FORCE OF ARMS

Nov. 5, 1918 Polish-Czech agreement on ethnic division of Cieszyn Silesia.

Nov. 7, 1918 Creation of Provisional Government of the Polish Republic in Lublin; Ignacy Daszynski prime minister; Edward Rydz-Smigly minister of war.

Nov. 11, 1918 Regency Council in Warsaw dissolving itself upon collapse of Germany; transferring its powers to Jozef Pilsudski, commander of Polish legions returning from internment in Germany (Magdeburg fortress).

Nov. 18, 1918 Jedrzej Moraczewski prime minister of a center-left cabinet.

Nov. 22, 1918 Government decree: Poland a republic; Jozef Pilsudski provisional head of state and commander-in-chief.

Nov. 24, 1918 Creation of a Provisional Governing Committee in Lwow after Polish Army gained control there.

Nov. 28, 1918 Government decree on general election to the Constitutional Seym.

Nov. 30, 1918 Poland admitted to peace negotiations by France and Great Britain.

Dec. 3–5, 1918 Provincial Seym in Poznan of 1403 deputies from Gdansk-Pomerania, Warmia, Mazuria, Silesia, Poznania and German areas populated by Poles; appointing a Supreme Peoples Council; demands that the Western Allies incorporate into Poland all of the lands annexed by Prussia in the partitions.

Dec. 26, 1918 Ignacy Paderewski (1860–1941) arriving in Poznan; expelling of the German garrison by a popular uprising.

Dec. 27, 1918 Supreme Peoples Council taking power in Poznan; war with Germany over the provinces of Greater Poland and Pomerania.

Jan. 10, 1919 Reorganization of the administration of Galicia and Cieszyn, Silesia.

Jan. 26, 1919 General Elections for Constitutional Seym; 230 deputies from Kingdom of Poland and Podlasie; 72 from western Lesser Poland; 20 from German Poland and 26 from Lesser Poland (previously elected to the German and Austrian parliaments respectively); eventually, with elections held in other districts, the total number reached 432 deputies on March 24, 1922.

Feb. 3, 1919 Signing in Paris of Polish-Czech border agreement on the basis of Nov. 5, 1918, ethnic division agreement.

Feb. 7, 1919 Decree on military draft to face Bolshevik "Target Vistula" offensive; first regular combat at Bereza Krtuska Feb. 14, 1919; war with Bolshevik Russia. Beginning of Pilsudski's diplomatic activity to form a federation of nations led by Poland and including Finland, Estonia, Latvia, Lithuania, Byelorussia, Ukraine, Don Cossacks, Kuban Cossacks, Georgia, Azerbaijan, and Armenia; the plan failed primarily because of British opposition out of fear that the new federation would be an ally of France; the British went on destroying the surrendered German arsenals rather than sending them to Poland faced with a life-and-death struggle against Bolshevik Russia. (Pilsudski's federation allied with the West offered a chance to stabilize the European continent and prevent the catastrophy of World War II.)

Feb. 16, 1919 Armistice with Germany; demarcation of border north of Silesia.

Feb. 20, 1919 Seym passing Provisional (Small) Constitution spelling out the powers of the Seym, government, and of the head of state.

Apr. 4, 1919 Agreement with France and Germany on transfer of the Polish Army from France.

Apr. 15, 1919 Dissolution of Polish National Committee in Paris, France.

Apr. 16, 1919 Polish Army occupation of Wilno (majority of inhabitants made up of Poles and pro-Polish Jews); war with Lithuania.

May 1919 Congress of Poles of Jewish Confession declaring loyalty to the Polish Republic despite ongoing conflicts between Zionists, who sought to persuade the Jews to leave Poland for Palestine, and extreme Polish nationalists who believed that assimilation of Jewish minority of 10 percent is impossible and propagated anti-Semitic policies (rejected by Pilsudski's government).

June 25, 1919 Supreme Allied Council transferring East Galicia to Poland.

June 28, 1919 Signing of the Peace Treaty at Versailles; for Poland Roman Dmowski and Ignacy Paderewski.

July 10, 1919 Seym reforming the agriculture; establishing maximum farm size.

Aug. 1, 1919 Seym Act of Incorporation of Greater Poland into Polish State.

Aug. 2, 1919 Seym Law on Standardization of the Polish Army.

Aug. 16–17, 1919 First Silesian uprising against German terror following a general strike in Upper Silesia; the first phase of war against Germany for Upper Silesia.

Dec. 8, 1919 Council of Allied Ambassadors proposing Soviet-Polish border on the River Bug and north to include Bialystock Region in Poland (a part of the "Curzon Line").

Dec. 13, 1919 to Apr. 9, 1920 Government of Prime Minister Leopold Skulski (1878–1940).

Jan. 15, 1920 Decree on standardization of the Polish mark as national currency.

Feb. 9, 1920 Gdansk becoming a free city; Office of General Commissioner of the Polish Republic starts functioning there.

May 7, 1920 Polish Army occupying Kiev in support of Ukrainian government of Hetman Semyon Petlura and to counteract imminent Soviet offensive from the north on the front line along Rivers Dvina, Berezina, and Dnieper. Soviet strike force included 800,000 men and three to one superiority in artillery.

May 10–12, 1920 General strike in Upper Silesia against German terror.

May 16, 1920 Elections to the Legislature of Gdansk.

June 23–July 24, 1920 Government of Prime Minister Wladyslaw Grabski.

July 1, 1920 Seym establishing Council of National Defense in face of Soviet offensive and imminent life-and-death struggle of over million and half of Soviet and Polish soldiers.

July 10, 1920 Spa Conference of Allied Ambassadors proposing provisional Polish-Soviet demarcation line including Lwow Region in Poland.

July 11, 1920 Falsification of the Spa Conference line in the office of British Prime Minister Lloyd George by shifting the border to include the Lwow Region in Soviet Russia as part of the proposed Curzon Line.

July 11, 1920 British anti-Polish decisions in the plebiscite in East Prussia (Powisle, Warmia, and Mazuria) during Soviet offensive towards Warsaw.

July 15, 1920 Seym laws on Silesian autonomy and on agrarian reform.

July 24, 1920 to Sept. 13, 1921 Government of National Defense of Prime Minister Wincenty Witos.

July 28, 1920 Allied ambassadors decision partitioning Cieszyn, Silesia, and leaving in Czechoslovakia a quarter of a million Poles in the strategic Moravian Gate (leading to Poland from southwest); Polish government protesting violation of the Polish-Czech border demarcation agreement of Feb. 3, 1919.

July 30 to Aug. 18, 1920 Soviet installation of Provisional Polish Revolutionary Committee of Julian Marchlewski, Feliks Dzierzynski, Edward Prochniak, Feliks Kon, Jozef Unszlicht, etc., in the occupied town of Bialystok.

Aug. 20–25, 1920 Second Polish uprising in Silesia against German terror despite Allied military presence; the second phase of war for Upper Silesia.

Oct. 12, 1920 Polish-Soviet Armistice signed in Riga, effective Oct. 18. Creation of Central Lithuania with a Polish majority by Gen. Lucian Zeligowski (1864–1946).

Oct. 27, 1920 Council of Allied Ambassadors proclaiming Gdansk a free city.

Nov. 15, 1920 Constitutional self-government established in Gdansk; treaty with Poland signed and guaranteed by the League of Nations.

Feb. 19, 1921 Signing of the Polish-French Common Defense Treaty.

Feb. 24, 1921 Signing in Riga of Polish-Soviet repatriation agreement including 400,000 Jews (actually about 800,000 Jewish refugees from U.S.S.R. entered Poland and were given Polish citizenship under this pact).

March 3, 1921 Signing of the Polish-Romanian Common Defense Treaty.

March 17, 1921 Seym Act: Constitution of the Polish Republic; bicameral parliament Seym and Senate; supreme power in the legislative branch, at any time producing a government crisis by failure to rally a majority to vote for confidence in the administration; regional self-government; independent judiciary; basic civil rights of all citizens, protection of life, personal freedom and property was guaranteed, as was freedom of speech, secrecy of correspondence and freedom of religion; voting rights of both sexes. Principal editor of the new constitution, Edward Dubanowicz (1881–1943). The Seym left to cope with an unworkable constitution (similar to the French).

March 3, 1921 Peace treaty signed with Soviet Russia and Ukraine at Riga; recognition of sovereignty of Soviet Republics of Ukraine and Byelorussia.

March 20, 1921 Inconclusive results of the plebiscite in Silesia.

May 2 to July 5, 1921 Third Polish uprising in Silesia led by Wojciech Korfanty (1873–1939) against German terror and an anti-Polish British project leaving a large Polish population on the German side.

June 22, 1920 League of Nations giving Poland the responsibility to defend the Free City of Gdansk and represent it internationally. Railroads of Gdansk becoming a part of Polish transportation system.

Oct. 12, 1921 League of Nations proposing Polish-German

border in Silesia accepted by the Council of the Allied Ambassadors Oct. 20, 1921.

Nov. 19–20, 2921 League of Nations drawing the demarcation line between Western and Central Lithuania.

Jan. 9, 1922 Elections to the Seym of Wilno representing Central Lithuania.

Feb. 20, 1922 Seym in Wilno voting for incorporation with Poland (the majority composed of ethnic Poles and pro-Polish Jews).

March 2, 1922 Act of incorporation of Central Lithuania into Poland.

March 24, 1922 Seym ratification of incorporation of Central Lithuania.

May 15, 1922 Signing of Polish-German border agreement in Silesia.

June–July, 1922 Establishing of Polish administration in eastern Upper Silesia.

Sept. 13, 1922 Seym approval of building of the port of Gdynia which in 1939 was the largest on the Baltic.

Dec. 9, 1922 National Assembly of the Seym and Senate electing Gabriel Narutowicz (1865–1922) to the presidency of Polish Republic.

Dec. 12, 1922 Assassination of President Gabriel Narutowicz.

Dec. 20, 1922 Election of President Stanislaw Wojciechowski (1869–1953).

March 14, 1924 League of Nations assigning to Poland peninsula of Westerplatte in Gdansk for handling of Polish defense materials.

Oct. 2, 1924 Poland signing the Charter of the League of Nations.

Nov. 15, 1924 Signing 180 million dollar war debt agreement with the United States.

Feb. 10, 1925 Commercial agreement with the United States; signing Concordat with Vatican; an increase of Church influence in Poland.

March 24, 1925 Anti-Polish speech by Lloyd George in Commons proposing revision of Polish-German border in favor of Germany; Poland viewed as an ally of France.

Oct. 5–16, 1925 Conference of Locarno; Germany questioning Polish borders; France and Poland signing agreement to counteract possible German aggression.

Oct. 28, 1925 Seym voting Social Security Law for white collar workers.

Dec. 1925 League of Nations authorizing stationing of Polish garrison in Gdansk on Westerplatte.

Dec. 28, 1925 Seym voting Agrarian Reform (until 1939 six million acres or 19 percent of land held in large estates were parcelled out to small farmers).

May 12–14, 1926 The military takeover of the government by Marshal Jozef Pilsudski in the name of stability after fifteen changes of government since the formation of the Second Polish Republic in 1918. President Stanislaw Wojciechowski and government resigning after struggle (about 200 dead and 1000 wounded).

May 31, 1926 Election of President Jozef Pilsudski who declined.

June 1, 1926 Election of President Ignacy Moscicki (1867–1946).

Aug. 2, 1926 Amendments to the Constitution of 1921. Presidential powers to include dissolving of the Seym and Senate and a rule by decree between parliamentary sessions (which could be delayed); limiting freedom of the press.

Sept. 16, 1926 Poland elected to temporary membership of the Council of the League of Nations.

July 6 and Oct. 20, 1927 Loans from the United States: $15 million for foreign exchange reserve and $66 million for economic stabilization; Thomas Dewey (1902–1971) joining the Supervisory Council of the Bank Polski.

Aug. 27, 1928 Poland signing the Briand-Kellog non-violence treaty.

1928–1929 Poland reaching prewar level of industrial production on the eve of the Great Depression.

March 17, 1930 Signing in Warsaw of commercial agreement with Germany to end twelve years of customs and trade war (amid demands by German politicians to expand Germany's territory at Polish expense).

Aug. 29, 1930 Dissolution of the Seym and Senate; call for new elections.

Sept. 10, 1930 Arrests and imprisonment of opposition leaders of the center-left coalition in the military prison in Brzesc on the Bug, followed by pacification of Eastern Galicia and tampering with election results.

Apr. 16, 1931 German provocations and terrorism in Gdansk.

Oct. 26, 1931 to Jan. 13, 1932 Trials and sentencing of opposition leaders, many of whom emigrate; Great Depression hitting Poland very hard; mass unemployment in towns and villages, hunger riots and strikes.

Apr. 18, 1932 Adolf Hitler demanding 1914 frontiers with Poland and France.

March 14, 1933 League of Nations approving an increase in Polish garrison on the Westerplatte peninsula in Gdansk to 200 men.

March 27, 1933 Government decree dissolving Dmowski's right wing party of the Camp of the Great Poland, organized in Dec. 1926, and including anti-Semitic propaganda; Alliance of Poles in Germany protesting persecution of Poles in Silesia.

May 5, 1934 Prolongation for the next ten years of the non-aggression treaty with Soviet Union and exchanging ambassadors, rather than legates.

Dec. 12, 1934 Creation of an internment camp in Bereza Kartuska for detainment of opposition activists by an administrative decision.

Sept. 13, 1934 Cancellation by Poland of treaty on ethnic minorities at the League of Nations (because Polish laws were "adequate").

March 23, 1935 New Constitution (signed by the president on April 23) increasing powers of presidency (trying to follow the American model); reducing the number of deputies from 444 to 208; removal of patronage quotas and electing all deputies by name; two-mandate electoral districts created for ethnic minorities (borrowing some features of the Seym of the First Republic); the president to be elected by joint session of the Seym and Senate; he was to appoint a prime minister and cabinet ministers responsible to him.

Apr. 28 to Oct. 12, 1935 Third government of Walery Slawek (1879–1939) issuing a liberal election ordinance for municipal self-government.

Apr. 5, 1935 Polish protest against anti-Polish demonstrations led by Herman Goering (1893–1946) and Josepf Paul Goebbels (1897–1945) in Gdansk.

Jan. 18, 1936 League of Nations warning the Senate of Gdansk that it violates its constitution; warning based on a well documented complaint by Polish high commissioner in Gdansk.

Feb. 7, 1936 Deputy Janina Prystor introducing a bill in the Seym requiring that animals be stunned before being slaughtered, Jewish politicians considering this law as "the first wedge into the constitutional equality of the Jewish population in Poland." Reports of pogroms in form of anti-Jewish boycotts and rioting without killings or desecrations of synagogues as was the case in Germany, Hungary, and Romania at the time.

Apr. 20, 1936 Presidential decree on the Fund for National Defense.

Aug. 31, 1937 German terror in Gdansk, also coercing Polish children to go to German schools.

Jan. 11, 1938 Stanislaw Kulczynski, the president of the University of Lwow, resigning in protest against anti-Semitic riots by extremist students who demanded imposition of proportional Jewish quotas, tried to impose regulations requiring that the Jews sit in the back of classrooms, and protested against "overcrowding" of the law and medicine fields by the Jews. Similar events occurred in other schools in 1938–39.

March 17, 1938 Polish ultimatum to Lithuania to normalize diplomatic relations in order to improve Polish position in the north while Hitler annexed Austria.

Sept. 30, 1938 Polish ultimatum to Czechoslovakia to return to Poland a part of Cieszyn, Silesia, populated by a quarter of a million Poles living in the strategic Moravian Gate of entry to Poland (while Great Britain and France were appeasing Hitler at Munich and Soviet Union was threatening to terminate the non-aggression pact with Poland).

March 31, 1939 Great Britain and France proclaiming their guarantee of Polish independence and inviolability of Poland's borders.

April 28, 1939 Germany terminating non-aggression treaty with Poland and demanding annexation of Gdansk and German-controlled highways and railroads through Poland to East Prussia; demands rejected by Poland.

May to Aug. 1939 Poland rejecting subordination to the Soviets under cover of a military alliance; refusing the passage of Soviet Army through Poland.

July 25, 1939 Poland giving Great Britain and France each a copy of linguistic deciphering electro-mechanical computer for German secret military code system Enigma, complete with specifications, perforated cards, and updating procedures. Thanks to the

Polish system for breaking of Enigma the British project Ultra was able to read for the Allies all German secret messages during the entire war of 1939–1945 (the Enigma deciphering computer was developed by linguists and mathematicians of the University of Poznan in 1932–38).

Aug. 23, 1939 to June 22, 1941 Soviet-German pact on non-aggression (setting the stage for the outbreak of World War II); secret clauses on partition of Poland; beginning of Hitler-Stalin partnership which resulted in obliterating Poland and conducting mass murders and deportations of Polish citizens.

Aug. 25, 1939 Signing of Polish-British Common Defense Pact against German aggression.

Aug. 31, 1939 German ultimatum to Poland by media (not delivered formally) demanding plebiscite in Gdansk, Pomerania, and annexation of the Free City.

Sept. 1, 1939 Beginning of World War II; German cruiser *Schleswig-Holstein* (while on a "good will" visit) opening fire on Polish positions in Gdansk on Westerplatte (200 Polish soldiers held out there against massive German attacks until Sept. 7). Air raids on the open Polish cities, airports, and railroads. Germans attacking Polish fortified positions with 70 divisions; two times more men that in incompletely mobilized Polish 40 divisions. Rare pure-cavalry engagement between German 1st Cavalry and Polish Mazowiecka Brigades. The horses were basically used for transportation and never in attacks against tanks or heavy machinegun fire. German forces depended primarily on horse-drawn supplies throughout World War II in which more horses were killed than in any other war in history. Beginning of perfidious German propaganda about Poles charging tanks with sabers, an absurdity since as all Polish cavalry brigades had light tank units and the men were very familiar with armor; cavalry represented 10 percent of Polish and 2 percent of German forces.

Sept. 3, 1939 During the battle on Poland's frontiers Great Britain and France declare war on Germany, but let the Polish Army fight alone.

Sept. 8–27, 1939 Siege of Warsaw.

Sept. 9, 1939 Polish-French agreement to form Polish Army units in France under General Wladyslaw Sikorski (two divisions and two brigades including one in Syria).

Sept. 9, 1939 Counterattack by armies of Poznan and Pomerania near Lodz.

Sept. 9–22 Counteroffensive on the Bzura River in central Poland derailing German pincer movement.

Sept. 11, 1939 Marshal Edward Smigly-Rydz orders Polish armies to re-group and form Romanian bridgehead to hold during the promised British-French offensive. Soviet mobilization announced amid communication breakdown among Polish forces; some confusion concerning which side the Soviets are on.

Sept. 14, 1939 Successful counterattack by the Army of Pomerania near Lowicz and Skierniewice causes concentration of German armor there after withdrawal from central Vistula; decisive German air superiority ends the battle on Sept. 17.

Sept. 17, 1939 Soviet attack on Poland; battles against Army Corps of Defense of (eastern) Borderlands; Soviets ground attack with 24 divisions and air support organized into Byelorussian and Ukrainian front (total Soviet force of about 60 divisions lined up against Poland).

Sept. 18–20, 1939 Counterattack of Army of Krakow near Tomaszow Lubelski; the largest Polish-German tank battle of the campaign.

Sept. 20–Oct. 2, 1939 Defense of Hel Peninsula.

Sept. 22, 1939 Surrender of Lwow to the Soviets after battle against Germans.

Sept. 27, 1939 Capitulation of Warsaw; organization of Polish resistance movement, first under General Michal Karaszewicz-Tokarzewski (1893–1964) in the Service of Poland's Victory *(Sluzba Zwyciestwu Polski)*, soon renamed Alliance for an Armed Struggle *(Zwiazek Walki Zbrojnej)*.

Sept. to Oct. Polish government resigning after crossing to Romania. President Ignacy Moscicki appointing Wladyslaw Raczkiewicz (1885–1947) as his successor; nomination of General Wladyslaw Sikorski as prime minister of Polish Government-in-Exile and commander-in-chief (Sept. 30, 1939, in France; after Apr. 19, 1940, in Great Britain).

Oct. 5, 1939 Battle of Kock; (Polish Army before collapsing destroyed one-third of German tanks and airplanes used against it, Polish Navy arriving intact to England and on Apr. 8, 1940, sinking the first German ship of W.W. II).

Oct. 1939 Partition of Poland along the Hitler-Stalin Line on the Bug River, as agreed on Sept. 28, 1939; annexation to Germany of 90,000 sq. km. with ten million population and formation of General Government of 100,000 sq. km. with twelve million people; annexation to Soviet Union of 200,000 sq. km. with fifteen million population, less the Wilno Region incorporated into Lithuania. Polish military losses: 66,300 troops killed, 133,700 wounded, 587,000 captured by the Germans and about 200,000 by the Russians; 100,000 escaped to Romania, Hungary, and the Baltic republics. German losses: 16,000 killed, 32,000 wounded. Soviet losses about 1000 killed and 2000 wounded. Polish civilian losses heavier than all combined military losses in the war theater. Mass murders of Polish civilians by German army and security forces; beginning of five-year German reign of terror in Poland and mass deportations to Soviet Union.

Dec. 9, 1939 Creation in Paris of National Council under Ignacy Paderewski, an advisory body to the President and Government-in-Exile.

Apr. 20, 1940 Declaration of Polish, British, and French governments condemning German mass murders and other violations of the international law in occupied Poland.

Aug. 5, 1940 Polish-British military pact integrating war effort of Polish forces under overall British command.

Oct. 2, 1940 Germans creating Warsaw ghetto by concentrating Jews and evicting Polish Christian population.

Nov. 11, 1940 London Declaration of Reconciliation by Polish and Czechoslovak governments in exile; beginning of plans for postwar Confederation which would eventually encompass the states between Germany and Russia, from Finland to Greece, including at first Poland, Czechoslovakia, Yugoslavia, and Greece and eventually Finland, Estonia, Latvia, Lithuania, Romania, Hungary, and Bulgaria. Creation of clandestine representation of Polish Government-in-Exile in occupied Poland.

May 5, 1941 Ottawa Declaration on formation of Polish armed forces in Canada for service in Europe.

July 30, 1941 Resumption of diplomatic relations between Poland and U.S.S.R.

Aug. 14, 1941 Polish-Soviet agreement to form a Polish army in U.S.S.R.

Nov. 1941 German preparations for a total genocide of the Jews in Auschwitz, Majdanek, Kholm, and other death camps. Jews assigned 250 calories per day.

Jan. 1, 1942 United Nations declaration on uniting all forces to defeat Nazi Germany and Fascist Italy.

Feb. 1942 Reorganization of resistance in Poland in Armia Krajowa, the Home Army under the Government-in-Exile in London as an armed force of the Second Republic; British agreement to form the First Polish Armored Division in Great Britain to participate later in 1944 invasion of France, Belgium, Holland, and Germany.

March 18, 1942 Start of evacuation of the Polish Army from Soviet Union to Near East through Iran allowed by the Soviets (because of their need for the Lend-Lease aid from the United States) and demanded by the Poles because of an impossibility to account for 15,000 Polish Army officers captured in 1939 and deported to Russia; suspicion of mass murders of Polish officers by the Soviets. (Evacuation first of 30,000 soldiers and 14,000 Polish civilians, former inmates of Soviet prison camps by Aug. 30; total of 110,000 Polish soldiers evacuated from Soviet Union to Iraq and Palestine).

June 3, 1942 Polish-Czechoslovak declaration of postwar Confederation (after Jan. 15, 1942 Greek-Yugoslav and Jan. 23, 1942, Polish-Czechoslovak pacts) to unite in one confederation the nations between Germany and Russia friendly to the United States; The Confederation was to be based on the Atlantic Charter.

July 1, 1942 United States extending Lend-Lease Act to Poland.

July 19, 1942 German Governments Decree signed by Heinrich Himmler (1900–45) on extermination of Jews in occupied Poland (organization of death camps of Belzec in March, of Sobibor in May, Treblinka in July, for Jews deported from ghettos organized by the Germans; continuation of mass murders on Polish population, especially in preparation of farmlands in Zamosc Region for colonization by Germans from Besarabia, Ukraine and Baltic states of Lithuania, Latvia, and Estonia; evacuation of 293 towns and villages of 110,000 people, including 30,000 children, to concentration camps in Auschwitz, Majdanek, etc.; arresting of 70,000 in Warsaw streets for mass deportation to concentration and labor camps in Germany.

Sept. 27, 1942 Founding in Warsaw of the Council of Assistance for the Jews by the Delegate of the Government-in-Exile, code name "Zegota" (unique in Europe, it included political organizations ranging from Catholics to socialists); organizing help for Jews in the ghettos, camps, and those hidden by the Poles in form of money, safe houses, food, clothing, medicine, false documentation (as non-Jews), over 100,000 Jews were helped.

Feb. 2, 1943 Turning point of World War II, capitulation of German Sixth Army in Stalingrad.

March 1943 Creation of Association of Polish Patriots including employees of Soviet security forces as a nucleus of pro-Soviet regime and Soviet controlled Polish People's Army.

Apr. 12, 1943 German announcement of discovery of mass graves of 4200 Polish officers in Katyn forest in Russia.

Apr. 19–May 16, 1943 Jewish uprising of 600 men in the Warsaw Ghetto prepared with help of Polish resistance in accumulation of weapons and construction of bunkers (since Jan. 1943) and with participation of Polish sharpshooters ending in a complete destruction of the ghetto and killing of 72,000 Jews by German forces of 2,000 under Gen. Jurgen Stropp, followed by Jewish uprisings in Lwow Apr. 3, Treblinka Aug. 2, Bialystok Aug. 16–20, Sobibor Oct. 14, 1943 and others.

Apr. 25, 1943 Soviet Union breaking diplomatic relation with government of Gen. Sikorski because of his inquiry into mass murder of Polish officers buried in Katyn forest in Russia (also Soviet opposition to his initiative to create the postwar Confederation of States between Germany and U.S.S.R. allied with the West).

May 9, 1943 Beginning of formation of a Polish Kosciuszko Division in U.S.S.R.; while in Great Britain Polish Army of 100,000, Airforce of 12,000 and Navy of 3,000 men under the Polish Government-in-Exile.

July 4, 1943 Death of Gen. Wladyslaw Sikorski near Gibraltar in a sabotaged British airplane followed on July 7 by nomination of Gen. Kazimierz Sosnkowski as Commander-in-Chief of Polish forces in the West and on July 14 formation of a new government-in-exile by Prime Minister Stanislaw Mikolajczyk.

Nov. 1, 1943 Moscow Declaration by the United States, Great Britain and U.S.S.R. on crimes committed by the Germans in occupied Europe and promise to punish the perpetrators.

Oct. 9, 1943 Founding of United Nations Relief and Rehabilitation Administration (UNRRA).

Nov. 28–Dec. 1, 1943 Teheran, United States and Great Britain accepting the Hitler-Stalin line on the Bug River as a postwar boundary between U.S.S.R. and Poland; inclusion of Poland in postwar Soviet zone of influence in exchange for Soviet participation in war against Japan (Roosevelt and Churchill secretly agreeing to the loss of independence of Poland); the U.S. and Britain promising to fight on a western front in France.

Dec. 1943 Formation in Poland of joint committee of the representatives of Government-in-Exile, the command of the Home Army (AK), and four democratic parties (excluding communists) for struggle for independence.

Dec. 31, 1943 to Jan. 1, 1944 Constitutional convention of pro-Soviet groupings proclaiming statute of Soviet style regional councils (Rady Narodowe) under a central council presided over by Boaleslaw Bierut (1892–1956), an employee of Soviet security forces (now K.G.B.) where he headed the Polish desk (he was a 1930 graduate of Lenin's International Academy in Moscow).

Dec. 1943–Feb. 1944 Relocation of the 2nd Polish Corps from Near East to Italy.

Jan. 9, 1944 Formation of Council of National Unity for an Independent Poland.

Jan. 17, 1944 Soviet offer to talk with Government-in-Exile on the basis of acceptance the Hitler-Stalin border on the Bug River, otherwise called the Curzon Line; Winston Churchill supporting the Soviet position in Commons on Feb. 22.

March 21, 1944 the First Polish People's Army organized by the Soviets; 80,000 men soon increased to 200,000.

May 11–18, 1944 Victory of 2nd Polish Corps at Monte Cassino, Italy, opening for allied advance the coastal road from the south to Rome.

June 6, 1944 Invasion of France under Gen. Dwight D. Eisenhower, Polish Navy participating.

July 15, 1944 Declaration of intention to continue the government of the 2nd Polish Republic after victory over Germany.

July 20–21, 1944 Crossing of Bug River by the 1st Polish People's Army under Soviet control and inclusion in it of the pro-Soviet underground People's Army.

July 21–22, 1944 Beginning of the 3rd Polish Republic within the Soviet bloc, creation of Polish Committee of National Liberation (controlled by the Soviets) to become a provisional government of Poland; proclamation of Manifesto to the Polish Nation calling for struggle against the Germans and for relocation of Polish western border to the Oder-Neisse River Line and eastern border to the Bug River, (the former Hitler-Stalin Line now referred to as the Curzon Line); formation of the command of pro-Soviet Polish Army with Soviet advisers and a Soviet security forces' employee Gen. Aleksander Zawadzki (1899–1964) as the chief political officer.

Aug. 1 to Oct. 2, 1944 Warsaw uprising proclaiming an independent Poland; Hitler ordering complete destruction of Warsaw; killed over 150,000 civilians (massacre of 40,000 in Warsaw-Wola alone) and 18,000 insurgents; wounded over 100,000 civilians and 25,000 insurgents; losses to the 1st Polish People's Army 3764 officers and soldiers; German losses 26,000 men. 87 percent of Warsaw destroyed (mostly after the combat by German Army Engineers) as the Soviet Army stood by across the Vistula River, deadly struggle between Germans and Russians did not prevent them from again joining hands against the Poles.

Aug. 6–7, 1944 Unsuccessful attempt by Winston Churchill and Joseph Stalin to form a "coalition government" including the Government-in-Exile of the 2nd Republic with the provisional government under Boleslaw Bierut organized by the Soviets; a second unsuccessful attempt Oct. 17, 1944.

Aug. 8–20, 1944 Polish First Armored Division decisive in the battle of Fallaise which led to liberation of France.

Sept. 6, 1944 Provisional government decree dividing 13,000,000 acres among one million farmers.

Oct. 2, 1944 Surrender of Warsaw by Gen. Tadeusz Bor Komorowski.

Dec. 31, 1944 Replacing the rule of Polish Committee of National Liberation by Provisional Government of Polish Republic, controlled by the Soviets and nominating as president Soviet security agent Boleslaw Bierut, formally recognized by the Soviets on Jan. 4, 1945, moved to Warsaw Feb. 1, 1945. Organizing 2nd Polish "People's" Army of 55,000, a total of 280,000 men under the Soviets.

Feb. 2–11, 1945 Yalta agreement (never ratified by the U.S. Congress), Roosevelt Churchill, and Stalin establishing Soviet domination in eastern and central Europe.

March 27, 1945 Gen. Leopold Okulicki (1898–1953), the last commander-in-chief of the Home Army (AK) and Jan Stanislaw Jankowski (1882–1953), former vice-premier and delegate of the Government-in-Exile arrested by the Soviets in Poland (sentenced to ten years imprisonment in Moscow in June 1945).

May 2–8, 1945 Fall of Berlin followed by an unconditional surrender of Germany; 6,028,000 Polish citizens killed by the Germans, including 644,000 in combat; plus 1,000,000 perished as a result of deportation of 1,700,000 to Soviet Union. Nearly three million Polish Jews were killed by the Germans; total of eleven million people of different nationalities were killed by the Germans in Poland.

THE THIRD POLISH REPUBLIC— RECENT EVENTS

June 28, 1945 Formation of Government of National Unity under Soviet control but including the former prime minister of the Government-in-Exile, Stanislaw Mikolajczyk (acting under British pressure).

July 5, 1945 Recognition of Soviet-sponsored Polish Government of National Unity by the United States and Great Britain and their withdrawal of diplomatic recognition from the Government-in-Exile of the Second Polish Republic.

July 17 to Aug. 2, 1945 Potsdam agreements by U.S.A., U.S.S.R., and Great Britain fixing the western border of Poland on the Odra-Nysa Line, closing it to returning 5,000,000 German refugees, authorizing evacuation of additional 3,200,000 Germans, and providing means for their transportation to designated resettlement areas in East and West Germany.

July 28–30, 1945 Re-organization of leftist Poles into Polish National Council in France followed by return of 60,000 Poles from France to Poland in 1946–1949.

Sept. 14, 1945 Signing an agreement with United Nations Relief and Rehabilitation Administration for delivery of supplies to Poland.

Oct. 16, 1945 Signing of the Charter of the United Nations (of Apr. 26, 1945) by Wincenty Rzymowski (1883–1950), foreign minister of Poland.

Nov. 25, 1945 Boleslaw Piasecki (1914–79), prewar leader of extreme right faction (advocating university quotas, economic boycott, and eviction of the Jews), in wartime resistance, sentenced for killing of Soviet guerrillas, in death row of N.K.V.D. prison, writing memorandum on ways to subvert the Catholic Church in Poland and subordinate it to the Soviets; starting "progressive" Catholic press (Today and Tomorrow, Pax Publishing House etc., not all of his publications were harmful to the Church).

Jan. 3, 1946 Act of nationalization of industry in Poland.

Feb. 14, 1946 Census: 23,929,757 inhabitants; 5,02,100 in northwestern areas (acquired from Germany in compensation for the loss of land to Soviet Union), including still about 2,000,000 Germans.

June 30, 1946 National referendum on abolition of the Senate, socialization of Poland, and acceptance of the Odra-Nysa frontier with Germany; Soviet tampering with the referendum, including staging of a massacre of 42 Jews on July 4, 1946, to distract attention of the foreign observers and to make them believe that Polish resistance to Sovietization movement perpetrated the crime.

Sept. 21, 1946 Enacting three-year plan for reconstruction (1947–1949).

Jan. 19, 1947 Election of Constitutional Seym under Soviet control.

Feb. 5, 1947 to Nov. 20, 1952 Boleslaw Bierut, the first president of the Third Polish Republic, a high ranking officer of Soviet security (for seven years the head of the Polish desk of N.K.V.D. or K.G.B.)

Feb. 6, 1947 Formation of the cabinet under Prime Minister Jozef Cyrankiewicz, former social democrat, converted to pro-Soviet orientation while imprisoned by the Germans in Auschwitz concentration camp.

Feb. 19, 1947 Enactment of Small Constitution as an amendment to the Constitution of 1921.

July 3, 1947 Seym act on reconstruction of Warsaw as the capital of Poland, amid intense liquidation of all resistance to Soviet supremacy.

Aug. 31–Sept 3, 1948 Poland confirmed as a one-party-state under Boleslaw Bierut, the first secretary of the Polish Workers Party and after Dec. 21, 1948, of the United Polish Workers Party which included a number of coerced social democrats from Polish Socialist Party (PPS); 1948–1956 severe Stalinist terror; Beirut in direct control of the Soviet-style terror apparatus in Poland.

Dec. 30, 1948 Integration of the administration of northwestern provinces with the rest of Poland (5,000,000 Poles settled there in four years).

Jan. 1, 1949 Formation of state farms (PGR)—a modern form of serfdom.

1949–1953 Intensive collectivization of Polish agriculture.

Jan. 25, 1949 Formation of the Council of Mutual Economic Aid of the Soviet Bloc.

Apr. 4, 1949 Founding of N.A.T.O.

Sept. 1, 1949 Founding of Catholic Chaplain Section in Soviet-controlled Veterans' Association ZBOWID.

Nov. 6, 1949 Boleslaw Bierut formally becomes the head of state and party chief. Polish-born Soviet Marshal K. Rokossowski becomes the defense minister.

March 20, 1950 Seym act on reorganization of territorial administration by local national councils.

Apr. 14, 1950 State-church agreement.

July 4, 1950 First Polish language broadcast of Radio Free Europe.

July 6, 1950 Signing of Polish-East German agreement on final demarcation of the border on the Odra-Nysa Line.

July 21, 1950 Seym enactment of the six-year plan (1950–1955).

July 29, 1950 Act of Zgorzelec: formalization of Polish-German border on the Odra-Nysa Line between Polish People's Republic and German Democratic Republic.

Dec. 3–9, 1950 National census of 25,008,000 inhabitants of Poland. Since 1945 3,789,000 people returned to Poland; 1,529,000 from U.S.S.R. and 2,260,000 from Germany and western Europe.

Jan. 26, 1951 Decree making permanent the provisional Church hierarchy in the northwestern provinces.

Jan. 27, 1951 Signing in Frankfurt of final demarcation of the Polish-German border on the Odra-Nysa Line with German Democratic Republic (East Germany).

May 26, 1951 Formation of Seym committee for writing a new constitution.

July, 1951 Arrest and imprisonment of Wladyslaw Gomulka for "rightist deviation" by Jozef Swiatlo, who defected to the West in 1953 and publically exposed communist corruption, tampering

with elections (1947 and 1952), and methods of terror (141 detailed reports on Radio Free Europe in 1954–55). Beginning of Soviet ordered purge of Jewish dignitaries in satellite regimes, starting with trial of Slanski and ten other "Zionist conspirators" in Prague, Czechoslovakia.

Jan. 27, 1952 Seym initiating a "national discussion" of the new constitution.

July 22, 1952 Seym enacting Constitution of Polish People's Republic, Soviet style; with Boleslaw Bierut as president; compulsory participation in elections enforced by police and based on a single list of party approved candidates. The Seym made (nominally) the supreme organ of the republic (Art. 15); in fact the most powerful were: the Politburo, Secretariat of the Soviet controlled party, and departments of party's Central Committee enforcing their rule by terror apparatus using tactics of organized crime.

Oct. 26, 1952 Election of a new Seym.

Nov. 21, 1952 to March 18, 1954 Government of Prime Minister Boleslaw Bierut. Aleksander Zawadzki, Moscow-trained N.K.V.D. officer sentenced to seven years in the Second Polish Republic for spying for U.S.S.R. (given a low sentence for high treason because of his "very limited intelligence"), now head of state of Polish People's Republic as the head of State Council (which also represented Poland abroad, Art. 25 of the Constitution of July 22, 1952).

March 5, 1953 Death of Stalin amidst a new purge at the top for reconsolidation of control over Soviet terror apparatus; also a new anti-church offensive ordered by the Soviets throughout the Satellites (in Poland show-trials of priests and communist takeover of Catholic press). Changing of the city name of Katowice to Stalingrad.

Aug. 5, 1953 Discovery of Europe's largest 4000 years old Stone Age chert mining complex near Opatow, dating back to the early Balto-Slavic period.

Sept. 1953 An act on reconstruction and expansion of Gdansk. Imprisonment of six Catholic bishops including sentencing for twelve years of Bishop Czeslaw Kaczmarek (Sept. 22) and arresting of the Polish Primate Stefan Cardinal Wyszynski (Sept. 26); terrorizing of the Church (unique in Polish history); publication of pro-communist declaration by Bishop Michael Klepacz (Sept. 28); smuggling out of Poland the May 8, 1953 letter of Polish Bishops to Beirut describing and protesting the anti-Church terror offensive; silencing of the Church; former fascist, now Soviet agent, Boleslaw Piasecki head of PAX anti-Church diversion in control of newly formed Priestly Commissions; terrorized Bishop Klepacz vowing obedience to communist rule (Oct. 17); while yielding under terror he basically remained loyal to the imprisoned Primate.

March 17, 1954 to March 12, 1956 Boleslaw Bierut appointed as the first secretary United Polish Workers Party (communist).

March 18, 1954 to Feb. 20, 1957 Government of Prime Minister Jozef Cyrankiewicz.

Apr. 18, 1954 Poland joining UNESCO (United Nations Educations, Scientific, and Cultural Organization).

July 8, 1954 Polish Academy of Sciences constructing and putting in operation of the first main-frame Polish-designed computer.

Sept. 28,–Dec. 28, 1954 Daily broadcast by RFE of Col. Swiatlo reports on Bierut's terror apparatus in Poland. Series of 141 reports ending in Spring 1955.

Dec. 13, 1954 Release from prison of W. Gomulka and hundreds of others after a purge and reorganization of the terror apparatus in Poland (Dec. 7).

Feb. 12, 1955 Start of balloon operation "Spotlight" to deliver 3,000,000 copies of Col. Swiatlo's report to Poland to overcome jamming of radio broadcasts.

May 11–14, 1955 Signing of the Treaty of Warsaw integrating military and economic forces of the entire Soviet bloc because of re-militarization of West Germany within NATO by the United States; severing of relations with Vatican.

July 31, 1955 Beginning of Soviet ordered radio campaign "Kraj" for the purpose to "liquidate by repatriation" the Polish emigration in the West amid massive release from Soviet "gulag archipelago" of German, Italian, Austrian, Spanish, and Belgian prisoners, all of whom testify that the Poles are the largest nationality in Soviet prisons.

Aug. 21, 1955 Founding of Nuclear Research Institute of Polish Academy of Sciences.

Oct. 18, 1955 Founding of Polonia Association for relations with Poles abroad; two million Poles, persecuted and under Russification pressure in U.S.S.R. excluded from the activities of Polonia.

March 12, 1956 Death of Boleslaw Bierut in Moscow (apparently shot in the neck, officially of flu) because of the end of his usefulness to the Soviets after serving for seven years as the head of the Polish desk of NKVD, head of Polish National Council, president of Polish People's Republic, and currently the First Secretary of the Communist Party (PZPR); apparently executed because of lack of an orderly succession procedure and because he knew "too much" and above all he compromised the Soviets by failing to insure the secrecy of the details of Communist rule by methods of organized crime (disclosed by Bierut's right-handman Col. Swiatlo in 141 reports on Radio Free Europe).

March 20, 1956 Edward Ochab (1906–), veteran Soviet security agent, becoming the first secretary of (communist) United Polish Workers' Party.

Apr. 27, 1956 Release of 30,000 prisoners by the Communist government in Poland.

May 1, 1956 First television station starts broadcasting (from Warsaw).

June 28, 1956 "Bread and Freedom" labor uprising in Poznan; two days' fighting workers and militia; death of 53 men; communist party offices destroyed; files of the secret police burned; Hungarian demonstrations in sympathy of events in Poznan leading to an uprising and Soviet invasion of Hungary; purge of Hilary Minc, the Stalinist tsar of Polish economy in a Soviet drive to stop all criticism of "Soviet advisors" and blame only their Jewish subordinates.

Aug. 27, 1956 Pilgrimage of one million Poles to the Catholic Monastery of Czestochowa vowing a massive support for the church (Poland 96% Catholic).

Oct. 19–21, 1956 Wladyslaw Gomulka first secretary of the (communist) United Polish Workers' Party; Soviet trained prewar communist; escaped mass purge of Polish communists in U.S.S.R. in 1937 while serving a sentence in Poland; after defeating an attempted coup by Konstanty Rokossowski, Polish born Soviet marshal who was deposed as Polish defense minister and commander-in-chief in a Krushchev-Gomulka deal amid rumors that the Polish Army, if attacked, was threatening to invade East Germany, demolish Soviet positions in Central Europe, and break through to the American lines in West Germany; increase of the autonomy of Poland conditioned on purging the armed forces of nationalists; beginning of the "Polish Road to Socialism"; end of Stalinist terror which was blamed by the Soviets on the large number of Jews in the party and security apparatus; cycles of Soviet policies selecting Jewish executioners and then turning them into victims with the propaganda benefit of blaming abroad Polish resistance to Sovietization as anti-Semitic; renegotiation of the legal status of Soviet forces stationed in Poland; short period of freedom as party factions struggle for power; Polish intellectual opposition pleading for a "likable socialism" (long before the Czechs called for "socialism with a human face"). Boleslaw Piasecki accused of using Mafia tactics with help of KGB; he apparently did not escape revenge as his only son, 16 year old Bogdan, was abducted and murdered in January 1957 by men purged from the security apparatus.

Oct. 23, 1956 New electoral law enlarging the party approved list to 722 for 459 seats, including non-party men; preservation of Party control through "Front of National Unity" (FJN) amid widespread public demands to bring back the masses of Poles still imprisoned in the Soviet Union while the Communists were staging their Moscow-ordered campaign to repatriate Poles from the West.

Oct. 28, 1956 Return of Stefan Cardinal Wyszynski from internment in Komancza.

Nov. 7–13, 1956 Passage of five year plan for 1956–1960; approved July 12, 1957.

Nov. 15–19, 1956 Negotiation in Moscow on decollectivization of agriculture to overcome food shortages; Soviet agreement on limited repatriation of Poles from Soviet Union; KGB coercing of Polish intellectuals, long term Soviet prisoners and considered "enemies" of U.S.S.R. to write memoranda on their possible service for the Soviets as a pre-condition of their release and return to Poland.

Nov. 21, 1957 Polish act of defiance against the Soviets in the U.N. by abstaining, and not voting against condemnation of U.S.S.R. for its invasion of Hungary.

Feb. 20, 1957 to Feb. 20, 1961 Seym "electing" again Aleksander Zawadzki, as head of state and Jozef Cyrankiewicz as prime minister of Polish People's Republic.

March 25, 1957 Polish-Soviet agreement on limited repatriation of Poles from Soviet Union (out of two million in U.S.S.R., 131,000 were permitted to repatriate).

March 1957 Catholic opposition to Soviet anti-Semitic policies. Catholic weekly *Tygodnik Powszechny* stating that "anti-Semitism is irreconcilable with Catholicism."

May 1957 Economic Advisory Council urging greater autonomy for individual enterprises.

June 7, 1957 Polish-American agreement on handling of American property in Poland and Polish property in the U.S.A.

Oct. 2, 1957 U.N. proposal by Polish Foreign Minister Adam Rapacki (1909–70) to form a nuclear-free zone out of Poland, Czechoslovakia, and both Germanys.

Oct. 1957 Gomulka's attack on "revisionists"; closing of dissident journal *Po Prostu (To Put It Plainly);* systematically diluting of effectiveness of worker's councils by subsuming them to official trade unions controlled by the communist government; blackmailing Polish population with threats of Soviet intervention.

Nov. 13, 1957 Reactivation of Administrative Supreme Control Chamber.

1957 Further decollectivization of Polish agriculture; growth of co-ops in form of agricultural circles; 90 percent of collective farms disappearing.

Dec. 25, 1957 Cardinal Wyszynski, the Primate of Poland, denied the right to broadcast the traditional Christmas message to the Polish people.

1957 Repatriation from U.S.S.R. including up to 40,000 Jews (soon applying for exit visas, thoroughly fed up with communism); Polish population generally sympathetic towards the Jews; Soviets continuing to flood Poland with successive waves of anti-Semitism in the tsarist tradition to disrupt the brotherhood between Christians and Jews in Poland, still full of memories of common suffering under the Nazi terror.

1958 Karol Wojtyla nominated Auxiliary Bishop of Cracow.

Feb. 25, 1958 Seym act on commemoration of 1000 years of Poland in 1960–1966.

March 17, 1958 Extraction of the one billionth ton of coal in postwar Poland.

Apr. 14, 1958 Activation of the first Polish atomic reactor in Swierk near Warsaw.

July, 1958
Jasna Gora monstery at Czestochowa raided by police.

Dec. 20, 1958 Seym law on employee self-management of enterprises.

Feb. 3, 1959 Return to Poland of national treasures from deposit in Canada.

Dec. 18, 1959 Signing in Moscow of agreement to build an oil pipeline from U.S.S.R. to Poland and East Germany to supply them with Soviet oil.

Apr. 9, 1960 Decree on tax reductions for private shops.

Apr. 14, 1960 Decree on a new code of administrative procedure.

Nov. 18, 1960 Admission of Poland to General Agreement on Tariffs and Trade.

Nov. 20–Dec. 21, 1960 Gomulka reintroducing nuclear-free zone proposed in 1957 by Adam Rapacki, attacking colonialism, and defending Odra-Nysa border.

Dec. 6, 1960 National census of 29,776,000 inhabitants of Poland.

1960 Another purge in the security service; kicking out Jews and people who would not vociferate against Jews.

Jan. 1, 1961 Return to Poland of the rest of national treasures from Canada.

Feb. 16, 1961 Seym approving of a five year plan for 1961–1965.

May 15–18, 1961 New Seym voting Aleksander Zawadzki president of the State Council and Jozef Cyrankiewicz prime minister.

July 15, 1961 Extending grade school program to eight years.

Aug. 13, 1961 Erection of the Berlin Wall, increasing isolation of Poland.

Dec. 15, 1961 Agreement on U.S. sale on credit of surplus grain to Poland.

1961 Worsening of Church-state relations; religion can no longer be taught in the schools.

June, 1963 Removal of last vestiges of the "Polish Spring in October of 1956;" shutting down of journals of "Nowa Kultura" and "Przeglad Kulturalny;" Mieczyslaw Moczar (of Ukrainian descent, born Nicolai Demko, recruited by NKVD in 1939 to campaign for the referendum to incorporate north-eastern Poland into Soviet Byelorussia) initiating special training courses for informers; the number of secret informers employed by the secret police alone reaching 300,000; police faction, under the name of "Partisans" led by Moczar, totally subservient to the KGB as Soviet leaders groom Moczar as Gomulka's potential successor; anti-Polish slanders such as Leon Uris' Exodus, Mila 18, etc., published in the West, used systematically in anti-Semitic propaganda of the Moczarite press.

June 6, 1963 First laser built in Poland on a synthetic ruby.

Oct. 22, 1963 Poland signing in Moscow agreement on exchange-rubles and on an International Bank of Economic Cooperation of the Soviet Bloc.

Apr. 22, 1964 Signing contract to deliver in 1966–70 to U.S.S.R. 175 oceangoing ships, total of one and half million tons capacity.

Apr. 1964 Official denunciations of "letter of thirty-four" intellectuals calling for greater freedom of expression protesting party's cultural policy; party's campaign against intellectuals and Jews.

Oct. 17, 1964 Seym voting a new Civil Code.

1964 Soviet Bloc Warsaw Pact achieving military parity with NATO; start on propaganda for international detente; strengthening of censorship after the fall of Krushchev.

Nov. 14, 1964 Arrest of Jacek Kuron and Karol Modzelewski after seizure of their manuscript on lack of democratic freedom under the pro-Soviet regime.

Nov. 24, 1964 Expelling of Modzeleweski and Kuron from the Communist Party; release by them of an "Open Letter to the Communist Party" with a detailed critique of the communist rule and its tyranny by bureaucratic centralism.

Jan. 1, 1965 National census of 31,339,000 inhabitants of Poland. German Evangelical Church publishing memorandum on the relations of the German people with their neighbors to the east.

March 31, 1965 Seym law on social security, industrial safety and hygiene; changing the laws on higher education, research institutes, scientific degrees, etc.

Apr. 5–9, 1965 Signing in Warsaw 20-year pact with U.S.S.R.

May 1965 Klaus von Bismarck, head of West German Radio leading German Protestant leaders to Warsaw for an exchange of views.

June 24–25, 1965 New Seym voting Edward Ochab president of the State Council and Jozef Cyrankiewicz prime minister.

Nov. 10–11, 1965 Seym law on taxation, retirement payments, and regulation on international private matters.

Nov. 18, 1965 New pact to increase trade with U.S.S.R. by 63 percent.

Nov. 18, 1965 Reconciliation letter of the Polish bishops to their German counterparts to forgive and forget in order to stop the use of German issue in Gomulka's propaganda; worsening of Church-state relations.

March 31, 1966 Pope Paul VI cancelling May 3 visit to Poland; Church-state relations worsen.

June 1966 Start of Chinese "Cultural Revolution" condemned by the Gomulka regime which organized protest demonstration outside Chinese embassy; Chinese retaliation by showing in their embassy, Nazi newsreels about unearthening of mass graves of 4200 Polish officers at Katyn.

July 21, 1966 Special session of the Seym commemorating 1000 years of Poland.

Oct. 21, 1966 Tenth anniversary of "Polish October" student demonstrations demanding the release of Kuron and Modzelewski; leading speakers Adam Michnik and Leszek Kolakowski, philosophy professor and former editor of Po Prostu, who condemned Gomulka for a decade of increasing repression, lack of democracy and intolerance of opposition.

Oct. 22, 1966 Adam Michnik suspended from school for one year; Leszek Kolakowski expelled from the Communist Party.

Oct. 26, 1966 Gomulka regime embarking on an anti-Semitic campaign in order to derail widespread demands for freedom of speech and general liberalization; Nina Krasow sentenced to three years imprisonment in a trial with anti-Semitic overtones (Gomulka using anti-Semitism despite the fact that his wife was Jewish). "Moczar's boys" or the "young guard" of the "anti-cultural" revolution in control of the security forces infiltrating party apparatus, terrorizing civil service; armed forces becoming testing ground of anti-Semitic policies as the Soviets woo Arab nationalists. Gen. Wojciech Jaruzelski nominated minister of national defense.

1967 Bishop Karol Wojtyla elevated to cardinal.

June 5–11, 1967 Israeli victory in the Six-Day War bringing widespread celebration in Poland (including government officials and Army officers) as "Polish Jews defeated Soviet Arabs;" Gomulka severing diplomatic ties with Israel. Strong pro-Israeli sentiment in Poland as the resistance to Sovietization is continued.

Sept. 6–12, 1967 Visit in Poland of French President Charles de Gaule, who served in Poland during Polish-Soviet war of 1919–1920.

Jan. 5, 1968 Alexander Dubcek regime in Czechoslovakia; suspension of censorship in Prague; liberalization within Czech Communist Party; Gomulka urging the Soviets to stamp out Dubcek's crisis before the "pest" spreads out to Poland.

Jan. 30, 1968 Closing down in Warsaw of 19th century drama of Adam Mickiewicz The Forefathers including phrases like "Every one sent here from Moscow is either a jackass, a fool, or a spy," which generated standing ovations. Attempts to stir anti-Semitism to split the protest movements; punitive action (the first in Polish history) against those who protested against Jew-baiting.

March 2, 1968 Polish Writers' Union passing a resolution condemning the state's cultural policy.

March 8, 1968 Student demonstrations in Warsaw protesting the closing of The Forefathers and Michnik's arrest and chanting pro-Dubcek slogans. The riot police making an unprecedented show of force; Moczar's faction using security apparatus to create an atmosphere of an imminent coup d'etat.

March 11, 1968 Eight-hour attack on the students of the University of Warsaw by police and "angry workers."

March 14, 1968 Student demonstration spread to Krakow and all the 104 campuses of universities and institutes of higher learning throughout Poland.

March 19, 1968 Gomulka appeals for calm and blames disturbances on Zionists; Moczar conducting anti-Semitic purges in the party causing emigration of some 20,000 Jews including many former Communist Party members and leaders as the power struggle rages within the party (which included the only substantial number of Jews still left in Poland).

March 25, 1968 Dismissal of Leszek Kolakowski from his job at the University of Warsaw.

March 28, 1968 Student demonstration and issuing of an ultimatum to the government to reinstate Professor Kolakowski by Apr. 22; closing of eight departments of the University of Warsaw and ordering the 1300 students to apply for re-admission; notification that if there are any demonstrations on Apr. 22, the University will be shut down indefinitely; preventive arrests of student leaders; Leszek Kolakowski and other purged academics leaving Poland.

April 12, 1968 Moczar's blunder in a televised interview (blaming the Soviets for giving to the Jews monopolistic right to leadership in postwar Poland); the Soviets retaliating by switching their support back to Gomulka; Moczar losing his bid for total power as Soviet viceroy in Poland.

June 19–30 Warsaw Pact maneuvers in Czechoslovakia; Soviets demand restriction of freedom of the press and an increase of Czech party discipline.

Aug. 3, 1968 U.S.S.R., Poland, and other five nations of the Warsaw Pact claim to respect the sovereignty of the Dubcek's regime after their conference with Soviet leaders.

Aug. 20–21, 1968 Invasion of Czechoslovakia by Warsaw Pact countries including Poland, but excluding Romania; restoration of Czech censorship; removal of Dubcek.

Oct. 16, 1968 Soviet-Czech treaty on indefinite placing of Soviet troops in Czechoslovakia; Hungary taking advantage of Soviet preoccupation with Czechs, starting on decentralization of planning, greater role for private sector of the economy which starts to prosper.

1969 Continuing power struggle in Poland between Gomulka and Maczar; Dubcek replaced by Gustav Husak; Gomulka launching a campaign for reaching an agreement with West Germany.

July 20, 1969 American man on the moon; Soviet loss of face in the space race, rejoicing in Poland.

June 26, 1970 Dubcek expelled from the Czech Communist Party; in Poland ostentatious prosperity of party bureaucracy disgusting to ordinary people; Soviet-sponsored anti-Jewish propaganda, under cover of "anti-Zionism" gradually driving Western Communist parties into anti-Semitism.

Sept. 1970 Gomulka regime faced with an economic crisis contriving a new Five-Year-Plan, including an incentive system which would result in reduction of wages of most workers.

Dec. 7, 1970 Treaty between the People's Republic of Poland and the Federal Republic of Germany signed in Warsaw by Wladyslaw Gomulka and Chancellor Willy Brandt, recognizing the Odra-Lusatian Nysa frontier and materially reducing the anxiety over German revengism.

Dec. 13, 1970 Increase in food prices accompanied by decrease in prices of luxury items.

Dec. 14, 1970 Demonstrations by workers of Lenin Shipyards in Gdansk; students do not participate because workers did not support them in 1968.

Dec. 15, 1970 Gdansk, Bloody Tuesday, officially 45 people killed and 1,165 injured in battle of workers against security forces; strike spreads to Paris Commune Shipyards in Gdynia and Warynski Shipyards in Szczecin.

Dec. 16, 1970 Tanks and helicopters used against workers.

Dec. 17, 1970 State of siege declared in Poland as battle against workers spreads to Gdynia and Szczecin (Stettin); total of 300 killed and 4500 injured.

Dec. 20, 1970 Gomulka resigning, replaced by a short-lived duumvirate of Gierek-Moczar; Edward Gierek (former coal miner in Belgium, born in Silesia, winning against Moczar without openly repudiating the anti-Semitic campaign).

Jan. 22, 1971 Gierek's nine-hour session in Szczecin shipyards, pleading successfully to be given a chance to govern.

Jan. 25, 1971 Gierek meeting with representatives of Gdansk shipyards including Lech Walesa (27-year-old electrician).

Feb. 7, 1971 Suspending of Gomulka's membership in the Central Committee.

Feb. 13, 1971 Strike of women textile workers in Lodz, demanding and achieving a rollback of December food-price increases.

June 24, 1971 Gierek's new economic policy of expansion of consumer sector based on massive foreign loans; revising of the Five-Year-Plan for 1971–75; crackdown on leaders of December labor strikes.

Sept. 1971 Soviet Bloc members, including Poland, pressed to amend their constitutions to proclaim their socialist character, emphasize the leading role of their Communist parties, and commit themselves to friendship and cooperation with Soviet Union.

Oct. 1971 Metalworkers convention under party's control; Edmund Baluka of Szczecin shipyards fired from union and his shipyard job.

1972 Liberalization of party's cultural policy; Wajda's film, *The Wedding*.

1973 Poland's debt to the West: $2.5 billion.

Oct. 6–24, 1973 Israeli victory in Yom Kippur War results in Arab oil embargo and an economic havoc which prevents an increase of export of Polish manufactured goods necessary to sustain Gierek's policy of borrowing from the West.

1974 Strikes in Gdynia and in Silesia bring some wage increases.

Aug. 1, 1975 Poland signing with 34 other nations the Helsinki Pact, recognizing existing boundaries as inviolable and guaranteeing freedom of thought, conscience, religion, and belief. Gradual linkage of Western credits to compliance with the Helsinki Pact. Guidelines for the next congress of the Polish Communist Party, calling for affirmation in an amendment to the constitution that Poland is a socialist state in which the Communist Party is a "leading force" cooperating with U.S.S.R. Church protesting the "totalitarian nature" of the proposed amendments.

Jan. 23, 1976 Seym Commission adopting a proposal for constitutional changes; Poland described as a "socialist state" "guided" by its Communist Party (PZPR), committed to "friendship and cooperation with U.S.S.R." and that "civil rights of the citizens depend on fulfillment of their responsibilities towards the Motherland."

Jan. 31, 1976 Author Jerzy Andrzejewski writing a letter of protest, signed by 101 persons, stating that "citizens' rights cannot be limited by any special conditions. . . ."

Feb. 10, 1976 Seym adopting the constitutional amendment as proposed on Jan. 23; party propaganda claiming that nothing has changed and that the constitution is nothing but a record of practical reality; party's treatment of the constitution confirming the basic illegality of the Communist rule, subservient to the Soviet Union against the will of Polish population.

1976 Poland's debt to the West: $11 billion.

June 24, 1976 Up to 60 percent increases in food prices; protest strikes; burning of party headquarters in Radom; casualties smaller than in 1956 and in 1970.

June 25, 1976 Rollback on price increases; end of strikes; mass arrests of strike leaders.

Sept. 23, 1976 Workers' Defense Committee *(Komitet Obrony Robotnikow)*, KOR, founded by Kuron, Michnik, and Jan Litynski to help brutally suppressed strikers and their families with legal, financial, and medical help as well as new jobs for the sacked. KOR receiving an initial subsidy of $10,000 from the American United Auto Workers' Union.

Nov. 2, 1976 Jimmy Carter defeats Gerald Ford in race for the presidency of the U.S. and states that his national security adviser will be Polish born Dr. Zbigniew Brzezinski.

Jan. 6, 1977 Human Rights Manifesto of 240 Czech intellectuals.

Feb. 1977 Wajda's film *Man of Marble* on tragic fate of a workers' hero exploited by the Stalinists and killed in the 1970 Gdansk massacre.

May 1977 Founding of NOWA, an underground publishing house; publishing some 50,000 copies of *What to Do in Contacts with Police*, plus Orwell's *1984*, works of Czeslaw Milosz, Aleksander Solzhnitsyn, etc.

Dec. 1977 Thaw in the Church-state relations; Gierek visiting Pope Paul VI.

Dec. 29–31, 1977 President Carter visit in Warsaw emphasizing human rights; Gierek limiting to 48-hour arrests in the harassment of KOR and NOWA activists in order to obtain American debt financing.

Feb. 1978 Formation of a Free Trade Union of Silesia in Katowice by Workers' Committee.

May 1978 Formation in Gdansk of a Baltic Coast Committee of Free Trade Unions by Andrzej Gwiazda, Anna Walentynowicz, and Lech Walesa.

Oct. 5, 1978 Nobel Prize for Literature given to Isaac Bashevis Singer, Polish-born writer in Yiddish, the language of the Judeo-Germanic sub-culture in Poland, based on a Germanic language and Jewish ethnic and religious tradition of the world's largest Jewish community (from 14th to 20th centuries).

Oct. 16, 1978 Karol Wojtyla, Archbishop of Cracow, elected as Pope John Paul II, strengthening the position of independent Catholics by making more difficult for the ruling Communist Party to continue persecuting them.

Dec. 16, 1978 Memorial service of the site of the Gdansk massacre of 1970 organized by Andrzej Gwiazda and Lech Walesa.

June 2–10, 1979 Pilgrimage to Poland by Pope John Paul II on the nine hundredth anniversary of martyrdom of St. Stanislaus; sermons on spiritual freedom to largest ever field masses in the history of Christianity; visit to Auschwitz commemorating martyrdom of the Jews and Christians killed there by the Germans during WW II.

June 17, 1979 Carter-Brezhnev agreement on Salt II (despite objections by Zbigniew Brzezinski, National Security Adviser, about inadequate verification. Disarmament negotiations strengthening Soviet Union; treating it as an equal of the United States and using exclusively U.S. estimates of Soviet strength rather than basing them on direct verification of Soviet missile production rates, actual number, and location; not one Soviet missile verified in a satellite-photographed silo; strong possibility that silos and missile containers are decoys cheaper to build by Soviet slave labor than to produce the actual missiles; the missiles aimed at the United States could be concealed at unknown locations, undetected by the satellite cameras which operate in daylight only. In 1976 Soviet Marshal of Aviation C. V. Zimin gave a high priority to measures prohibiting intelligence gathering by satellites thus making ill-advised U.S. dependence on outside monitoring, without on-site verification. Soviet exploitation of the atomic balance of terror and public pressure on Western democracies to achievement peace through disarmament).

Sept. 1979 Charter of Workers' Rights published by KOR in underground journal *Robotnik*.

Oct. 1979 Formation in Szczecin (Stettin) of the Committee for the Free Trade Union of Western Pomerania followed by protests of poor safety conditions and of irregular work shifts by Silesian coal miners; two-day strike in Gdansk against a new wage system.

Dec. 16, 1979 Memorial service on the site of the Gdansk massacre of 1970 organized by Andrzej Gwiazda and Lech Walesa; demands for an official memorial or a permit to build one by volunteers; arrest of many participants.

Dec 27 Soviets' attention drawn away from Poland by their invasion of Afghanistan which resulted in American-led boycott of the Moscow Olympics and an embargo on grain sales to U.S.S.R.

May 3, 1980 Commemoration in Gdansk of the May 3, 1791, Constitution; arrest and jailing of two organizers.

June 18, 1980 Workers' protest of poor safety in Gdansk shipyards after an explosion killing eight and injuring six.

July 1, 1980 Decree on 100 percent rise of meat prices causing protest strikes throughout Poland.

July 2, 1980 KOR becoming a clearing house of strike information.

July 11, 1980 Industrial managers told in Warsaw to buy social peace at any price following disclosure by the government media of the catastrophic economic situation.

July 16, 1980 Protest strike in Lublin against export of meat to U.S.S.R. for the upcoming Olympics; writing of 35-point demands (anticipating 21 points of the Gdansk strike), but not yet demanding free trade unions; strike ending in a compromise negotiated by vice-Premier Mieczyslaw Jagielski.

July 21, 1980 Pay raises given in Radom to prevent workers' strikes which so far affected 100 enterprises.

July 27, 1980 Gierek leaving for U.S.S.R. to confer with Leonid Brezhnev.

July 29, 1980 Work stoppages breaking out on the Baltic coast followed by 48-hour arrest of Lech Walesa on July 31.

Aug. 1, 1980 Memorial service in Warsaw Powazki Cemetery commemorating 4200 Polish officers executed by the Soviets in 1940 at Katyn.

Aug. 4, 1980 Warsaw garbage collectors' strike.

Aug. 5, 1980 Arrest and release of Jan Litynski, editor of *Robotnik*.

Aug. 7, 1980 Anna Walentynowicz, crane operator at Gdansk shipyard, sacked after she went home sick; dissatisfaction of her co-workers.

Aug. 8, 1980 KOR operated strike information service expanded to act as a contact center of strike committees formed in some 150 factories.

Aug. 9–10, 1980 Gdansk Free Trade Unionist and KOR leaders discussing a protest strike on behalf of Anna Walentynowicz.

Aug. 11, 1980 Arrest of strike leader of garbage collectors in Warsaw. Printing in Gdansk of 6000 copies of initial strike demands.

Aug. 12, 1980 Polish debt exceeding $20 billion as West German and American banks extend $1.5 billion loan to Poland.

Aug. 14, 1980 Celebration in Warsaw at the Tomb of the Unknown Soldier, the sixtieth anniversary of the great victory of Polish Army led by Marshal Jozef Pilsudski over Soviet invasion (the battle involved over 1.5 million soldiers and prevented Soviet linkup with German Communists in 1920).

Aug. 15, 1980 A total of 50,000 workers on strike in Gdansk in a communication blackout, as all telephone lines are cut; Gierek returns citing Soviet "concern." Cardinal Wyszynski's sermon on Assumption Day at Czestochowa on bread as the property of the whole nation and on tactful and dignified ways the Poles are demanding it. Soviet TASS announcing "routine maneuvers" of Warsaw Pact armies in the Baltic area, including East Germany.

Aug. 16, 1980 Beginning of an occupational strike by 16,000 workers in Gdansk Shipyards, demanding erection of a memorial to the martyrs of 1970, reinstatement of Anna Walentynowicz and other fired workers, and the right to form a union independent of government or party control (broadcasting of negotiations with local party secretary).

Aug. 16, 1980 Forming in Gdansk of Interfactory Strike Committee, MKS, to represent strikes which spread throughout Poland.

Aug. 17, 1980 Field Mass at the shipyard gate; decorating of members of the strike committee with medals of Pope John Paul II by Gdansk Bishop Kaczmarek; Vice-Premier Tadeusz Pyka sent to Gdansk to negotiate while Litynski of KOR is arrested.

Aug. 18, 1980 Gierek postponing a trip to West Germany.

Aug. 19, 1980 Strike in Szczecin shipyards; parallel, but separate, negotiations begin; Walesa elected as a leader of Gdansk Interfactory Committee while students contribute 10,000 zlotys to his strike fund.

Aug. 20, 1980 Kuron, Michnik arrested together with other 12 KOR leaders.

Aug. 21, 1980 A 15-member presidium elected by 500 delegates from 261 striking factories; 24 activists arrested; Jagielski replacing Pyka as government negotiator.

Aug. 22, 1980 Solidarity, *Solidarnosc* (so-lee-dar-noshch), daily bulletin of Gdansk MKS now representing 400 factories. Pope John Paul II offering a Mass for Poland.

Aug. 23, 1980 Jagielski arriving at Gdansk shipyards; receiving 21-Point Demands and an ultimatum to restore communication links with the rest of Poland if the negotiations are to continue.

Aug. 24, 1980 Hard-liners Stefan Olszowski and Tadeusz Grabski move up in Politburo; Prime Minister Babiuch replaced by Jozef Pinkowski; TV tsar Maciej Szczepanski fired; Gierek surviving.

Aug. 26, 1980 Negotiations with Jagielski resume after restoration of communications and arrival from Warsaw of seven experts on law and economics to assist MKS negotiators (now numbering 1000 delegates); party broadcasting of selectively edited sermon of Cardinal Wyszynski, urging workers to return to work, Church protesting.

Aug. 27, 1980 Third session of negotiation with Jagielski producing next day an appeal by Walesa to stop the spreading strikes for four days to allow time to achieve agreement in negotiations.

Aug. 30, 1980 Breakthroughs in Szczecin in the morning and in Gdansk in the afternoon; Central Committee ratifying the agreement brought by Jagielski; Andrzej Wajda visiting Gdansk; accepting suggestion to film *Man of Iron* about shipyard workers as a follow up to the *Man of Marble*; arrests continue.

Aug. 31, 1980 Signing of final agreement; Walesa using a souvenir pen with an image of the Pope under a crucifix hanging on the wall; sanctioning of a free and independent union with the right to strike; improved health and working conditions; Saturdays off; Catholic Masses to be broadcast over radio and TV; loosening of political repression and censorship. Walesa threatening resumption of strikes if activists are not released, government complying (to buy time).

Sept. 1, 1980 Strikes end in Gdansk and Szczecin but continue elsewhere waiting for clarification that the Gdansk provisions apply everywhere in Poland. Walesa installed in a new union office in Gdansk; release of remaining dissidents.

Sept. 2, 1980 Government press giving full text of the accord; 5,000,000 zlotys donated to the new trade union by new members and well-wishers.

Sept. 3, 1980 Jastrzebie agreement in Upper Silesia with 350,000 strikers. Pope John Paul II broadcasting his support for Poland's moral right to independence; U.S.S.R. granting loans and food supplies to Poland.

Sept. 4, 1980 Exposing of financial corruption of the media-tsar M. Szczepanski.

Sept. 5, 1980 First postwar open parliamentary debate; Central Committee replacing Gierek with Stanislaw Kania (formerly in charge of the secret police, the Army, and Church-state relations).

Sept. 7, 1980 Lech Walesa received at home of Cardinal Wyszynski.

Sept. 8–15, 1980 Lifting government ban on critical documentary films including *Workers' 80* on the August strikes by Andrzej Chodakowski and Andrzej Zajaczkowski; screening attended by Walesa, the Archbishop of Gdansk, and deputy Minister of Culture.

Sept. 11, 1980 Jagielski reporting to Brezhnev in Moscow.

Sept. 15, 1980 Gdansk accords declared by the government to be applicable throughout Poland while the courts process the official registration of the new union.

Sept. 21, 1980 First radio transmission of the Sunday Mass in postwar Poland.

Sept. 22, 1980 Birth of Solidarity in Gdansk as thirty-six regional independent unions unite; Karol Modzelewski, history professor at Wroclaw University, elected official national press spokesman of Solidarity.

Sept. 24, 1980 Solidarity applies for registration with Warsaw court; tension building up as the court delays.

Oct. 3, 1980 One-hour warning strike staged nationwide by Solidarity to protest government's failure to honor fully the Gdansk accords and to show the union's strength; strike effective; TV coverage of the strike.

Oct. 9, 1980 Nobel Prize for Literature awarded to Czeslaw Milosz, dissident poet living in exile in the U.S. and becoming a national hero whose works start to appear in underground publications; changes in government leadership.

Oct. 24, 1980 Ultimatum by Solidarity (membership reaching eight million) for complete court registration by Nov. 12 under threat of general strike; court insisting on inclusion in the union charter recognition of "the leading role of Communist Party in Poland;" crisis escalating.

Oct. 29, 1980 East Germany leading in anti-Polish regulations, travel restrictions, etc.

Oct. 30, 1980 Consultations: Stanislaw Kania, head of the party and Jozef Pinkowski, prime minister, conferring in Moscow with Brezhnev while Cardinal Wyszynski conferring with Pope John Paul II.

Nov. 4, 1980 Jimmy Carter defeated in presidential elections by Ronald Reagan whose political program included the lifting of grain embargo against the Soviet Union and strengthening of the arsenal of Chinese Nationalists on the island of Taiwan. Weakening prospects for Solidarity.

Nov. 8, 1980 Romania's warning against foreign (Soviet) interference in Poland. Solidarity's registration crisis intensifying.

Nov. 10, 1980 Legalization of Solidarity charter by Polish Supreme

Court, without making a reference to the leading role of the Communist Party.

Nov. 12, 1980 Formal apology by the Senate of the University of Warsaw to the victims of anti-Semitic purges conducted in 1968 under party orders.

Nov 21–24, 1980 Hard-line party bureaucrats defend their privileged position by provoking wildcat strikes to paralyze Poland's economy; Warsaw Steel Plant, Huta Warszawa, in crisis over jailing of two printers; strike averted by mediation led by Walesa and Kuron and leading to the release of the two printers.

Nov. 22, 1980 Party purge; sacking of 35 percent provincial first secretaries.

Nov. 29, 1980 Independent student union officially registered at the Warsaw University as a concession to end students' sit-in.

Dec. 1, 1980 Soviet military moves on Poland's western frontier in apparent preparation to isolate and invade Poland; increasing tension. Col. Wladyslaw Kuklinski, the liason officer between the Polish army command of Gen. Wojciech Jaruzelski and Warsaw Pact forces of Marshal Viktor Kulikov disclosing Soviet invasion plans and date to the government of the United States—acting for patriotic reasons without any compensation.

Dec. 3, 1980 President Carter expressing concern; nine European common market countries issue warnings.

Dec. 5, 1980 Stanislaw Kania and Stefan Olszowski report to Warsaw Pact meeting in Moscow.

Dec. 7, 1980 Warning by U.S. government that the Soviets have completed military preparations for invasion of Poland.

Dec. 10, 1980 Italian Communists voice an opposition to Soviet invasion.

Dec. 12, 1980 Polish Catholic Church warning against acts by extremists which endanger the very statehood of Poland. American Secretary of State Edmund Muskie (Polish-American, family name originally Marciszewski) leading a NATO meeting in Brussels; issuing an official warning to U.S.S.R. not to invade Poland.

Dec. 13, 1980 U.S.S.R. easing the tension; letting the Polish Communists handle the situation in Poland; accusing the United States of making a false alarm when in reality American disclosures prevented Soviet invasion of Poland.

Dec. 14, 1980 Rural Solidarity registration drive by 1000 delegates gathered in Warsaw.

Dec. 16, 1980 Dedication in Gdansk of a monument commemorating the martyrs of 1970 on the tenth anniversary of their death; three huge crosses, each with a crucified symbol of hope—the ship's anchor; the ceremony attended by representatives of Solidarity, Church, and government; in Warsaw Moczar staging a comeback, bitterly criticized by cultural leaders who demand investigation of Moczar's role in anti-Semitic party actions in 1968.

Dec. 31, 1980 Poland's debt to the West reaching $23 billion. Government urging an end to labor unrest while communist hard-liners continue to provoke wildcat strikes.

Jan. to Feb. 1981 Struggle for an official registration of Rural Solidarity; sit-in strike in Rzeszow; minor confrontations over the implementation by the government of the agreements with Solidarity.

Jan. 12, 1981 Beginning of showing the documentary film *Workers' 80* on strikes of Aug. 1980; movie houses packed with enthusiastic audiences.

Jan. 24, 1981 Solidarity encouraging workers to take this Saturday off.

Jan. 25, 1981 Gierek resigning from the Central Committee; wildcat strikes continue; in Bielsko-Biala demands to oust a corrupt governor.

Jan. 30, 1981 Agreement on five-day work week in 1982.

Feb. 3, 1981 Solidarity threatening one-hour strike if Rural Solidarity is not granted official registration; government sending a negotiation team to Rzeszow; negotiations filmed in a documentary, *Farmers '81*.

Feb. 7, 1981 Cardinal Wyszynski receiving a delegation from Rural Solidarity.

Feb. 8, 1981 Beginning an official investigation of KOR.

Feb. 9, 1981 Defense Minister Wojciech Jaruzelski takes over as prime minister.

Feb. 15–17, 1981 Stanislaw Kania visiting with Gustav Husak in Czechoslovakia and Erich Honecker in East Germany.

Feb. 17, 1981 Rzeszow sit-in suspended by Rural Solidarity as the registration negotiations seem to make progress.

Feb. 23, 1981 Kania and Jaruzelski attending Soviet Communist

Party Congress in Moscow; Brezhnev still cautious on the subject of Solidarity.

March 8, 1981 Rally of 3000 students and professors of the University of Warsaw commemorating the 1968 demonstrations and protesting anti-Semitic party policies; party provocateurs publish attacks on Stalinist Jews who tortured Polish patriots in 1940s and on Jews affiliated with KOR; an attempt to tinge the resistance against Sovietization of Poland with anti-Semitism in world opinion in order to weaken the support for Solidarity abroad; strong protest by Solidarity against these party tactics.

March 9, 1981 Rural Solidarity congress in Poznan pressing for an official recognition.

March 11, 1981 Moscow announcing large-scale maneuvers by Warsaw Pact forces in preparation of Soviet invasion of Poland; plans and date of the invasion disclosed again to the United States government by Col. W. Kuklinski.

March 13, 1981 Catholic bishops warn against extremists endangering Poland.

March 19, 1981 Rural Solidarity sit-in broken up by police in Bydgoszcz; injured Mariusz Labentowicz and Jan Rulewski; their pictures reproduced on posters throughout Poland; beatings represented in rumors (spread by the government) as done by hard-liners trying to oust General Jaruzelski; Solidarity demanding, under threat of nationwide strike on March 31, that the guilty of police violence be punished.

March 20–29 Walesa negotiating on Bydgoszcz police violence with Deputy Prime Minister Mieczyslaw Rakowski; tension increasing.

March 27, 1981 Four-hour warning strike by Solidarity while the March 31 strike is being prepared midst rumors of an impending Soviet invasion of Poland; publication by the United States of Soviet plans preventing the invasion; the Soviets again accusing the United States of spreading false alarm.

March 30, 1981 Walesa reaching compromise with Rakowski and calling off the nationwide strike in spite of some disagreement in Solidarity leadership. Power struggle within the Party's Central Committee; defeated hard-liners Olszowski and Grabski saved by direct Soviet intervention.

Apr. 1, 1981 Establishing within Solidarity of a study committee on police violence in Bydgoszcz, on the way the protest strike was suspended; resignation Karol Modzelewski as Solidarity press spokesman; beginning of meat rationing in Poland.

Apr. 2, 1981 Jagielski negotiating emergency aid with Vice President Bush in Washington; U.S. government warnings on impending Soviet intervention in Poland.

Apr. 7, 1981 End of Warsaw Pact maneuvers during Czech Communist Party Congress where Poland was represented by Kania and Olszowski; Gustav Husak warning that the Warsaw Pact forces will intervene to save Communist rule in Poland; Brezhnev confident that the Communist government in Poland has means to solve its problems with Solidarity.

Apr. 10, 1981 Seym resolution on two-months suspension of strikes in Poland because of an economic crisis; party hard-liners continue to fight for their political life by provoking wildcat strikes.

Apr. 15, 1981 Pro-Solidarity Communist Party members in Torun calling for democratic reforms within the Party.

Apr. 17, 1981 Government's agreement to proceed with court registration of Rural Solidarity during the month of May.

Apr. 26, 1981 Rescheduling of payments on Poland's $25 billion debt by the West followed by liberalization of Polish passport regulations.

May 1, 1981 Party leadership marching in the May Day parade instead of reviewing it; food rationing extended to a number of products.

May 3, 1981 Polish constitution of 1791 commemorated in a huge celebration for the first time since 1947; it was the first modern constitution in Europe—a unique voluntary extension of civil rights to all including the Jews; May 3 was a national holiday in the Second Polish Republic after 1918.

May 9, 1981 Lech Walesa leaving for Japan, invited there by the Japanese trade unions to see Japanese worker-participation systems in action.

May 12, 1981 Rural Solidarity officially registered by Warsaw court.

May 13, 1981 Pope John Paul II seriously wounded in Vatican by a Turkish terrorist apparently recruited by Bulgarian secret police on behalf of Soviet KGB in order to intimidate Solidarity in Poland and aggravate relations between Turkey and its western Christian allies in NATO. Illness of Cardinal Wyszynski.

May 26, 1981 Spreading of corruption investigations leading to suicide death of two former cabinet ministers.

May 27, 1981 Golden Palm won at the Cannes Film Festival by Wajda for *Man of Iron*, recently completed and shown in Poland in full without censorship.

May 28, 1981 Death of Cardinal Stefan Wyszynski at age seventy-nine; state funeral attended by Solidarity leaders and hundreds of thousands of mourners.

June 1981 Apparent KGB plant: Katowice Forum a hard-line Communist propaganda source favorably quoted by Soviet state news agency TASS.

June 5, 1981 Walesa speech to International Labor Organization in Geneva.

June 6, 1981 Communist Party infighting before Party congress; "liberals" criticizing "hard-liners."

June 7, 1981 Triumphal return of Czeslaw Milosz, Nobel laureate, receiving honorary doctorate at Catholic University of Lublin and visiting the Gdansk 1970 Memorial on which his poetic translation of the Psalms is engraved.

June 10, 1981 Kania managing to stay as Party's first secretary in spite of hard-liners' attempt to remove him.

June 13, 1981 Defacing of a Soviet war memorial in Lublin; a likely provocation by communist hard-liners denounced by Walesa.

June 21, 1981 Opinion poll by *Kultura* magazine; Solidarity ranking as the most respected institution in Poland, after the Catholic Church, followed by the Army, presented to the public as a "truly patriotic" Polish defense force (which it was to a considerable extent in 1956); Communist Party ranking as fourteenth.

June 28, 1981 Dedication in Poznan of a monument, consisting of two crosses as a memorial to the martyrs of the 1956 labor uprising, attended by 150,000.

July 7, 1981 Pope John Paul II naming Bishop Jozef Glemp of Warmia as the new primate of Catholic Church in Poland.

July 9, 1981 Four-hour strike by employees of the state airline LOT to protest government passing over their choice for the manager.

July 14, 1981 Communist Party Congress in Warsaw of 2000 delegates, including members and sympathizers of Solidarity, for the first time in the Soviet bloc, elected by a free and secret ballot; voting to use secret balloting in election of a new Party leadership; Kania re-elected Party's first secretary.

July 27, 1981 Wajda's film *Man of Iron* released in Warsaw, uncensored.

July 25–Aug. 10, 1981 Nationwide elections of delegates for Solidarity annual congress in September; government attacks on anti-Socialist character of Solidarity amid widespread food shortages (widely suspected as staged by the government in order to blame it on Solidarity).

Aug. 3, 1981 Walesa's statement of sympathy with 12,000 air-traffic controllers fired by President Reagan, moving to decertify their union.

Aug. 14–20, 1981 Solidarity delegation led by Lech Walesa obtaining an audience with the pope and visiting the Monte Cassino cemetery of Polish soldiers.

Aug. 19, 1981 Solidarity demanding access to media; wildcat strikes by printers protesting government's media attacks on Solidarity; Kania reporting to Brezhnev in Crimea on the situation in Poland.

Aug. 26, 1981 Opinion polls showing some drop in popularity of Solidarity (estimated as having 14 million members including four million in the Rural Solidarity, Poland's population 36 million); the drop resulting from government anti-Solidarity propaganda playing up threats of Soviet invasion and a famine in the coming winter.

Aug. 27, 1981 Compensation won for workers injured in 1976 in Radom under a threat of a strike there.

Aug. 29, 1981 Walesa and three other Solidarity panelists obtain 20-minutes program on TV on Sept. 1 to speak on upcoming Solidarity national congress.

Aug. 31, 1981 Celebration of the anniversary of Gdansk accords; Solidarity completing the giant job of canvassing its ten million members in the process of selecting delegates for national congress.

Sept. 1981 Showing of many Polish patriotic films with anti-Soviet overtones including *Farmers '81*; Festival's Grand Prize given to Agnieszka, Holland's *Fever*, a film on preparations for an anti-Russian insurrection in 1905.

Sept. 4, 1981 Beginning of Soviet Navy war games off Polish Baltic coast.

Sept. 5, 1981 Beginning of Solidarity's First National Congress of Delegates with a Mass celebrated by Archbishop Jozef Glemp, the new primate of Poland; Lech Walesa opening address including doubts about government's sincerity in dealing with Solidarity; banning from the congress hall of government's TV because of refusal to grant Solidarity's request for its own slots in covering the congress.

Sept. 5–7, 1981 Solidarity sending mediators to defuse a new Bydgoszcz crisis resulting from a prison break and a takeover.

Sept. 5–10, 1981 First session of Solidarity's National Congress dealing with the authority of union's central leadership; an alternate "worker self-management bill" to counter before Seym of the rigged government's version; a demand for national referendum to decide between government's and Solidarity's version of "worker's self-management" bill; a decision to hold the national referendum by Solidarity if government refuses to do it; a demand of open and free voting procedures in the elections for the next year Seym; sending a letter of support to workers trying to form free trade unions throughout the Soviet Bloc countries, two weeks adjournment for delegates' consultations with their constituents.

Sept. 11, 1981 Soviets producing a counterletter from Moscow ZIL truck plant workers in answer to Solidarity; Soviet press describing Solidarity congress as an "anti-Soviet, anti-Socialist orgy."

Sept. 12–22, 1981 Solidarity and government negotiating the issue of "worker self-management" amid rising tension and fierce government propaganda attacks on the free union (as Soviet leaders sent a warning letter to Polish Party leaders threatening drastic reduction in delivery of petroleum and other critical supplies).

Sept. 15, 1981 Pope John Paul II issuing encyclical *On Human Work* supporting many Solidarity positions stating that means of production cannot be possessed against labor, but that they should serve labor.

Sept. 22, 1981 Tension easing as "worker self-management" compromise bill is approved by the Seym allowing some worker voice in selection of managers outside of "key security enterprises."

Sept. 26, 1981 Solidarity's national congress resuming amid criticism of the "worker self-mananagement" compromise and its undemocratic aspects; after airing of reservations, the compromise approved.

Sept. 28 "Founding father" of KOR, 93-year old economist Edward Lipinski, announcing disbanding of KOR and stating that the government is anti-Socialist and violates Socialist principles.

Oct. 2, 1981 Lech Walesa winning the chairmanship of Solidarity by 55 percent majority to head a national commission (more radical than he was).

Oct. 3, 1981 Solidarity offering a two-year program for national economic recovery including limiting of military spending and special people's courts to deal with government corruption.

Oct. 4, 1981 Solidarity opposing steep price increases on food and tobacco announced by the government; wildcat strikes follow; Oct. 15 Solidarity winning a temporary price rollback.

Oct. 18, 1981 General Wojciech Jaruzelski consolidating his grip on power as he is elected to replace Kania as the first secretary and head of the Polish Communist Party, in addition to being prime minister and defense minister of Poland; first such concentration of power in hands of a professional military man in the history of Soviet Bloc; the fact that Soviets ordered this to happen despite their fear of "Bonapartism" indicates the degree to which Polish Communist Party was bankrupt. First act of the new first secretary was to lead the Central Committee to ban labor strikes in Poland.

Oct. 19, 1981 Walesa, while opposing the strike ban, also expresses opposition to the wildcat strikes which were provoked by the communist hard-liners as a tactic to discredit Solidarity.

Oct. 20, 1981 Police provocation of a violent street riot by arresting union members during routine distribution of legal Solidarity publications.

Oct. 23, 1981 Jaruzeski sending Army patrols of three of four throughout the country under the guise of helping the rural administrators with food collection and distribution, while in reality rehearsing for a military coup d'etat to break Solidarity by imposition of marshal law in Poland.

Oct. 24, 1981 Nationwide protest; one-hour strike by Solidarity.

Nov. 1981 Sosnowiec coal mine takeover by the miners called an "active strike" in which the miners take over the mine management, set working hours, supervise production and distribution of coal (which they sent directly to farmers and day care child nurseries).

Nov. 1, 1981 All Saints' Day commemoration in Warsaw in Powazki Cemetery of 1940 mass execution of Polish officers in Katyn forest by the Soviets, attended by thousands.

Nov. 4, 1981 Polish summit meeting of Solidarity's Lech Walesa, Party's Wojciech Jaruzelski, and Primate Bishop of Poland Jozef Glemp.

Nov. 7, 1981 Huge wildcat strikes in Zielona Gora to protest firing of an activist seen as a provocation by the government by 160,000 strikers and other 200,000 who threaten to join the strike. Escape from Poland of Col. Wlodzimierz Kuklinski to the United States with complete plans and date of proclamation in Poland of state of war in order to destroy Solidarity, the only free labor union within Soviet Bloc. This time the United States refusing to make public Soviet plans to subjugate Poland by imposition of martial law and to forewarn Solidarity by means of any public or private channels.

Nov. 9, 1981 Publishing of Solidarity's agenda for immediate negotiations with the government: 1. Social control of economic decision making; 2. Solidarity's access to mass media; 3. Economic reform; 4. Democratization of government at provincial and district level; 5. Reform of legal system; 6. Reform of pricing system. Government's counterproposal to buy time: a "front on national accord."

Nov. 10, 1981 Poland applying for membership in the International Monetary Fund to get credit to pay debts to Western banks; Soviet Union suspending an earlier veto; IMF requiring a complete audit of Poland's economy.

Nov. 10, 1981 Nationwide student protest strike over government's appointment of a new president of the Radom Politechnical Institute.

Nov. 11, 1981 First postwar commemoration of Poland's Independence Day on Nov. 11, 1918, and a massive tribute to the memory of Marshal Jozef Pilsudski.

Nov. 12, 1981 Wildcat strikes in Zielona Gora end; other wildcat strikes, mostly provoked by communist hard-liners as a tactic to defend their privileges, strikes including nearly 300,000 people throughout Poland.

Nov. 13, 1981 Government's statistics indicate 15 percent drop in industrial production and 25 percent drop in exports to the West from the year before.

Nov. 15, 1981 Selection of candidates for local government councils by members of Silesian branch of Solidarity.

Nov. 17, 1981 Agenda for government talks with Solidarity set to discuss possible formation of a Front of National Accord.

Nov. 19, 1981 Withdrawal of the Army patrols sent throughout Poland on Oct. 23.

Nov. 22, 1981 Visit to Bonn of Leonid Brezhnev, finding out that there is no support for Solidarity in Chancellor Helmut Schmidt's government.

Nov. 22, 1981 Jacek Kuron's home raided by police.

Nov. 23, 1981 Protest resignations of officials of Solidarity and Rural Solidarity over "too conciliatory attitude" of their top leadership (possibly influenced by Primate Glemp).

Nov. 24, 1981 Gen. Jaruzelski's consultations with Marshal Victor Kulikov, Soviet commander of the Warsaw Pact forces, in Warsaw.

Nov. 25, 1981 Strike of firefighter cadet school for exemption from police duties and academic rights, becoming a test case for a renewed use of force by the government.

Nov. 26, 1981 Stalemate in government-Solidarity negotiations.

Nov. 27, 1981 Attempts to eliminate Communist Party's organizations in twenty-one out of forty-nine provinces of Poland; government seeking emergency legislation including a ban on strikes.

Dec. 2, 1981

Helicopter-supported police attack on the firefighter school in Warsaw; removal of 300 striking cadets, denunciated by Solidarity whose telephone and telex communications were disconnected during police raid on firefighters.

Dec. 5, 1981 Rural Solidarity proposing a merger with Solidarity and Student Union to form one organization. A total of 70 out of 104 institutions of higher learning in Poland on strike in support of the students of Radom Politechnical Institute. Walesa and Archbishop Glemp discuss the deteriorating political situation.

Dec. 6, 1981 Warsaw Solidarity calling for worker guards to protect strikers and setting Dec. 17 to protest police takeover of firefighter cadet academy and eviction of 300 cadets.

Dec. 7, 1981 Warsaw radio accusing Walesa of advocating overthrow of the government.

Dec. 8, 1981 Primate Archbishop Glemp asking Jaruzelski and Walesa to resume negotiations.

Dec. 10, 1981 Soviet warning note to Polish Central Committee. Walesa stating, "We can not retreat anymore."

Dec. 11, 1981 Solidarity promising 24-hour nationwide strike if new emergency laws are passed; Jurczyk of Szczecin calling for free elections to Seym on March 31, 1982. Start of first summit meeting between East and West Germany by Helmut Schmidt and Erich Honecker discussing the implications of Solidarity crisis for Germany.

Dec. 12,1981 Film *Man of Iron* submitted for the American Academy Award.

Dec. 12, 1981 National leadership of Solidarity voting Dec. 17 nationwide strike to protest police action at the firefighter's academy and to hold national referendum on: 1. vote of confidence in Jaruzelski's government; 2. establishing of a temporary government to conduct free elections; 3. providing military guarantees to U.S.S.R. in Poland; 4. whether the Polish Communist Party PZPR can represent the entire Polish society in delivering such guarantees to U.S.S.R. A few hours later all communication lines not under military control were cut.

Dec. 13, 1981 Gen. Jaruzelski declaring a "state of war" in Poland.

Dec. 13, 1981 Coup d'etat by Communist Military Junta led by Gen. Wojciech Jaruzelski; the first military takeover within the Soviet bloc; violation of Polish constitution, 1980 Gdansk accords with Solidarity, and 1975 Helsinki Pact on human rights by imposition of state of war in Poland (eleventh anniversary of 1970 killings of protesing workers in Gdansk and in other Polish ports on the Baltic).

Heart attacks and other treatable conditions bringing death to thousands throughout Poland as a result of telephone communication blackout and a complete breakdown of emergency medical aid and ambulance service.

Execution of precisely planned military operation prepared under supervision of Marshal Victor Kulikov, Soviet commander of Warsaw Pact forces. All telephone lines disconnected; all cities and towns sealed by troops; roundup by the police of Solidarity leaders gathered in Gdansk for their meeting of national commission; mass arrests of Solidarity's regional leaders and associated intellectuals such as writers, journalists, expert advisers, and some priests on this Sunday morning; Solidarity calling for a general strike.

1 A.M. Telephone message from Polish Embassy in Rome to Pope John Paul II notifying about the planned military takeover and giving false assurances for purpose of obtaining statements by Catholic hierarchy in Poland condemning armed resistance and violence and appealing that "Poles do not start fighting against Poles," as in fact Archbishop Glemp did say later in his morning sermon.

6 A.M. Radio address by General Jaruzelski declaring state of war and takeover of the government by a military junta of twenty-one Army generals and commissars acting as Army Council of National Salvation (*Wojskowa Rada Ocalenia Narodowego*, WRON, soon called "wrona" meaning "the crow."

In the name of defense of socialism WRON decreeing: 1. Temporary suspension of freedom of speech, press, assembly, access to communications and other basic civil rights. 2. Except for religious gatherings banning of all public gatherings such as demonstrations, strikes, sport games and artistic events. 3. Curfew from 10 P.M. to 6 A.M. 4. Banning of use of any printing equipment and distribution of any publications without prior government approval. 5. Mail and telephone conversations placed under censorship. 6. Strict enforcement of carrying of I.D. cards at all times and prohibition to leave one's residence for more than 48 hours without an official permission. 7. Blocking of all civil and commercial traffic across Polish frontiers and airspace. 8. All broadcasting restricted to one official TV and radio channel based in Warsaw. 9. Closing of all educational institutions for an indefinite period. 10. Placing under direct military control of police, civil defense, and fire department, as well as thousands of industrial enterprises related to national security. 11. Official legalization of use by the military of "coercion to restore peace, law and order." 12. Decree on immediate penalties including death for any violations of the martial law.

Telephone communication blackout making impossible emergency calls for first aid and ambulance services causing thousands of preventable death throughout Poland.

West German Chancellor Helmut Schmidt extending his stay in East Germany, avoiding public comments on the situation in Poland and trying to assist East Berlin government in benefiting from the Polish crisis; growth of neutralist mood in West Germany expressed in the belief that trade with the Soviets and loans are more important to West Germany than the American atomic umbrella and a notion that the U.S.S.R. does not plan to change West European governments into communist ones because that would destroy Soviet sources of desperately needed high technology and commercial credits; German fear that the Soviets may not be able to control the Polish Army with its 3000 tanks, strong air force and rocketry; concern that the 17 crack Polish divisions, in case of struggle with the Soviets, may break through East Germany into West Germany and upset the precarious balance between East and West; neutralist fears alleviated as the true nature of the military takeover became more apparent amid reports that no one in Poland can be promoted to the rank of a general (in a sensitive spot) without serving at the same time as an officer in Soviet KGB; soon West Germany leading western Europe in giving Soviets assurances that no sanctions would be imposed no matter what happens to Poland and Solidarity, and that the business would be as usual.

Dec. 14, 1981 (Monday) High precision execution of the military takeover and a complete news blackout astonishing Western news media whose telex lines were cut. Government troops encircling shipyards, steel mills, and countless factories occupied by workers throughout Poland; the actual brute work of strikebreaking, beatings, using water cannons, and coercion by force assigned to the 56,000 Internal Security Forces (which included convicted criminals serving main parts of their sentences in the riot police called ZOMO) mass arrests continuing; the government claim of 4000 arrests rejected by Solidarity as being about 10 percent of the actual total of all arrests.

Rescheduling of Poland's debt considered at a meeting of Western bankers in Paris, as previously planned; hopes expressed that the military rule in Poland will restore normal economic activity and produce hard currency exports to pay foreign debts; suspension of $100 million in economic assistance to Poland by the United States.

Dec. 15, 1981 ZOMO forces crushing occupational strikes one by one; evicting the occupying workers and at first not letting them back in; passive resistance and slowdown tactics spreading throughout Poland as communication blackout is continuing with telephone lines cut between cities.

Sudden reversal in food supply; huge quantities of food in stores convincing the Poles that recent food shortages were used by the government as a coercion tactic and part of artificially created acute crisis, falsely blamed on Solidarity. Dollar value almost doubling on the black market within one day.

Arrest of hundreds of scientists in the police raid on Polish Academy of Sciences in Warsaw.

Dec. 16, 1981 ZOMO forces battling workers and the public around the Gdansk shipyard, hundreds injured there; seven killed by the ZOMO at the Wujek mine in Silesia. List of 57 arrested dissidents broadcast by Warsaw radio including names of three people visiting in the West, an indication that the list was prepared during the advance planning of the military takeover long before.

Archbishop Glemp calling for national prayer, an end to martial law, freeing of prisoners, and revival of free labor unions.

American diplomats continue being grounded in Poland; U.S. retaliating by restricting movements of Polish diplomats to 25 miles.

Dec. 17, 1981 Tear-gas attacks on demonstrators; violence continuing, especially in Gdansk and Warsaw.

Dec. 18, 1981 Archbishop Glemp smuggling out a letter to Paris stating that Poland is under a reign of terror; workers' strongholds are gradually eliminated by ZOMO forces in spite of such obstacles as wiring with explosives, etc.

Dec. 19, 1981 Leonid Brezhnev on his 75th birthday receiving thanks from general Jaruzelski for his help in current crisis in Poland.

Dec. 20, 1981 Polish ambassador to the United States, Romuald Spasowski, resigning his post in protest against the military takeover in Poland, a few days later followed by Zdzislaw Rurarz, Polish ambassador to Japan and Philippines; both receiving political asylum in the United States and later sentenced to death in absentia and stripped of Polish citizenship by a Warsaw court.

Dec. 21, 1981 Nearly 3000 miners still barricaded deep inside two coal mines in Silesia.

Dec. 22, 1981 Rejection by Western banks in Paris of Poland's request for $350 million for interrest payment on loans from the West and due on Dec. 31, 1981. The first meeting of Politburo of the Polish Communist Party (PZPR) since the proclamation of the state of war. Lifting of curfew for midnight Mass on Dec. 24.

Dec. 23, 1981 President Reagan announcing punitive sanctions for breaking the free labor union movement of Solidarity by the Communist military junta under Soviet orders. U.S. sanctions aimed primarily against Poland in spite of the recognition of Soviet primary responsibility for the breaking of Solidarity. Polish public hit harder by the sanctions than the government of General Jaruzelski. An indefinite suspension of American policy of helping Poland economically by giving credits, custom duty reductions, and foreign aid. A change from the policy based on assumption that Poland would become more independent if treated as a fully independent country.

Miners' strikes continuing; beginning of negotiations between government and the Church soon to be joined by an envoy from Vatican.

Dec. 24, 1981 Address by General Jaruzelski to the people of Poland justifying his imposition of the state of war as a lesser evil than a fratricidal conflict which "stood on our threshhold." Since Solidarity was unarmed and committed to non-violence, the fratricidal conflict might have occurred in case of Soviet invasion of Poland with Polish armed forces split, some resisting it while others remained under Soviet orders. Jaruzelski stated that there would be a place for independent trade unions in Poland; at the same time all the leaders of Solidarity, the only independent Polish trade union since 1939, were imprisoned; many of them brutally treated and detained under horrible conditions.

Midnight Masses becoming a massive pro-Solidarity demonstration throughout Poland.

POLAND'S INDIGENOUS DEMOCRATIC PROCESS

COMPOSITION OF THE NATIONAL PARLIAMENT
THE POLISH SEYM DURING:
POLISH CONSTITUTIONAL MONARCHY (1493–1569) AND IN
THE FIRST POLISH REPUBLIC (1569–1795)

AN EARLY MODERN POLISH CIVILIZATION was unique in Europe. It was shaped by an indigenous democratic process which matured in the 15th century. The Democracy of Polish nobility (about 10 percent of population) was based on a representative form of government and a clear understanding of its legality. It took a form of a parliamentary system controlled from below.

Polish cultural and social life centered on the nationwide parliamentary activities rather than on the royal court and town. In this Poland differed from all of Europe where the king and his court were actually dictating the course of development of cultural, social, and artistic life of their countries. Thus, Poland was unique in that the parliament was the center of cultural and social life. Polish culture and civilization was led by a nationwide group of free citizens who were independent from the central government of a king.

National and regional parliaments became catalysts of social and cultural life of Poland, a role played in the rest of Europe by the royal court and the town. Precisely, because parliamentary form of government had such a crucial role in development of the unique Polish civilization, it is important to become familiar with the composition of the national parliament (the Seym) and its procedures such as the order of debates, adoption of bills, and evolution of the principle of unanimity, all described here in detail.

The Polish National Parliament, or the General Seym, *Seym Walny* (seym val-ny), became bicameral in 1493, composed of the Chamber of Deputies, *Izba Poselska* (eez-ba po-sel-ska) and the Senate. Seym's composition remained unchanged unitl the Constitution of May 3, 1791. Warsaw was the permanent seat of the National Parliament since the founding of the First Polish Republic in 1569. The General Seym was composed of:

An Elective King

An elected king was head of the state and head of the executive branch of the government. He was also the presiding officer of the Senate where he was usually represented by the Grand Marshal of Poland until 1569, and then alternatively by the grand marshals of Poland and Lithuania. If both marshals were absent, their powers were taken over by a marshal of the Court, from Poland or Lithuania.

The Senate (a permanent body)

The Senate, formerly the Royal Council, in 1493 included 81 senators: 2 archbishops, 6 bishops, 68 territorial officers (13 provincial governors, or Voivodes, and 55 Castellans) and 5 government ministers (Grand Marshal or the senior minister, Chancellor, Vice-Chancellor, Treasurer, and Marshal of the Court). Upon the founding of the First Polish Republic in 1569, the number of senators reached 140; 113 from Poland (13 bishops, 22 Voivodes, 73 Castellans, and 5 government ministers) and 27 from Lithuania (2 bishops, 9 Voivodes, 1 Starosta of Samogitia, 10 Castellans, and 5 government ministers).

The order of precedence for senators corresponded to their rank in the Church hierarchy and the importance of their region, starting with the Castellan of Krakow (Cracow). At the founding of the Republic in 1569, the order of precedence was fixed so that each Polish senator was followed by a Lithuanian senator of equal rank.

The Chamber of Deputies (created anew with each election)

The Chamber of Deputies or *Izba Poselska* (eez-ba po-sel-ska) was composed of the representatives elected by regional legislatures or *Sejmiki Ziemskie* (sey-mee-kee zhem-ske). In 1493 there were 40 deputies; in 1569 the number grew to 174 (114 from Poland, 48 from Lithuania, and 12 from Prussia); in 1768 the number grew to 236 and in 1790 to 354 deputies. The city of Cracow was represented permanently by two deputies while the towns of Poznan, Lwow, Lublin, Kalisz, Sandomierz, Wislica, and Biecz were represented only when town-related matters were dealt with by the Chamber of Deputies. In theory the number of deputies was of no importance since the National Parliament did not adopt decisions by a majority vote.

Regional Legislatures (*Sejmiki Ziemskie*)

These regional bodies usually sent two representatives each; however some sent as many as six. The number of regional legislatures grew with the incorporation of new territories. The government tried to limit the number of deputies, citing the growth of expenses of the sessions while in reality it was uncomfortable with the programs formulated by the Chamber of Deputies and its mounting criticism of government's policies. The Act of Parliament of 1520 limited to six the number of representatives from each district, whose expenses would be paid by the government, however, each Region, or Voivodship, could send as many as they wished at their own expense.

Legislators in regional legislatures decided the fate of the national parliament. They were secured against terrorism by the local armed forces commanded by their speaker, the local *starosta*. During any session of the Legislature, all private armed forces were ordered out of town. The King's message convening the national parliament and summarizing the state of external and internal affairs of the Republic and the issues facing the next Seym, was read. The required solutions were also indicated. After the King's emissary presented the government's program for the next Seym, the local senators evaluated the government's proposals and left in order to allow the citizens to act as a regional legislature. The citizen's body debated and formulated the instructions for the deputies and petitions. When this was done, the regional legislature elected the deputies for the national parliament. At this point the senators would return to the legislature and verify that the deputies were instructed and elected in accordance with the law and the true expression of the will of the assembled citizens.

All debates followed well-defined rules. The senators spoke in the same order as they did in the Senate. After their departure the speaker, or marshal, asked the citizens to speak according to their place in the circle. If there was a dispute about the conclusion, a free discussion clarified the situation. If a unanimous conclusion could not be agreed upon, the region would lose its chance to speak in the national parliament. It should be noted that the citizens were armed during the the debates and elections. Poland was the most militarized society of Europe and the political nation of free and noble citizens of the First Polish Republic numbered in various regions from eight to as high as twenty percent of the total population.

Sixteenth century legislative debates in Poland were primarily political arguments of a moral and legal nature: praise of the Republic's freedom and civil liberties and one's readiness to sacrifice for them one's life and property. The political orations often displayed a mature theory of democracy, always insisting that the King and his government should be equally subject to the law with the aristrocrats and all noble citizens, the barefoot nobles, indeed, the whole political nation (which numbered about one million people).

Polish politicians acquired their education by listening to and learning government debates in the regional legislatures and in the national parliament, all of which were opened to the public. Texts important to the training of politicians included works on history and government by ancient and modern writers, especially the history of Poland; studies on contemporary Poland; and collections of the laws of the Polish Republic, especially laws that were in force. Legal skills of the deputies were high, and there were many experts in law among them. (See the preceding chapter "Chronology" for the record of Laws and Regulations created by the Seym).

PARLIAMENTARY PROCEDURE DURING POLAND'S CONSTITUTIONAL MONARCHY (1493–1569) AND THE FIRST POLISH REPUBLIC (1569–1795)

Joint Session of the Entire Parliament—The Seym

Parliamentary procedure in Poland was shaped by custom and, to a lesser extent, by constitutional acts. Initially the lack of comprehensive rules caused waste of time as the same procedural questions had to be settled repeatedly. Gradually binding procedural laws were established. The Senate was a permanent body while the Chamber of Deputies was elected for each session.

Each parliamentary session, called a Seym, was constituted separately for a specific time interval. Traditionally the session would start with a solemn Mass celebrated by the bishops. It included a sermon on the issues to be dealt with in that session.

The Procedure of the National Parliament—The Seym

1. The new Chamber of Deputies elected the speaker or marshal, alternately from Greater and Lesser Poland. The speaker of the preceding session conducted the election of the new speaker. Re-election of the former speaker was permissible. Until the end of the 17th century the speaker was rewarded for his services with a territorial office called *starostwo*, later his remuneration was fixed by the parliament.

The speaker controlled the agenda because he decided on the order of the parliamentary proceedings and, therefore, his election was contested. The speaker's deputy would report to the king when the election was concluded and would receive an appointment for the king's meeting with the new Chamber of Deputies.

2. Verification of the validity of the election of the deputies followed, especially in cases when two men claimed victory for the same seat. The Chamber of Deputies was required to decide such issues.

3. A formal greeting of the king was delivered by the speaker in a political speech during a joint session of the Senate and the Chamber of Deputies. Then the king or, in his name, the chancellor would congratulate the new deputies on the election of the speaker. Each deputy, then, would formally greet the king. The Senate, being a permanent body, did not require periodical renewal, as did the Chamber of Deputies.

4. Following the greeting, the chancellor presented the government's reasons for calling the parliamentary session and a proposal for an agenda of the most important issues. The chancellor reviewed the state of the Commonwealth (or the Republic) since the last meeting of the parliament. From 1693 on, he also read pertinent state documents giving a full account of recent important events, the effects of bills passed by the previous session, and decisions taken by the resident senators (of the watchdog committee) advising the government. Instructions given to the envoys sent abroad were also disclosed.

5. The speaker then presented his rules, known as the Marshal's Articles, concerning orderly debates and his penalties for breaking them. After 1669 the Marshal's Articles were printed for distribution. From then on the *Pacta Conventa* were read to remind the Deputies of the contractual obligation assumed by the new elected king to serve as a chief executive of the Republic. *Pacta Conventa* constituted a social contract between the elecotrate and the king-elect, since late 16th century.

6. Territorial and other vacant offices were conferred early so that the government could not use the appointments later for political bargaining. An act of 1588 required that the vacancies be filled during the first eight days of the parliamentary session. After 1690, the Chamber of Deputies established what vacancies were available and named the candidates to fill them.

7. *Vota* or opinions of the senators were then presented. These vota explained the government's proposals for the benefit of the newly elected and less experienced deputies. Listening to the senatorial opinions became a mere formality as the real power shifted to the Chamber of Deputies. Generally, the vota were followed by a formal, concluding speech by the king.

8. Since 1573, the chancellor appointed a watchdog committee of sixteen senators to serve, four at a time, as resident advisers of the king on constitutional matters and to fulfill the social contract with the electorate—by then the social contract included both the *Pacta Conventa* and *Henrician Articles*.

9. The Marshal of Poland appointed several senators to be responsible for drawing up the texts of enacted bills as they become available.

10. The Marshal of Poland appointed a committee of several senators to receive and check the financial reports from the treasury and from the army, in particular from the general commanding the artillery.

11. A summary of the national defense problems by emissaries from the army followed.

12. Foreign envoys then presented their proposals, complaints, etc. This ended preliminary debates. All components of the Seym participated, namely, the king, in his dual capacity as the chief executive of the Republic and as the presiding officer of the Senate, the Senate itself, and the Chamber of Deputies. The exit of the deputies to their own chamber for seperate deliberations followed.

Debates in Separate Chambers—Adoption of Bills by the Chamber of Deputies

The king deliberated with the Senate during the parliamentary session early in the period of the Constitutional Monarchy (1493–1569) on judicial matters, foreign policy issues and, when the Chamber of Deputies broke up in protest for some reason. As the Chamber of Deputies became the supreme power in the Republic (1569–1795), the king had to concentrate on the debates of the deputies.

The speaker, or marshal, of the Chamber of Deputies had the following duties:

1. Ordering and adjourning the meetings.
2. Determining who will speak.
3. Editing the adopted decisions and formulating them diplomatically to prevent unnecessary opposition to a bill.
4. Receiving the submitted bills.
5. Guiding the proposed bills through the debate to passage.
6. Nominating members to parliamentary commissions.
7. Nominating members for deputations.
8. Keeping the debates orderly. For this, he used his ornate gavel-staff to call for attention by knocking loudly on the floor.
9. Steering the debates with skill and restraint, curbing unnecessary clashes of opinions, and keeping the debates on the right course. This was especially important considering the exceptional freedom of speech that was permitted to the deputies and their freedom to decide the course of a debate which the speaker had no power to close since every curtailment would have been regarded as a restriction of a deputy's rights.
10. Representing the deputies outside the Chamber.
11. Leading the Chamber to the king and Senate.
12. Addressing the king and the Senate on behalf of the Chamber of Deputies.
13. Presenting conclusions.
14. Stating what decisions had been adopted under the tradition of unanimity.

Note: The speaker or marshal was the most important member of the parliament as he could direct a debate in favor or against any proposed bill. The passage of a bill depended on his skill. All the political parties and the king were most anxious to have their own candidate elected as the speaker.

The unlimited freedom of speech of each deputy required extraordinary skill and restraint to avoid violent clashes of opinions and to bring a debate to a successful conclusion, a task complicated by the principle of unanimity.

The debates were conducted by speaking in order of sitting, called *vota*, always starting with the representatives of Cracow and Poznan. After each round of *vota* speeches the speaker summarized the points on which consensus had been reached. When two or three rounds of *vota* speeches did not produce results, a free discussion or *interlocutorium* would result in free and spirited exchange of opinions until agreement or disagreement was reached.

Clerks summed up the arguments for each side of an issue to make it easier for the deputies to take a stand. Once an agreement was reached, the speaker would ask for a plenary session with the king in the Senate chamber and would lead the deputies there. The king, or more often the chancellor, would reply to the decision by the Chamber of Deputies after consultation with the Senate.

The senators could give the king whispered advice or state their opinions openly for the deputies to hear. If an open debate of the senators took place, the chancellor would summarize it and state whether unanimity was achieved. In the 17th and 18th centuries, the Polish parliament was controlled by the Chamber of Deputies and the deputies ceased to consult with the Senate.

Parliamentary committees dealt with specific problems, such as, appropriations, treasury expenditures, and the drafting of bills to make sure that the version approved by the Chamber of Deputies actually was written into the new law. Elected representatives from the Chamber of Deputies and from the Senate verified and signed the enacted bills.

In the middle of the 17th century, preliminary sessions of separate general legislatures of Greater Poland, Lesser Poland, and Lithuania were convened prior to the session of the national parliament. The general legislatures were presided over by a senior senator and served to prepare the work of the upcoming Seym through a process of free discussion. These preliminary sessions were called Sessions of Nations.

Conclusion of the Seym

During the period of the Constitutional Monarchy (1493-1569), consultations of the Chamber of Deputies with the Senate and the king were important to establish whether agreement could be reached. During the years of the Republic (1569–1795), the Chamber of Deputies acquired supremacy and the consultations were abandoned.

It became necessary to set aside the last five days for a plenary session of the entire Seym in order to fix the wording of newly passed bills before the deadline. Nobody had the right to depart. When the debates ended, the speaker would address the king in a joint plenary session; then, each of the deputies would formally greet the king. If the legislative work was successful, the entire Seym went to church and sang the hymn of thanksgiving *Te Deum Laudamus*.

There was a possibility that an unfinished debate would be postponed until a second meeting of the Seym with the same deputies present. This practice was declared illegal in 1726 because each Seym was considered an entity unto itself and each deputy had a mandate for only one Seym of a specified duration. Thus, every Seym had to be preceded by elections.

The Principle of Unanimity

The accountability of deputies to their constituencies was only political, and not legal. The instructions from the regional legislatures were observed because of each deputy's honor and honesty and not because of any legal sanctions. Customary types of instructions given to deputies were:

1. Unlimited power to exercise judgment, or
2. A specific order to obtain concessions, or
3. A specific prohibition to agree to new obligations (taxes, etc.) or
4. A conditional-restrictive mandate.

These instructions, combined with the principle of unanimity, crippled the parliament's freedom of decision during 100 years out of the 300 years of life of the bicameral Polish Seym (1493–1795). The principle of unanimity could be legally circumvented by forming a parliamentary confederation in which majority vote ruled. This was done quite frequently. There was no law sanctioning the principle of unanimity and it was dealt with successfully for 200 years.

It should be noted that the total consent was regarded as the basic guarantee of freedom. The deputies defended the will of their electors. They respected tradition and precedent which served as an example or justification, sometimes stronger than law. They strived for full agreement and the commitment of all.

A rule by majority vote was considered an expediency. During the 16th century, Poles felt that the efforts to secure a majority were generally dishonest. They felt that these efforts were like the "pork barrel" which consisted of bestowing undeserved titles, dignities, leases, etc. They felt that minority rights had to be respected and that in general "better" was not necessarily "more numerous." They respected the consensus reached by "brotherly entreaties." On the other hand on many occasions, a dissenting deputy was "shouted down;" all were not willing to perish because of the obstinacy of one region.

The fact that the parliament session might end without coming to a decision was accepted. Polish politicians felt that the Seyms had a dual responsibility. One was to adopt new laws, and the other, no less important, was to correct any abuses and infringements of the law by the government.

Uncontested bills were passed while questioned bills were postponed or abandoned. One hundred and sixty years after Polish parliament became bicameral in 1652, for the first time, a successful protest against one question by one deputy exercising a Liberum Veto led to the breaking up of the entire session of the Seym and created a disastrous precedent.

The stage was set for this very harmful event when the Respect for the Law Movement of the middle and lower nobility lost the power struggle against political machines of the landed magnates. At the same time, general elections for the head of state admitted foreign candidates to the Polish throne and as a result became a vehicle for the foreign interference in the internal affairs of the Republic.

Political machines of the landed magnates were set up in regional legislatures in order to gain control of the Republic's government from below and to destroy the Cossack self-government in Ukraine (and turn the Cossacks themselves into serfs). Cossack rebellion of 1648 critically weakened the Republic.

The disastrous legal precedent created the Liberum Veto by default when a member of the political machine of a fabulously wealthy dissident governor of Wilno, registered a formal veto with the Crown Secretariat and immediately left Warsaw. His sudden departure violated the parliamentary rule that nobody had the right to depart during a session of the Seym and that absentee votes were traditionally considered unacceptable.

At that point the speaker, Andrzej Maximilian Fredro (1620–1679), author of libertarian "paradoxical philosophy of anarchy," decided that the Liberum Veto (registered as an absentee vote of an illegally departed deputy) was in fact legal and valid. This extremely harmful precedent was followed for about one hundred years, long enough to be one of the main causes of the fall of the First Polish Republic. The breaking of Seyms by a single vote, dissent in form of the Liberum Veto, was sponsored by the internal and external enemies of the Polish Republic.

The absolutist countries used subversion for the preservation of the Liberum veto, participation of foreign candidates in general elections, and the anarchistic "Golden Freedom" or *Zlota Wolnosc* (zwo-ta vol-noshch). By the time the Republic was weakened critically and could not defend her sovereignty the whole process of general elections for the head of state degenerated and became a vehicle of foreign interference in the internal affairs of Poland. The enemies were able to corrupt with bribes individual deputies in order to have them execise the *Liberum Veto* and paralize the Seym.

Numerous secret pacts were concluded by the absolute regimes of the neighboring countries in order to subvert the open parliamentary government of the Polish Republic and foster anarchy in Poland by interfering in the Seym and especially by preventing the passage of urgently needed reforms and defense appropriations.

The secret pacts of the foreign absolutist enemies of the Polish Republic included treaties signed in 1675 by Austria and Russia, in 1686 and 1696 by Sweden and Brandenburg, in 1886 by Austria and Brandenburg, and in 1720 by Russia and the "Kingdom of Prussia," which was the new name for Brandenburg created in 1701 in order to exploit the troubles that the First Polish Republic had with the Russian Empire.

EVOLUTION OF POLISH IDENTITY
THE MILESTONES

600–840 Polish-Polabian Beginnings of a Nation

Pre-Piast period of transition from the tribal military democracies to tribal federations within the Polish-Polabian language area (the basins of the Elbe, the Oder, and the Vistula rivers). Transformation from elective military leaders to hereditary tribal aristocracy. Beginning of early feudal forms and a personal loyalty to the ruler. Local patriotism. Establishment of permanent agriculture based on the use of plough. Beginning of towns in Poland. Separation of crafts and trades from agriculture. Early medieval beginnings of a nation-state.

840–966   The Early Establishment of the Polish Nation

Early Piast period of transition from tribal loyalty first to the local ruler then the development of personal loyalty to the monarch within the area of the common Polish-Polabian language and culture. Unification of the Polish tribes. Early consolidation of the boundaries by political and military actions. Soliciting the Pope for the royal crown as a sign of Polish independence from the Holy Roman Empire.

966–1138   The Foundation of the Polish Nation

Formulation of an early national ambition and realization of an early role-model for the Polish state within the European context. Expansion of local patriotism to include loyalty to the king crowned in 1025. Pride in the national ruler. Beginning of the national cult of St. Adalbert in 1000, then after 1075, of St. Stanislas.

1138–1306   Poland During Feudal Fragmentation of Europe

Attempts to reunite Poland. The Polish Church providing the main impulse. Loyalty to the regional ruler. Local patriotism combined with medieval nationalism described in early chronicles. In 1264 legal protection of the Jews from persecution by their fellow immigrants from Germany. Beginning of formation of world's largest autonomous, Yiddish-speaking Jewish community in Poland.

1306–1370   The Concept of *Corona Regni Poloniae*

Transition of loyalty from regions to the national territory of the lands rightfully held by the crown of the Polish Kingdom and to the person of the king. Emergence of the Polish political nation composed of the masses of the lower and middle gentry who were obliged to defend the country on the basis of their ownership of land. Strengthening of Polish intellectual leadership by founding of the University of Krakow in 1364.

1370–1493   Development of the Polish Political Nation

Partnership of the political nation of the nobility (about 10 percent of population) with the king against the power of aristocracy. Establishing of the original Polish model of government by the democratic process. Growth of power of the lower and middle nobility. National and regional parliaments becoming catalysts of the social and cultural life in Poland. Parliament becoming a forum for the competition of talents. Transfer of the concept of Poland from the person of the king to the "national territory."

1493–1569   The Indigenous Democratic Process in Poland

Participation by 10 percent of population (the largest in Europe) in government of the constitutional monarchy in Poland by an indigenous democratic process. The concept of the *Civis Polonus* an expression of pride in Polish citizenship and Polish democratic process. Polonization occurs as a voluntary acculturation, not denationalization based on the use of force and fraud. Free citizens of Polish culture throughout Poland, Lithuania, Byelorussia, and Ukraine. National and regional parliaments act as catalysts of social and cultural life. Beginning of Polish political literature. Development of popular book market for Polish language.
Maturity of Polish indigenous democratic process. Elective constitutional monarchs allied with the nobility against aristocracy. Golden age of the nobility throughout the multinatioinal commonwealth. Golden age of the Yiddish-speaking free and autonomous Jewish Talmudic nation in Poland (8 percent of the population of the Commonwealth and 80 percent of world Jewry). Development of a "full work" *(folwark)* manorial system resulting in deterioration of the legal status of peasantry east of the Elbe River, including Poland. Serfs tied to the land providing cheap labor to produce grain for export. Burghers east of the River Elbe become second class citizens. "Low brow" unifying myth that all the people of the Polish Commonwealth allegedly descended from Sarmatians (legendary inhabitants of Poland).

1569–1795   Beginnings of Territorial Nationality

The 16th century wealth, strength, and freedom of the political nation of nobility is a sharp contrast to the neighboring countries. Polonization of the nobility and upper classes of Byelorussia, Lithuania, and Ukraine. Intense pride of membership in the Polish Republic by all nationalities. The concept of *Antemurale Christianitatis*. Polish Republic viewed as the shield of Western Christianity against Moslems and Russian Orthodox.
The 17th century golden age of huge land owners, the magnates. Successful opposition of the magnates to the inclusion of Ukrainian Cossacks in the political nation of the free citizens leading in

1648 to the rebellion in Ukraine and destruction of the multinational federal system in the Polish Republic.

Contradictory trends: rationalism of the Polish Brethren vs. Sarmatian irrationalism. Reshaping of the Sarmatian myth by exclusion of the lower social classes from the ancient Sarmatian links. The 1696 replacement of the official Byelorussian language by Polish in Lithuania, Byelorussia, and Ukraine.

The 17th century, a unified Polish-speaking noble nation throughout the multinational Republic; Polish patriotism: *Gente Rutheni, Natione Poloni*. During 1768–1772 the first modern nationalist movement in Europe, the Confederation of Bar for the national liberation from Russian subversion and abuse of the Polish Republic.

In 1775 patriotism centering on the parliamentary republic of the nobility of all her territories, consolidation of a unique Polish civilization of one million strong noble nation, still the most militarized society of Europe. May 3, 1791, Constitution: the first in Europe; a modern, formal constitution including for the first time a voluntary extension of civil rights to towns people and, in a more diluted form, to the peasantry, "more moderate than the French and more progressive than the English." The first step towards territorial nationality later developed in France, Great Britain, and the United States of America, interrupted in Poland by the partitions, which obliterated the First Polish Republic. In 1794 Kosciuszko uprising based on the belief that complete emancipation of the peasants is the key to national idependence.

1795–1918 Vertical Growth and Territorial Contraction of the Polish Identity

Survival of the Polish identity under foreign rule. Persecution of the Poles results in Polish resistance and a national awakening that produces the growth of Polish identity which encompasses the entire Polish ethnic and linguistic community. Further expansion of the Polish identity after emancipation of the peasants from serfdom, 1807–1864.

Polish peasantry alienated by serfdom but never denationalized. By 1900 ever deeper roots of Polish identity among peasantry. False hopes generated by the Napoleonic campaigns for armed aid from the west to fight for the cause of an independent and democratic Poland. A hope for an alliance of all oppressed people of Europe to overthrow despotism and liberate Poland.

Radical orientation takes the form of people risking death in the struggle for independence. Conservative and extreme left orientation takes the form of tri-loyalism. All in presence of reaffirmation of the Polish identity by cultural nationalism.

Dissatisfaction with limited self government leading to an abortive uprising in 1864. Commitment to organic work and efforts to achieve prosperity. General rejection of tri-loyalism in the face of German chauvinism in the west and forced Russification in the east.

National identity in common language, literature, and historic past reinforced by political parties functioning within the entire Polish ethnic area. Patriotism includes the inactive majority of law-abiding citizens of the three partitions. Polish identity based on the idea of free Poland in the new industrial population led by declassed nobles, the transmitters of Polish national tradition. Failure of denationalization programs of forced Germanization and Russification.

Formulation of Polish populist program of national freedom based on democracy and national culture. The hope to overcome ethnic differences of Poles, Ukrainians, Byelorussians, Lithuanians, and Jews, in reality Polish populism actually helps the formulation of the emerging ethnic nationalism of these nations which was exploited by the partitioning powers.

1918–1945 The Grand Battle for Reorientation of the Polish Identity

The Second Polish Republic led by Jozef Pilsudski who believed in the Jagiellonian idea of an anti-Russian and anti-German federation of Poland, Lithuania, Ukraine, Byelorussia, and Latvia. Opposition led primarily by Roman Dmowski who aggravated the national minorities of 35 percent by denial of national identity of the borderland nations which he wanted to Polonize. He proposed eviction of the Jews as impossible to assimilate because of their Judeo-Germanic culture. Failure to generate a federal nationalism of all the nationalities of the First Republic in the Second Republic because of inconsistent policy of placating them interrupted by sporadic suppression. An inadequate industrialization, the cause of socio-economic difficulties. Horrible war losses of over six million people or 20 percent of the population. Over five million killed by the Germans and one million died under Soviet occupation. Martyrdom of three million Polish Jews, mostly executed in German gas chambers.

1944– The Polish Democratic Tradition Confronted by Soviet Coercion

Incomplete sovereignty of the People's Republic of Poland, the most homogenous nation of Europe, resettled on the original Piast lands, recently held by the Germans. Struggle of the Polish will for independence and expression of national individuality against Sovietization while recovering from the Nazi terror, which was by far fiercer and lasted longer in Poland than anywhere else in Europe. Clash of Polish voluntarism with Russian coercion.

Territorial and cultural losses in eastern Polish borderlands because of lack of support by the Western Powers and growing, during the war, Soviet military strength. Polish situation complicated by the emergence of national identity of Ukrainians, Byelorussians, and Lithuanians. In 1980–1981 Solidarity non-violent mass movement demonstrated the scope and maturity of Polish national consciousness. It broke forever forty-year-long continuity of official distortions of Polish history, both past and present. Solidarity was based on the Polish traditional values of human dignity, patriotism, personal freedom, democracy, toleration, and striving for the truth.

THE ATLAS

Poland Within Western Civilization
966–1986

AN INTRODUCTION

THE AREA BETWEEN RUSSIA AND GERMANY RANGING FROM FINLAND TO GREECE IS NOW CALLED "EASTERN EUROPE" OR "EAST-CENTRAL EUROPE." IN THIS PART OF THE WORLD POLAND IS THE LARGEST COUNTRY. THERE A VITAL PART OF WESTERN CIVILIZATION WAS BORN. EAST-CENTRAL EUROPE REMAINS VITAL FOR CONTINUA-TION AND SURVIVAL OF WESTERN CIVILIZATION.

Poland Within Western Civilization 966-1986

POLAND IN WESTERN CIVILIZATION 1004, 1201, 1493, 1618, 1717, 1815, 1922, & 1986 (8-map two page plate)

Map: 800-1986 THE RANGE OF BORDERS OF POLAND IN THE MIDDLE GROUND OF EUROPE.

Map: THE POLISH LANDS.

Map: 1986 POLAND.

GRAPH: A COMPARISON OF POLISH POPULATION GROWTH WITH ALL OF EUROPE (since the year 1000).

I. Poland—Hereditary Monarchy (840–1370)

The Piast Dynasty

BUILDING OF THE NATION

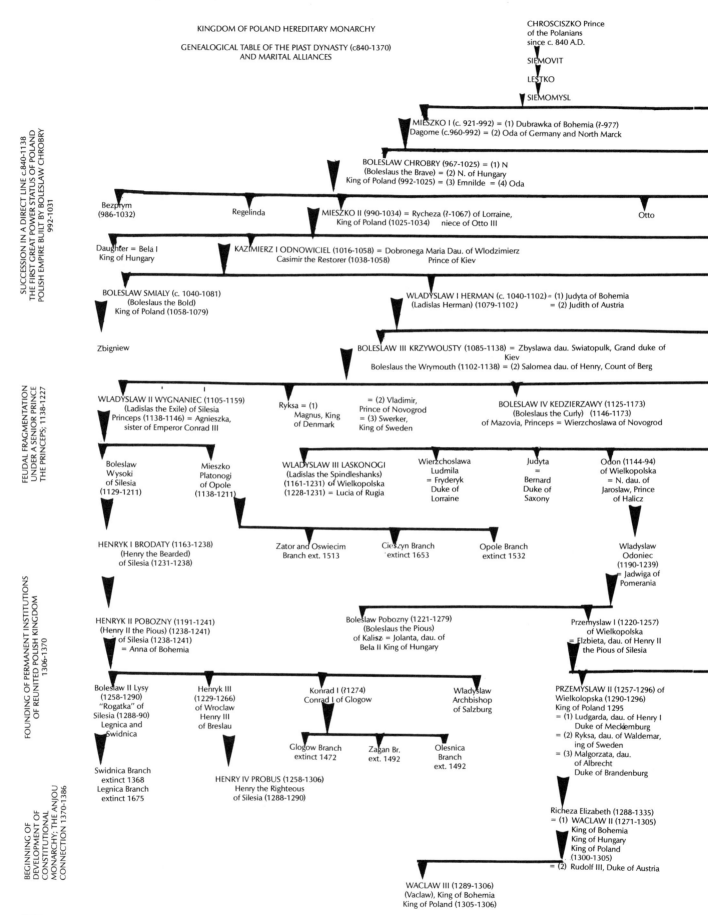

Genealogical table of the Piast (pyast) Dynasty and marital alliances.

The Piast Dynasty

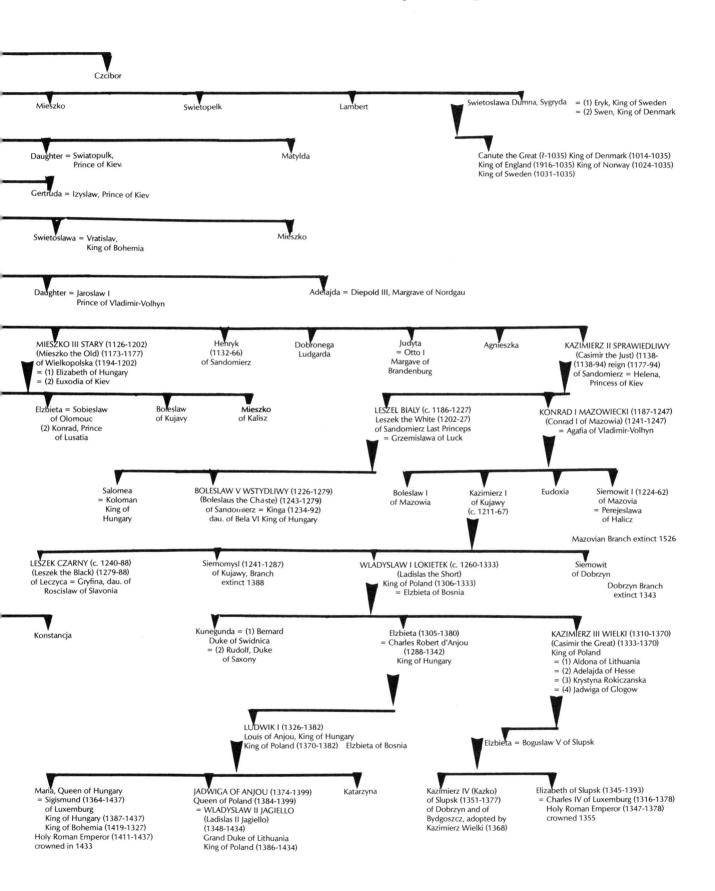

Czcibor

Mieszko   Swietopelk   Lambert   Swietoslawa Dumna, Sygryda   = (1) Eryk, King of Sweden
= (2) Swen, King of Denmark

Daughter = Swiatopulk,   Matylda   Canute the Great (?-1035) King of Denmark (1014-1035)
Prince of Kiev   King of England (1916-1035) King of Norway (1024-1035)
King of Sweden (1031-1035)

Gertruda = Izyslaw, Prince of Kiev

Swietoslawa = Vratislav,   Mieszko
King of Bohemia

Daughter = Jaroslaw I   Adelajda = Diepold III, Margrave of Nordgau
Prince of Vladimir-Volhyn

MIESZKO III STARY (1126-1202)   Henryk   Dobronega   Judyta   Agnieszka   KAZIMIERZ II SPRAWIEDLIWY
(Mieszko the Old) (1173-1177)   (1132-66)   Ludgarda   = Otto I   (Casimir the Just) (1138-
of Wielkopolska (1194-1202)   of Sandomierz   Margave of   (1138-94) reign (1177-94)
= (1) Elizabeth of Hungary   Brandenburg   of Sandomierz = Helena,
= (2) Euxodia of Kiev   Princess of Kiev

Elzbieta = Sobieslaw   Boleslaw   Mieszko   LESZEL BIALY (c. 1186-1227)   KONRAD I MAZOWIECKI (1187-1247)
of Olomouc   of Kujavy   of Kalisz   Leszek the White (1202-27)   (Conrad I of Mazowia) (1241-1247)
(2) Konrad, Prince   of Sandomierz Last Princeps   = Agafia of Vladimir-Volhyn
of Lusatia   = Grzemislawa of Luck

Salomea   BOLESLAW V WSTYDLIWY (1226-1279)   Boleslaw I   Kazimierz I   Eudoxia   Siemowit I (1224-62)
= Koloman   (Boleslaus the Chaste) (1243-1279)   of Mazowia   of Kujawy   of Mazovia
King of   ot Sandomierz = Kinga (1234-92)   (c. 1211-67)   = Perejeslawa
Hungary   dau. of Bela VI King of Hungary   of Halicz

Mazovian Branch extinct 1526

LESZEK CZARNY (c. 1240-88)   Siemomysl (1241-1287)   WLADYSLAW I LOKIETEK (c. 1260-1333)   Siemowit
(Leszek the Black) (1279-88)   of Kujawy, Branch   (Ladislas the Short)   of Dobrzyn
of Leczyca = Gryfina, dau. of   extinct 1388   King of Poland (1306-1333)
Roscislaw of Slavonia   = Elzbieta of Bosnia   Dobrzyn Branch
extinct 1343

Konstancja   Kunegunda = (1) Bernard   Elzbieta (1305-1380)   KAZIMIERZ III WIELKI (1310-1370)
Duke of Swidnica   = Charles Robert d'Anjou   (Casimir the Great) (1333-1370)
= (2) Rudolf, Duke   (1288-1342)   King of Poland
of Saxony   King of Hungary   = (1) Aldona of Lithuania
= (2) Adelajda of Hesse
= (3) Krystyna Rokiczanska
= (4) Jadwiga of Glogow

LUDWIK I (1326-1382)   Elzbieta = Boguslaw V of Slupsk
Louis of Anjou, King of Hungary
King of Poland (1370-1382)   Elzbieta of Bosnia

Maria, Queen of Hungary   JADWIGA OF ANJOU (1374-1399)   Katarzyna   Kazimierz IV (Kazko)   Elizabeth of Slupsk (1345-1393)
= Sigismund (1364-1437)   Queen of Poland (1384-1399)   of Slupsk (1351-1377)   = Charles IV of Luxemburg (1316-1378)
of Luxemburg   = WLADYSLAW II JAGIELLO   of Dobrzyn and of   Holy Roman Emperor (1347-1378)
King of Hungary (1387-1437)   (Ladislas II Jagiello)   Bydgoszcz, adopted by   crowned 1355
King of Bohemia (1419-1327)   (1348-1434)   Kazimierz Wielki (1368)
Holy Roman Emperor (1411-1437)   Grand Duke of Lithuania
crowned in 1433   King of Poland (1386-1434)

FOUNDING OF POLISH-POLABIAN PIAST (PYAST) DYNASTY OF THE POLANIANS

A.D. c. 840
FOUNDING OF POLISH-POLABIAN PIAST (PYAST) DYNASTY OF THE POLANIANS

Map: A.D. c.840 Founding of Polish-Polabian Piast Dynasty of the Polanians.

Map: 822-907 Great Moravia; 896 Arrival of the Hungarians.

Map: 989 Unification of Ethnic Poland by Mieszko I.

A.D. 1004
POLISH EMPIRE
WITHIN
WESTERN
CHRISTIANITY

Europe's population about 22 million, of which Kievian Ruthenia 4.5 M.
German Empire 3.4 M.
Polish Empire 2.0 M.
Including Poles 1.125 M.
Czechs and Moravians 0.475 M.
Lusatians 0.15 M.
Slovaks 0.25 M.

Attempt to bring the Prussians into the Polish Empire by sponsoring St. Adalbert (999) and St. Bruno (1009) Missions to them by Boleslaus I.

Frontier of Western Christianity

INDEPENDENT METROPOLITAN SEE OF POLAND

ATTEMPT TO UNIFY WESTERN SLAVS BY BOLESLAUS THE BRAVE

Map: 1004 Polish Empire within Western Christianity (Population numbers).

Map: 1004 Polish Empire of Boleslaus the Brave: Military Successes

A.D. 1004 ATTEMPT TO UNIFY WESTERN SLAVS BY BOLESLAUS THE BRAVE

★ Polabian pagan state of the Obodrits and Veleti was crucial in the unification plan of Boleslaus the Brave.

In A.D. 983 the Polabians reduced a number of German missionary fortresses and bishoprics including Hamburg, which they destroyed.

Refusal of the Polabians to abandon their Slavic pagan religion and to accept Christianity from Poland prevented unification of the Western Slavs.

Eventual conversion to Christianity by the Germans destroyed the Polabian state and Slavic ethnic identity of Polabians.

Map: 1004 Attempt to unify the Western Slavs by Boleslaus the Brave.

Map: 1018 Empires of Poland and Denmark within the trade routes.

A.D. 1031 INDEPENDENT METROPOLITAN SEE OF POLAND

ARCHBISHOPRIC ↑ ← BISHOPRIC

997 Mission of St. Adalbert-Wojciech (voy-chekh) to the Prussians. Reliquary of Martyred St. Adabert at Gniezno Cathedral until 1039 sacking of Gniezno by Bretislas II of Bohemia. St Adalbert patron of Poland in the 11th and 12th centuries.

1009 Mission to Prussia of St. Bruno. Successful defense of the independence of Polish church hierarchy from the attempts to impose German control.

End of the Heroic Age of the Slavs and Vikings. Varangians-Slavs-Greek and Baltic trade falling off.

Recurring crisis of feudal fragmentation throughout Europe and succession problems typical of the period affecting Poland.

1031 First Russo-German alliance against Poland prevented unification of western Slavs.

Piast (pyast) coronations marked the periods in which Polish hereditary monarchy was free from political sphere of influence of German ruled Holy Roman Empire.

Piast Coronation Dates:

Male Line Succession		Female Line Succession	
1025	Boleslaus I the Brave	1300	Vaclav II
1025	Mieszko II	1305	Vaclav III
1076	Boleslaus I the Bold	1370	Louis I of Anjou
1295	Premislas II	1384	Jadviga of Anjou
1320	Ladislas the Short		
1333	Casimir the Great		

BALTS

BALTIC SEA

POLABIA

KOLOBRZEG 1000

BRENNA 946-983

GDANSK 997

LEBUS 1124

POZNAN 968

GNIEZNO 1000

PLOCK (pwotsk) 1076

KINGDOM OF POLAND

WROCLAW 1000

KRAKOW 1000

OLOMOUC 1063

MISNIA 968

PRAGUE 973

MERSEBURG 896

HAMBURG 848

HOLY ROMAN EMPIRE

OSTRZYHOM 1001

DUCHY OF HUNGARY

SLOVENES

DUCHY OF KIEV A.D. 1031

VLADIMIR 991

TUROV 1072

KIEV 988

BLACK SEA

CRIMEA

AZOVS

INDEPENDENT METROPOLITAN SEE OF POLAND A.D. 1031

Map: 1031 Independent Metropolitan See of Poland.

A.D. 1102-1138 BRILLIANT MILITARY SUCCESSES OF BOLESLAUS III

Feudal crisis of fragmentation was slowed down by Boleslaus III thanks to successful operations unifying Gdansk and Western Pomerania with Poland. Boleslaus III relied on alliances with Ruthenia and was successful in defeating German invasion of 1109 by winning the battle of Psie Pole and defending the fortress of Glogow. In 1115 unsuccessful attempt to conquer Prussia; 1135 paid hommage for Dymin and Rugia. Gallus Anonimus, contemporary biographer of Boleslaus III the Wry Mouth.

RUTHENIAN DUCHIES

POLAND

BALTIC SEA

GERMAN RULED ROMAN EMPIRE

Polish victories and operations
German invasion
Czech attacks
Polish Fortifications

A.D. 1102-1138 BRILLIANT MILITARY SUCCESSES OF BOLESLAUS III
1109 DEFEAT OF GERMAN INVASION OF HENRY V
AND
1121 RECOVERY OF POMERANIA

UNIFICATION OF ETHNIC POLAND

Map: 1102-1138 Military Successes of Boleslaus III.

FEUDAL CRISIS OF FRAGMENTATION SPREADS TO POLAND

Failure to unify the Western Slavs and to produce state of equal potential' to Germany resulting in varying degree of Poland's participation in the political sphere of interests of the Holy Roman Empire controlled by the Germans.

1138–1227 Polish duchies ruled be a senior duke, the "Princeps". Cycles of increased fragmentation and unification attempts ending with 1320 coronation of Ladislas the Short.

Seniorial Duchy or Province.

BALTIC SEA

RUTHENIAN DUCHIES

VLADIMIR

YAIVINGS

PRUSSIANS

P O L A N D

WIZNA

LUBLIN

PLOCK (pwotsk)

SIERADZ WOLBORZ

CRACOW

GDANSK

OPOLE

SZCZECIN

POZNAN

WROCLAW

MORAVIA

HUNGARY

ROZTOKA

DYMIN

VELETI

BRENNA

LUSATIA

MISNA

MILSKO

BOHEMIA

A.D. 1138
FEUDAL CRISIS OF FRAGMENTATION SPREADS TO POLAND
TESTAMENT OF BOLESLAUS III THE WRY MOUTH

HOLY ROMAN EMPIRE BECOMING A LOOSE FEDERATION OF MAGNATES

Map: 1138 Feudal Crisis of Fragmentation Spreads to Poland.

FEUDAL CRISIS OF FRAGMENTATION A.D. 1138 TESTAMENT OF BOLESLAUS III

1138-1227 Polish Duchies ruled by a Senior Duke the "Princeps". Cycles of increased fragmentation and unification attempts ending in 1320 Coronation of Ladislas the Short.

Central Province of the Senior

1. Mazovia and Kujawy
2. Sandomierz Lesser Poland
3. Silesia
4. Wielkopolska, Greater Poland
5. Gdansk, Pomerania
6. Szczecin, Pomerania

1227 Death of the last Senior Prince or Princeps, Leszek Bialy (1186-1227). The Seniorate system did not work as it was intended by Boleslaus III. It was followed by unification efforts of the Silesian Piasts.

EUROPE'S CENTRAL MERIDIAN

BALTIC SEA

PRUSSIANS

MAZOVIA

PLOCK ①

GDANSK ⑤

SZCZECIN ⑥

POZNAN ④

WROCLAW ③ SILESIA

GNIEZNO

SIERADZ

LECZYCA

SANDOMIERZ ②

LESSER POLAND

CENTRAL PROVINCE OF THE SENIOR THE SENIORATE PROVINCE

CRACOW

HOLY ROMAN EMPIRE BECOMING A LOOSE FEDERATION OF MAGNATES

FRAGMENTED HOLY ROMAN EMPIRE

A.D. 1138-1227
PLAN OF
BOLESLAUS III
THE WRY MOUTH

100 KM

50

0

Map: 1138-1227 Senioral System designed by Boleslaus III (not fully implemented).

**Map: 1201 Fragmented Poland within Western Civilization. Beginning of German Aggression in the Baltic at Riga.
(Population numbers).**

10th TO 13th CENTURY ROMANESQUE ARCHITECTURE WITHIN THE POLISH BORDERS

Introduction of fired bricks to Poland by the beginning of 13th century revolutionized construction; soon original Polish patterns of brick laying were introduced in construction of walls and vaults; for example, nine triangle solution within a rectangular space. Brick used at first in Romanesque architecture became an important element in Polish or Vistula Gothic style of built-in buttresses necessary in Polish climate. This resulted in efficient use of bricks with respect to the enclosed space. Large construction projects were built in Poland beginning in the second half of the 13th century, including churches, town halls, and urban defense walls. Early Vistula Gothic ornate buildings were built at the beginning of the 14th century. A huge construction program of Casimir the Great followed. Early 14th century Gothic mural paintings date from that period.

BALTIC SEA

KINGDOM OF POLAND

CORONA REGNI POLONIAE

WARSZAWA (WARSAW)

KRAKOW (CRACOW)

WROCLAW (BRESLAU)

POZNAN

GDANSK

SZCZECIN (STETTIN)

LOCATION OF
10th TO 13th CENTURY
ROMANESQUE ARCHITECTURE
WITHIN THE BORDERS
OF THE
POLISH KINGDOM
THE
CORONA REGNI POLONIAE

Map: 10th-13th century Romanesque architecture within the borders of the Polish Kingdom known as the Corona Regni Poloniae.

1226 Temporary land grant by Konrad of Mazovia to the Order of Teutonic Brethren in return for help in converting Prussians and including them in the Polish Metropolitan See. 1234 Falsification by the Brethren of the Teutonic Order of the temporary land grant to read as a permanent one. Beginning of German genocide of the Balto-Slavic Prussians under the cover of Christianization.

BALTIC SEA

RUTHENIAN DUCHIES

LITHUANIANS

MAZOVIA

PRUSSIA

TEUTONIC KNIGHTS

LUBLIN

SANDOMIERZ

PLOCK

CRACOW

OPOLE

GDANSK

GNIEZNO

POZNAN

WROCLAW

SILESIA

POMERANIA

SZCZECIN

LUSATIA

BRANDENBURG

KINGDOM OF HUNGARY

CZECH KINGDOM

ROZTOKA

A.D. 1232
THE STATES OF
SILESIAN AND MAZOVIAN
PIASTS

HOLY ROMAN EMPIRE
A LOOSE FEDERATION OF MAGNATES

Map: 1232 The States of Silesian and Mazovian Piasts.

Map: 1241 A Double Threat: The Mongol Empire and German Monastic States.

A.D. 1308 BETRAYAL BY THE TEUTONIC ORDER. THE MASSACRE OF GDANSK

German aggression in the Baltic. Falsification of a temporary land grant as a permanent one by the German Brethren.

1259 Second Tartar invasion

1255-1306 Lithuanian invasions

1287-8 Third Tartar invasion

Brandenburgian Invasions

1308-1309 Betrayal and massacre in Gdansk of Polish people by allied German Brethren

1306 Ladislas the Short successful attempt to unify Poland

1288-1290 United Polish duchies of Henry IV of Silesia

1289-1294 United Polish duchies of Ladislas the Short

1294-1296 Kingdom of Poland of Przemyslaw II

BALTIC SEA

PREGOLYA R.

MONASTIC STATE OF THE GERMAN BRETHREN OF 1228-1285

ROZTOKA

SZCZECIN

ODRA (ODER R.)

BRANDENBURG

LUSATIA

ŁABA

FRAGMENTED FEUDAL GERMANY

GDANSK

(VISTULA R.)

NOTEĆ

SANTOK

POZNAN

GNIEZNO

VARTA

PLOCK

WARSAW

SIERADZ

ODRA

WROCŁAW

NYSA (NEISSE R.)

CZECH KINGDOM

WISLA

LUBLIN

SAN

KIELCE

PILCA

SAN

K. OF HUNGARY

100 KM

50

0

A.D. 1308 AGGRESSION AGAINST POLAND AND BETRAYAL BY THE TEUTONIC ORDER THE MASSACRE OF GDANSK

Map: 1308 Aggression against Poland, Betrayal by the Teutonic Order; The Massacre of Gdansk.

Map: 1320 Kingdom of Poland of Ladislas the Short.

1333–1370 POLISH DEFENSES AND FOREIGN AGGRESSION AGAINST POLAND

POLISH
DEFENSES
1333–1370
AND
FOREIGN
AGGRESSION

- Fortified lines
- Fortified perimeters
- Towns and castles
- Tartar Invasions
- Lithuanian Invasions
- Czech Attacks
- Brandenburgian Attacks
- Teutonic Brethren's Attacks

1325 Second alliance with Lithuania. Marriage of Casimir the Great to Aldona, daughter of Giedymin, Grand Duke of Lithuania resulting in the release of 26,000 Polish prisoners.

GRAND DUCHY OF LITHUANIA

GERMAN MONASTIC STATE

BALTIC SEA

POMERANIA

BRANDENBURG

LUSATIA

CZECH KINGDOM

POLISH DUCHY

KINGDOM OF HUNGARY

MOLDAVIA

A.D. 1370
KINGDOM OF POLAND OF CASIMIR THE GREAT

S. BUG R.
DNIESTR R.
PRUT R.
TISA R.
SAN
WARTA R.
NOTEC R.
ODRA R.
ELBE R.
NEMAN R.

200 M
100 M
200
100 KM
KILOMETERS
MILES
0

Map: 1370 Kingdom of Poland of Casimir the Great; Polish defenses 1333-1370.

Legend:

Area of intensive agriculture

Area of intensive colonization

Industrial Centers

Weaving — W

Iron Works — I

Glass Works — GL

Mining — M

Amber — A

Copper — C

Gold — G

Iron Ore — I

Lead — L

Silver — SI

Salt — S

Main routes of German, Dutch and Jewish Immigration

1333

Note: Towns chartered :

before 1333 — 116

In 1333-1370 — 133

Fortified Towns — 77

1333 Beginning of Judeo-Germanic cultural presence of about 10% of population on Polish ethnic lands for the next six centuries.

BALTIC SEA

A.D. 1370 KINGDOM OF POLAND OF CASIMIR THE GREAT

Map: 1370 Kingdom of Poland of Casimir the Great; Agriculture, Mining, Industry, Towns, Immigration Routes.

POLISH ETHNIC BORDERS

:::::::::: FRONTIERS OF THE POLISH KINGDOM AND THE DUCHY OF JAWOR-SWIDNICA

→ POLISH OPERATIONS 1340-50

By 1340 began centuries-long Polish political presence east of the Polish ethnic lands.

Polish ethnic area is also known as the Land of the Piasts or *Ziemie Piastowskie* (zhem-ye-pyas-tov-skie) related to the Piast concept of the Polish Nation State on the Polish ethnic area in contradistinction to the Jagiellonian concept of a multi-national commonwealth of nations between German and Russian ethnic area.

GERMAN MONASTIC STATE OF THE TEUTONIC ORDER OR TEUTONIC KNIGHTS

GRAND DUCHY OF LITHUANIA

BALTIC SEA

POMERANIA

BRANDENBURGB

SANTOK

BYDGOSZCZ

GNIEZNO

POZNAN

PLOCK

WARSAW

SIERADZ

KALISZ

WROCLAW

SWIDNICA

LUSATIA

CZECH KINGDOM

OPOLE

KRAKOW

CRACOW

SANDOMIERZ

LUBLIN

BREST

BRZESC

VLADIMIR

PRZEMYSL

LWOW

TREMBOWLA

HALICZ

KAMIENIEC PODOLSKI

KINGDOM OF HUNGARY

TISA R.

200 KM

100

0

200 M

100

0

A.D. 1370 KINGDOM OF POLAND OF CASIMIR THE GREAT

Map: 1370 Kingdom of Poland of Casimir the Great & Polish Ethnic Borders.

Poland – Hereditary Monarchy 840-1370

A.D. 800-1370
TERRITORIAL DEVELOPMENT OF POLAND AS A HEREDITARY MONARCHY

800	....
989&1138	▬▬▬
1018	▬ ▬ ▬
1370	✱✱✱✱✱✱

Hereditary monarchy: the Piast Dynasty (840-1370) owned the Polish State for the first few centuries, all along having to struggle against independently rich powerful lords claiming a share in power.

Townsmen of alien ethnic origin mostly immigrants from Germany lost a power struggle against the king who had the support of the entire ethnic Polish society including the peasants.

Rulers of Poland protected the Jews from persecution by their fellow immigrants from Germany who often formed the patriciate of Polish towns.

BALTIC SEA

PREGOLYA R.
NEMAN R.
VLADIMIR
KAMIENIEC PODOLSKI
DNESTR R.
PRUT R.
HALICZ
TISA R.
PRZEMYSL
SAN R.
BUG R.
WIEPRZ R.
LUBLIN
SANDOMIERZ
VISTULA R.
CRACOW
PLOCK
WARSAW
PILICA R.
SIERADZ
VISTULA R.
GDANSK
NOTECH R.
GNIEZNO
WARTA R.
KALISZ
POZNAN
ODRA R.
WROCLAW
OPOLE
KROSNO
VAH R.
MORAVA R.
DANUBE R.
SZCZECIN
ROZTOKA
BERLIN
ODER R.
ELBE R.
PRAGUE
ELBE R.
VIENNA
DANUBE R.

0	100	200	KM
0	100	200	M

A.D. 800-1370

TERRITORIAL DEVELOPMENT OF POLAND AS A HEREDITARY MONARCHY

Map: 800-1370 Territorial Development of Poland as a Hereditary Monarchy.

II. Poland—Transition to Constitutional Monarchy (1370–1493)

The Jagiellonian Dynasty

THE MULTINATIONAL
COMMONWEALTH

EUROPE'S LARGEST TERRITORY

GENEALOGICAL TABLE OF THE JAGIELLONIAN AND VASA DYNASTY

EVOLUTION OF CONSTITUTIONAL MONARCHY IN THE MULTINATIONAL COMMONWEALTH
LED BY THE POLES 1370-1492. UNDER THE JAGIELLONIAN DYNASTY 1386-1492

Evolution of Constitutional Monarchy 1370-1493

CONSTITUTIONAL MONARCHY 1492-1569

POLAND-LITHUANIA 1569-1648

GREAT POWER STATUS OF THE REPUBLIC OF

POLAND'S GOLDEN AGE 1492-1586

GREAT POWER STATUS OF POLAND 1386-1648

BEGINNING OF OLIGARCHIC
TENDENCIES WITHIN THE REPUBLIC

DELUGE OF
INVASIONS
1648-1668

GIEDYMIN c.1275-1341
GEDIMINAS
Grand Duke of Lithuania
(1316-1341)

Monwid

Narymunt Gleb

YEVNUT IVAN
Grand Duke of Lithuania
(1341-1345)

OLGIERD ?-1377
ALGIRDAS
Grand Duke of Lithuania
(1345-1377)
=(1) Maria of Vitebsk
=(2) Juliana of Twersk

Andrzej

Dymitr

Vołodimir

Skiergiello

Korybut

JOGAILA, c.1350-1434
WLADYSLAW JAGIELLO
Ladislas Jagiello
Grand Duke of Lithuania
(1377-1401)
King of Poland (1386-1434)
=(1) JADWIGA OF ANJOU 1374-1399
=(2) Anna
=(3) Elzbieta
=(4) Zofia Sonka

Bonifacja

Jadwiga

WLADYSLAW III WARNENCZYK 1424-1444
Ladislas of Varna
King of Poland (1434-1444)
King of Hungary (1440-1444)

KAZIMIERZ IV JAGIEL LONCZYK 1427-1492
Casimir Jagiellon
Grand Duke of Lithuania (1440-1492)
King of Poland (1446-1492)
= Elizabeth of Austria

Wladyslaw II
1456-1516
King of Bohemia
(1471-1516)
King of Hungary
(1490-1516)
= Anne de Fair

JAN OLBRACHT
John I Albert
King of Poland
(1491-1501)

Zofia
= Friedrich von
Hohenzollern
of Anspach

ALEKSANDER I 1461-1506
Grand Duke of Lithuania,
King of Poland (1501-1506)

Fryderyk
Bishop of Cracow
Archbishop of Gniezno
Cardinal

Louis II 1506-1526
King of Bohemia
and Hungary (1516-1526)
= Maria de Castille

Anna
= Ferdinand
of Habsburg
Holy Roman
Emperor (1556-1564)

Albrecht von Hohenzollern
Grand Master of the
Teutonic Order,
Duke of Prussia
(1526-1568)

Jadwiga
= Joachim III
Elector of
Brandenburg

ZYGMUNT AUGUST 1520-1572
Sigismundus Augustus
Grand Duke of Lithuania
King of Poland (1548-1572)
The last of the Jagiellonian Dynasty
Presided over the founding of the
Republic of Poland-Lithuania in 1569
= Elizabeth of Habsburg
= Barbara Radziwill 1520-1551
= Catherine of Habsburg

Izabella 1519-1559
= Jan Zapolya
King of Hungary
1457-1540

Zofia
= Heinrich
Duke of Brunswick

Anna 1523-1596
= Istvan Bathory
1533-1586
Prince of Transylvania
STEFAN BATORY
Elected King of Poland-
Lithuania (1575-1586)

Karol Ferdynand
Prince of Opole
and Raciborz
Bishop of Breslau
and Plock

Aleksander Karol

WLADYSLAW IV 1595-1648
Ladislas Vasa
Elected King of Poland-
Lithuania (1632-1648)
King of Sweden (1632-1648)
Tsar of Russia (1610-1634)
=(1) Cecylia Renata
of Austria
=(2) Marie-Louise Gonzaga

JAN KAZIMIERZ 1609-1672
John Casimir Vasa
Elected King of Poland-
Lithuania (1648-1660)
King of Sweden (1648-1660)
= Marie Louise Gonzaga
Abdicated 1668

Note:
Names of ruling monarchs in capital letters

JAGIELLONIAN AND VASA DYNASTY
**Genealogical table of the Jagiellonian Dynasty (c.1275-1572 including the Vasa Dynasty
and marital alliances).**

JAGIELLONIAN
AND VASA DYNASTY

NOTE: NEGOTIATED SUCCESSION OF THE JAGIELLONIAN KINGS. THE SECOND POLISH DYNASTY
DURING FORMATION OF THE CONSTITUTIONAL MONARCHY IN POLAND. (1386-1572)

Kiejstut 1297-1382
Prince of Troki

Koriat
Prince of Novogrod

Princess of Podolia

Lubart Dymitr
Prince of Vladimir
and Sluck

Vignut

SVIDRIGAILA
SWIDRYGIELLO
Grand Duke of
Lithuania (1430-1432)

VITOVT 1350-1430
WITOLD
Grand Duke of Lithuania
(1401-1430)
=(1) Anna
=(2) Julianna of Holstein

Tovtivil
Prince of
Novogrod

ZYGMUNT
Grand Duke of
Lithuania (1432-1440)

Elzbieta Bonifacja 1399-1399 — an infant. The last direct descendant of the Piast Dynasty born to a reigning king and queen
of Poland. The end of the Piast blood line in the Polish royal succession.

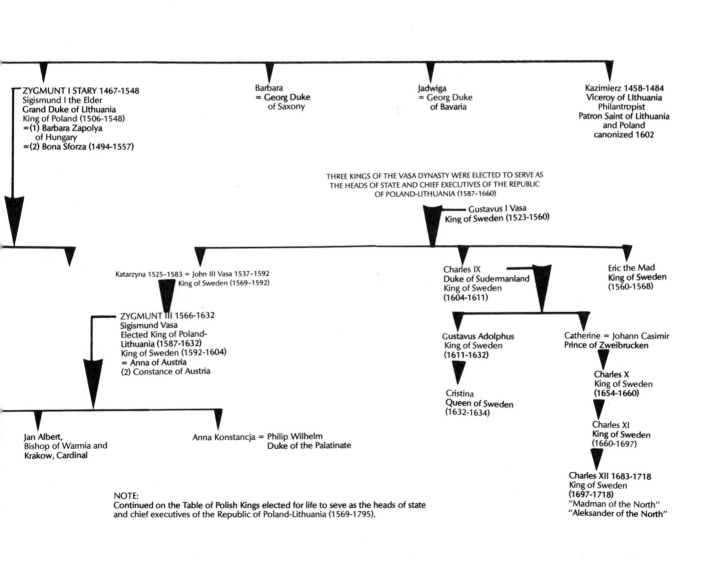

ZYGMUNT I STARY 1467-1548
Sigismund I the Elder
Grand Duke of Lithuania
King of Poland (1506-1548)
=(1) Barbara Zapolya
of Hungary
=(2) Bona Sforza (1494-1557)

Barbara
= Georg Duke
of Saxony

Jadwiga
= Georg Duke
of Bavaria

Kazimierz 1458-1484
Viceroy of Lithuania
Philantropist
Patron Saint of Lithuania
and Poland
canonized 1602

THREE KINGS OF THE VASA DYNASTY WERE ELECTED TO SERVE AS
THE HEADS OF STATE AND CHIEF EXECUTIVES OF THE REPUBLIC
OF POLAND-LITHUANIA (1587-1660)

Gustavus I Vasa
King of Sweden (1523-1560)

Katarzyna 1525–1583 = John III Vasa 1537–1592
King of Sweden (1569–1592)

Charles IX
Duke of Sudermanland
King of Sweden
(1604-1611)

Eric the Mad
King of Sweden
(1560-1568)

ZYGMUNT III 1566-1632
Sigismund Vasa
Elected King of Poland-
Lithuania (1587-1632)
King of Sweden (1592-1604)
= Anna of Austria
(2) Constance of Austria

Gustavus Adolphus
King of Sweden
(1611-1632)

Catherine = Johann Casimir
Prince of Zweibrucken

Charles X
King of Sweden
(1654-1660)

Jan Albert,
Bishop of Warmia and
Krakow, Cardinal

Anna Konstancja = Philip Wilhelm
Duke of the Palatinate

Cristina
Queen of Sweden
(1632-1634)

Charles XI
King of Sweden
(1660-1697)

NOTE:
Continued on the Table of Polish Kings elected for life to seve as the heads of state
and chief executives of the Republic of Poland-Lithuania (1569-1795).

Charles XII 1683-1718
King of Sweden
(1697-1718)
"Madman of the North"
"Aleksander of the North"

Map: 1370-1382 The first union of Poland with Hungary.

A.D. 1403
GERMAN AGGRESSION
IN THE BALTIC
A CAUSE FOR
UNIFICATION WITHIN
SCANDINAVIA
AND OF POLAND
WITH LITHUANIA

State of the Brethren of the Teutonic Order becoming the largest wheat merchant of Europe by controlling the commerce of the deltas of Vistula, Niemen, and Dvina rivers. It was the main force in the Hanseatic system of trade.

A.D. 1403 POLAND & LITHUANIA THREATENED BY THE MONASTIC STATE OF THE TEUTONIC ORDER

Map: 1403 German Aggression in the Baltic a Cause for Unification within Scandinavia and of Poland with Lithuania.

CONSOLIDATION OF POLAND & LITHUANIA

Rise of Poland and Lithuania. Lithuania taking Christianity from Poland to prevent subjugation by the Teutonic Brethren. Mortal danger of a major crusade organized by the Teutonic Brethren with volunteers from Western Europe. Competition to fill the power vacuum created by the decline of the Mongol Empire.

Grand Duchy of Lithuania a Lithuano-Ruthenian state; elite speaking the old Byelorussian language. 1385 Krewo. Marital alliance, King Jagiello to convert to Roman Catholicism and to unify with Poland the lands of Lithuania and Ruthenia in return for the Polish Crown. 1413 Union of Horodlo (kho-ro-dwo) strengthening the Treaty of Krevo establishing the office of Wojewoda as provincial governor and commander. Polish clans extending the use and privileges of their coat of arms to Lithuanian clans. 1399 Mongol victory at Vorskla discouraging Lithuanian separation from Poland.

A.D. 1403 CONSOLIDATION OF POLAND & LITHUANIA BETWEEN DECLINING GERMAN & MONGOL EMPIRES WHILE THREATENED BY THE MONASTIC STATE OF THE TEUTONIC ORDER

DECLINING GERMAN & MONGOL EMPIRES

Map: 1403 Consolidation of the Union of Poland and Lithuania (while the German and the Mongol empires were in decline and the Monastic State of the Teutonic Order became a deadly threat).

DEFEAT OF THE AGGRESSION BY GERMAN MONASTIC STATE AT TANNENEBERG

TANNENBERG = STĘBARK

PHASE 1

Phase 2

STĘBARK

Phase 3

GRÜNWALD

GRUNWALD

STĘBARK

STĘBARK

LODWIGOWO

LODWIGOWO

ULNOWO

L. Lubien

Lake Lubien

ULNOWO

LODWIGOWO

N

Phase 1: Breakthrough Lithuano-Ruthenian lines;

plunder of Lithuanian camp by Germans; Ruthenians struggle back to Polish lines.

Phase 2: Germans commit 100% of their reserves; attack to split Poles. After 6 hours, Poles encircle the German south wing.

Phase 3: Counter-attack of Polish and Lithuanian reserves traps the Germans in two encirclements; slaughtered German commander-in-chief, the Grand Master of Teutonic Brethren; all 51 German banners captured; cavalry in pursuit of the panic-stricken Teutonic Knights; Polish infantry reducing the Teutonic camp; Teutonic missionary propaganda discredited.

Polish-Lithuanian forces: 50 Regiments under provincial banners. Ruthenians, Czech allies, and volunteers. Tartar auxiliary light cavalry: 45,000 troops *plus servants.* German armed monks, plus guest knights, the volunteer crusaders from Western Europe: 40,000 troops, 51 regiments under provincial banners plus servants.

End of fashionable Western European apprenticeship to knighthood in the service of the German Monastic State. Myth of invincibility of Teutonic Order ended. Population of Prussia starts to throw off the yoke of the German Monastic State. Polish command was in control of the day-long battle of about 100,000 men. Throughout the battle King Jagiello systematically concentrated his forces for a decisive attack.

Pontoon bridge prefabricated earlier by the Poles for a surprise crossing of the Vistula River was a technological feat of medieval military engineering. Polish-Lithuanian victory changed the balance of power in Northern Europe. It prepared for the downfall of the Monastic State of the Teutonic Brethren and the end of German aggression in the Baltic for several centuries. Teutonic Order escaped the full consequences of the crushing defeat thanks to Western support obtained by deceitful propaganda covering up the crimes of the Brethren.

CAMPS: German Armed Monks
Poles
Tartars
Allied Forces

Lithuanians III
Ruthenians rrr
German forces +++

German artillery

Poles ppp

REP. OF NOVGOROD

RUSS-DS

GRAND DUCHY OF LITHUANIA

WILD PLAINS

WARSAW

K. OF POLAND

K. OF HUNGARY

HOLY ROMAN EMPIRE

FRAGMENTED

BOSNIA

SERBIA

ALBANIA

OTTOMAN SULTANATE

BLACK S.

ADRIATIC

MEDI-TERRA-NEAN SEA

NAPLES

PAPAL STATE

ARAGON

NORTH SEA

BALTIC SEA

K. OF DENMARK

PSKOV

OKA R.

**A.D. 1410
BATTLE OF GRUNWALD
STĘBARK-TANNENBERG
DEFEAT OF
THE AGGRESSION BY
GERMAN MONASTIC STATE
AGAINST
POLAND & LITHUANIA**

Map: 1410 Battle of Grunwald; Defeat of the German Monastic State; defeat of German aggression against Poland & Lithuania.

Defeat and killing of King Ladislas III Jagiellon by the Moslems resulting in the fall of Constantinople in 1453

A.D. 1444
BATTLE OF VARNA
THE END OF THE SECOND
UNION OF
POLAND WITH HUNGARY
1439 — 1444

1444 Battlefield death of King Ladislas Jagiellon by the Moslem Turks. Polish-Hungarian defeat at Varna leading to the fall of Constantinople in 1453 and a complete Turkish recovery from the 1402 defeat by Timur the Lame (Tamerlane) who captured Sultan Bajazet I and compelled him to raise siege of Constantinople.

After an initial success against Turkish cavalry— a decisive charge by Polish cavalry was led by the King before Hungarians could fully participate. On the verge of victory, the King and his knights were surrounded and slaughtered by the Janizary infantry.

King Ladislas' army of 20,000 was outnumbered by 60,000 Turks because papal fleet failed to prevent crossing at Dardanelles of Turkish forces from Asia Minor.

After 1438 Hapsburgs were emperors of the fragmented Roman Empire in Germany.

1444 Battle of Varna

Map: 1444 Battle of Varna; The End of the Second Union of Poland with Hungary 1439-1444; (Defeat and killing of King Ladislas III Jagiellon by the Moslems resulting in the fall of Constantinople in 1453).

Map: 1454-1466 The Thirteen Year War, Recovery of Gdansk Pomerania and Establishment of the Polish Fief of Prussia.

A.D. 1454-1466 THE THIRTEEN YEAR WAR, RECOVERY OF GDANSK-POMERANIA, AND ESTABLISHMENT OF THE POLISH FIEF OF PRUSSIA

GRAND DUCHY OF LITHUANIA IN UNION WITH POLAND

NIEMEN RIVER

BIALYSTOK

RAGNETA

TYLZA

KNIPAWA
KROLEWIEC
KOENIGSBERG

BRANIEWO

ILAWA

POLISH FIEF OF PRUSSIA

KETRZYN

MAZURIAN LAKELAND

ELK

PISZ

SZCZYTNO

MAZOVIA

NAREW RIVER

BUG RIVER

WARSZAWA
WARSAW

Polish toleration towards Teutonic Order in allowing it to remain in Prussia later led to creation there of the craddle of Hohenzollern Prussia, the initiator of partitions of Poland in 1772-1795.

Polish Victories:
Vistula Delta, Sept. 16, 1463
Swiecino, Sept. 17, 1463

Teutonic Victory:
Chojnice, Sept. 18, 1454
Towns under Polish siege:

WARMIA

LIDZBARK

ORNETA

OLSZTYN

OLSZTYNEK

NIDZICA

Protracted war was fought amid financial difficulties. It brought modernization of Polish armed forces and the beginning of Polish Navy, Marine Infantry, and Military Engineering Service. It proved the need for professional military formations.

PLOCK

VISTULA RIVER

K M

MILES

50

30

0

0

LUSIN
1454-55

RADZYN

LUBAWA

GRUDZIADZ

CHELMNO

TORUN

1464-65

NOWE

STAROGARD

1465-66

GDANSK POMERANIA

GDANSK

PUCK

SWIECINO

BAY OF GDANSK

VISTULA DELTA

BALTIC SEA

SLUPSK

WESTERN POMERANIA

CHOJNICE
1454-66

KINGDOM OF POLAND

KUYAVY

PILA

POZNAN

WARTA RIVER

War was started by general uprising in Gdansk, Pomerania, and Prussia by the burghers, nobles, and peasants against the yoke of the Tuetonic Brethren. Vast majority of the Prussian population wanted to unite in freedom with Poland. Main centers of uprising against the Teutonic Order: Gdansk, Krolewiec-Koenigsberg.

1466 Victory over the German Monastic State; incorporation of Prussia into Poland

Map: 1464-1466 An Attempt by Poland, Bohemia, and Hungary to form an Organization of United Nations of Europe (complete charter recorded in Metryka Koronna of 1463).

1475 Crimea Tartars becoming a vassal state of the Ottoman Empire and a terrorist vanguard of Moslem aggression against Poland. 1478 Muscovy renunciation of allegiance to the Golden Horde. 1478 Muscovy conquest of Novgorod Republic 1480, mass deportation of 10,000 Novgorodians to the Urals enlarging the Muscovy domain and breaking down the resistance to Moscovite rule. Maturity of Muscovy political engineering, a beginning of 500-year tradition of empire building by coersion, deportations and despotism.

Hapsburgs acquiring Burgundy and Netherlands by Marriage. Hapsburg possessions.

A.D. 1480
POLAND IN DYNASTIC UNION
WITH LITHUANIA AND BOHEMIA
ALLIED WITH HUNGARY
AGAINST MOSLEM AGGRESSION
OF OTTOMAN TURKS AND
THEIR CRIMEAN VASSALS

THE END OF GERMAN MIGRATION
TO POLAND AND EAST BALTIC

DEMOCRACY OF THE MASSES OF CITIZEN-SOLDIERS

KHANATE OF KAZAN
KIRGHIZ-KAZAK-TURKS
CASPIAN S
URAL R.
VOLGA R.
SARMATIAN ALLANS
CAUCASUS MTS.
K. OF GEORGIA
ARAS R.
KURA R.
EMIRATE OF THE WHITE SHEEP TURKS
TIGRIS R.
EUPHRATES R.
MAMLUKE SULT
ARAB. SULT

RIAZAN
KHANATE OF THE GOLDEN HORDE
DON R.
GRAND DUCHY OF MOSCOW
DNIEPER R.
BLACK SEA
OTTOMAN TURKISH SULTANATE

PSKOV
PSKOV
KINGDOM OF POLAND-LITHUANIA
MOLDAVIA
VENICE

EUROPE CENTRAL MERIDIAN
TEUTONIC MONASTIC STATE OF LIVONIA
BALTIC SEA
K. OF DENMARK
K. OF HUNGARY
ADRIATIC

NORTH SEA
HOLY ROMAN EMPIRE FRAGMENTED INTO 300 SELF-GOVERNING STATES
K. OF BOHEMIA
AUSTRIA
VENETIAN REPUBLIC
PAPAL STATE
GENOA
K. OF NAPLES

RHINE R.
ALPS
SEINE R.
LOIRE R.
K. OF ENGLAND
K. OF SCOTLAND
ATLANTIC OCEAN
K. OF FRANCE
GARONNE R.
PYRENEES MTS.
EBRO R.
K. OF NAVARRE
K. OF ARAGON
MEDITERRANEAN SEA

1469 MARITAL ALLIANCE OF FERDINAND OF ARAGON AND ISABELLA OF CASTILLE
K. OF CASTILLE
DUERO R.
K. OF PORTUGAL
WATTASID SULTANATE

Map: 1480 Poland in Dynastic Union with Lithuania and Bohemia Allied with Moslem aggression by Ottoman Turks and their Crimean Vassals.

III. Poland, the Constitutional Monarchy (1493–1569)

The Jagiellonian Dynasty

THE MULTINATIONAL

COMMONWEALTH

**DEMOCRACY OF THE MASSES OF
CITIZEN-SOLDIERS**

Map: 1493 Polish Jagiellonian Realm the Shield of Western Christianity (population numbers).

A.D. 1493
POLISH JAGIELLONIAN
REALM
THE SHIELD OF
WESTERN CIVILIZATION

Europe's Population in Millions	
Polish Jagiellonian Realm	14.5M
France	14M
Germany	10M
Spanish Domain	8M
Italy	8M
European Turkish Empire	6M
(Christians 5M + Moslems 1M)	
England	3.5M
Russia	3M
Netherlands	2.75M
Kingdom of Denmark	2M
Portugal	1M
Tartars and Turkmen	0.5M
Irish	0.75M
Scotland	0.5M
Alan-Cherkies	0.25M
Georgia	0.5M
Livonia	0.5M
A.D. 1493 Europe 77 Millions	

Polish-Jagiellonian Realm	
Constitutional Kingdom of Poland	14.5M
Poles 3.25M	7.5M
Ukrainians	2.5M
Lithuanians	0.5M
Byelorussians 1.25M	
Kingdom of Hungary	3.5M
Hungarians + Slovaks + Croats + Serbs	
Czechs Kingdom	2.75M
Czechs + Moravians + Lusatians + Silesians	
Moldavian Fief	0.75M

A.D. 1493

POLISH JAGIELLONIAN REALM ON THE FRONT OF TURKISH AGGRESSION GERMAN AND ITALIAN POWER VACUUM DECLINE OF THE GOLDEN HORDE

HABSURG POSSESSIONS

1490–1526 Largest territorial extent of the Jagiellonian Realm. 1493 Maturity of Polish Constitutional Monarchy. Polish parliament becomes bicameral. 1505 Constitution "Ninil novi" ("nothing new about us without us.") Beginning of the movement for respect, execution, and enforcement of the law. Beginning of the "Golden Age." Maturity of Polish indigenous democratic process. Holy Roman Empire fragmented into 300 self-governing German states. Grand Duchy of Moscow under the sovereign "Gosudar of all Russia."

Since 1475 Turkish aggression spearheaded by terrorism of Crimean Tartars. 1484 Loss of South Moldavia or Budziak to the Turkish Empire.

Map: 1493 Polish Jagiellonian Realm on the Front of Turkish aggression; German and Italian power vacuum; Decline of the Golden Horde.

Maturity of Polish Constitutional Monarchy; German Empire fragmented into 300 self-governing states; unification of Spain.

Map: 1493 The Jagiellonian Realm (Dates).

Map: 1493 The Jagiellonian Realm of the Second Polish Dynasty within Trade Routes of Europe.

A.D. 1495 CONSTITUTIONAL KINGDOM IN POLAND A SANCTUARY OF THE WORLD'S LARGEST JEWISH COMMUNITY

Sources of Polish Toleration: Pluralistic Society Governed by an open Parliamentary Government based on the democratic process of Europe's largest political nation of free citizens, and on difficulties with political activities of immigrants from Germany who brought with them a tradition of anti-Semitism and pogroms. 1264 Act on General Jewish Liberties and civil rights becoming the law in Poland: Development of an extensive Jewish autonomy patterned after Polish republican institutions. Freedom of religion; no Jewish serfs or slaves, no obligation for defense of Poland or to speak Polish. Formation of Yiddish speaking autonomous Jewish nation based on the Talmudic law and education. Beginning of 16th century Golden Age of the Jews in Poland. Jewish immigration to Poland to escape severe persecution and mass murders in Western Europe.

Polish Eagle protecting the Star of David in the Crest of Namyslow

Jewish Communities and date of Expulsion

Direction of the Flight of Expelled Jews, Mostly to Poland

Borders of the Realm of the Second Polish Dynasty, the Jagiellons

A SANCTUARY OF THE WORLD'S LARGEST JEWISH COMMUNITY IN THE KINGDOM OF POLAND

Map: 1495 Constitutional Kingdom of Poland a Sanctuary of the World's Largest Jewish Community of Judeo-Germanic sub-culture.

A.D. 1510 COPERNICAN UNIVERSE THE BIRTH OF MODERN ASTRONOMY

A.D. 1510
COPERNICAN
UNIVERSE
THE BIRTH OF
MODERN
ASTRONOMY

Copernicus formulated his astronomical theory by 1504 and circulated it in 1510 in Commentariolus; his main astronomical work, De Revolutionibus Orbium Coelestium was written 1515–1530 and published in 1543 the year he died. The Church encouraged publication of Copernicus theory in 1536 after studying it since 1533. Luther and Calvin condemned Copernican astronomy.

Copernicus, a native leader of Polish Renaissance, established his revolutionary astronomical theory in Poland the freest and most tolerant state of Europe after passage of the constitution Nihil Novi in 1505. Portrait of Copernicus shown within borders of the Realm of the Polish Jagiellonian dynasty.

Copernican Universe
1. Sphere of immobile stars
2. Saturn 30 years orbit
3. Jupiter 12 years orbit
4. Mars 2 years orbit
5. Earth 1 year orbit
6. Venus 9 months orbit
7. Mercury 80 days orbit
   Sun at the center

Signature:

Nicolaus Copernicus
Mikolaj Kopernik
(mee-ko-way ko-per-neek)
1473–1543

LIFE OF COPERNICUS
1. 1473-1490 Torun, Poland
2. 1491-1496 University of Krakow, Poland, College of Astronomy
3. 1496-1500 University of Bologna, researcher
4. 1500-1501 Lecturer on astronomy in Rome
5. 1501-1503 Law School, University of Ferrara
6. 1503-1506 University of Padua, Medical School
7. 1507-1512 Physician in Lidzbark, Poland
8. 1512-1521 Chancellor and military commander of Warmia in Olsztyn
9. 1521-1543 Legislator and astronomer in Grudziadz and Frombork, Poland

Copernicus. Founder of modern astronomy in establishing theory that earth rotates daily on its axis and that planets revolve in orbits around the sun.

Copernican calendar, accurate within two minutes of the correct year length: gave Christians their first chance to date realiably resurrection of Christ and Easter holidays. It remained in use even after the Church placed Copernican works on the index of forbidden books 1616-1828

Thirty years after death of Copernicus the 1572 supernova fiery death of an exploding star first indicated to astronomers that there is movement outside the Solar System.

Map: 1510 Copernican Universe - The Birth of Modern Astronomy.

Constitutional King of Poland Sigismund Jagiellon received the homage from his nephew Albrecht of Hohenzollern, the former Grand Master of the defunct Order of the Teutonic Brethen or Knights. He was an upstart Duke of Prussia newly converted to Protestantism. West Prussia or Warmia was a Polish province while east Prussia with capital in Krolewiec or Koenigsberg was a Polish fief. During the Golden Age of Sigismund Jagiellon religious toleration flourished in Poland. And it was there the first in history formal state act between a Catholic king and a Protestant vassal occurred. The Hohenzollerns later betrayed Poland and grew into an international parasite at the expense of Poland. Eventually they were the initiators of the crime of partitions which obliterated the Polish state for a century 1795-1918.

In 1641 the last homage to Poland was paid by Frederick William of Hohenzollern at the Castle of Warsaw. He was the direct ancestor of the emperors of the short lived German Hohenzollern Empire (1871-1918).

A.D. 1525
THE HOHENZOLLERN HOMAGE IN CRACOW
BEGINNING OF A LONG SERIES OF
HOHENZOLLERN VASSAL HOMAGES
TO POLAND
THE FIRST FORMAL ACT IN HISTORY
BETWEEN A CATHOLIC KING
AND A PROTESTANT VASSAL

POLISH JAGIELLONIAN REALM

1525 The Hohenzollern Homage in Cracow

Map: 1525 The Hohenzollern Homage in Cracow; Beginning of a long series of Hohenzollern homages to Poland; the first formal act in history between a Catholic king and a Protestant vassal.

A.D. 1526
DISASTER AT MOHACZ
POLISH JAGIELLONIAN REALM
UNDER PRESSURE FROM TURKS, RUSSIANS, AND AUSTRIANS

1502 Disintegration of Golden Horde. The great reversal in the steppes of Eurasia. Final collapse of the Mongol empire due to the advent of firearms and the end of the superiority of a mounted archer over footsoldier, creating a huge power vacuum gradually filled by Russians. Early decline of the Mongol Empire gave a chance to create the great Polish Jagiellonian Realm; Mongol collapse became foundation of the Russian Empire.

1515 Treaty of Vienna giving priority to Hapsburg female claim of succession to the Czech and Hungarian throne in case of death of the ruling Jagiellonian king in return for cessation of Hapsburg-Muscovy alliance and an end of Hapsburg support for the defeated Teutonic Order in Prussia.

1514 Muscovite troops take Smolensk; Polish Lithuanian victory at Orsha won by artillery.

1526 Defeat by the Turks at Mohacz and death of the second Jagiellonian king in battle against the Turks resulting in passing of the Czech and Hungarian Crown from Polish to Austrian dynasty and a partition of Hungary between Austria and Turkey. Rise of Turks as a military machine based on Janizary elite (of captured Christian children brought up as fanatical Moslems) and an adaptation of European firearms technology from the Greeks. 1475 Crimean Tartars becoming Turkish vassals used against Poland as Moslem terrorist vanguard.

1525 Conversion of Prussian monastic fief into the Duchy of Prussia and homage paid to Polish King Sigismund by Albrecht Hohenzollern as First Duke of the Polish Duchy of Prussia.

1526 Loss to Austria of the Croatian access to the Adriatic Sea.
1526 Loss to Turkey of the Ukrainian access to the Black Sea.

Rise of the Hapsburgs and support of the Church given them in the 1504 marriage of Juana of Spain to Philip of Austria.

Map: 1526 Disaster at Mohacz; death of Louis II, the second Jagiellonian king killed in battle against Moslems; Polish Jagiellonian Realm under pressure from Turks, Russians, and Austrians.

1526 Disaster at Mohacz; death of Louis II, the second Jagiellonian king killed in battle against Moslems

80,000 Russian Cavalry under Ivan Cheladnin

Pol. Inf.

Ambush Force

Artillery

ORSHA, Sept. 8, 1514

Russ.

Fake Retr.

2 MILES

Russian Rear Guard

Main Force

Vanguard

Frontal Force

Polish Main Force

Lith.

Russ.

Pontoon Bridge Crossing Sept. 7

Dnieper River

Polish-Lithuanian forces surprised the enemy by constructing and using a pontoon bridge and hiding an ambush force on the east side.

Phase 1: Russian diversionary attack on the west wing was halted by the Polish cavalry. Russian encircling attack on the Polish east wing encountered a fake retreat, leading the Russians into an ambush.

Phase 2: Polish artillery and infantry fire from ambush caused the Russian east wing to panic.

Phase 3: Frontal attack led by Polish heavy cavalry; capturing of Russian command and inflicting casualties of approx. 50,000 killed, wounded, and captured. The breaking of Muscovy support for the Hohenzollerns of Berlin; beginning in 1525 of a century of Hohenzollern homages to Poland.

OKA R.

MUSCOVY RUSSIA

DNIEPER R.

PRYPET R.

DNIEPER R.

NEMAN R.

KINGDOM OF POLAND-LITHUANIA

DNIESTR R.

CARPATHIAN MTS.

TISZA R.

DANUBE R.

TURKISH EMPIRE

BLACK S

BALTIC

DVINA R.

NORTH SEA

FRAGMENTED GERMANY

ELBER R.

ODER R.

NYSSA R.

WESSER R.

MOSELA R.

RHINE R.

SEINER R.

FRANCE

K. OF ENGLAND

ATLANTIC OCEAN

OBERTYN, Aug. 22, 1531

WALACHIANS

POLES

3

1

2

Phase 1: Poles in a ring of battle-wagons withstood 5 hr. of artillery fire then eliminated an enemy foray on the north side.

Phase 2: Polish cavalry attack through west gap was helped by enemy panic caused by a Polish squadron approaching the camp from northwest.

Phase 3: The shifting of Walachian forces to the north-west weakened their southern force which was then destroyed by the Polish main force. 10,000 Walachians were killed, wounded or taken prisoner.

1514 Victory of Orsha over Muscovy army of 80,000 cavalry by 20,000 Polish regulars and 15,000 Lithuanians under Konstanty Ostrogski (c. 1460-1530)

1531 Victory at Obertyn over Turkish attack of 20,000 Walachian cavalry and 50 cannons by 4,800 Polish cavalry, 1,200 Polish infantry, and 12 cannons under Jan Tarnowski (1488-1561)

Map: 1514 Battle of Orsha; 1531 Battle of Obertyn — Two Victories

IV. The First Polish Republic of Kingdom of Poland and Grand Duchy of Lithuania (1569–1795)

Polish Nobles' Republic

ONE MILLION CITIZENS

POLAND FACING TURKISH AND RUSSIAN EMPIRES

WHILE TINY BRANDENBURG AND SAXONY, ACTING AS INTERNATIONAL PARASITES, GRADUALLY BROUGHT ABOUT THE OBLITERATION OF THE POLISH STATE IN 1795. THIS EVENT LED TO UNIFICATION OF GERMANY FRAGMENTED FOR CENTURIES INTO 350 SELF-GOVERNING STATES. IN 1871 GERMANY WAS UNIFIED UNDER THE "BLOOD AND IRON" HEGEMONY OF THE BERLIN GOVERNMENT.

GOVERNMENT STRUCTURE OF THE POLISH REPUBLIC

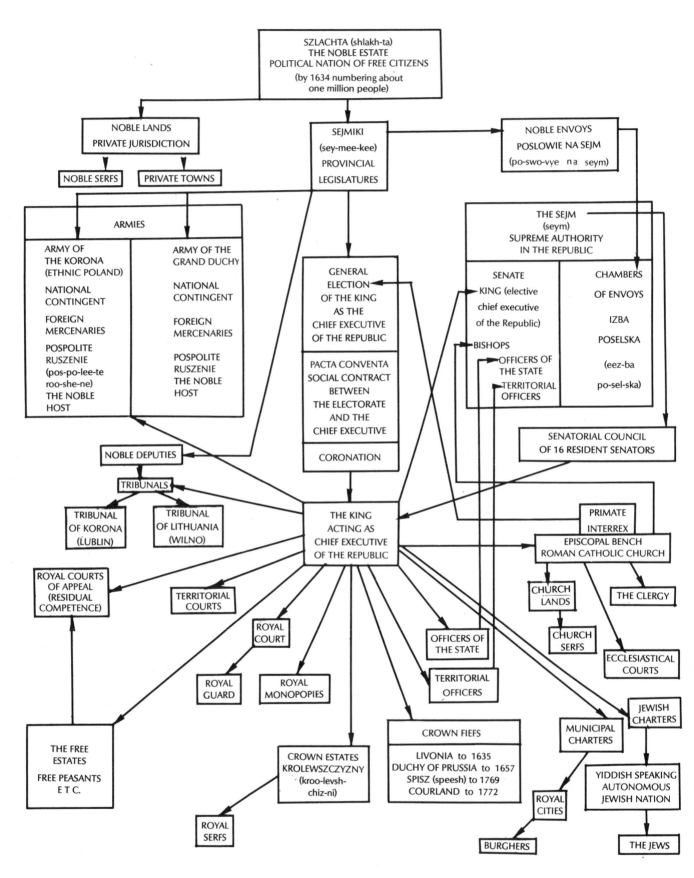

CENTRAL INSTITUTIONS OF THE FIRST POLISH REPUBLIC 1569-1795

Diag. of Government Structure of the Polish Republic.

TABLE OF GENERAL ELECTIONS

NOTE: GENERAL ELECTIONS OF KINGS TO SERVE AS HEADS OF STATE AND CHIEF EXECUTIVES OF THE REPUBLIC OF POLAND-LITHUANIA 1569-1795

CANDIDATES PRESENTED TO AND APPROVED BY THE POLISH PARLIAMENT KNOWN AS THE CONVOCATION SEYM

Left margin notes: NOTE: POLAND'S GOLDEN AGE TILL 1586 — GREAT POWER STATUS OF POLAND TILL 1648 — DECLINE DURING DELUGE OF INVASIONS 1648-1674 — 1674-1696 RECOVERY LED BY SOBIESKI — 1697-1717 CRITICAL DISINTEGRATION — 1717-1768 CRISIS OF SOVEREIGNTY — 1768-1795 AGONY OF THE REPUBLIC

YEAR OF GENERAL ELECTION	KING ELECT OF POLAND-LITHUANIA				
1573	HENRYK WALEZY Henri Valois 1551-1589 Duke of Anjou Later Henri III King of France	Ernest Habsburg Archduke of Austria	Ivan IV Tsar of Russia "Ivan the Terrible"	John III Vasa King of Sweden	Stephen Batory Prince of Transylvania, Hungary
1575	STEFAN BATORY Istvan Ba thory 1533-1586 Prince of Transylvania, Hungary	Maximilian II Holy Roman Emperor, King of Germany		John III Vasa King of Sweden	Alphonso II Duke de Ferrara
1587	ZYGMUNT III VASA Sigismund Vasa 1566-1632 King of Sweden	Feodor III Tsar of Russia (the last of the Ruriks)		Andreas Bathory of Hungary	Maximilian Habsburg Archduke of Austria
1632	WLADYSLAW IV VASA Ladislas Vasa 1595-1648 King of Sweden 1632-1648 Tsar of Russia 1610-1634	single candidate, unopposed			
1648	JAN KAZIMIERZ John Casimir Vasa 1609-1672 King of Sweden Abdicated in 1662		Karol Ferdynand Vasa Charles Ferdinand Vasa of Poland		Sigismund Rakoczy Prince of Transylvania, Hungary
1669	MICHAL KORYBUT WISNIOWIECKI 1640-1673 of Poland	Philip Wilhelm of Neuburg	Charles V of Lorraine and Bar		Charles Bourbon d'Longueville
1674	JAN III SOBIESKI John III Sobieski 1629-1696 Army Commander Hetman Wielki Koronny	Charles V of Lorraine and Bar.	James Stuart Duke of York later King of England, Scotland and Ireland as James II	Francois Louis de Bourbon- Conti	Charles Hohenzollern of Brandenburg, Germany	George Prince of Denmark
1697	AUGUST II MOCNY Augustus Wettin 1670-1733 of Saxony	Francois Louis de Bourbon- Conti	Jakub Sobieski James Sobieski of Poland	Max Emmanuel of Bavaria, Germany	Livio Odescalchi Duke of Ceri	Louis Margrave of Baden, Germany
1733	AUGUST III August Wettin 1696-1763 of Saxony, Germany		STANISLAW LESZCZYNSKI 1677-1766 King of Poland-Lithuania (1704-1711 and 1733-1736) Abdicated in 1736		Emmanuel of Portugal
1764	STANISLAW AUGUST Stanislaw Antoni Poniatowski 1732-1798 of Poland founder of Ministry of Education in 1773 Presided over passing of the Constitution of May 3, 1791 Abdicated in 1795	Frederic Christian Wettin of Saxony Germany	Adam Kazimierz Czartoryski Political writer of Poland		Jan Klemens Branicki Hetman Wiellki Koronny, of Poland

Note: Ten General Elections for the Head of State and Chief Executive of the First Polish Republic 1569-1795

Table of General Elections.

AUTONOMOUS JEWISH GOVERNMENT

NOTE: JEWISH PARLIAMENTARY GOVERNMENT UNIQUE BETWEEN SANHEDRIN OF ANTIQUITY
AND KNESSET OF THE STATE OF ISRAEL
SELF GOVERNMENT OF YIDDISH SPEAKING JEWISH TALMUDIC NATION IN POLAND
WHICH NUMBERED 1,000,000 YIDDISH SPEAKERS BY 1795

GENERAL CHARTER OF RIGHTS AND PRIVILEGES GUARANTEEING FREEDOM AND SECURITY OF THE JEWS
BASED ON THE ACT OF KALISZ OF 1264

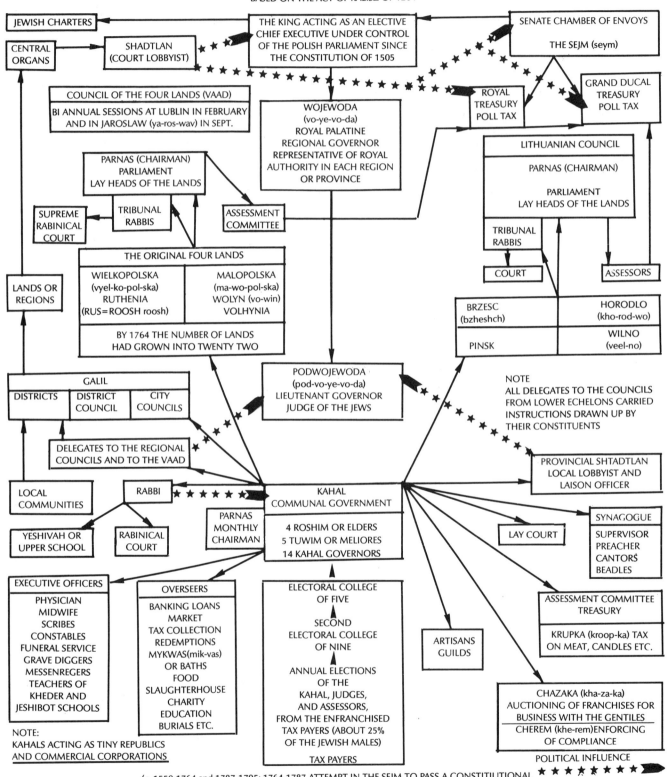

(c. 1550-1764 and 1787-1795; 1764-1787 ATTEMPT IN THE SEJM TO PASS A CONSTITIUTIONAL
AMENDMENT FOR A COMPLETE JEWISH EMANCIPATION IN THE POLISH REPUBLIC).

THE ORGANS OF JEWISH REPRESENTATIVE GOVERNMENT

Diag. of Autonomous Jewish Government in the Polish Republic.

Democracy of the numerous Polish gentry (10% of population) created the most democratic society of Europe governed by an indigenous democratic process. By 1493 constitutional monarchy was achieved when the supreme political power in Poland, the Polish parliament, became bi-cameral. Gradually the king became the chief executive in charge of the executive branch of the government. The last Jagiellonian king, Sigismund August, was childless. He became the founder of a united republic of Poland and Lithuania which included Ukraine and Byelorussia. He instituted in 1559 Polish-style national parliament in the Grand Duchy of Lithuania and in 1564 provincial legislatures patterned after the Polish model. Common Polish culture of the leadership community of both states and common danger from Russia and the Moslems made it possible. "Freemen with free. Equals with e-qual" were joined in one republic with one national parliament, one currency, and one elective chief executive with title of the "king." The Lithuanians were to have their own law, their own administration, their own army and their princely families could keep their titles. Ukraine became a part of Poland. On July 1, 1569, the act of union was sealed in Lublin creating "the Republic of Good Will" governed by the noble political nation of free citizens numbering nearly one million people. It was the first republic based on general elections before creation of the United States of America.

A.D. 1569 UNION OF LUBLIN

FOUNDING OF
THE FIRST
POLISH REPUBLIC

AMIDST ABSOLUTIST EUROPE

KILOMETERS

MILES

200 400 600

400

Map: 1569 Founding Of The First Polish Republic amidst Absolutist Europe.

"The Republic of Good Will...Free Men with Free. Equals with Equal..."

The 1561 monastic state of the Livonian Brethren known as "Knights of the Sword" offered Livonia, as a fief of Poland-Lithuania in return for guarantees of self government, freedom to convert to Protestantism and to disband the Order. Southern Livonia became the Duchy of Courland and Semigalia and Northern Livonia became a joint dominion of Poland-Lithuania.

The 1563-1570 Seven Year War fought with varying success brought a dangerous concession to Brandenburg in exchange for Hohenzollerns' support against Muscovy and Sweden. They obtained the right to succeed the childless Albrecht of Hohenzollern as dukes of Polish fief of Prussia. Thus the chance of Prussia becoming a regular province of Poland was lost in 1563.

A.D. 1569
LANDS
OF THE FIRST
POLISH REPUBLIC

Conflict over Livonia brought alliance of Poland with Denmark and Muscovy with Sweden.

DEMOCRACY OF THE MASSES OF CITIZEN-SOLDIERS

Map: 1569 The Lands of the First Polish Republic.

REPUBLIC OF POLAND-LITHUANIA

A.D. 1569

POLITICAL SITUATION AT FOUNDING OF THE REPUBLIC OF POLAND-LITHUANIA

Ivan IV's (The Terrible), first to call himself Tsar of all Russia.

conquests:

1552 Khanate of Kazan
1556 Khanate of Astrakhan
1558 Invades Livonia proclaiming Moscow the third and last "Rome". Gatherer of Slavic lands.
1561 Muscovy-Sweden Alliance.

1561 Sweden evicts Denmark from Estonia. Denmark seeks support of Poland.
1561 secularization of the Monastic State of Livonia until 1513 a part of German Monastic State of Prussia.
1561 Livonia offers itself as a fief of Poland-Lithuania for guarantee of self-government and freedom of religon for its new Protestant faith.

Turkish Moslem Empire consolidated by the rule of Suleiman the Magnificent (1520-1566).

The 1569 transfer of Ukraine from Lithuania to Poland, called the "Korona" or "the crown."
In 1569 Warsaw became a permanent capital of the national parliament of the new republic for the next two hundred twenty-six years.
Note: The entire territory of the Monastic State of the Teutonic Order of German Brethren created by German aggression on the Baltic now was within the borders of the First Polish Republic with the exception of North Estonia.

LOCATION OF MAIN ARSENALS

Map: 1569 Political Situation during the founding of the Republic of Poland-Lithuania.

Poland acts as a great power under leadership of Batory mobilizing adequate forces to defeat Russian invasion of Livonia by Ivan IV "The Terrible." **1)** Polish operations remove Muscovy's forces from Livonia. In **2)** 1577 reduce Dvinsk (Duneburg); 1578 Wenden decisive operations; **3)** 1579 reducing Polock 22,000 Knights in 100,000 force: raiding deep into Polesie **4)** Reducing Vyelkye Luki Stara Russa, building road to Polock.

Siege of Pskov by a force of 170,000 men against 60,000 defenders reducing Rzhev, Staritsa Staraya Russa, Dorpat, Wenden, and Riga. Raiding Upper Volga and up to the shores of Lake Ladoga, Muscovy loses 300,000 men. Ivan IV suing for peace Ten-year truce at Jam Zapolski

A.D. 1576-1582

POLAND'S VICTORIOUS CAMPAIGN

IN WAR WITH

MUSCOVY RUSSIAN EMPIRE

OVER LIVONIA

Deep raids by Polish cavalry tying up Muscovy's main forces

Map: 1576-1582 Poland's Victorious Campaign in War with Muscovy Russian Empire over Livonia.

In 1585 Bathory plans to conquer Russia, to form a huge united Slavic state under Polish leadership, and free the Balkan Christians (Slavs, Hungarians, Moldavians, Vlachs, and Greeks) from the Moslem terror-rule. Support of Pope Sixtus V (1521-1590) for the Polish plan and for Polish King Stefan I Bathory to be the supreme commander of Christian forces allied into an anti-Turkish league organized to free Southern Europe from Turkish Moslem yoke. In hopelessly fragmented Europe, Spain was the strongest anti-Turkish power. Philip II of Spain gave initial support to the Polish plan but Spanish war for the Netherlands against the English and the Dutch weakened Philip's participation in the Polish plan. The plan failed because of the death of King Stephan Bathory (1533-1586) possibly by poisoning. Disbanding of Polish mobilization for campaign against Muscovy Russia and growing opposition of the Seym to appropriate money for military operations abroad.

Missed opportunity to elect to the Polish throne of Bathory's "Alterrex," "The Grand Hetman Jan Zamoyski (1542-1605)Chancellor of the Polish Nobles' Republic political leader of Polish Renaissance and former president of the University of Padua, Italy. Death of Bathory marks the end of Poland's Golden Age.

Year 1584 marks conclusion of peace treaty between Turkish and Persian empires giving the Turks a chance to concentrate on further expansion into Europe.

A.D. 1585-1586

UNREALIZED POLISH PLAN

TO UNIFY ALL SLAVS,

FREE THE BALKANS,

AND EVICT THE MOSLEMS

FROM EUROPE

PROPOSED COMPAIGN

POLISH REPUBLIC

Map: 1585-1586 Unrealized Polish Plan to Unify All the Slavs, Free the Balkans, and Evict the Moslems from Europe - the Proposed Campaign.

NALEVAYKO'S COSSACK UPRISING

The 1596 Union of Brest between Catholic and Orthodox Churches attempted to subordinate the Orthodoxy to Rome and to strengthen the ties of Byelorussians and Ukrainians with Poland. It was supported by the Orthodox Metropolites who hoped to obtain seats in the Senate of the Polish Republic. This was blocked by the Catholic clergy. The Union of Brest broke up the Ruthenian population into Uniates and Disuniates. It contributed to major Cossack uprisings against the Republic.

Nalevayko's uprising had religous and economical motives. Nalevayko was executed in Warsaw in 1597.

1594-1596

NALEVAYKO'S UPRISING FOR CIVIL RIGHTS UKRAINIAN COSSACKS

Arenda leases were concluded between the noble estate owners and Jewish financiers. The leases fueled the expansion of noble estates and were a major factor in Cossack uprisings.

Arenda system of prepaid leases of limited duration was leading to short term intensive exploitation of the leased estates and its peasants — often associated with the right to collect and even impose taxes and such payments as church fees for funerals, baptisms, weddings, etc., in the Ukraine and to a lesser extent in Poland.

See Chmielnicki (khmyelnitsky) Uprising
See "Kolishchina" Uprising

NALEVAYKO'S COSSACK UPRISING

Map: 1594-1596 Nalevayko's Uprising for Civil Rights of Ukrainian Cossacks.

1590: Jan Zamoyski (1542-1605) Chancelor and Defence Minister (Grand-Hetman) of the Polish Republic won the support of the Seym to extend Polish defence line to the Danube River by securing Moldavia and Wallachia as fiefs in order to prepare for a new round in the struggle against Turkish advance into Europe. Oct.20.1600 Hetman Zamoyski led armed intervention to defend the Moldavian and Wallachian vassals of Poland Simon and Jeremi Mokhyla.

Jan Zamoyski one of the most talented political leaders in Polish history was educated in Poland, France and Italy where in 1563 he served as president (rector) of the University of Padua. He was one of the founders of the First Polish Republic and the political leader of the Polish Renaissance.

A.D. 1600
JAN ZAMOYSKI'S DEFENSE LINE ON THE DANUBE RIVER IN PREPARATION FOR THE NEXT WAVE OF TURKISH MOSLEM AGGRESSION AGAINST CENTRAL AND EASTERN EUROPE

POLISH NOBLES' REPUBLIC'S FIEFS OF MOLDAVIA AND WALLACHIA 1595-1616

1 MOLDAVIA
2 WALLACHIA
3 TRANSYLVANIA

Map: 1600 Jan Zamoyski's Defense Line on the Danube River.

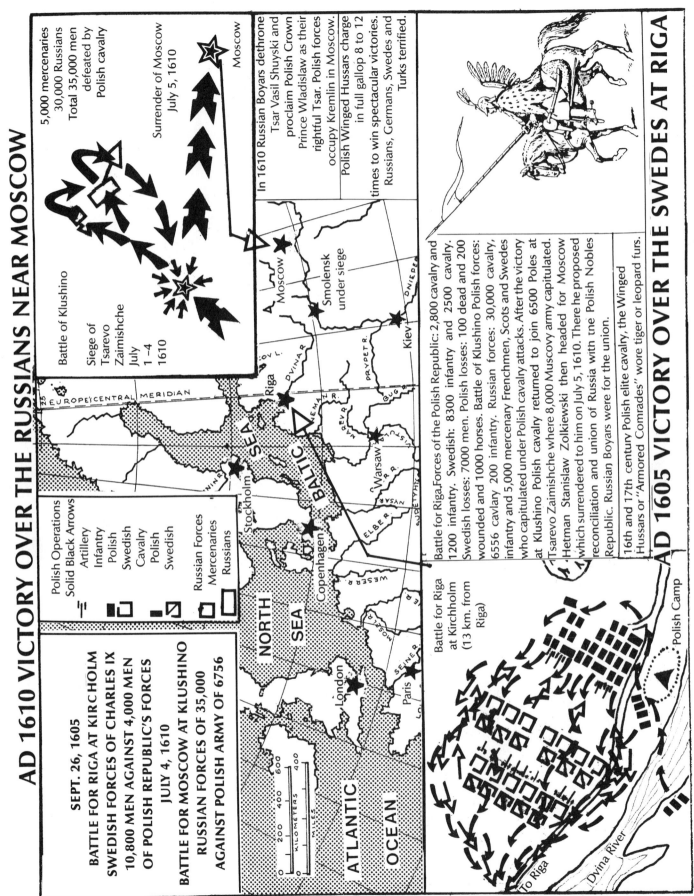

AD 1610 VICTORY OVER THE RUSSIANS NEAR MOSCOW

5,000 mercenaries
30,000 Russians
Total 35,000 men
defeated by
Polish cavalry

Surrender of Moscow
July 5, 1610

Moscow

Battle of Klushino

Siege of
Tsarevo
Zaimishche
July
1 - 4
1610

In 1610 Russian Boyars dethrone Tsar Vasil Shuyski and proclaim Polish Crown Prince Wladislaw as their rightful Tsar. Polish forces occupy Kremlin in Moscow. Polish Winged Hussars charge in full gallop 8 to 12 times to win spectacular victories. Russians, Germans, Swedes and Turks terrified.

Moscow

Smolensk
under siege

Kiev

DNIEPER

PRYPET R.

NAREV R.

BUG R.

Warsaw

VISTULA R.

NYSAR.

ELBE R.

SUDETY MTS.

Riga

DVINA R.

NIEMAN R.

SEA

BALTIC

EUROPE'S CENTRAL MERIDIAN

25

Stockholm

Copenhagen

NORTH
SEA

WESER R.

MOSEL R.

Lo...

London

Paris

SEINE R.

ATLANTIC
OCEAN

MILES

KILOMETERS

0   200   400   600

0   200   400

Polish Operations
Solid Black Arrows

Artillery

Infantry
Polish
Swedish

Cavalry
Polish
Swedish

Russian Forces
Mercenaries
Russians

SEPT. 26, 1605
BATTLE FOR RIGA AT KIRCHHOLM
SWEDISH FORCES OF CHARLES IX
10,800 MEN AGAINST 4,000 MEN
OF POLISH REPUBLIC'S FORCES
JULY 4, 1610
BATTLE FOR MOSCOW AT KLUSHINO
RUSSIAN FORCES OF 35,000
AGAINST POLISH ARMY OF 6756

Battle for Riga. Forces of the Polish Republic: 2,800 cavalry and 1200 infantry. Swedish: 8300 infantry and 2500 cavalry. Swedish losses: 7000 men. Polish losses: 100 dead and 200 wounded and 1000 horses. Battle of Klushino Polish forces: 6556 cavalry 200 infantry. Russian forces: 30,000 cavalry, infantry and 5,000 mercenary Frenchmen, Scots and Swedes who capitulated under Polish cavalry attacks. After the victory at Klushino Polish cavalry returned to join 6500 Poles at Tsarevo Zaimishche where 8,000 Muscovy army capitulated. Hetman Stanislaw Zolkiewski then headed for Moscow which surrendered to him on July 5, 1610. There he proposed reconciliation and union of Russia with the Polish Nobles Republic. Russian Boyars were for the union.

Battle for Riga
at Kirchholm
(13 km. from
Riga)

16th and 17th century Polish elite cavalry, the Winged Hussars or "Armored Comrades" wore tiger or leopard furs.

AD 1605 VICTORY OVER THE SWEDES AT RIGA

Polish Camp

To Riga

Dvina River

TWO GREAT VICTORIES : BATTLE FOR MOSCOW AT KLUSHINO AND **BATTLE FOR RIGA AT KIRCHHOLM**
Map: 1605 Victory over the Swedes at Riga-Kirchholm and 1610 Victory over the Russians near Moscow at Klushino; occupation of Moscow (battle maps).

Sigismund Vasa signed the social contract to preserve the Polish constitution and serve as chief executive of the Polish Republic. Zebrzydowski's uprising was against the absolutist tendencies of Sigismund III, his violation of the social contract of the Republic and his efforts to remove the chamber of deputies as the supreme power.

The Populist Party led by Mikolaj Zebrzydowski (1553 – 1620) declared uprising in 1606 to impeach Sigismund III, restore religious toleration, and cancel the Union of Brest of 1596 which affected badly relations between the Republic and Orthodox Ruthenians.

The Seym of Jan.-Feb. 1609 passed an amnesty for the members of the uprising, confirmed freedom and in-violability of general elections for the king as the head of the Nobles Republic and assigned a permanent Senate watch-dog committee to preserve the constitution.

July 6, 1607 defeat of the Zebrzydowski uprising at Guzow.

A.D. 1606 – 1609
CIVIL WAR TO UPHOLD THE CONSTITUTION AND SOCIAL CONTRACT OF THE REPUBLIC LED BY ZEBRZYDOWSKI

K. OF SWEDEN

The 1587 election of Sigismund Vasa brought an end to the Golden Age of Poland (and of the lower and middle gentry). By 1586 the respect-for-the-law movement disintegrated. Huge land owners, the magnates, started to build their political machines in the regional legislatures. The 17th century became the Golden Age of Magnates who attempted to convert the Republic into an oligarchic federation of huge estate owners. When Sigismund Vasa could not break the social contract, he tried secretly to abdicate in favor of Ernest Habsburg for 400,000 Guilders. His ambition was to be the King of Sweden. The election to head of the Polish Republic he treated, at first, as a stepping stone to the Swedish throne.

Map: 1606-1609 Civil War to Uphold the Constitution and Social Contract of the Republic Led by Zebrzydowski.

1621 THE OTTOMAN ARMY AT CHOCIM WAR WITH TURKEY

1620 defeat at Cecora of Polish Army of 9000 by 14,000 Tartars and 7,000 Turks. Death of Hetman Zolkiewski

1621 Inconclusive battle of Chocim by 26,000 Poles and 20,000 Cossacks against 100,000 Turks and Tartars ends the attempted Turkish invasion of Poland.

The 1610 Russian alliance with Sweden. In 1609–1611 Polish siege of Smolensk. On July 4, 1610, Polish cavalry victory of 7000 men over 35,000-man Russian army at Kluszyn. Polish occupation of Moscow. Taking prisoner of Tsar Vasil IV Shuyski. Negotiation to place on the Russian Throne Polish Prince Ladislas as rightful Tsar.

A.D. 1609 – 1618 POLISH VICTORIES IN WAR WITH RUSSIA.
PLANS FOR UNIFICATION OF RUSSIA WITH POLAND

A.D. 1619 – 1621
INCONCLUSIVE WAR WITH TURKEY. TERRORIST RAIDS, PLUNDERING, AND MASSIVE TAKING OF HOSTAGES FOR RANSOM BY CRIMEAN TARTARS.

INCONCLUSIVE WAR WITH TURKISH OTTOMAN EMPIRE

Turkish Moslem Ottoman Empire   Turkish invasion 1621
CECORA 1620 Death of Hetman Zolkiewski

A.D. 1609 – 1618 POLISH VICTORIES IN WAR WITH RUSSIA. PLANS FOR UNIFICATION OF RUSSIA & POLAND

Map: 1609-1618 Poland's Victory in War with Russia; 1619-1621 Inconclusive War with Turkey.

THE HEIGHT OF SUCCESS OF DEMOCRACY OF THE MASSES OF CITIZENS-SOLDERS

"Freemen with free. Equals with equal"

Population of Europe 97 million

France 15½M.	Habsburg
Germany 12M.	Austria 7M.
Republic of	Netherland 1½M.
Poland 11½M.	Belgium 1½M.
Italy 11M.	Portugal 1½M.
European Turkey 9½M.	Scotland 1M.
Russia 8M.	Sweden 1M.
Spain 8M.	Ireland 1M.

"POLISH EYES ON PARIS; POLISH HEARTS ON ROME; POLISH SABRES ON RUSSIA."

Republic of Poland 11.5M.
Poles 4.4M.
Byelorussians 1.5M.
Lithuanians 0.75M
Prussians 0.75M.
Livonians 0.5M.

"the Republic of Good Will"

A.D. 1618
REPUBLIC OF POLAND
THE
BASTION OF
WESTERN CIVILIZATION

REPUBLIC BASED ON TOLERATION AND FREEDOM OF SPEECH
A.D. 1618 HEIGHT OF POLAND'S SUPERIORITY OVER RUSSIA.
A FEDERATION BASED ON AUTONOMY AND FREEDOM
OF ALL ETHNIC AND RELIGIOUS GROUPS INCLUDING THE JEWS

Map: 1618 Republic of Poland-Lithuania The Bastion of Western Christianity (population numbers).

Note the growth of grain exports during Poland's Golden Age 1492-1586. Poland's Vistula trade reflected her political fortunes and a shift of the center of international trade away from the Baltic and to the Atlantic. The index of Republics economy: Vistula grain trade through Gdansk.

Republic's territory: 1,000,000 square kilometers. Population: 11M Szlachta (shlkh-ta) The Noble Nation — the political nation of one million free citizens of people forming the Polish Republic

The luxury of burghers and the noble class contrasting with the growing poverty of the peasants.

BALTIC SEA

BLACK SEA

AZOV'S

CRIMEA

DORPAT
RIGA
EUROPE'S CENTRAL MERIDIAN
MEMEL
WILNO
POLOCK
WITEBSK
SMOLENSK
LUND
COPENHAGEN
MALMÖ
STETTIN
BERLIN
HAMBURG
DREZDEN
WROCLAW
POZNAN
GDANSK
TORUN
CRACOW
KIELCE
RADOM
LUBLIN
WARSAW
BUDAPEST
OCZAKOW

Vistula Grain Trade

300,000 Tons per year

200,000 Tons

100,000 Tons

-1618-

YEARS
The Index of Republic's Economy

1500 1600 1700 1800

-1772-
-1795-

A.D. 1618
WATER WAY
TRANSPORTATION
OF EXPORT GRAIN
OUT OF THE
POLISH REPUBLIC
AT THE HEIGHT OF
THE BALTIC TRADE

Map: 1618 Grain Export - Waterways and Trade - The Index of Poland's Economy. (1604-1619 the last period of booming economy in Poland and relatively high efficiency in Polish agriculture.)

THE INTERNATIONAL TRADE ROUTES AT THE HEIGHT OF THE BALTIC TRADE

A.D. 1618
THE FIRST POLISH REPUBLIC WITHIN THE INTERNATIONAL TRADE ROUTES AT THE HEIGHT OF THE BALTIC TRADE

Beginning of decline of agricultural efficiency east of the Elbe river and south of the Pyrenees as the West converts from serfdom to rents.

Table of return per one grain planted

	End of 16th century	End of 17th century
The Netherlands	7.5	13.1
England	4.6	9.8
West Germany	4.4	5.3
Poland	4.0	3.3

Russia until the 20th century 3.0

Four hundred years of Tartar Terrorism turned the Southern Ukraine into "Wild Plains."

Export of Polish grain reached 300,000 tons/year.

Taxes were the land tax collected from peasants and nobles: Pobor (po-boor)

Property tax from the burghers and from clergy "shos" tax.

Beverage tax‡Chopowe (cho-po-ve)

Poll Tax

Custom Duties.

Port Dues at Gdansk, Elblag, and Riga.

Revenues from mining of salt, copper, silver, and lead.

Profits of the mint.

Seym granted each tax separately.

Note: critical average temperature drop and frequent draught in 1600–1860 in East-Central Europe was adverse for Polish agriculture as were the subsidized Russian exports through Arkhangelsk from the beginning of 17th century.

1618–1648 Thirty Year War economic crisis in Western Europe gave an impulse for the down trend in Poland's economy which went into a deep crisis followed by a century of stagnation especially pronounced during the Saxon Period (1697–1763) preventing rebuilding and recovery from destructive wars, invasions and plunder.

ON THE EVE OF A MAJOR REVERSAL FROM BALTIC TO ATLANTIC TRADE

POLAND WITHIN TRADE ROUTES OF EUROPE

Map: 1618 The First Polish Republic within International Trade Routes.

Map: 1618 Fortresses and Defense Castles.

Nobility of 10% and burghers of 15% spoke Polish throughout the multinational Republic; 450,000 Jews spoke Yiddish — a Germanic language (300,000 Jews lived in towns and 150,000 in the villages). For listing by size of the community of other language groups see the summary in the left bottom corner.

A.D. 1618
LANGUAGES
OF THE MULTINATIONAL REPUBLIC

Republic's Languages
Estimated total population of
11,000,000 on one million
square kilometers:

Polish   40%, 4.4M
Ukrainian   30%, 3.3M
Byelorussian   15%, 1.7M
Lithuanian   5%, .7M
Others: Approx. 1.5M
Yiddish, German, Latvian,
Russian, Estonian, Armenian,
Prussian, Tartar, Livonian,
Slovak, Czech, and Gypsy
listed by group size.

M = millions

Map: 1618 Languages of the Multinational Republic.

TERRORIST RAIDS, PLUNDERING, AND MASSIVE TAKING OF HOSTAGES FOR RANSOM BY CRIMEAN TARTARS.

Cossacks: East Slavic peasant frontiersmen adapted to the struggle against terrorism of the nomads, especially Tartars. (Russian Cossacks conquered Siberia)

The cause of Ukrainian Cossacks was opposed by huge landowners who wanted to convert them to serfs working on manorial farms.

Frustrated Cossacks were ready to win their civil rights by force when they could not get them by participation in the campaign against the Moslem.

SICZ (sheech) CAPITAL OF THE AUTONOMOUS COSSACK GOVERNMENT

Trails of the Terrorist Tartar attacks

Strike force on Dnieper River: Fleet and planned overland attack on Constantinople

A.D. 1644-1647 UNREALIZED PLANS TO ELIMINATE TARTAR TERRORISM AND TO FREE THE BALKANS FROM MOSLEM YOKE

Ukrainian Cossack support for the campaign was secured by a promise of freedom from serfdom and full civil rights and inclusion of the Cossacks in the political Nation of Free Citizens of Polish Republic.

Campaign plans were torpedoed at the Seym of 1646 and 1647 by the huge landowners who dominated provincial legislatures and tried to create in the Polish Republic a federation of strong dominions of magnates; they felt that military success would strengthen the executive branch of the government.

Meanwhile, Christian allies of Poland against Moslems were letting her down. Muscovy concluded a treaty with the Tartars while Rome and Venice failed to provide any effective assistance, France did nothing.

SHARIFATE OF MARAKESH

MOSCOVY RUSSIAN TSARDOM

MOSCOW

REPUBLIC OF POLAND

WARSAW

KIEV

CRIMEAN TARTARS THE "HORNETS NEST" OF TERRORISM

CONSTANTINOPLE ISTAMBUL

MOSLEM OTTOMAN EMPIRE

VIENNA

VENICE

ROME

NORTH SEA

BALTIC SEA

ADRIATIC SEA

MEDITERRANEAN SEA

CASPIAN S.

EUROPE'S CENTRAL MERIDIAN

1644-1647 UNREALIZED PLANS TO ELIMINATE TARTAR TERRORISM — FREE THE BALKANS

Cossacks were ready to participate in an anti-Turkish crusade. When the Polish plans failed Cossack uprising broke out.

Map: 1644-47 An Unrealized Plan to Eliminate Tartar Terrorism and to Free the Balkans from the Moslem Yoke.

Ukrainian Cossacks rebelled against attempts to convert them into serfs and change their religion into Greek Catholic. Cossacks were ready to participate in an anti-Turkish crusade. When the Polish plans failed Cossack uprising broke out. Bohdan Chmielnicki (1595-1652) assumed the leadership; he was a former officer-scribe in the army of the Polish Republic (he failed to get satisfaction in court for his grievances against other Ukrainian nobles and himself committed an act of treason and desertion for which he faced a death sentence). 1648 march of the joint Cossack-Tartar forces started after concluding an alliance with the Khan of Crimea.

Muscovites supported Chmielnicki with men and money in order to weaken Poland and eventually annex Ukraine into the Muscovy-Russian Empire. Defeated by the army of the Republic, Chmielnicki accepted Muscovy protectorate which eventually led to abolition of Cossack self-government.

Crimean Tartars — a Moslem vanguard of the Turkish Empire intended to weaken the Polish Republic but prevent rising of an independent Ukrainian Cossack state. Prolonging the war gave Tartars an additional opportunity to loot and take people for ransom. Tartars broke with the Cossacks at Zborow and Zwaniec while at Beresteczko they simply ran from the battlefield and left the Cossacks to suffer a crushing defeat.

A.D. 1648-1651
COSSACK UPRISING
— THE END OF GREAT
POWER STATUS OF
POLISH NOBLES' REPUBLIC
UKRAINIAN COSSACK
UPRISING EXPLOITED BY
MUSCOVY RUSSIA, SWEDEN
BRANDENBURG AND TURKISH
MOSLEM OTTOMAN EMPIRE

COSSACK UPRISING LED BY BOHDAN CHMIELNICKI (KHMELNYTSKYY)

Map: 1648-1651 Cossack Uprising - The End of Great Power Status of the Polish Nobles' Republic.

POWER STATUS OF POLISH NOBLES' REPUBLIC

1648-1651 COSSACK UPRISING — THE END OF GREAT

Huge human losses including 120,000 Jews murdered and starved by the Cossacks, the largest massacre in Jewish history to date. Tartars murdering at Batoh of an entire captured Polish division after the Cossacks demanded the killings and refunded the ransom value of the Poles; huge losses of life and property throughout the area of Cossack uprising.

1648 MARCH OF COSSACKS AND THEIR TARTAR ALLIES

Cossack Uprising

Cossack March

A.D. 1648-1651 COSSACK UPRISING LED BY BOHDAN CHMIELNICKI (KHMELNYTSKYY) BATTLES AND PACTS

ENCOURAGING MUSCOVY ATTACK

UKRAINIAN COSSACK UPRISING EXPLOITED BY MUSCOVY RUSSIA, SWEDEN BRANDENBURG AND TURKISH MOSLEM OTTOMAN EMPIRE

BATTLES AND PACTS
1. May 1648   Yellow Waters
2. May 1648   Korsun
3. Sept. 1648   Pilawce
4. July-Aug. 1649   Zbaraz Siege
5. Aug. 1648   Zborow Pact
6. June 1651   Beresteczko
July 1651   Beresteczko
8. Sept. 1651   Biala. Cerkiew Pact
9. June 1652   Batoh
10. Dec. 1653   Zwaniec pact
11. Oct. 1653   Moscow Sobor on annexation of Ukraine by Muscovy-Russian Empire
12. Jan. 1654   Perejeslaw pact between Cossacks and Muscovy on annexation by Russia of Ukraine east of the Dnieper River.

TURKISH MOSLEM OTTOMAN EMPIRE

Bohdan Chmienlicki (1595-1652) assumed the leadership

Ukrainian Cossacks rebelled against attempts to convert them into serfs and change their religion into Greek Catholic.

Map: 1648-1651 Cossack Uprising - Battles and Pacts.

Summer 1654 Muscovy Russian northern army invades Polish Republic in a drive to annex Ukraine and Byelorussia; occupy (1.) Smolensk, (2.) Byelorussia, and (3.) part of Lithuania with Wilno; Southern army joins the Cossacks; (4.) Polish victory at Ochmatow (Jan. 1655) Chmielnicki's offensive: (5.) Siege of Lwow (Sept.-Nov., 1655) (6.) Cossack advance to the lower Vistula River (7.) Tartar attack on Cossack Muscovy stores and capture of Hetman Chmielnicki resulting in capitulation of the Cossacks at Jezierna and a formal declaration of allegiance to Poland by Bohdan Chmielnicki. Sweden domination of the Baltic Sea a threat to Muscovy. Russian access to the Baltic causing the Muscovites to stop the offensive against Poland in order not to help the Swedish invasion against Western and Northern Poland starting in July 1655. See next map.

End of Cossack Tartar alliance: Turkey opposing the growth of strength of Muscovy Russian Empire as well as any form of an independent Ukrainian state led by the Cossacks of Zaporozhe. Turkey orders a limited support to Poland by Crimean Tartars.

A.D. 1654-1656
INVASION OF THE
POLISH REPUBLIC BY
MUSCOVY RUSSIAN AND
COSSACK ARMIES STOPPED
BECAUSE OF MILITARY
SUCCESS OF SWEDISH
ATTACK AGAINST POLAND

Map: 1654-1656 Muscovy and Cossack Invasion.

Swedish invasion precipitated by Muscovy successes in Ukraine and in war against Poland starting in 1654. Swedish preparations helped by traitor Hieronim Radziejawski (1623-67) who reported on weaknesses of the Republic and persuaded the command of Polish forces to surrender 10,000 men to 40,000 Swedish forces, veterans of the Thirty Years War.
(1.) July 1655 Surrender of Poznan
(2.) Aug. 1655 Surrender of Lithuania
(3.) Sept. 1655 Surrender of Warsaw
(4.) Oct. 1655 Surrender of Krakow after a fierce fight (5.) Rise of guerrillas against Swedish mass murders and plunder (6.) Nov./Dec. 1655 siege of Castle Shrine of Czestochowa, lifted by advance of guerrillas (7.) Dec. 1655, formation of patriotic confederation of Tyszowce (8.) Feb. 1656, Polish forces surrounding King Charles X Gustavus in the fork of San and Vistula. Polish victory at Warka (9.) June 1656, recovery of Warsaw by Polish army of 40,000.

Jan. 1656 Polish vassal Frederic Wilhelm Hohenzollern becoms Swedish vassal of Prussia. Sweden discussing Brandenburgian plans for a partition of Poland. Coordination of army operations with the Guerrillas, July 1656; 20,000 from Brandenburg joining the Swedes, fall of Warsaw for three weeks; defeat of Brandenburgians and plundering of Prussia by the Tartars. Nov 1656, Polish-Russian pact against Sweden and Swedish-Brandenburgian pact against Poland.

A.D. 1655-1657
SWEDISH INVASION TO CONQUER
BALTIC PROVINCES OF
THE POLISH REPUBLIC
AMIDST TREASON OF MAGNATES WHO
HOPED TO MAINTAIN POLITICAL DOMINANCE
AND REGAIN ESTATES IN UKRAINE
WITH HELP OF SWEDEN
"THE PLUNDERER OF EUROPE"

EXTENT OF SWEDISH ADVANCE

Dec. 1656 Pact of Radnot of Brandenburg, Sweden and Transylvania for partition of Poland, independent Cossack Ukraine, separate Duchy of Lithuania and Swedish annexation of the Baltic Coast — opposed by Poland, Russia, Austria, Denmark, and Holland — leading to Transylvanian invasion — ended by Polish Army retaliatory raids in Transylvania. May 1657 Polish Austrian treaty of defense,
June 1657, Denmark entered war against Sweden.

Map: 1655-1657 Swedish Invasion and Treason of Magnates.

A.D. 1656 – 1657 TROOP MOVEMENTS SWEDISH INVASION JOINED BY BRANDENBURGIANS AND TRANSYLVANIANS POLISH COUNTER OFFENSIVES

The 1657 treaties of Welawa-Bydgoszcz release Polish-Prussian fief to Brandenburg despite widespread opposition of the inhabitants of Prussia (in return for Brandenburgians ending alliance with Sweden). Formation of a parasitic stranglehold on Vistula delta by the tiny Duchy of Brandenburg.

Range of plundering and devastation by the Swedes. Polish spring offensive of 1656 by Hetmans Stefan Czarnecki (1599–1665) and Jerzy Lubomirski (1616–1667). Victory at Warka, April 1656.

July 1656 March of 20,000 Brandenburgians to join the Swedes in the Battle of Warsaw which resulted in 3-weeks occupation of Polish capital.

Jan. – July 1657, Transylvanian invasion prolonging war, plunder, and devastation, ending in July 1657. Capitulation of the Transylvanian army – retaliatory raids into Transylvania.

SWEDISH "THE PLUNDERER OF EUROPE"

A.D. 1656 – 1657 TROOP MOVEMENTS SWEDISH BRANDENBURGIAN AND TRANSYLVANIAN

Map: 1656-1657 Invasion by Sweden, Brandenburg, and Transylvania.
Polish Counteroffensives.

Map: 1658-1667 the Republic of Poland-Lithuania-Ruthenia (including Byelorussia and Ukraine). 1665-1666 Rebellion Against Constitutional Reforms Led by Jerzy Lubomirski; Rebellion Preventing the Recovery of Eastern Ukraine and Byelorussia.

Map: 1587-1660 Swedish Expansion and Plunder.

A.D. 1587 – 1660
SWEDISH EXPANSION
AND
PLUNDER
DYNASTIC ENTANGLEMENT
WITH
POLISH NOBLES' REPUBLIC

Swedish Expansion and Plunder

1. 1561 Estonia (1598 Nominally ceded to Poland).
2. 1617 Karelia   3. 1617 Ingria
4. 1629 Livonia occupied by Sweden
   Livonia Polish fief 1561–1660
5. 1629–1635 Ducal Prussia under Sweden—Polish fief
   1525–1657
6. 1645 Islands of Gotland and Oesel
7. 1645 Jämtland and Hariedalen
8. 1645 Halland
9. 1648 Western Pomerania (Stettin)
10. 1648 Bremen and Werden
11. 1658 Scania   12. 1658 Borhus 1592–1604

Sweden in personal union with Polish Nobles' Republic. In 1635 Peace of Sztumska Wies (Stumdorf) Warmia. Sweden returns to Poland all Polish and Prussian ports in return for Swedish hold on Livonia. Sweden enters the Thirty Year War to plunder in Pomerania and Germany.

Protestant Swedish Vasas mobilizing forces twice the size of the Polish army out of population 1/5 of that of the Polish Republic. In 1626 plundering Polish Baltic ports and successfully tapping Vistula trade to pay Swedish army despite the breaking of the Swedish blockade by Polish naval victory at Oliwa in 1627. Sweden taking over Polish fief of Ducal Prussia (1629–35) after truce at Altmark, Warmia.

A.D. 1657 - 1667
TERRITORIAL AND POPULATION LOSSES
OF THE REPUBLIC

CAUSED BY 1648 COSSACK UPRISING

1655 SWEDISH INVASION

1666 CIVIL WAR

1648 - 1657 Polish Republic's population losses of about 4,000,000 people caused by "The Deluge" of invasions, civil wars, mass murders, devastation, natural disasters, and important territorial losses shown on this map.

MUSCOVY RUSSIAN EMPIRE

SMOLENSK 1667 ANDRUSZOW

KIEV

WILD PLAINS

CRIMEA TARTARS

BLACK SEA

CRIMEA

AZOV S.

POLISH NOBLES' REPUBLIC

RIGA

WILNO

LWOW

WELAWA 1657

WARSAW

CRACOW

AUSTRIA

OLIWA 1660

GDANSK

BYDGOSZCZ

POZNAN

BALTIC SEA

K. OF DENMARK

BRANDENBURG

BERLIN

SAXONY

HAMBURG

1. 1657 Treaties of Bydgoszcz Welawa; losses to Brandenburg
2. 1660 Peace Treaty of Oliwa confirming 1629 Truce of Altmark – losses in Livonia to Sweden
3. 1667 Pact of Andruszow confirmed in 1686 Peace Treaty by Grzymultowski (1620–87)
4. Zaporozhe or Wild Plains a part of an independent Ukrainian state of Hetman Chmielnicki, the original area of development of the Cossack type of population and elective self government.

THE LOSS   CAUSED BY 1648 COSSACK UPRISING 1655 SWEDISH INVASION 1666 CIVIL WAR   TURKISH MOSLEM OTTOMAN EMPIRE

A.D. 1657 – 1667 TERRITORIAL AND POPULATION LOSSES OF THE REPUBLIC
Map: 1657-1667 territorial and population losses of the Republic.

In 1648 Bogdan Chmielnicki elected Hetman of the Zaporazhian Host of the Polish Republic to press demands for civil rights of the Cossacks (by ennoblement). Bitter fighting made the compromise impossible.

A.D. 1648 – 1672
THE DELUGE OF INVASIONS
AND TERRITORIAL LOSSES OF THE
REPUBLIC BY 1667

As the Republic wavered under Cossack attack the vultures descended on her territory.

1. Zaporozhian Cossacks (and Tartars) 1648 and 1651
2. Muscovites (and Cossacks) 1654 – 1657
3. Swedes 1655 – 1658
4. Brandenburgians 1656
5. Transylvanians 1656 – 1657
6. Ottoman Turks 1672 – 1673

A.D. 1648 – 1672

THE DELUGE OF INVASIONS AND TERRITORIAL LOSSES OF THE REPUBLIC BY 1667

Map: 1648-1672 The Deluge of Invasions and Territorial Losses of the Republic by 1667.

(1.) Hetman of Ukrainian Cossack Piotr Doroshenko declares himself Turkish vassal causing 1666 Polish-Turkish war. (2.) The 1667 crushing of Cossack-Tartar army at Podhajce by Hetman John Sobieski. (3.) 1672 Turkish invasion by Sultan Mohammed IV reducing Kamieniec Podolski. (4.) 1672 surrender of Podolia and part of Ukraine to Turkey at Buczacz. (5.) 1673 great Polish victory at Chocim won by Hetman John Sobieski. (6.) 1674 Polish victory won by King John III Sobieski at Zurawno and recovery of Ukraine, an end of ransom. (7.) 1675 Polish victory over Tartars at Lwow and defense of Trembowla. (8.) 1674 inconclusive Battle of Zurawno, truce and recovery of the rest of Ukraine, not Podolia. (9.) Habsburgs under the threat of annihilation of their empire signing a common defense treaty with Poland and extending foreign aid of 1,200,000 ducats to the exhausted Republic.

King John III Sobieski to be the supreme commander of the Allied Christian Army in case of Turkish invasion, 1683. (10.) Turkish siege of Vienna and a crushing victory over the Turks by King John III Sobieski bringing the end of Turkish expansion into Europe and beginning of liquidation of the Turkish yoke in Southern Europe; strengthening the struggle for national independence of the Balkan Christians.

**A.D. 1667-1683
WAR WITH TURKEY
AFTER LOSS OF PODOLIA AND
HUMILIATION AT BUCZACZ

THE LAST TWO GREAT VICTORIES
OF THE ARMY OF POLISH REPUBLIC

1673 ANNIHILATION OF
THE OTTOMAN ARMY AT CHOCIM

1683 VICTORY AT VIENNA ENDING
TURKISH EXPANSION INTO EUROPE**

Map: 1667-1683 War with Turkey after the Loss of Podolia. The Last Two Great Victories of the First Polish Republic: Chocim and Vienna.

A.D. 1683 POLAND FACING TURKISH AND RUSSIAN EMPIRES

Frontier of the Domain of Western Christianity

TURKISH AGGRESSION AGAINST POLAND AND AUSTRIA

1683 VICTORY AT VIENNA ENDING TURKISH EXPANSION INTO EUROPE

1672 invasion of Poland and fall of the fortress of Kamieniec Podolski resulted in the Treaty of Buczacz which the Poles considered a shame and disgrace. It made Podolia a Turkish fief (1672-1699) and obligated Poland to pay ransom. Instead the Republic armed herself and elected Jan Sobieski, an experienced military commander, as the king and chief executive of the Polish Nobles' Republic. Poland faced a large increase of the length of her border with Turkey and a possible Turkish attack on Rome and the Vatican. All this made war with Turkey inevitable when the Turks laid siege on Vienna. Turkish threat and insistence to hold part of Poland as a fief paralyzed the treaty of April 11, 1675, made in Jaworow between John III Sobieski, Sweden and Louis XIV of France for the purpose of evicting the Hohenzollerns of Berlin from Prussia. This plan was not realized because of successful lobbying in the Seym by Austrian and Brandenburgian diplomats, and by huge Polish landowners who feared an increase of the power of the central government of the Republic. Brandenburg-Prussia (see map) where it conducted parasitic economic policies and eventually could become a powerful state at the expense of Poland. 1683 Turkey - a military machine at the height of her territorial expansion was on the verge of overrunning Austria and destroying the Habsburg state. For the victorious campaign of King John III Sobieski acting as the supreme commander of Allied Christian Armies against the Turks see next pages.

1673 ANIHILATION OF THE OTTOMAN ARMY AT CHOCIM

BRANDENBURG - PRUSSIA

A.D. 1683
TURKISH EMPIRE AT THE ZENITH OF TERRITORIAL EXPANSION WHILE THE RUSSIAN EMPIRE GRADUALLY FILLS THE POWER VACUUM LEFT AFTER COLLAPSE OF THE MONGOL EMPIRE

Map: 1683 Poland Facing Turkish and Russian Empires

Map labels: KAMCHATKA, PACIFIC OCEAN, ANADIRSKY OSTROG 1649, NIZHNYEKOLIMSK 1644, YERKHOYANSK 1618, JAKUCK 1632, LENA RIVER, NERCHINSK 1659, CHINESE EMPIRE, RUSSIAN EMPIRE, YENISEY RIVER, YENISEYSK 1681, TOMSK 1604, OB RIVER, TOBOLSK 1587, ARCTIC OCEAN, NOVAYA ZEMLIA, MOGUL EMPIRE, PERSIA, CASPIAN SEA, PERSIAN G., ORMUZ, INDIAN OCEAN, RED SEA, VOLGA RIVER, MOSCOW, BLACK SEA, ISTAMBUL, MEDITERRANEAN SEA, OTTOMAN EMPIRE, TROPIC OF CANCER, ARCTIC CIRCLE, ATLANTIC OCEAN, NORWAY, SWEDEN, BALTIC, NORTH SEA, ENGLAND, FRANCE, SPAIN, DANUBE, VIENNA, PAPAL STATE, POLAND

AUG. SEPT. OCT. 1683
SOBIESKI'S
VICTORIOUS
CAMPAIGN
AGAINST TURKEY

Christian Allies:
Austrains 18,000
Germans 28,000
Poles 22,000

1683 King John III Sobieski the Supreme Commander of Allied Christian Armies lifts the Siege of Vienna.

Map: 1683 Aug.-Sept. Sobieski's Victorious Campaign Against Turkey.

1683 King John III Sobieski the Supreme Commander of Allied Christian Armies lifts the siege of Vienna.
Map: 1683 Sept.12 5a.m.-2p.m. Sobieski's Victory at Vienna.

SOBIESKI'S VICTORY AT VIENNA SEPT. 12, 1683

2 p.m. — 4 p.m.

Polish Cavalry
Polish Infantry

Austrian Cavalry
Austrian Infantry

German Cavalry
German Infantry

Allied's Positions

Turkish Camps
Turkish Fortifications
Turkish Main Force
Turkish Advanced Positions
Turkish Counterattacks
Turkish Retreats
Austrian Villages

elevation in meters

0 1 2 3km

KAHLENBERG

FORESTS
WOODS
Danube River
Danube
Danube lowlands
Danube
MOLDAVIANS
Lowlands
WALACHIANS
Danube

Polish Winged Hussar

Vienna Austria UNDER SIEGE

VIENNA

creek

PRINCE CHARLES
IBRAHIM PASHA
KARA MUSTAFA
HUSEIN
ABAZY SARY
JABLONOWSKI
SIENIAWSKI
SOBIESKI
WALDECK

Vienna River

Tartars

creek

1315
423
483
542
492
454
420
460
386
415
310
386
350
388
300
507
295
463
389
348
286
350
310 420

1683 King John III Sobieski the Supreme Commander of Allied Christian Armies lifts the Siege of Vienna.
Map: 1683 Sept.12, 2p.m.-4p.m. Sobieski's Victory at Vienna.

Polish elite cavalry, the Winged Hussars or "Armored Comrades" wore tiger or leopard furs.

SOBIESKI'S VICTORY AT VIENNA SEPT. 12, 1683

4 p.m.   10 p.m.

Polish Cavalry
Polish Infantry
Austrian Cavalry
Austrian Infantry
German Cavalry
German Infantry

Allied's Positions

Turkish Camps
Turkish Fortifications
Turkish Main Force
Turkish Advanced Positions
Turkish Counterattacks
Turkish Retreats

Austrian Villages

elevation in meters

0   1   2   3 km

FORESTS

WOODS

Polish Winged Hussar

Danube lowlands

Danube River

Danube

MOLDAVIANS

WALACHIANS

Lowlands

Vienna Austria UNDER SIEGE

VIENNA

PRINCE CHARLES

KARA MUSTAFA

WALDECK

SIENIAWSKI

SOBIESKI

JABLONOWSKI

HUSEIN

ABAZY SARY

Vienna River

Tartars

KAHLENBERG   483

315

423

492

542

454

420

386

415

310

350

460

507

388

300

386

463

295

286

389

348

415
295

Map: 1683 Sept.12 4p.m.-10p.m. Sobieski's Victory at Vienna.

1683 King JohnIII Sobieski the Supreme Commander of Allied Christian Armies lifts the Siege of Vienna.

DECLINE OF POLISH NOBLES' REPUBLIC–THE SAXON NIGHT OF DEGRADATION AND ANARCHY OF MAGNATES

A.D. 1697-1763
RAPE OF THE POLISH ELECTION
A CENTURY OF AN OPEN ABUSE
BY FOREIGN GOVERNMENTS
OF POLAND'S DEMOCRATIC PROCESS
BEGINNING WITH THE RAPE OF
POLISH ELECTIONS OF 1697
BY RUSSIA AND SAXONY RESULTING IN
THE CRISIS OF SOVEREIGNTY
OF 1697-1763

POLAND EXHAUSTED BY WARS WITH TURKEY

Invasion of Poland by Russia and Saxony resulting in the loss of control of the coronation site in Cracow and installation on the Polish throne of a minority candidate, Augustus II Wettin of Saxony, later in 1733 followed by his son Augustus II. Both Saxons fell into the hands of Russia throughout their struggle to stay on the Polish throne (1697-1763). The rape of Polish elections of 1697 permitted the Hohenzollerns of Berlin to found in 1701 a "Kingdom of Prussia" and shift to Berlin the balance of power in fragmented Germany.

Augustus' II machinations bringing into discredit the idea of Polish-Saxon union.

ECONOMIC REGRESSION (1697-1763) PREVENTING RECOVERY FROM WAR DESTRUCTION OF 17TH AND EARLY 18TH CENTURY

RAPE OF THE POLISH ELECTION BY FOREIGN GOVERNMENTS

A.D. 1697-1795 A CENTURY OF AN OPEN ABUSE OF POLAND'S DEMOCRATIC PROCESS

Map: 1697 Rape of the Polish Election.

THE CRISIS OF SOVEREIGNTY

DECLINE OF THE POWER STATUS

Endless power struggle between political machines of the magnates and subversion by Austria, Brandenburg, and Russia leading to a double election. The first decisive role of Russia in the Polish royal election on Sept. 15, 1697. Crowning of the minority candidate as a result of Russian and Saxon invasion and control of the coronation site in Cracow. Crowning of Augustus II Wettin of Saxony as king of Poland and chief executive of the Polish Nobles' Republic. Beginning of critical weakening of the Republic's defenses and of economic exploitation for the benefit of Saxony, deepening of anarchy and growth of obscurantism. Peter the Great becoming the patron and benefactor of the wretched Saxon administration while converting Russia into a Spartan military machine. Arch-Lutheran Augustus II Wettin converting to Roman Catholicism — the Republic was "worth a mass". Seym of 1699 accepting the Saxon *fait accompli* the same year as the war with Turkey ended and Podolia returned to the Polish Republic.

Augustus II "catching tiger by the tail" by trying to create great power status out of the union of tiny well governed Saxony and a huge oligarchic Polish Nobles' Republic. He faced resistance of the political nation of free citizens of the Republic and that of the neighboring powers committed to maintain anarchy in Poland for their own aggrandizement. Failure of Augustus II leading him to high treason and secret proposals of partition of Poland in exchange for keeping a part of her territory as his sovereign hereditary monarchy.

ECONOMIC STAGNATION UNDER ABSENTEE RULERS (1697-1763)

A.D. 1697
POLAND EXHAUSTED BY WARS WITH TURKEY AND ANARCHY OF MAGNATES SUCCUMBING TO THE SAXON NIGHT OF DEGRADATION (1697-1763)
PERSONAL UNION OF SAXONY WITH POLAND-LITHUANIA
DECLINE OF POLISH NOBLES' REPUBLIC

Augustus' II machinations bringing into discredit the idea of Polish-Saxon union.

Economic stagnation and exploitation by Saxony

THE RAPE OF POLISH ELECTIONS OF 1697 BY RUSSIA AND SAXONY
PERSONAL UNION OF SAXONY WITH POLAND-LITHUANIA (1697-1763)
Map: 1697 Poland Succumbing to the Saxon Night of Degradation, Plunder of Polish Resources, and Nearly a Century of Economic Stagnation.

17th century is Golden Age of the owners of huge estates; their success in political struggle to achieve oligarchy of the magnates is one of the main causes of downfall of the First Polish Republic at the very end of 18th century. The magnates fought to be the supreme arbiter in the Republic, when they failed the arbitration was done by Peter the Great in 1717.

During the Saxon Night of Polish history, 1697-1763, the competition for vacant offices and benefices became the main driving force in political activity.

BORDERS IN 1699-1772

BORDERS IN 1618

K. OF SWEDEN

MOSCOW

OKA R.

MUSCOVY RUSSIAN EMPIRE

ZAPO ROZHE

CRIMEAN TARTARS

BLACK SEA

CRIMEA

KIEV

GRAND DUCHY OF LITHUANIA

POLISH NOBLES' REPUBLIC

MOLDAVIA

PRUT R.

SERET R.

BALTIC SEA

PRUSSIA

WARSAW

K. OF POLAND

AUSTRIA

TRANSYLVANIA

TISA R.

SAMOS R.

AUSTRIA

K. OF DENMARK

COPENHAGEN

HAMBURG

BRANDENBURG

300 GERMAN STATES

BERLIN

SAXONY

DRESDEN

ODER

ELBE R.

TURKISH OTTOMAN EMPIRE

SEVENTEENTH AND EIGHTEENTH CENTURY

HEADQUARTERS OF POLITICAL MACHINES

AND PALACIAL RESIDENCIES OF THE MAGNATES

WHO FOUGHT TO MAKE THE POLISH REPUBLIC INTO AN OLIGARCHY

Map: 17th and 18th Century Headquarters of Political Machines.

A.D. 1700-1721
SWEDISH-RUSSIAN WAR IN POLAND
DECLINE OF THE POWER STATUS
OF POLAND AND SWEDEN
DESPITE OF THE
SPECTACULAR CAMPAIGNS
OF CHARLES XII

July 12, 1704, Election of King Stanislaus Leszczynski in a camp surrounded by Swedish soldiers 1705 Polish-Swedish Treaty of Warsaw 1706 Swedish attack on Dresden, abdication of Augustus II, withdrawal of Saxony from the Northern War 1707 Agreement with Hetman Mazepa (Russian vassal) to unify the Ukraine.

Ukraine to be under suzerainty of the Polish Nobles' Republic 1708, Swedish attack on Russia with Polish and Cossack help, defeated July 8, 1709, at Poltava. 1710 Seym restoring Augustus II to the Polish throne, the first widespread use of confederacy as a vehicle of foreign intervention in Poland to "legalize" it. Saxons the first kings never at home in Poland — absentee rulers.

France backs Polish-Swedish alliance; looting by Swedes resulting in 1702 Pro-SaxonConfederation of Warsaw; civil war pro "Las" Leszczynski and pro "Sas" Wettin; foreign military operations legalized in Poland. By 1704 Polish-Russian treaty at Narva and 1705 Polish-Swedish treaty at Warsaw degrading of the power status of Poland on the international scene after the Northern War.

A.D. 1700-1721

SWEDISH-RUSSIAN WAR IN POLAND

Armies:

Turkish

Russian

Swedish

Map: 1700-1721 Swedish-Russian war in Poland.

THE LAST GREAT RALLY OF THE DEMOCRACY OF POLISH CITIZENS-SOLDIERS

A.D. 1713-1717
THE SAXON COUP
TO DESTROY
POLISH NOBLES' REPUBLIC AND
IMPOSE AN ABSOLUTIST REGIME ON
POLAND-LITHUANIA AMIDST EFFORTS TO
STRENGTHEN THE REPUBLIC
ARBITRATION BY PETER THE GREAT
BEGINNING OF 50 YEARS OF RUSSIAN
SUBVERSION OF THE REPUBLIC

Saxon Augustus II, the absentee king attempting an absolutist coup d'etat. Not calling the Seym from 1703-1710. Weakening of the central government of the R;public by the King who swore to uphold the constitution and serve as chief executive of the Nobles' Republic. 1713, bringing the Saxon army into Poland under the pretext of Turkish danger, in reality to provoke crisis, conduct brutal pacification and establish an absolute regime. 1714 riots throughout southern Poland where gentry and peasants joined in the drive against Saxons. 1715, forming the General Confederation of Tarnogrod to preserve the Republic soon joined by the army of the republic – a three-way struggle. Masses of the gentry—nation fighting to preseve the Republic against an absolutist king and the Russian-controlled military command defending the status quo and the political machines of the magnates.

Peter the Great arbitrates, invades Poland with 18,000 troops, surrounding the Seym in Warsaw and forcing a silent approval of treaty limiting to 1200 the Saxon guard and establishing 12,000 man standing army out of proportion to needs of the Republic. The "Dumb Seym" froze in atrophy of the legislature and accepted Russian guarantee. Evacuation of Russian forces, 1719-1720, reassured the public.

BEGINNING OF 50 YEARS OF RUSSIAN SUBVERSION AMIDST EFFORTS TO STRENGTHEN THE REPUBLIC

A.D. 1713-1717

THE SAXON COUP TO IMPOSE AN ABSOLUTIST REGIME–ARBITRATION BY PETER THE GREAT

Map: 1713-1717 The Saxon Coup - Beginning of 50 Years of Russian Subversion of the Republic.

Population of Europe 120 Million

France 19M	Republic of Poland 9M
Russia 15M	Portugal 2M Spain 9M
Italy 14M	Netherlands 2M
Germany 13M	Belgium 1½M
Austria 11M	Swiss 1½M
European Turkey 10M	Sweden 1½M
Great Britain 9½M	Denmark 1½M

Republic of Poland 9M
Poles 4½M, Jews 0.5M
Ukrainians 1½M
Byelorussians 1.2M
Lithuanians 0.8M
Others 0.5M

A.D. 1717

REPUBLIC OF POLAND IN CRISIS OF SOVEREIGNTY WITHIN WESTERN CHRISTIANITY, EXHAUSTED BY WARS, SUBVERSION, ANARCHY, AND ECONOMIC REGRESSION

Frontier of Western Christianity

Decline of Poland, the Athens of Slavic Europe in face of the rise of Russian Sparta

Map: 1717 Republic of Poland within Western Christianity. Crisis of Sovereignty. Poland Exhausted by Wars, Subversion, Anarchy and Economic Regression (population numbers).

Election of Stanislas Leszczynski the author of "A Free Voice Insuring Freedom"

A.D. 1733-1735

WAR OF POLISH SUCCESSION
ABOLISHING BY RUSSIA OF
KING STANISLAS LESZCZYNSKI
REPLACING NATIVE
INDEPENDENCE MOVEMENT WITH
A RUSSIAN PUPPET
SAXON ADMINISTRATION
OF KING AUGUSTUS III,
THE ABSENTEE MONARCH

1733 Election of King Stanislas Leszczynski. Invasion by Saxon and Russian armies forcing King Stanislas to leave Poland through Gdansk. Confederation of Dzikow supporting King Stanislas overwhelmed by 30,000 Russians and 10,000 Saxon. Rigged election of Augustus II Wettin. France, Spain, and Sardinia attacking Austria. 1738, peace treaty profitable to France and honorable to King Stanislas Leszczynski retaining the title of King of Poland for life and receiving the Duchy of Lorraine with capital of Nancy from his son-in-law King Louis XV of France. "Pacification Seym" of 1736 recognizes Russian puppet August III as King of Poland. Chronic succession crisis during the reign of Augustus III.

Demilitarization and neutralization of the Polish Nobles' Republic stabilized by inertia of a system of "anarchy" caused by unrestrained licence of the magnates. Status quo in Poland maintained by neighboring powers. A regular army was viewed as potential tool to install royal absolutism or despotism of Hetmans in control of the military establishment. End of wars in Ukraine brought prosperity in former Wild Plains.

Economic stagnation and exploitation by Saxony

Restoring the unworkable union of Poland and Saxony

1735 ABOLISHING BY RUSSIA OF KING STANISLAS LESZCZYNSKI
WAR OF POLISH SUCCESSION   REPLACING   NATIVE   INDEPENDENCE   MOVEMENT WITH
A RUSSIAN PUPPET   SAXON ADMINISTRATION   OF   THE ABSENTEE   KING AUGUSTUS III

Map: 1733-1735 War of Polish Succession.

Silesia was lost for good by the conglomerate Habsburg Empire where a small minority of Germans ruled over Slavic majority (and Hungarians) Polish Republic was neutralized by the success of the political machines of the magnates who achieved an omnipotent oligarchy in the internal affairs of the Republic. They used the influence of foreign governments in their own internal intrigues: they became accustomed to accepting foreign money.

Absentee Saxon king who swore to act as a chief executive of the Republic was incapable of forming a central government. Truly Polish policy could not come from Dresden. Saxons had fallen into Russian control from the beginning of their fraudulent accession to the Polish throne. Saxons were imposed by force. They had only a minority support in Poland. Task of neighboring governments to deepen the anarchy in Poland was made easy by the ongoing power struggle among the members of the oligarchy.

War chest of Berlin government built up by parasitic tapping of the Polish Vistula trade and by severe taxing of Brandenburgians and Prussians. 1740 Beginning of two decades of wars which almost destroyed the new Kingdom of Prussia. Prussian conquest of Silesia brought an end to Saxon plan to acquire Silesia as a "bridge" to Poland.

A.D. 1740
DEMILITARIZED, NEUTRALIZED POLISH NOBLES' REPUBLIC OUT-FLANKED BY CONQUEST OF SILESIA BY THE BERLIN GOVERNMENT OF PRUSSIA

Map: 1740 Demilitarized and Neutralized Polish Republic Outflanked by the Conquest of Silesia by the Berlin Government of the New Prussia of The Hohenzollerns.

Concept of a Polish buffer state limiting the German power by Poland's physical presence in the path of German expansion east reappeared several times in different versions. It was actually implemented two hundred years later by Stalin in 1945. A low cost strategic advantage for Russia by situating the Poles in such a way that their natural defenses would be beneficial to the Muscovites (and in process Sovietize Poland in 1945).

1745-56, Plans formulated by Alexis Bestuzhev-Riumin,(1693-1766). Poland to get (1) (East) Prussia in return for Russian acquisition of (2) Podolia or parts of Byelorussia. These plans were one version of the overall "Piast" concept of restoring to Poland the original Polish ethnic areas conquered by the Germans,

In the "Jagiellonian" concept Poland is the leader of a multinational federation between German and Russian ethnic areas. 1745, Poland paralyzed by foreign subversion and anarchy of the magnates opted for the status quo.

First of a number of Russian plans to shift Poland westward against expanding Germans, thus improving the strategic position of Russia. Plan consisted of restoration to Poland of the original Prussia (East Prussia) in return for ceding Podolia to Russia.

1745-1756
UNREALIZED RUSSIAN PLAN TO SHIFT POLAND WEST AND USE HER AS A BUFFER AGAINST AN EXPANDING GERMAN STATE

MAGNATES OPPOSING THE EXCHANGE OF FERTILE PODOLIA FOR PRUSSIAN LAKELAND

Map: 1745-1756 Unrealized Russian Plan to Shift Poland West by Evicting Hohenzollerns from East Prussia in exchange for Podolia, part of Ukraine or Byelorussia.

WAR AGAINST RUSSIAN TERRORISM

Feb. 29, 1768, Bar Confederation. Oct. 8, 1768, Declaration of war by Turkey against Russia in support of Poland. Fall 1769, Formation of a unified command of Bar Confederacy at Presov. Oct. 22, 1770, Proclamation of impeachment of King Stanislas Augustus. 1770, High point of guerrilla warfare by the Bar Confederacy led by Casimir Pulaski (1747-1779) and Michael Oginski (1728-1800). May 1771, defeat of Col. Charles Dumouriez at Lanckorona. Sept 1771, Defeat of Oginski at Stolowicze. July 1771, Austro-Turkish alliance against Russia.

The 1768 "Kolishchizna" uprising in Ukraine for an end of policies encouraging colonization of former Wild Plains, serfdom and service by shifts (Koley). Killing of 200,000 Catholics and Jews. Feb. 1769, Berlin plan for Russia to buy off Austria and Prussia by joint partition of Poland. Summer 1769, Austro-Prussian negotiations. Russia the only sure and permanent guarantor of Berlin's acquisitions in Poland. Russia giving up Moldavia and Valachia won from the Turks as a price of peace with Austria.

The 1769-1772, Bar Confederacy in protest of Russian terrorism and subversion; fifty years of Russia's tactics to impose on Poland her protectorate resulting in a crisis of sovereignty and an open abuse of Poland's democratic process by Russia, Prussia and Austria, especially since Jan. 30, 1717 imposition of arbitration on the Silent Seym by Peter the Great of Russia and his guarantees for the Orthodox in Poland.

A.D. 1768-1772

WAR OF THE FIRST PARTITION

FOUGHT BY THE BAR CONFEDERACY

FOR INDEPENDENCE OF POLAND

AND

AGAINST RUSSIAN TERRORISM

BIRTH OF MODERN

POLISH NATIONALISM

Thousands of Poles deported to Siberia

1768-1772 WAR OF THE FIRST PARTITION FOUGHT BY THE BAR CONFEDERACY FOR INDEPENDANCE OF POLAND

Map: 1768-1772 War of The First Partition - Fought by the Bar Confederacy.
The Birth of Modern Polish Nationalism (the first in Europe).

THE END OF RUSSIAN PROTECTORATE

Austria, Russia and Prussia strive to make out of the Polish Nobles' Republic "The Republic of Anarchy" perverting Polish democratic process and traditional Polish republican institutions by an expert use of Polish constitution and bill of rights making a travesty out of them and using them to legalize destructive policies by such means as Seym Confederations and Liberum Veto.

Paralysis of the Republic fomented and exploited by neighboring powers was not curable by the democratic process. Tragedy brought by the victory of the political machines of the magnates in the regional assemblies(caused by the economic decline of the middle and lower gentry,primarily due to the 17th century deluge of invasions).Paradox of the once most militarized society of Europe unable to defend itself.

Prussia controlling the vital Vistula trade, an economic blockade of Gdansk Sept. 30, 1773, Partitions Ratified by the Seym controlled by Russia. King Stanislas Augustus protests the illegality of the partition and solicits Western help.

1790,False alliance of Prussia with Poland (betrayed by Prussia on Aug. 7, 1792 in exchange for participation in the Second Partition of Poland), a move to stiffen Polish position towards Russia and provoke the Polish Russian war of 1792.

Aug. 5, 1772, First partition of Poland. Austria 83,000 sq. km. and 2,650,000 population. Prussia 36,000 sq. km. and580,000 population. Russia 92,000 sq. km. with 1,300,000 people.

THE AGONY OF

THE FIRST REPUBLIC

AMIDST NATIONAL REBIRTH

AND ENLIGHTMENT

A. D. 1772

THE FIRST PARTITION

OF POLAND

THE END OF

RUSSIAN PROTECTORATE

Thousands of Poles deported to Siberia

A. D. 1772 THE FIRST PARTITION OF POLAND THE AGONY OF THE FIRST REPUBLIC AMIDST NATIONAL REBIRTH
Map: 1772 The First Partition of Poland During National Rebirth.

Oct. 14, 1773, Seym founded the Ministry of Education, named Commission for National Education. 1775, Created Association for Elementary Textbooks for preparation of standardized textbooks and school programs in Polish language.

1783, Polish Republic divided into two school provinces: the Kingdom of Poland under the University of Cracow and Grand Duchy of Lithuania under the University of Wilno. In 1776 the school system became financially autonomous. Jewish population preferred separate Talmudic schools in Hebrew and in Yiddish.

■ Two universities
▷ Nine junior colleges under universities
■ Main high schools. Seventy four main high schools under junior colleges
1600. elementary schools under high schools. Elementary schools were run by parishes
▲ Additional 14 private junior colleges of the Piarist fathers 1781–1790 about 17,000 pupils attended the 74 high schools annually. Half of the students were not from the gentry.

Under conditions of sovereignty the Seym passed on May 3, 1791, the first modern constitution in Europe ; voting appropriations for a 100,000-man army.

A.D. 1773

ENLIGHTENMENT IN POLAND

THE SCHOOL SYSTEM UNDER THE FIRST MINISTRY OF EDUCATION IN EUROPE

Map: 1773 The School System under the First Ministry of Education in Europe.

TREASON OF MAGNATES

1790, False alliance of Prussia with Poland (betrayed by Prussia on Aug. 7, 1792 in exchange for participation in the Second Partition of Poland), a move to stiffen Polish position towards Russia and provoke the Polish Russian war of 1792. Under conditions of sovereignty the Seym passed on May 3, 1791, the first modern constitution in Europe abolishing all the constraints which were basic for the Russian protectorate; voting appropriations for a 100,000-man army.

Jan. 9, 1792, End of Russo-Turkish War making available the Russian army against Poland. Feb 1792, Austro-Prussian anti-revolutionary alliance against France. April 27, 1792, Signing in St. Petersburg of the Act of Confederation dated falsely on May 14, 1792, at Targowica; condemning the "Democratic Revolution of May 3, 1791," by Russia's henchmen. Prussian blockade making impossible buying of arms for Poland.

1792 POLISH-RUSSIAN BATTLES

1 April 10 Mir
2 April 15 Boruszkowce
3 April 18 Zielence
4 July 4   Zelwa
5 July 18   Dubienka
6 July 23   Brzesc
7 August, 1792. Surrender of Warsaw by King Stanislas Augustus to "save unnecessary suffering."
8 March 28, 1793, surrender of besieged Gdansk to Prussian army; population rioting in protest.

A.D. 1792-93
WAR OF THE SECOND PARTITION OF POLAND
in 1793 FOUGHT IN DEFENSE OF THE CONSTITUTION OF MAY 3, 1791, BY 36,000 POLES AGAINST 97,000 RUSSIANS

Map: 1792-1793 War of the Second Partition.

Catherine II of Russia issues assurances that there will not be a Second Partition of Poland, the lie making conservative supporters of the Confederation of Targowica politically bankrupt. Jan. 23, 1793, Russo-Prussian Pact for the Second Partition of Poland signed in St. Petersburg during the war of Austria and Prussia against revolutionary France. Russia initiated the anti-French action.

Russia pays Prussia for war effort against France with participation in the robbery of Polish territory after lengthy parasitic economic growth at Poland's expense, the upstart Kingdom of Prussia became a European power with acquisition of Polish ethnic lands of Masuria, West Pomerania, Silesia, Gdansk Pomerania, and Greater Poland or Poznania.

Jan. 23, 1793, Second Partition of Poland
Russia takes 250,000 sq. km. and 3,000,000 people.
Prussia takes 51,000 sq. km. with 1,000,000 people.
Austria not participating in the Second Partition of Poland, trying to get Prussian and Russian support in her plans to annex Bavaria which was allied to the revolutionary France and thus was saved from annexation by the Austrian Empire.

A.D. 1793
SECOND PARTITION OF POLAND
ABOLITION OF THE CONSTITUTION OF MAY 3, 1791
RESTORATION OF LIBERUM VETO, FREE ELECTIONS AND RETURN TO ALL CONSTRAINTS MAKING POLAND A RUSSIAN PROTECTORATE

Map: 1793 The Second Partition of Poland.

Pressure to disarm the Republic was generated by fear of Russia, Prussia, and Austria of a potential revolution in Poland while Polish resistance offered opportunity for a final annexation of Polish lands, giving them total of over one million sq. km. and thereby making stable for a long time the alliance of the partitioning powers cemented by common criminal act against Polish Republic.

Battles of 1794
1 April 4, Raclawice
2 April 17, Warsaw
3 April 22, Wilno
4 May, Polaniec
5 June 6, Szczekociny
6 June 8, Chelm
June 30, Lublin
8 July 7-10, Raszyn
9 July 27-Sept. 5,
   Prussian attacks on
   Warsaw repulsed
10 August, uprising in
   Poznania
11 September 17, Krupczyce
12 September 19, Terespol
13 September 30, Gniezno
14 October 2, Bydgoszcz
15 October 10, Maciejowice
November 9, fall of
   Warsaw to the Russians
   amidst massacre of
   population

"War to Death Against Muscovite Tyranny" for "Liberty, Integrity, Independence," Proclamation of insurrection and a new constitution freeing peasantry from servitude. Call for 100,000 infantry and 10,000 cavalry supplied by newly organized production of gunpowder, guns, and ammunition in response to an order of Feb. 21, 1794 to reduce the army from 50,000 to 15,000 men.

A.D. 1794
WAR OF THE THIRD PARTITION
OF POLAND
IN DEFENSE OF INDEPENDENCE,
THE CONSTITUTION, AND
SOCIAL CONTRACT OF
THE POLISH REPUBLIC LED BY
TADEUSZ KOSCIUSZKO AGAINST
PRUSSIA, RUSSIA AND AUSTRIA

Map: 1794 War of the Third Partition - Kosciuszko Insurrection.

Nov 25, 1797 the final treaty of partition by Russia, Prussia and Austria including clause that the name of Poland "shall remain suppressed as from the present and forever ... " Partitions of Poland were condemned as an international pillage exposing illegitimacy of the Russian and Austrian empires and of Prussia where the lives of the people, their freedom and property were determined by the whims of despots.

1795 Annexations:
Russia 120,000 sq. km. with
1,200,000 people
Prussia 48,000 sq. km. with
1,000,000 people
Austria 47,000 sq. km. with
500,000 people
Annexations since 1772
Russia 463,200 sq. km. or
63.15% with
11,250,000 people
Prussia 141,000 sq. km. or
19.27% with
2,580,000 people
Austria 128,900 sq. km. or
17.57% with
3,150,000 people
Population numbers are a
sum of people present
at the time of each
annexation in 1772, 1793,
and 1795.

Polish fault of allowing "Golden Freedom" to become "Last Refuge of Scoundrels" a tool of foreign domination. Partitions were the answer of Russia, Prussia, and Austria to Polish efforts to reform the Republic. Vast Polish majority in the new Prussia resulting in Berlin's drive to acquire a German majority and thereby unify Germany under Prussia. Unique Jewish sanctuary and autonomy (since 1264) ended in Poland; 150 years of persecution by Russia begun to be ended by German perpetrated mass genocide of the Jews.

A.D. 1795
THE THIRD PARTITION
OF THE POLISH REPUBLIC
OBLITERATING THE ONLY HOPE
OF SELF-DETERMINATION
AND RULE BY CONSENT
OF THE GOVERNED
FOR PEOPLES BETWEEN GERMAN
AND RUSSIAN ETHNIC AREAS

RUSSIAN EMPIRE

OTTOMAN EMPIRE

FRAGMENTED GERMANY

BALTIC SEA

1795 THE THIRD PARTITION

Map: 1795 The Third Partition of Poland.

A.D. 1795 TOTAL OBLITERATION OF THE REPUBLIC — TERRITORIAL LOSSES

Polish Democracy of the Gentry 10% of population 1370-1648, Rise 1648-1772, Decline 1772-1795, Fall and Agony
1618 Territory of Polish Republic 1,060,000 km.sq. (including Livonia 50,000 and Ducal Prussia 20,000 km.sq.)
1686, Territory of Polish Republic 727,000 sq.km. (loss to Russia 311 km.sq., loss to Brandenburg-Prussia 22,000 sq.km. Partitions of Poland:
(1.) 1772 First (2.) 1792. Second (3.) 1795. Third)

1493. Polish Constitutional Commonwealth 1,270,000 sq.km. (including fiefs: Moldavia 105,00 sq.km. Mazovia 30,000 sq.km., and Prussia 20,000 km.)
1493, Polish Jagiellonian Realm 1,800,000 sq.km. (including Czech Kingdom 135,000 sq.km. and K. of Hungary 395,000 sq.km.)

1370-1795 Polish Commonwealth area of the greatest freedom in Europe — for about 400 years expanded on the basis of a voluntary union of Poland and Lithuania. Price of freedom: — government opened to internal and external abuse-democratic process fragile.

A.D. 1795 TOTAL OBLITERATION OF THE REPUBLIC TERRITORIAL LOSSES SINCE 1618
TO RUSSIA 773,000 sq.km. OR 73%
TO PRUSSIA 157,000 sq.km OR 15%
TO AUSTRIA 130,000 sq.km OR 12%

parasitic growth of Prussia at Poland's expense.

Map: 1795 Total Obliteration of the Republic - territorial losses since 1618.

A.D. 1795, As Poland sunk and the vultures of Austria, Prussia and Russia tore up her body, for about ten years German states achieved their maximum penetration into Slavic Europe. From then on each successive peace settlement starting in 1815 brought to the Germans a loss of land. This process continued as Austria disintegrated in 1918 and Germany in 1945, in 1795 Polish speakers represented over 60% of the population of the Kingdom of Prussia; Western and Southern Slavs constituted by far the majority in the German Habsburg Empire. In 1806 France abolished the Roman Empire of the German Nation which in reality was composed of 350 self-governing German states.

Polish struggle to preserve national culture: 1800, Founding of library and research center of Society of Friends of Science in Warsaw 1802, Reopening of the Polish University in Wilno; further growth of indigenous Polish scientific terms. 1805, Founding of Polish Liceum of Krzemieniec, a center of Polish culture in Ukraine.

1797-1803 Polish legions join the French revolutionary forces with hope to fight for the cause of an independent Poland against Austria, Prussia and eventually Russia. 1797, Widespread underground independence movement throughout Poland; mass imprisonments of Austrian and Russian Poles. 1806, Napoleon in conquered Berlin seeking Polish support.

Partitions of Poland did not have to happen. They were caused by parasitic growth at Poland's expense of the Hohenzollerns of Berlin, who were the initiators of the crime of partitions. Without their initiative and provocations Polish State would have survived undivided under Russian domination until Napoleonic campaigns - then in 1812 Poland could have tipped the scales in favor of France in war against Russia and thus, preserved Polish independence.

EUROPE AFTER A.D. 1795
OBLITERATION OF POLAND
BY AUSTRIA, PRUSSIA AND RUSSIA
RISE OF THE FRENCH REPUBLIC
SHORT LIVED
HIGH WATER MARK
OF GERMAN EXPANSION
ON THE SLAVIC TERRITORY

POLAND 1618

EUROPE AFTER A.D. 1795

Map: 1795 Europe after Obliteration of Poland. The Short Lived High Water Mark of German Expansion on the Slavic Territory.

PARTITIONS OF POLAND 1772 – 1795

ARCTIC OCEAN

ALASKA

KAMCHATKA

PACIFIC OCEAN

RUSSIAN EMPIRE

CHINESE EMPIRE

GREENLAND

ARCTIC CIRCLE

GR. BRITAIN

FRANCE

SPAIN

POLAND

PERSIA

OTTOMAN EMPIRE

AFRICA

INDIAN OCEAN

ARCTIC OCEAN

CANADA

1775 – 1783 AMERICAN WAR OF INDEPENDENCE

TROPIC OF CANCER

ATLANTIC OCEAN

THE EQUATOR

TROPIC

SOUTH AMERICA

sonal freedom and civil rights of the individual, freedom of religion, the value of self reliance, and prevention of the growth of authoritarian power of the state. These ideals formulated in the 15th and 16th century Poland were shared by Americans fighting for independence. Many Poles volunteered to serve the American cause motivated by common ideals and not to make money, as were most of the professional soldiers from Western Europe, with few exceptions.

Poles gave money and jewelry to the American cause. Most prominent among them were Generals Casimir Pulaski (1747-1779) and Tadeusz Kosciuszko (1746-1817). At different times each of them saved American Revolution from catastrophy. Kosciuszko did it by engineering October 17, 1777, the first major American victory at Saratoga without which the French would not join the war against the British. General Pulaski did it by preventing the impending surrender of Charleston, May 11, 1779, which was about to bring a catastrophic collapse of the American position in the South. General Pulaski, "The Eagle" of the Bar Confederacy had to face treason on both continents. Polish forces were divided between patriots and political machines of the aristocrats controlled by Russia, while American forces were divided between patriots and loyalists controlled by Britain. It was a loyalist named James Curie who deserted to the British and forewarned them. The American battle plan became a death trap. General Pulaski was killed on October 11, 1789. The tragic problem of disunity was weathered successfully in America thanks to the favorable geography. It ended with a mass exodus of loyalists to Canada. In Poland, attacked from all sides by greedy despotic regimes, disunity was one of the main causes of Polish tragedy and of the death of the First Republic. General Kosciuszko defined precisely the devastating problem of disunity in his Manifesto of Polaniec 1794.

First banner in history bearing the initials of the United States was made for the Casimir Pulaski Legion in 1778. Amidst the Era of Enlightenment, the tragedy of partitions of Poland shocked patriotic Poles. They believed in ideas such as: general elections, the social contract between government and the citizens, the principle of government by consent, per-

A.D. 1768 – 1794 THE STRUGGLE FOR LIBERTY IN POLAND AND AMERICA

POLAND, THE ATHENS OF SLAVIC EUROPE 1370 – 1795

Map: 1768-1795 Struggle for Liberty in Poland and America.

CANADA

UNITED STATES

ATLANTIC OCEAN

NEW YORK

JULY 23, 1777
BOSTON-MARBLEHEAD
ARRIVAL OF CASIMIR PULASKI

GEN. PULASKI
CAVALRY COMMANDER,
IN BATTLES:

1 Sept. 11, 1777
Brandywine
2 Oct. 4, 1777
Germantown
3 Oct. 14, 1777
Egg Harbor
4 April 11; 23, 1777
Chesnut Hill
5 March 1, 1778
Cooper's Ferry

OCT. 10,1 1779 Death of
Casimir Pulaski, the only
American general killed
in battle in the
War for Independence

6 April 1778 Baltimore founding of Pulaski's
Legion

7 May 11 - 12, 1779 Charleston, Pulaski preventing
surrender

8 Oct. 10, 1779 Battle of Savannah

9 Oct. 11, 1779 Death of General Casimir
Pulaski, Burial at sea

Oct. 22, 1779. Public funeral;
Nov. 29, 1779, Congressional committee
to erect Pulaski Monument;
Pulaski's epitaph by
King of Poland Stanislas Augustus Poniatowski:
"Pulaski has died as he lived—a hero—
but an enemy of kings."

BATTLEFIELD OF SARATOGA ON HUDSON RIVER

Kosciuszko chose and fortified the Saratoga site; he drew and
signed the plan above. Tadeusz Kosciuszko engineered the
American victory at Saratoga; his most important fortification
was West Point which he suggested for a military academy.
October 13, 1784 Tadeusz Kosciuszko was made Brigadier
General by the United States Congress followed by decoration
of General Tadeusz Kosciuszko with the prestigious Order of
Cincinnati — one of only three foreigners. July 1784 departure
from New York for Poland where Gen. Kosciuszko served as
division commander in the 1792 war of the second partition of
Poland and commander-in-chief in the 1794 war of the third
partition of Poland.

A. Kosciuszkes plan under
a. Kosciuszkes
B. Negdo Angielskie

Order of
Cincinnati

Decoration
for the Leaders
of the American
War for Independence

1777 TICONDEROGA
1777 SARATOGA
1777 VAN SCHAIK

1778-80 WEST POINT
NEW YORK 1776

PHILADELPHIA 1776

JULY 1776

ATLANTIC OCEAN

HALIFAX

GUILFORD

CHARLOTTE

FORT NINETY SIX

TRIUMPHAL ENTRY TO
CHARLESTON, DEC. 14, 1783

A.D. 1776 - 1783
CAMPAIGNS OF
POLISH SOLDIERS OF LIBERTY
SERVING IN AMERICAN
War of Independence

1778–1779 General Pulaski's Legion
1780–1782 Kosciuszko in the South

Fortification by
Tadeusz Kosciuszko

Maps: 1776-1783 Campaigns of Polish Soldiers of Liberty in American War of Independence.

A.D. 1386 – 1772

POLAND, THE ATHENS OF SLAVIC EUROPE 1370 – 1795

In 1634, the First Polish Republic (1569 – 1795) at the height of her success with a territory of one million square kilometers, still Europe's largest with population of 11½ million of which over one million were noble members of the Politi-cal Nation of Free Citizens of the Republic, in Polish, Rzeczpospolita (zhech-pos-po-lee-ta).

CASPIAN S.

1386-1454

1634

1667-1772*

BLACK SEA

LIVONIA 1561-1625

VILNO

KIEV

PODOLA

PSKOV

RIGA

BALTIC SEA

PRUSSIA 1454-1657

WARSAW

CRACOW

1386-1772

NORTH SEA

ADRIATIC

MEDITERRANEAN SEA

ATLANTIC OCEAN.

Development of civil liberties in Poland (1228 – 1791)

A.D. 1386 – 1772
TERRITORIAL DEVELOPMENT OF THE UNION OF POLAND–LITHUANIA

The area of the greatest political and religious freedom in Europe (1386 – 1795)

Turkish occupation of Podolia after the disgrace of Buczacz. OTTOMAN Turkish infringement on the Polish territory in Podolia caused the War of Mutual Attrition between Poland and Turkey. Both became the sick men of Europe. Polish plans of an alliance with France and eviction of the Brandenburgian Hohenzollerns from Prussia were torpedoed. This gave the Hohenzollerns a chance to continue their parasitic economic growth at the expense of the Polish Republic. Tiny Brandenburg was to initiate the plans for partitions of Poland. The exhaustion in Turkish wars led to imposition on Poland a minority candidate from Saxony as the head of state when Russian and Saxon troops grabbed the coronation site in Cracow and forced on Poland a disastrous Saxon administration. The "Saxon Night" brought in 1717 the crisis of sovereignty on the Republic; formalized by the "Seym Niemy", the Silent Seym which under duress of Rus-sian occupation did not voice an objection to the assumption by Peter the Great the role of an arbiter between the parliament of the Polish Republic and, the imposed upon her, Saxon administration.

TERRITORIAL DEVELOPMENT OF THE UNION OF POLAND-LITHUANIA

The area of the greatest political and religious freedom in Europe (1386 – 1795)

Map: 1386-1772 Territorial Development of the Union of Poland-Lithuania.

V. Century of Partitions of Poland (1795–1918)

The Struggle For Independence

THE PUŁAWY PLAN

THE "SLAVIC CARD" AND ADAM CZARTORYSKI PLAN

Adam Czartoryski (1743-1823) Proposed to attack neutral Prussia with over 60% Polish population to recover Polish lands and restore Poland in union with Russia under Tsar Alexander. Polish aristocracy welcomed the Tsar in Puławy in 1805 when he was in reality on his way to sign a pact with Prussia, blackmailed into cooperation by the Slavic card of Russia shown in four stages on this map. 140 years later Stalin was able to unite all Slavs in the Russian bloc—but this time instead of defending the old feudal order, he was able to enforce the modern feudalism Soviet-style. He did it with American and British help.

Polish Soldiers, while disgusted with the ugly pacifications which Napoleon made them do, believed that France was the only true opponent of the partitioning powers cemented by their common robbery of one million square kilometers of land of the Old Polish Republic. They believed that Russian use of the Slavic card would not bring restoration of a free Poland true to the traditional Polish values.

Playing the Slavic card, Tsar Alexander permitted reopening of the Polish university at Wilno and college at Krzemieniec. Both became flourishing centers of Polish culture. In 1806 there was

published the huge dictionary of the Polish language which then was equally developed as was the German. Polish then was the most advanced among Slavic languages of Europe, including Russian.

UNREALIZED PLAN OF ADAM CZARTORYSKI

THE "SLAVIC CARD" AND ADAM CZARTORYSKI PLAN

A.D. 1800

UNREALIZED PLAN OF ADAM CZARTORYSKI KNOWN AS THE PUŁAWY PLAN

BECOMING A PART OF THE "SLAVIC CARD" PLAYED BY TSAR ALEXANDER I

TO WHIP IN LINE

THE ANTI-FRENCH ALLIANCE OF RUSSIA, AUSTRIA, AND PRUSSIA

Area populated by the Slavs outside Russian Empire

CASPIAN S.

RUSSIAN EMPIRE

CAUCASUS MTS.

KURA R.

KIZIL R.

RUSSIAN EMPIRE

VOLGA R.

DON R.

BLACK SEA

OTTOMAN EMPIRE

DNIEPER R.

KRZEMIENIEC

WILNO

PRYPET R.

RIGA

DVINA R.

PSKOV L.

RUSSIAN EMPIRE

RUSSIAN EMPIRE

EUROPE'CENTRAL MERIDIAN

K. OF SWEDEN

BALTIC SEA

K. OF PRUSSIA

VORMARK

GULF OF BOTHNIA

NORTH SEA

K. OF GREAT BRITAIN

FRAGMENTED GERMANY

AUSTRIAN EMPIRE

DANUBE R.

OLT R.

ADRIATIC

PAPAL STATE

K. OF NAPLES

ALPS

RHINE R.

MOSEL R.

FRENCH REPUBLIC AND DEPENDENCIES

SEINE R.

LOIRE R.

GARONNE R.

PYRENEES MTS.

EBRO R.

K. OF SPAIN

ATLANTIC OCEAN

MEDITERRANEAN SEA

TUNIS

ALGIERS

SHARIFATE OF MOROCCO

KILOMETERS

MILES

0 200 400 600

0 200 400

THE "SLAVIC CARD" PLAYED TO WHIP IN LINE THE ANTI-FRENCH ALLIANCE OF RUSSIA–AUSTRIA–PRUSSIA

Map: 1800 The "Slavic Card" and Adam Czartoryski Plan.

"STRUGGLE FOR THE RIGHTS OF MAN"

Nov. 9, 1799, Napoleon seized power
Dec. 2, 1805 Crowned emperor
July 12, 1806 Abolished Roman
Empire of Germany jigsaw of 350 states
into French controlled Confedera-
tion of the Rhine.

Napoleon's Victories:
1 Oct. 20, 1805, ULM (Austrians)
2 Dec. 2,1805 Austerlitz (Austro-
Russian)
3 Oct. 17, 1806 Jena and Auerstadt
(Prussians)
4 June 14, 1807 Friedland (Russians)
Victories won by superior tactics.

Seeing French exploitation of the Polish
cause, Jozef Pawlikowski (c. 1770–1829), associated with General Tadeusz Kosciuszko, published the program for national liberation
and improvement of the lot of all (the publication of 1800 immediately confiscated by the
French police.)

July 7, 1807, Peace of Tilsit creates out of Polish
provinces taken by Prussia in the second and third
partition a Grand Duchy of Warsaw (less Bialystok
taken by Russia) as a French protectorate.

1797-1803 POLISH LEGIONS

★ Centers of Formation of Polish Legions
→ Movements of Polish Troops
⊙ Siege by Polish Troops
⬤ Movements of French Troops

A.D. 1807
GRAND DUCHY OF WARSAW
A FRENCH PROTECTORATE

BEGINNING OF EXPLOITATION BY NAPOLEON
OF POLISH STRUGGLE FOR INDEPENDENCE

1797-1803 POLISH LEGIONS IN THE
"STRUGGLE FOR THE RIGHTS OF MAN"
USED TO PUT DOWN ITALIAN REVOLTS
LOSING 6,000 MEN IN PUTTING DOWN
NEGRO REVOLT IN HAITI 1802-3

Jan. 9, 1797, Founding of Polish Legions by
Napoleon in Lombard. Within a year 10,000 men
(total of 20,000 passed through the Legions.)

A.D. 1807 GRAND DUCHY OF WARSAW — A FRENCH PROTECTORATE

■→ Sea Transport of Polish Troops

BEGINNING OF EXPLOITATION BY NAPOLEON OF POLISH STRUGGLE FOR INDEPENDENCE

Map: 1807 Grand Duchy of Warsaw - A French Protectorate.

Map: 1809 Invasion by Austria.

A.D. 1812 THE "SECOND POLISH WAR" OF NAPOLEON FAILURE OF NAPOLEON'S CONQUEST OF EUROPE

Map: 1812 "The Second Polish War" of Napoleon - conquest of Moscow.

Population of Europe 200 Million

Russia 50M.   Spain 13M.
France 30M   Eur. Turkey 11M.
Austria 30M.   Low Countries 6M.
Germany 23M.   Portugal 3½M.
Britain 19M.   Sweden 3½M.
Italy 14M.   Denmark 1½M.
   Suiss 2M.

Poland Partitioned Into:
1 Kingdom of Poland under Russia
2 Kingdom of Galicia and Lodomeria
    Grand Duchy of Poznan under Prussia.
3 Free Republic of Krakow (Cracow),
    other Polish lands directly incor-
    porated into Russia, Prussia, and Austria.

11M. Poles in partitioned Poland
4M. Polish Kingdom under Russia
3½M. Northwestern Provinces (Poznania,
    Pomerania Masuria and Silesia).
3M. Southern Provinces (Cracovia,
    Galicia, Silesia)
1½ M. In Russian Provinces (Lithuania,
    Latvia, Ukraine, Byelorussia).

A.D. 1815
Truncated
POLISH CONSTITUTIONAL KINGDOM
WITHIN
THE RUSSIAN EMPIRE

1806 Napoleon Abolishes
Holy Roman Empire

Map; 1815 Polish Constitutional Kingdom within Russian Empire (population numbers).

**A.D. 1815
ABUSE OF POLAND
AT THE CONGRESS OF VIENNA**

Poland not represented, abused.

West and south to be Germanized;
Eastern part to be Russified
central part to be the only
constitutional kingdom
inside autocratic Russian Empire

Grand Duchy of Poznan with a make believe "Autonomy" under the yoke of Prussia

1815, Poland in a vicious circle, each of the parties to the congress committed to make Polish lands as useless as possible to the power of the others. Patchwork area of fragmented Germany reduced for the benefit of Prussia starting the process of reducing the Polish majority within the Prussian state. "Kingdom of Poland," "Congress Poland or "Congress Kingdom" "Forever" united with Russia made out of a cut down area of the Grand Duchy of Warsaw. The Tsar promises expansion of the Kingdom on other Polish lands within the Russian Empire.

Kingdom of Poland constitution written by Adam Czartoryski, autocratic corrections by Tsar Aleksander I, has provisions to abolish serfdom and establish equl rights for all before the law, personal freedom, and freedom of the press. Under a figure-head viceroy: "Namiestnik (namyest-neek) while real power in hands of commander of the army, The Grand Duke Constantine and the "Imperial Commissioner" Nikolai Novosiltsov, both opposed to the constitution. Autonomy lasted from 1815 to 1831.

Kingdom of Galicia and Lodomeria under the Austrian yoke named with Ukrainian names to foment Polish-Ukrainian difficulties within the conglomerate Austrian Empire.

Turkish Ottoman Empire continuing as "The sick man of Europe" ever since the 1683 defeat in the Battle of Vienna by Polish King John III Sobieski.

Poland not represented.

Neutral Republic of Cracow "Guaranteed" by Russia, Prussia, and Austria, weak. Free enough to serve as a fuse to provoke a national uprising for more benefit to the West than to Poland.

A.D. 1815 ABUSE OF POLAND AT THE CONGRESS OF VIENNA

Map: 1815 Abuse of Poland at the Congress of Vienna.

NOVEMBER UPRISING

Nov. 19, 1830, Mobilization order in Warsaw: Russia moving to uphold the "Holly Alliance" of 1815, readying the Polish army against the French. Revolution of July 1830, and upheaval in Belgium. Russian troops to be moved to Poland. Nov. 19, 1830, revolution in Warsaw by patriotic gentry students and cadets leaving selection of leadership to the democratic process; Seym controlled by conservaties; Seym slow to change the government and army command to dedicated patriots committed to struggle for independence as the supreme national goal; wasting of time by indecisive leadership of conservative generals. Nov. 30, 1830, revolutionary throngs attack Warsaw arsenal and engage Russian garrison in combat. Nov. 30, 1831, old town of Warsaw in control of the revolutionaries. Aristocrats led by Czartoryski and Lubecki, fear social reforms, conspire against the revolution. Select hero of Napoleonic wars Gen. Jozef Chlopicki (1771-1854), a conservative dictator who did not believe that war with Russia was possible since Polish military success would revive the anti-Polish alliance of Russia, Prussia and Austria. Dec. 5, 1830, law and order restored. Russian army permitted to leave Poland unmolested; secret negotiations with the Tsar who in Jan. 1831, demanded an unconditional surrender, Chlopicki yielding his authority to the Seym. Dethronement of the Tsar as a King of Poland. "For freedom ours and yours" written on Polish banners. Gen. Jan Skrzynecki (1787-1860) elected commander in chief after several Polish victories trying to get reconfirmation of constitution of 1815 and evacuation of Russian army from Poland. Fumbling Gen. Pradzynski's plan for defeat of Russian army. Oct. 11, Gen. Henryk Dembinski (1791-1846) nominated commander in chief; suspected traitors executed by revolutionaries. Sept. 8, 1831, surrender of Warsaw to Russian forces vastly superior in numbers. Oct. 5, 1831, 20,000 Poles under Gen. Maciej Rybinski (1784-1874) cross the Prussian border. Oct. 9, surrender of Modlin. Oct. 21, 1831, surrender of Zamosc. Tsar Nicolas abolishing the Seym and liquidating the Polish army. Russification intensified; building of a citadel-prison in Warsaw.

Total of 23 battles fought in 1831; four main battles: 1. Feb. 24-25, Warsaw-Praga; 2. Apr. 10, Iganie; 3. May 26, Ostroleka; 4. Sept. 6-7, Warsaw-Wola Polish army the best trained in Europe by veterans of Napoleonic campaigns; brilliant tactical plans by Gen. Ignacy Pradzynski (1792 – 1850) whose classical plans were not used by conservative Generals.

A.D. 1830 – 1831
Revolution in Warsaw

WAR WITH RUSSIA

Armies: Polish 40,000
vs. Russian 120,000

↑ Russians

↓ Polish main force

⤹ Polish Guerilla

campaign of Gielgud, Chlapowski
and Dembinski; Gen. Gielgud ◢
Gen. Dembinski

NOVEMBER UPRISING 1830-1831

A.D. 1830 – 1831 Revolution in Warsaw—War against Russia–Armies: Polish 40,000 vs. Russian 120,000
Map: 1830-1831 November Uprising; Revolution in Warsaw; Polish-Russian War.

1848 SLAVIC CONGRESS OF PRAGUE

1844-1848 Peasant Riots in Silesia

1846 Revolution of Cracow
1848 Uprising in Poznania

1846 Peasant Uprising in Galicia Pogrom of 450 Manors

Battles under Polish Generals

Jozef Bem (1794-1850)
Henryk Dembinski (1791-1864)

Wojciech Chrzanowski (1793-1861)
Ludwik Mieroslawski (1814-1878)
Franciszek Sznayde (1790-1850)

Battles Participation of Poles Polish Legion and Volunteers

Polish Military Camps Forming Centers of Polish Forces

1846 Abolition of Cracow Republic annexation by Austria

1849 Austro-Hungarian Conflict Polish Generals in command defeated by Russian invasion of Hungary

Threat of Polish national uprising led by patriotic gentry was averted in 1846 rising in which 450 manorial estates were destroyed in Galicia. In order to weaken Polish national strength, Russia permitted annexation of Cracow by Austria, thusexcluding the ancient Polish capital and center of Polish culture from the territory of Kingdom of Poland.

CENTERS OF POLISH POLITICAL EMIGRATION

A.D. 1844-1849 POLES LEADING IN THE REVOLUTIONS

A.D. 1844-1849
POLES LEADING IN THE REVOLUTIONS AFTER 1830-1831 WAR WITH RUSSIA
CENTERS OF POLISH POLITICAL EMIGRATION
1848 SLAVIC CONGRESS OF PRAGUE

Map: 1844-1849 Poles Leading in European Revolutions.

Map: 1850 Industry on the Polish Lands.

JANUARY UPRISING

Clandestine government collected taxes, kept order by its police force and penetrated Russian administration and military garrisons. Polish diplomatic activity reached all capitals of Europe. Emissaries were sent to all parts of pre-partition Republic of Poland-Lithuania. Polish revolutionary nationalism became a role model for the Byelorussians, Ukrainians and Jews.

1860 Resistance to serf labor on 160,000 farms in Kingdom of Poland, the last Polish area where serfdom was not abolished Jan. 14, 1863, National uprising and intense conspiratorial activity in Warsaw forced into the open by forced conscription of Poles to the Russian army. Heaviest fighting was in central Poland, south of Kielce. Uprising became strong in Lithuania. Most effecient leadership by Romuald Traugutt (1826-1864), Oct. 17, 1863, became a dictator; did not expect intervention from the West; issued a peasant emancipation decree and started conversion to regular warfare based on total mobilization including peasants. After arrest, executed on Aug. 5, 1864. Uprising ended in spring of 1865 in Podlasie. Total of 1229 battles and engagements were fought in the guerrilla war. Uprising started by urban revolutionaries ended with guerrilla struggle of peasant volunteers.

Well organized clandestine command in Warsaw in control of a guerrilla war which kept the Russian army (the largest in Europe) at bay for sixteen months. The first European campaign of urban guerrilla forerunner of the Polish Revolution of 1905-1907 and World War II struggle against the German terror.

A.D. 1863-1864
JANUARY UPRISING
A GUERRILLA WAR
IN KINGDOM OF POLAND
LITHUANIA, UKRAINE AND BYELORUSSIA

AGAINST RUSSIA
WEAPONS AND VOLUNTEERS FROM AREAS OF AUSTRIAN AND PRUSSIAN PARTITION OF POLAND:

1864 massive deportation to Siberia of insurgents.

Map: 1863-1864 January Uprising - Guerrilla War Against Russia - Final Elimination of Serfdom.
(Coinciding with abolition of slavery in America.)

November 1830 vs. January 1863. Insurrection started by gentry patriots vs. town people, total 120,000 soldiers vs. 200,000 revolutionaries. Maximum under arms, 87,000 vs. 25,000 guerrillas. The 1831 defeat brought the end of autonomy, abolition of the constitution and seym, and liquidation of the Polish army. Massive emigration. 1864 defeat brought an intense Russification; Russian in schools and courts; massive deportation to Siberia of insurgents.

Net effect of both insurrections was a tremendous strengthening of Polish national identity and of commitment to the cause of national independence, after November insurrection Poles were in the forefront of the struggle of national liberation in Central and Western Europe and provided it with professional military leadership during the Spring of the Nations of 1848.

After January insurrection, the independence movement gained the support of the peasant masses. Emancipation of the peasants by the Polish revolutionary government forced the Tsar of Russia to accept the emancipation of Polish peasants. Liquidation of serfdom brought modern industrialization and labor movement. Emancipation of peasants brought their commitment to the cause of national independence. Rise of labor movements throughout Europe brought during World War I the collapse of partitioning powers of Russia, Austria, and Germany. The movement of Polish labor of peasant stock blossomed in solidarity, the 10,000,000-man Free Labor Union of 1980.

Kingdom of Poland 128,500 sq.km.
Population: 75% Poles, 10% Jews, 7.5% Germans, 5% Lithuanians, 2.5% Others

Polish Population Numbers:
1830 - 1 Kingdom: 4,300,000; Warsaw: 135,000
1863-4 Kingdom: 5,000,000 Warsaw: 223,000

A.D. 1830-1864
JANUARY UPRISING 1863-1864
A GUERRILLA WAR
COMPARED WITH: 1830-1831
NOVEMBER UPRISING
A CONVENTIONAL WAR

AREA OF INTENSE FIGHTING:
JANUARY UPRISING
SUPERIMPOSED ON THE
NOVEMBER UPRISING

Map: 1830-1864 A Comparison of November and January Uprisings.

Map: 1900 Industry and Railroads in Polish Lands.

RUSSIFICATION PROGRAM IN POLISH AREAS

RUSSIAN EMPIRE

PRUSSIAN EMPIRE SINCE 1871

CHELM

WARSAW

KINGDOM OF POLAND

BALTIC SEA

AUSTRIAN EMPIRE

Legalized German Discrimination Against Poles

GERMAN COLONIZATION COMMISSION AGAINST POLISH LANGUAGE AND LAND OWNERSHIP

A.D. 1905-1907
THE STRUGGLE TO PRESERVE
POLISH LANGUAGE AND
LAND OWNERSHIP
AGAINST ACTIVITIES OF THE
GERMAN COLONIZATION COMMISSION
AND RUSSIFICATION PROGRAM
IN POLISH AREAS

German Colonization Commission 1886-1917 Total Appropriation of 995,000,000 marks for acquisition of Polish-owned land for Germans

Peasants strike for Polish language in schools and in rural self-government against Russification program

Polish the official language in Galicia in Government and schools since 1861 after Austrian defeat in Italy in 1859

Universities: Language of Instruction:

German or Russian

Polish

Polish Scientific Societies

Struggle for the use of Polish language in secondary Education

Center of Polish intellectual life. Polish press and secondary schools

Chelm Region separated from the Polish Kingdom in 1912.

Map: 1905-1907 Struggle to Preserve Polish Language and Land Ownership.

A.D. 1905-1907 REVOLUTION- URBAN GUERRILLA AND MASSIVE PEASANT STRIKES

700 Peasants Strikes Armed resistance to police; demands for Polish as the official language in Poland.

Jan. 28, 1905, four-week general strike by 400,000, 1905-1906, 6,991 work stoppages involving 1,300,000 people. Urban guerrillas bomb tsarist officials and eliminate criminal element in Warsaw.
May Day 1905, 45 killed, 105 wounded. Dec. 29, 1906, execution of 105 urban guerrillas. Fighting on barricades, police terror gaining upper hand.

Important center of major strikes in Prussian and Austrian Polish provinces before 1905.

Important centers of strikes in Prussian and Austrian Poland in 1905-1907.
Oct. 13, 1904, First shots fired by demonstrators in Warsaw Jan 22, 1905, "Bloody Sunday" in Petersburg.

Sept. 1905, Russia signing humiliating treaty ending the war with Japan.
Polish language reinstated in schools.

Oct. 30, 1905, Tsarist government agreeing to general elections and legislative powers of parliament. Duma — recognition of the basic civil rights of inhabitants of the Russian Empire.

Map; 1905-1907 Revolution, Urban Guerrilla, and Massive Peasant Strikes.

HAWAII 0/0-0/5%

100
MILES

Note: 1980 census results indicated that of the Americans fully or partly of Polish descent 8.2 million still identified themselves as Polish.

2-4%

4-6%

4-6%

6%+

6%+

ALASKA
0.0-0.5%

6%+

0.5-2%

Polish-
-Americans
by states
of highest
density in
1980 census:

0 200 400
MILES

Wisconsin	11%
Connecticut	10%
Michigan	10%
New Jersey	9%
Illinois	9%
Pennsylvania	8%
New York	8%
Massachusetts	7%

0 300 600
KILOMETERS

A.D. 1914
POLISH-AMERICANS AS
A PERCENT OF POPULATION
Note: 1980 census results

POLISH EMIGRATION 1870-1914

RUSSIA
300,000

UNITED STATES
2,600,000

2

OTHER AMERICAN STATES 200,000

A.D. 1914
POLISH
EMIGRATION
1870-1914

1000 2000
KILOMETERS

1 GERMANY 400,000
2 WESTERN EUROPE 100,000

Map; 1914 Polish Americans as a Percent of Population - compared to 1980; 1870-1914 Polish Emigration.

VI. The Second Polish Republic (1918–1945)

REBUILDING OF THE NATION

POLAND'S VICTORY OVER THE SOVIETS IN 1920, DURING

THE REVOLUTION IN GERMANY, DELAYED COMMUNIST ADVANCE

INTO CENTRAL EUROPE FOR A QUARTER OF A CENTURY.

Map: 1918 Demands for Rebuilding the Polish Republic.

Map: 1918-1922 Comparison of Demanded and Actual Frontiers.

A.D. 1918-1922
COMPARISON OF DEMANDED
AND ACTUAL FRONTIERS

BORDERS:
Actual
Demanded

COMPARISON OF DEMANDED AND ACTUAL FRONTIERS

Borders of the Polish Republic vs.
Romand Dmowski Line demanded at the
Paris Peace Conference in 1918.

SWEDEN
BALTIC SEA
VITEBSK
DWINA
KIEV
LUBLIN
DNIESTER R.
BEREZYNA
MINSK
PRIPET R.
ZBRUCZ R.
LITHUANIA
VILNO VILNIUS
GRODNO
BARANOWICZE
PINSK
PRIPET R.
ROWNE
LUCK
ZLOCZOW
TARNOPOL
DNIESTER R.
KOVNO KAUNAS
BIALYSTOK
BUG R.
ZAMOSC
SOKAL
LWOW
PRZEMYSL
GALICIA
KOENIGSBERG
OLSZTYN
MAZURIA
SIEDLCE
WIEPRZ R.
PULAWY
SAN R.
RZESZOW
KROSNO
VISTULA DELTA
NAREW RIVER
WARSAW
WISLA R.
RADOM
KIELCE
SANDOMIERZ
WISLA R.
GDANSK POMERANIA
TORUN
MAZOVIA
LODZ
CRACOW
SILESIA
WEST POMERANIA
POZNAN
POZNANIA
SILESIA
STETTIN
BERLIN
BRANDENBURG
DRESDEN DREZNO
PRAGUE

KILOMETERS
MILES
200
100
50
100
0

BUG R.

A.D. 1918-1922 SIX CONCURRENT WARS ON THE BORDERS OF POLAND

6. Soviet-Polish War started with Soviet advance on Vilno, Nov. 1918; fought by Poles to maintain the independence of Poland the Baltic states, Byelorussia, and Ukraine against Soviet recreating of the Tsarist empire under Communist Government and against spreading of the revolution to the countries of Western Europe. It continued until October 18, 1920 and ended with the treaty of Riga, March 19, 1921. Polish army casualties 250,000; 48,000 dead; Soviet casualties considered higher.

1. Ukrainian war Nov. 1918 to July 1919, ended with the collapse of the West Ukrainian Republic and Polish control over Galicia to the River Zbrucz.

4. Lithuanian War for Vilno (Vilnius), July 1919, to Oct. 1920, ended without a peace treaty.

2. Poznanian War with Germany, Dec. 27, 1918, June, 28, 1919.

German terror causing Polish uprising in Silesia

3. Silesian War with Germany; three uprisings; Aug. 16-24, 1919; Aug. 19-25; 1920; and May 2-July 5, 1921; settled in Geneva in 1922 in Silesian Convention.

5. Czechoslovak War of Cieszyn (Tesin); Czechoslovak invasion in violation of a local agreement. During Soviet advance on Warsaw terminated by Allied arbitration July 28, 1920, giving to the Czechs Zaolzie with over 200,000 Poles and 400 sq. miles of rich industrial and mining area located in the strategic Moravian Gate to Poland. (Poland recovered this area in 1938 to prevent Germany from occupying it). Questionable timing even though the operation followed Polish-Czech agreement in face of Nazi advance.)

SIX CONCURRENT WARS ON THE BORDERS OF POLAND

Map: 1918-1922 Six Concurrent Wars for the Borders of Poland.

A.D. 1919-1920 DEMOCRATIC UNION OF STATES PROPOSED BY MARSHAL JOZEF PILSUDSKI A FEDERATION OF NATIONS BETWEEN GERMANY AND RUSSIA BASED ON SELF-DETERMINATION

Nov. 1917 Finnish Bolsheviks occupied South Finland were defeated by Finnish army under Tsarist General Mannerheim who controlled all Finland by mid-1918. Estonia won independence from Russia in 1918, served as a base for the unsuccessful attack on Petrograd, 1919 by Yudenich. Latvia independent from Russia: 1918, Poles captured Dvinsk for Latvia and received Latvian support for federation plan. Vilno claimed by Poland and Lithuania was inhabited by Polish majority; occupied by Poles April 1919; by Bolsheviks July 19, 1920; the Poles in Oct. 1920. Regional parliament of Middle Lithuania voted for incorporation with Poland; Byelorussia, part of Poland unitl 1795, occupied by the Poles in 1919, invited to join Pilsudski's federation. Ukraine formerly part of Polish-Lithuanian state until 1795. Emerging weak nationalism did not give full support to the free Ukrainian government of Semion Petlura allied with Poland.In May 1920 Poles captured Kiev; Bolsheviks drove the Poles out June 1920.

Lithuania independent from Russia 1918; until 1795 in union with Poland refused to renew the union.

Poland rewon its independence in 1918; had token French, but not British support, in its struggle against the Bolsheviks.

British government of Lloyd George considered Poland an ally of France; as George was motivated by fear of France and was receptive to anti-Polish views of Lewis Namier. Namier apparently falsified the decision of the Allied Commission by secretly redrawing the Curzon line at a critical moment to exclude the city of Lvov from Poland.

Jozef Pilsudski, head of state of the Polish Republic proposed federation based on freedom and self-determination against Soviet violence and brutality. Federation failed primarily because the Ukrainians did not support their government of Semion Petlura. Because England fearing growth of French power as the traditional ally of Poland, refused to support with weapons the federation plan of a powerful democratic union capable of stabilizing Central and Eastern Europe and preventing World War II.

East Galicia of urban Polish majority and rural Ukrainian majority occupied by the Poles in 1919 against the wishes of the Paris Peace Conference.

Kuban base of anit-Bolshevik army of Denikin who refused to cooperate with the Poles and recognize the Polish state.

Crimea 1919-1920; a base for the anti-Bolshevik army of Wrangel.

Don Cossacks, allied with the Poles, formed the first volunteer White Army.

Republics of Georgia Armenia and Azerbaijan received envoys from Poland in February 1920, but were conquered by the Bolsheviks in 1920-1921

DEMOCRATIC UNION OF STATES— A FEDERATION OF NATIONS

Map: 1919-1920 Pilsudski's Federation Plan of Nations Between Germany and Russia.

Map: Nov.1918-Mar.1919 Polish Soviet War. Failure of Soviet "Target Vistula" Offensive.

MAR. – DEC. 1919 – POLISH COUNTEROFFENSIVE. POLISH SOVIET WAR – 1919-1920

The First round leading to massive operations and life and death struggle for survival of Soviet Russia and of the Republic of Poland Transition from the trench warfare to a highly mobile war.

"Psychological Warfare by Disinformation. Sept. 3, 1919, Soviets form "Bureau of Illegal Activities" for subversion and sabotage behind Polish lines using appeals of the Polish prisoners.

Polish objectives reached by the end of August. Pilsudski rejects the idea of a fall march on Moscow.

Soviets sue for peace in order to achieve victory in civil war. Territorial concessions to Poland meaningless since Europe is on the verge of Communist revolution. Peace negotiations start secretly in June 1919. Nov. 2 Soviets agree to return Polish hostages; Nov. 9, exchange of civilian prisoners; Nov. 3, Pilsudski's conditions for a ceasefire include the front line as a new Polish Soviet border: Soviet evacuation of Dvinsk; Soviet recognition of the free Ukrainian government of Hetman Petlura.

On Dec. 14, 1919, Lenin refuses to accept Polish demands on behalf of the Ukrainians resulting in the break off of the peace negotiation, preparations for a huge military showdown in 1920

Beginning of struggle for survival of Second Polish Republic and Soviet Russia A major source of Polish intelligence is Polish underground military organization formed in 1914 in Byelorussia and Ukraine with cells from Riga in Latvia to Rostov on Don and Stavropol in the Kuban.

First the Tsarist Generals more dangerous to Polish independence than the Soviets.

Main Polish Operations
1. Operation Wilno, Apr. 1919
2. Operation Minsk, Aug. 1919
3. Operation Luniniec Polesie Feb. to Sept. 1919
4. Operation Vholyn Dec. 1918, Against Ukrainian Directory; Summer 1919 Against the Soviets; Autumn against Denikin
5. Operation Galicia, April-July 1919, against West Ukraine and then against the Soviets
6. Operation Dvinsk, Jan. 3, 1920 against Soviets to capture Dvinsk for the Latvians
Latvian order December 2, 1920, to be executed by Dec. 15th

Dec 16 Soviets enter Kiev

Dec. 1919, Polish Front in Ukraine

PETLURA'S RETREAT

KAMIENIEC

POLOCK

SWIECIANY

BORISOV

MINSK 2
SEPT 1919

BOBRUJSK

BARANOWICZE

SEPT 1919 LUNINIEC 3

PRIPET R.

VOLHYN 4

SEPT 1919 GALICIA 5

DNIESTER R.

WILNO

MARCH 1919

GRODNO

BIALYSTOK

PINSK

PRIPET R. DEC 1919

BRZESC

Chelm

LWOW (LVOV) MARCH 1919

JAN. 3, 1920 6

KOVNO KAUNAS

KROLEWIEC KOENIGSBERG

BAY OF GDANSK

GDANSK

BRANDENBURG

WARTA R.

POZNAN

KALISZ

WARSAW

MAZOVIA

LODZ

RADOM

KIELCE

KRAKOW (CRACOW)

RZESZOW

SAN R.

LUBLIN

LUKOW

SIEDLCE

WIEPRZ R.

MINSK MAZOWIECKI

SILESIA

KILOMETERS
MILES
0 50 100
0 100 200

Map: Mar.-Dec. 1919 Polish Soviet War - Polish Counteroffensive.

POLISH COUNTER OFFENSIVES

SOVIET POLISH WAR 1918-1920

BATTLES OF MINSK AND DVINSK

By the end of Aug. 1919, cities with large Polish population: Vilno, Minsk, and Lwow secured as were the eastern areas of Polish settlement occupied by the Polish army and secure for Poland. Pilsudski rejects the idea of a fall march on Moscow and accepts armistice talks with the Soviets.

Developing pincer movement concentrated attacks strategy by the Poles for the mobile war against the Soviets; Polish Soviet war fought on World War I surplus material. The war was conducted by Polish veterans of World War I.

End of August 1919 stabilization of the Soviet-Polish front line from the Dvina River in the north to the Zbruch and Dniester River in the south.

SOVIET BYELORUSSIA

A.D. 1919-1920
BATTLES OF MINSK AND DVINSK

SCALE:
KILOMETERS
0 20 40 60 80 100 120 140 160
0 20 40 60 80 100
MILES

Polish Soviet War 1918-1920
Mobile war a change from the trench warfare. Polish Front Sept. 1919.
Operation Minsk July 20, Aug. 1919
Operation Dvinsk Jan. 1920 "Operation Winter" Jan. 3 at -25C on Jan. 5, 1920, completed and ended the Polish Soviet campaign of 1919.

Ignorance and confusion in the Western capitals concerning the situation on the Soviet-Polish front. Wrong notion about Lenin's "Peace Party". Poor reading of the Polish and Soviet Potential. Hostility of the Tsarist Whites towards the Poles.

Note Bialystok region occupied by the German army until Aug. 1919, in accordance with the Polish-German Agreement of Feb. 5, 1919.

Jan. 1920, Conference of the Baltic states presented with Pilsudski's plan of a federation of the border states and breakaway Russian provinces. General fear to join without strong allied support; only Ataman Semyon Petlura's free Ukrainian government joined the cause of anti-Soviet alliance.

BATTLES OF MINSK AND DVINSK

Map: 1919-1920 Battles for Minsk and Dvinsk.

APRIL – MAY 1920 POLISH OFFENSIVE ON KIEV

SOVIET POLISH WAR 1918-1920

Polish Invasion of Ukraine to win time causing Poland to prepare pre-emptive attacks.

Polish preparations to cut Soviet supply line at Mogilev and Zlobin.

The Mozyr Operation March 5-7 Gen. Sikorski takes large stores of weapons and armored trains in the Mozyr operation.

Soviets deploy vastly superior forces

One and half million men deployed on the front stretching from Latvia to Romania.

Soviets committing 800,000 men; Poles 750,000 men.

Four Polish armies against : 25 Soviet divisions in six armies

KK = Kavkor=Cavalry Corps

XV, April 28, Start of Soviet preparation of offensive under Gen. Tukhachevsky to cross Dvina and Berezina rivers with 700,000 men

March 10, 1920, Soviet order for a major offensive to the West. British supplies for Denikin taken over by the Soviets.

March 19, Soviet attack from Zlobin using airplanes and tanks.

Soviet armies: III IV XV XV KK

May 7 Polish Army in Kiev

April 28, 1920 Polish Offensive on Kiev

April 23, 2nd Galician brigade of the Soviet XII army of Kiev going over to the Polish side followed by the 3rd Galician Brigade, total of 11,000 men, paralyzing Soviet forces.

April 25, start of the Polish offensive. Dislocation of XII and XIV Soviet Armies saving them from destruction.

April 14, Polish army raised to the state of readiness.

April 17, order to launch the offensive against Kiev to form there an independent Ukrainian state.

April 21, 1920, signing of a formal alliance with Ukrainian government of Hetman Petlura.

April 24, signing of the Polish Ukrainian military convention.

Pilsudski's conviction that the Soviets intend sooner or later to conquer the border states and Poland by force. Poland could destroy the Soviets and conquer Moscow with extensive aide in form of World War I surplus from the United States, England and France and transfer of German arsenals.

Allied decision not to support Poland British notion to kill Communism by kindness. Rather see Russia Bolshevik than Britain bankrupt.

Success of Soviet peace offensive in the West blocking deliveries of war material to Poland.

May 7, 1920, Polish army entering Kiev.

POLISH SOVIET WAR 1918-1920

ZLOBIN, MOZYR GROUP

MOGILEV

XIV

BORISOV

MINSK

BYELORUSSIA

BOBRUJSK

PRIPET R.

MOZYR

APR. 25

APR. 26

APR. 28 FRONT

APR. 27

KIEV

XII

UKRAINE

XIV

III

KK

IV

XV

Polish 1st Army

SWIECIANY

Polish 4th Army

BARANOWICZE

BEREZA KARTUSKA

PINSK

ROVNO

VLADIMIR VHOLYNSK

LUCK

RAWA RUSKA

SAN R.

GALICIA

ROMANIA

VILNO (VILNIUS)

LIDA

Polish Reserve Army

GRODNO

BIALYSTOK

OSTROLEKA

WYSZKOW

NAREW RIVER

BUG RIVER

WIEPRZ R.

MINSK MAZOWIECKI

LUKOW

WARSAW

PULAWY

KIELCE

SANDOMIERZ

VISTULA R.

CZECHOSLOVAKIA

HUNGARY

CIESZYN

SILESIA

CRACOW

KRAKOW

TOMASZOW MAZOWIECKI

LODZ

KONIN

POZNAN

TORUN

VISTULA RIVER

WEST POMERANIA

POMERANIA

PUCK GDANSK

BRANDENBURG

SCALE:
100   200
KILOMETERS
0   50   100
MILES
0

Map: 1920 Apr.-May Polish Offensive reaching Kiev. A Move to Forestall the New and Massive Soviet Offensive in the North. Soviet Strike Forces of 800,000 vs. 700,000 Poles.

Map: 1920 May-June Battle of the Berezina and the Soviet Counteroffensive at Kiev.

Map: 1920 May-June Details of the Battle of the Berezina.

MAY – JUNE 1920
DETAILS OF THE BATTLE OF
THE BEREZYNA
SOVIET POLISH WAR 1918-1920

May 15 to June 8, 1920
Battle of the Berezyna

KILOMETERS
0 20 40 60 80 100 120 140 160
MILES
0 20 40 60 80 100

STRIKE FORCE OF 700,000 MEN

SOVIET BYELORUSSIA

VITEBSK

DVINA

POLOCK

DVINA

LATVIA

Dvinsk
Duneburg

DVINA

Reserve Army

Polish Reserve Army

MOGILEV

Unsuccessful Soviet Attack North of Zlobin

ZLOBIN

BEREZYNA

BATTLE OF THE BEREZYNA

BOBRUJSK

Polish 4th army

BEREZYNA

BORISOV

MINSK

Polish attacks scheduled to start May 19, 1920.

Frontline June 8, 1920 produced by Polish pincer attacks threatening to encircle the attacking Soviet forces

MOLODECZNO

POLISH 1ST ARMY

POLAND

Hard-fought Battle of the Berezyna, a Soviet diversion to gain time to complete preparation for the grand march to the west, take Warsaw and bring support to the German Communists in Berlin and prevent encirclement by the Polish army, which was preparing pincer movement from the beachheads of Borisov and Bobrujsk to cut Soviet supply railroad.

SLUCK

NIEMEN

BARANOWICZE

LIDA

SLONIM

SZCZARA

Polish Soviet War 1918-1920

VILNO
VILNUS

VILIJA

MOSTY

WOLKOWYSK

GRODNO

NIEMEN

LITHUANIA

NIEMEN

KOVNO
KAUNAS

SUWALKI

SEJNY

AUGUSTOW

BIALYSTOK

NORTH-EASTERN POLAND

Map: 1920 July. Soviet Breakthrough in Byelorussia.
Soviet Order signed by Leon Trotsky:
"To the West over the corpse of Poland on the road to worldwide conflagration."

Map: 1920 July. Soviet Advance during Plebiscite in Mazuria. "Polish Soviet."

Map: 1920 Aug. Soviet Advance on Warsaw.

POLISH SOVIET WAR 1918-1920 Soviet Invasion of Poland

NORTH CENTRAL POLAND Soviet Advance on Warsaw

INVASION TO CONQUER THE POLISH REPUBLIC

POLISH DEFENSE

SOVIET ADVANCE

Warsaw defenses holding the initial attack repulsed by Aug. 18.

SOVIET ARMIES

KAVKOR = KK CAVALRY CORPS = KK

NIEMEN R.

BALTIC S.

GDANSK DANZIG

ELBLAG

TCZEW

INOWROCLAW

TORUN

W LOCLAWEK

VISTULA R.

PLOCK

NASIELSK

CIECHANOW

OSTROLEKA

LOMZA

BIALYSTOK

SUWALKI

GRODNO

LIDA

BEREZA KARTUSKA

BRZESC (BREST)

MOZYR GROUP

KOVEL

DROHICZYN

SIEDLCE

LUKOW

DEBLIN

RADZYMIN

WYSZKOW

PULTUSK

BUG R.

POLAND

WARSZAWA (WARSAW)

POLISH RESERVE ARMY

POLISH STRIKE FORCE

WIEPRZ R.

PILICA R.

VISTULA R.

RADOM

MILES
KILOMETERS
50   25
0
100   50
0

JULY 4, 1920
SOVIET ORDER "TO THE WEST OVER THE CORPSE OF POLAND ON THE ROAD TO WORLD WIDE CONFLAGRATION."

Border of Plebiscite Area

July 11, 1920 Plebiscite Mazuria, Warmia, Powisle

Regrouping of the Polish army, forming an assault force on the Wieprz River.

SOVIET ADVANCE AGAINST POLISH DEFENSE Aug. 1920

Soviet Advance Through Poland: Real goal Germany

Polish rearguard actions delaying the Soviet advance shifting the center of gravity of the Soviet attack on Warsaw north, thereby separating the Northern and Southern Soviet fronts and weakening the center of the Soviet invasion forces gaining time to regroup and form a central front of the strike force on the Wieprz River. The miracle of the Quartermaster Gen. Sosnkowski in face of four weapons systems in use by the Polish army. Gigantic job of sorting out the ammunition during high speed reorganization and massive regrouping of the Polish armies. A race against time Soviets delayed, miss the target date of Aug. 12, to capture Warsaw.

the critical phase of the campaign

POLISH COUNTER OFFENSIVE
August 1920

the rout of Soviet armies advancing on Warsaw

Polish victory in the race against time

100,000 Soviet prisoners taken 40,000 Soviet soldiers fleeing into East Prussia

Flight of the Soviet armies

Poles successful in the use of mobile tactics.

One and half million men deployed on the front streching from Latvia to Romania. Soviets committing 800,000 men; Poles 750,000 men.

Mobile Soviet Polish War of 1920

NORTH CENTRAL POLAND

THE BATTLE OF WARSAW

THE POLISH REPUBLIC

Warsaw defenses holding the initial attack; repulsed by Aug. 18, the entire Soviet northern front encircled.

Aug. 1920 French Gen. Weygand ignored by the Poles as a useless trench war specialist and advocate.

Regrouping of the Polish army, forming an assault force on the Wieprz River.

BALTIC S.

GERMANY EAST PRUSSIA

THE REPUBLIC OF LITHUANI.

LIDA

BYELORUSSIA

BEREZA KARTUSKA

BRZESC

Mozyr Group

Aug. 16

DROHICZYN

BUG R.

SIEDLCE

LUKOW

Aug. 16

WIEPRZ R.

Polish Strike Force

DEBLIN

RADOM

MINSK M.

RADZYMIN

BUG R.

WARSZAWA (WARSAW)

MODLIN

VISTULA R.

KUTNO

PLOCK

NASIELSK

CIECHANOW

OSTROW MAZOWIECKI

PULTUSK

NAREV R. LOMZA

NAREV R.

BIALYSTOK

III

SUWALKI

GRODNO

XV

Aug. 26

KK

KK

KK

IV

Aug. 26

OLSZTYN

Warmia,

Mazuria,

Powisle

TORUN

INOWROCLAW

WLOCLAWEK

XV

III

XVI

VISTULA R.

DANZIG GDANSK

KILOMETERS 0   25   50

MILES

VICTORY OVER THE RUSSIANS NEAR WARSAW

Map: 1920 Aug. The Rout of Soviet Armies advancing on Warsaw.

The life and death struggle for survival of Soviet Russia and of the Republic of Poland.

Gen. Sikorski armored attack on Kovel, Sept. 10-12, 1920, history's first "Blitzkrieg" of armored tanks, cars, and motorized infantry.

Aug. 16, start of the Polish counteroffensive in the Battle of Warsaw.

Note: In 1928 Gen. Sikorski wrote in his "future war" a handbook on pincer movement attacks by offensive use of tanks. Sikorski's forecast was realized in World War II.

Soviet Army Positions and Operations
Soviet Concentrations
and Attacks
Soviet Armies III IV XII XIV

Polish army positions and operations
Polish armies and divisions :
Cavalry Brigade
Reserve Brigade
Division of Volunteers

Zamosc Ring
the demise of the Soviet First Cavalry Army of Budyonny, last pure cavalry battle of European history is Komarow, Aug. 31, 1920

Aug. 30 to Sept. 2, 1920

Aug. 15-20, 1920
Battle of Lwow (Lvov)
Polish 6th Army

Sept. 10, start of the Polish counteroffensive on the Southern front.

Locations of the Soviet First Cavalry Army of Budyonny

Front Line Aug. 12.

7th Ukrainian Army

Konarmia
Cavalry Army
Cavalry of Budyonny

XIV

Battle of Brody Aug. 12

Konarmia
Sept. 13 Retreat

Cavalry Army
Cavalry of Budyonny

ROWNE
ROVNO

LUCK

LWOW

KOMAROW

Zamosc

CHELM

XII

KOWEL
Kovel Sept. 13,

BUG R.

Aug. 16

Aug. 20

Aug. 16

Aug. 16

Aug. 16

Polish Strike Force

Polish 3rd Army

LUBLIN

RADOM

WIEPRZ R.

VISTULA R.

PILICA R.

VISTULA R.

SAN R.

GALICIA

SLOVAKIA

CRACOW

LODZ

WARSAW

PINSK

TO PINSK

PRIPET R.

Sept. 20

Front Line Aug. 12.

100   50   50   25   0
KILOMETERS   MILES
0   50   0

Mobile Soviet Polish War of 1920

SOUTH-CENTRAL POLAND   Defeat of Soviet cavalry army

DEFEAT OF
ATTACK AGAINST POLAND
Aug. 31 Defeat of Soviet cavalry army at Zamosc
Zamosc Ring Aug. 30 to Sept. 2, 1920

POLISH SOVIET WAR 1918-1920   INTENSE FIGHTING:

Map: 1920 Aug.-Sept. Defeat of the Soviet Cavalry Army at Zamosc.

POLISH OFFENSIVE

Sept 1920

Polish Victory on the Niemen River;
Road to Moscow opened to the Poles

POLISH SOVIET WAR – 1919-1920

Retreat of XV, XVI, and IV Sóviet armies permitted them to escape damaged, but intact. Three Soviet armies were annihilated

Lenin suing for peace; Poles saving Europe from the subversive Soviet tyranny.

Soviet Front Sept. 20
Polish Front Oct. 1

Sept. 20, 1920, Decisive campaign began with the Battle of the Niemen. Red Army's orders were still to take Warsaw. The Red Army retreated towards the stores and reinforcements. Its effectives were growing daily; its forces about equaled total of Aug. 1; Pilsudski's forces had first-class morale, initiative and momentum.

Gen. M. Weygand arrived in July without invitation, was ignored and played no significant role in the Polish victory over the Soviets.

the rout of Soviet armies

Map: 1920 Sept. Polish Victory on the Niemen River.

NORTH-EASTERN POLAND   Polish Victory on the Niemen River; Road to Moscow opened to the Poles **SOVIET POLISH WAR 1918-1920**

Sept. 20 to Oct. 18, 1920
Polish Offensive in Byelorussia
Pilsudski's Victory
Battle of the Niemen

Creation of
"Middle Lithuania"

Armistice signed Oct. 18 and Polish Soviet border becoming quiet for the next nineteen years.

Oct. 18, all areas of consolidated Polish settlement, except Vilno, held by the Poles.

Oct. 8, Zeligowski Mutiny of the first Lithuano Byelorussian Division entering Vilno to popular rejoicing and declaring a new state of "Middle Lithuania" which in a plebiscite opted for incorporation into Poland in March 1922.

Effect of Polish victories on the Niemen and at Zamosc resulting in general Polish advance on the entire front from Zbrucz River in the South to Dvina River in the North.

Oct. 12 Tukhachevsky's order "Death or Victory" his revolutionary strategy misfired.

SOVIET BYELORUSSIA

MOGILEV

VITEBSK

DVINA

POLOCK

BEREZYNA

BORISOV

MINSK
Oct. 18

BEREZYNA

ZLOBIN

BOBRUJSK

SLUCK

DVINA

LATVIA

DVINSK
DUNEBURG

DVINA

DVINA

Oct. 12
ARMISTICE

POLAND

LAKE NAROCZ

SWIECIANY
Oct. 10

MOLODECZNO
Oct. 12

NEMAN

IV XV XVI

BARANOWICZE

NIEMEN

SZCZARA

SLONIM

SOVIET ARMIES IN RETREAT

LITHUANIA

"MIDDLE LITHUANIA"

OCT. 1

OCT. 8
VILNO
VILNIUS

SEPT 27 LIDA

MOSTY

KILOMETERS

MILES

VILIA

KOVNO
KAUNAS

NEMAN

SUWALKI

SEJNY

AUGUSTOW

SEPT 23
GRODNO

NIEMEN

2nd
Polish Army

WOLKOWYSK

BIALYSTOK

VICTORY OVER THE SOVIETS

Map: 1920 Sept.-Oct. Polish Offensive in Byelorussia.

Lord d'Abernon wrote that Polish victory saved Europe from the Soviet tyranny.

SOVIET BYELORUSSIA

SOVIET UKRAINE

KIEV

Begin. of June 1920

End of Dec. 1919

End of Oct. 1920

End of May 1919

ROMANIA

A.D. 1919-1920
Frontlines of the Soviet-Polish War

LITHUANIA

WILNO

GRODNO

End of BIALYSTOK March 1919

Aug. 12, 1920

P O L A N D

LWOW

ZAMOSC

GALICIA

200 KILOMETERS

100 MILES

100

50

50

0

0

EAST PRUSSIA

GERMANY

GDANSK DANZIG

MAZURIA

POMERANIA

WARSAW

RADOM

KIELCE

SLOVAKIA

CZECHOSLOVAKIA

HUNGARY

BALTIC SEA

WEST POMERANIA

STETTIN SZCZECIN

GERMANY

BRANDENBURG BRANIEWO

POZNAN

KALISZ

CRACOW KRAKOW

BRESLAU WROCLAW

SILESIA

PRAGUE

CZECHO-SLOVAKIA
Transition from the trench warfare .o a highly mobile war.

POLISH SOVIET WAR 1918-1920 Pilsudski's Victory

Polish Borders Settled In 1919-1922
Polish Soviet Fronts
End of March 1919
End of May 1919
End of Dec. 1919
Begin. of June 1920
End of Oct. 1920

Map: 1919-1920 The Frontlines of Soviet-Polish War.

A.D. 1922 POLAND THE MAIN BARRIER AGAINST COMMUNISM

A.D. 1922
POLAND VICTORIOUS
IN THE WAR
AGAINST SOVIET RUSSIA

BECOMING THE MAIN BARRIER
AGAINST COMMUNISM

Communist Revolutions
in Germany and Hungary

Population of Europe 485 Millions

(Eur.)Soviet	Holland 7M.
Russia 120M.	Greece 6M.
Germany 64M.	Portugal 6M.
U.K.(Britain)45M.	Bulgaria 5.5M.
France 40M.	Sweden 5.5M.
Italy 39M.	Swiss 4M.
Poland 27M.	Finland 3.5M.
Spain 20M.	Denmark 3.2M.
Romania 16M.	Norway 2.5M.
Czechoslovakia 13M.	Lithuania 2.3M.
Yugoslavia 9M.	Latvia 1.7M.
Hungary 8M.	Eur. Turkey 1.9M.
Austria 8M.	Estonia 0.9M.
Belgium 7.7M.	Albania 0.8M.

Republic of Poland 27M.
Poles 17M. Ukranians 4.5M.
Jews 2.5M. Byelorussians 2M. Others 1M.

Map: 1922 Poland in Western Civilization. The Main Barrier Against Communism (population numbers).

SOVIET BYELORUSSIA

SOVIET UKRAINE
Murderous collectivization campaign (1928-1932)
Terror Famine
Millions starved to death
Hunger used as a weapon (1932-1933)

U.S.S.R

KIEV

MINSK

LITHUANIA

SWIECIANY

WILNO

KAUNAS (KOVNO)

GRODNO

BIALYSTOK

PINSK

LWOW

STANISLAWOW

ROMANIA

KOENIGSBERG

EAST PRUSSIA

GERMANY

DANZIG GDANSK

GDYNIA

POLAND

WARSAW

LODZ

CRACOW

POZNAN

BYDGOSZCZ

CZECHO-SLOVAKIA

HUNGARY

STETTIN

BERLIN

BRANDENBURG
GERMANY

DRESDEN

KILOMETERS
MILES
200
100
100
50
0
0

A.D. 1931
DENSITY OF POPULATION
IN POLAND

20 TO 60 PER SQ. KM.

60 TO 500 PER SQ. KM.

ABOVE 500 PER SQ. KM.

A.D. 1931 POLAND–DENSITY OF POPULATION

Map: 1931 Poland - Density of Population (census of 1931).

The great depression and lack of investment capital brought the rural unemployment to a near crisis level of 8,000,000 people. 70% of Polish population was rural and 30% was urban. This ratio was reversed some 40 years later after postwar relocation of Poland west to the Oder-Neisse frontier accompanied by massive reconstruction and industrialization which made Poland one of the ten most industrialized nations in the world in the seventies.

Millions killed by Soviet military and police forces to subjugate Ukrainians, limit their number and to kill the dream of an independent Ukraine.

A.D. 1931
AGRICULTURAL POPULATION
AS PERCENT OF THE TOTAL

0-65%	
65-80%	
80-93%	

A.D. 1931 Agricultural Population as Percent of the Total

Map: 1931 Poland - Agricultural Population as a Percent of the Total

Map: Aug.31,1939 Polish, German, and Soviet Order of Battle.

Soviet order of battle

III–V. I. Kuznetsov
Obj.:Wilno

XI–N.P.Medvedev
Reserve

X–I.G.Zakharin
Reserve

Byelorussian Front
I.V. ABodin
Minsk

IV–V.I.Chuikov
Obj.:Bug River

SOVIET
BYELORUSSIA

60 divisions
Soviet preparation
for "hyena" tactics
against Poland

KIEV

SOVIET UKRAINE

Ukrainian front
S.K.Timoshenko

V–I.G.Svetnikov
Obj.:Lublin

XII–I.V.Tiukenov
Res.

VI–F.I.Golikov
Obj.:Lwow

Aug. 23, 1939, Secret
German-Soviet pact for
a partition of Poland.
Hitler-Stalin line
finalized Sept. 28,1939,
on the Bug River

Aug. 25, 1939,
common defense pact
of Poland, Great Bri-
tain, and France

ROMANIA

LITHUANIA

WILNO

GRODNO

Polish
fortified
defense
perimeter

BIALYSTOK

Polish Objective: to hold the Germans for up to two weeks until 70
French and 40 British divisions
launch a major offensive across
the Rhine. Western Allies had not
fired a shot in defense of Poland.

LUCK

LWOW

DNIESTER R.

German:
armies
front

EAST
PRUSSIA

KUCHLER

DANZIG
GDANSK

WARSAW
Marshal
E. Smigly Rydz
total of 40
divisions

BUG. RIVER

WIEPRZ R.

SLOVAKIA

BALTIC SEA

VON BOCK

GERMANY

VON KLUGE

Berlin
Von Brauchitsch
100 divisions

POZNAN

SILESIA

BLASKOWITZ

REICHENAU

VON RUNSTEDT

LODZ

CRACOW

LIST

0   100   200
KILOMETERS

0   50   100
MILES

N

Aug. 31, 1939 Polish, German, and Soviet order of battle.
Polish and German Armies Before Battle.

Tanks: German 2,600 vs. Polish 150

Warplanes: German 2,000 vs. Polish 400.

German military manpower readied for invasion
twice larger than Polish defense forces.

30 infantry di-
visions on the
French border

70 divisions in-
cluding all armor
against Poland

Polish forces

German forces

Polish armies: 1. Pomorze, Gen. W. Bortnowski 2. Poznan, Gen. T. Kutrzeba 3. Lodz,
Gen. J. K. Rommel 4. Krakow, Gen. A. Szylling 5. Karpaty Gen. K. Fabrycy 6. Lwow,
Gen. Langer 7. Modlin. Gen. E. Kurkowicz-Przedzymirski 8. Group Narew, Gen. C.
Mlot-Fiialkow ski, Group Grodno, Gen. J. Olszyna-Wilczynski 9. Prusy, Gen, Dab-
Biernacki 10. Group, Wyszkow, Gen. W. Kowalski 11. Group Polesie, Gen. F. Kleeberg,
12. Korpus Ochrony Pogranicza, Gen. W. Orlik-Ruekemann, South Front, Gen. K. Sosnkowski

Aug. 31 1939 Polish, German, and Soviet order of battle. Polish and German Armies Before Battle.

AGGRESSION BY GERMANY

German invasion of Poland marking the beginning of World War II(1939-1945)

Sept. 1-3, 1939 Battle of the borders.

German forces in very heavy fighting lining up for the first and the second encirclement maneuver midst violent counterattacks.

4:40 A.M. Sept. 1, 1939, First shots of World War II fired by German battleship *Schleswig-Holstein* on 182-man garrison of Polish fort on Wester Platte in Danzig-Gdansk. Week-long German attacks by 3,500 men, 65 artillery pieces, and 20 airplanes ended on Sept. 7. Polish garrison surrendered after running out of ammunition and suffering 65 casualities.

Attacking Germans suffered nearly 400 casualities of dead and wounded. German naval units fired their 15-inch guns on the Poles while on a good-will visit in Danzig-Gdansk.

Polish fortified defense perimeter penetrated in the south-west against heavy fire and frequent counterattacks. German invading force of 70 division lining up the first pincer toward Warsaw and the second towards the big bend of the Bug River; in the north by breaking out from Silesia through out-gunned Polish defenses toward Warsaw and later with the second pincer from Slovakia toward the Bug River. Polish Command realized that the French and the British were likely to betray Poland. Still the freedom loving Polish people made their choice to go with Western democracies rather that to join the Nazis or the Soviets. Thus all that was left to Polish soldiers was to sell their lives dearly and to defend their honor heroically for the record of history and the pride of future Polish generations. And heroically fight they did. They counterattacked at night and regrouped during the day. They inflicted on the Germans heavy casualities. The antiquated Polish planes dove down on the faster moving German planes and won many proud air victories. Polish airforce dispersed to secret wartime bases. Most of the fighting was done by infantry, the backbone of Polish army. Once again Poles had to rely on improvisation. 75 M.M. cannons had proven to be surprisingly effective against German tanks. Germans started mass executions carried out by the Wehrmacht and different security units. German airforce proceeded with terror bombing of civilian population on a massive scale while German propaganda hid the true numbers of German casualities and spread lies about Polish cavalry charges on tanks.

Germans gamble successfully on a feeble French and British response leaving second rate 30 infantry divisions facing the potential assault of 110 French and British divisions. Germans attacked Poland with an invasion force equivalent to 70 divisions. It included all of German armor and the best trained troops. Delusions of a Thousand-Year Reich started the Germans on the road to the worst crimes and most disastrous defeat in their history.

Sept. 1-3, 1939 Battle of the borders— a feeble French and British response

Polish fortified defense perimeter

BALTIC SEA · STETTIN · BERLIN · BRANDENBURG · DRESDEN · GERMANY · EAST PRUSSIA · DANZIG · WILNO · GRODNO · WOLKOWYSK · BIALYSTOK · PINSK · KOVEL · LUCK · BUG RIVER · PRIPET R. · BUG R. · REPUBLIC OF POLAND · WARSAW · WIEPRZ R. · LUBLIN · SAN R. · KIELCE · LODZ · POZNANA · VISTULA R. · LWOW (LVOV) · DROHOBYCZ · HUNGARY · SLOVAKIA · CRACOW · WROCLAW (BRESLAU) · SILESIA · ROMANIA

0   50   100 KM
0   50   100 M

Map: Sept.1-3,1939 Battle of the Borders.

German invasion of Poland marking the beginning of World War II(1939-1945)

Sept. 3, 1939, France and Britain finally declare war on Germany in keeping with their common defense treaty obligation to Poland. Tough encounter between German invaders and Polish defenders continued. German propaganda portraying the Polish campaign as an easy walkover fabricating stories of Polish cavalry charges against tanks and hiding the extent of German casualties. Polish airplanes once the fastest climbing fighters, had nonretractable landing gear and therfore were slower than more recent German planes. German airforce in control of Polish skies proceeded to terror bomb open cities and disrupt communications. Both Poles and Germans made a number of tactical mistakes during the complicatied maneuvering of the critical campaign. Poles fought heroically but their cause was doomed from the beginning. Abandonment by Western Allies gave Germans a chance to use against Poland a crushing superiority. When German pincer heading for Warsaw bypassed Army Poznan and Army Pomorze, Polish counteroffensive began in the evening of Sept. 9 under Gen. Tadeusz Kutrzeba. German divisions were quickly routed and on Sept. 10 broke down in total disorder. Poles took several thousand prisoners. Germans diverted their best armor from the Warsaw pincer and amassed numerical superiority over Poles. On Sept. 12, the Polish offensive bogged down. Polish forces regrouped behind the Bzura River on Sept. 16; part of the encircled Poles broke through to Warsaw; the rest fought until Sept. 18, when they exhausted their supply of ammunition. By Sept. 21 nine infantry divisions and two cavalry brigades were crushed by nineteen German divisions including two panzer and three light armored, supported by a huge artillery barrage and devastating dive bomber attacks. Meanwhile on Sept.17, 1939, Soviet invasion of Poland began as a part of the Hitler-Stalin partnership at the Polish expense. It collapsed Polish defense and brought mass murders and deadly deportation of Poles on a gigantic scale after the battle of the Bzura River. Devastating air and ground attacks on Warsaw intensified The Polish capital fell on Sept. 29.

Sept. 3-6, 1939
German blitzkrieg tactics maturing in Poland
Battle for Piotrkow
Major Encounter of Polish and German Armor won by the Poles
Polish defensed stretched to a breaking point

German pincer advance within 125 KM. off Warsaw. German guerrilla action suppressed at Bydgoszcz on Sept. 3. Massacre of Polish civilians by the Wehrmacht on Sept. 5. Fall of Cracow and Poznan. German armor wedging in between armies of Lodz and Cracow. Army Modlin stopping the north pincer on the Vistula 60 KM. from Warsaw. A Major upset to Polish defensive plans. Sept. 6, in the evening crisis began with the rupture of the front at Piotrkow to Warsaw Highway.

Polish defenses: stretched to a breaking point

Map labels: BALTIC SEA, POMERANIA, GERMANY, STETTIN, BERLIN, DRESDEN, SILESIA, BRESLAU, ODER R., NOTECH R., POZNAN, CZECHS, SLOVAKIA, CRACOW, LODZ, BZURA R., WARSAW, RADOM, LUBLIN, VISTULA R., WIEPRZ R., SAN R., HUNGARY, ROMANIA, DNIESTER R., LWOW, LUCK, PRIPET R., BUG RIVER, BIALYSTOK, WOLKOWYSK, GRODNO, WILNO, LITHUANIA, EAST PRUSSIA, KOENIGSBERG, GDANSK, HEL PEN.

Scale: 0 — 50 — 100 KM

Map: Sept.3-6,1939 German Blitzkrieg Tactics Maturing in Poland.

Map: Sept.7-Oct.6 German Pincers, Polish Counteroffensive, Soviet Invasion.

Map: Sept.28,1939 Hitler-Stalin Line of Partition of Poland.

1939 PARTITION OF POLAND

Hitler-Stalin partnership enforcing a policy to destroy Polish intellectual elite, political and business leadership, as well as the lowest levels of organized national and social life by mass murder and deportation of millions up until June 22, 1941, when German invasion of Russia terminated the partnership.

Memel annexed by Germany from Lithuania in March 1939

Oct. 27, 1939, Lithuanian entry to Wilno after six weeks of Soviet terror and plunder.

June 15, 1940, fall of Paris to the Germans and Soviet occupation of Lithuania, Latvia, and Estonia followed by Bessarabia and Northern Bukovina

Massive Soviet supplies of petroleum and grain for Germany in fulfillment of Hitler-Stalin treaty of friendship and cooperation of Aug. 23, 1939

Poles and Jews declared sub-human by Hitler

Hitler-Stalin line of Sept. 28, 1939

The General Protectorate

Mass Deportations

Sept. 28, 1939, Finalization of the partition of Poland by Hitler and Stalin

Germany controlling 189,000 sq.km. with 21,800,000 population
90,000 sq.km. annexed into Germany with 10,000,000 9.5% Polish and 0.5% German
99,000 sq.km. a protectorate with 11,800,000 population
U.S.S.R. controlling 200,500 sq.km. a protectorate with 11,800,000 population
U.S.S.R. controlling 200,500 sq.km. with 13,400,000 population — over 5,000,000 Poles

GERMANY EAST PRUSSIA

KOENIGSBERG

LITHUANIA

KOVNO

WILNO

ANNEXATIONS

MINSK

U.S.S.R.

BEREZYNA R.

PRIPET R.

KIEV

DNIEPER RIVER

GRODNO

BIALYSTOK

Mass Deportations

ANNEXATIONS

LWOW (LVOV)

DNIESTER R.

ANNEXATIONS

BESSARABIA

N. BUKOVINA

ANNEXATIONS

VISTULA R.

WARSAW

RADOM

LUBLIN

ANNEXATIONS

POMERANIA GERMANY

GDYNIA

BYDGOSZCZ

POZNAN

LODZ

ANNEXATIONS

CRACOW

SILESIA

SLOVAKIA

HUNGARY

CZECHS

GERMANY

STETTIN

BERLIN

ODER-NEISSE RIVERS

KILOMETERS

MILES

Map: 1939 Hitler-Stalin Partnership - Partition of Poland.

Deportations by the Soviets: 200,000 Sentenced 150,000 Illegally Drafted to Soviet Army 140,000 Illegally Drafted to Soviet Industry Feb. 10, 1949, 220,000 Polish officials and their families Apr. 13, 1940, 325,000 families of previously deported June-July 1940, 240,000 war refugees from Western Poland June 1941, 300,000 at least 60% Poles, then Ukrainian nationalists, Byelorussians and Jews 15,000 murders of prisoners in prisons and in columns marching east during Soviet evacuation in June 1940. During the 20-month Hitler-Stalin partnership the Soviets eliminated 1,700,000 people from Poland. By Oct. 1, 1942, 900,000 of them were dead, including 15,000 Polish army and police officers imprisoned in camps: 1. Starobelsk, 2. Kozelsk 3. Povelishtchev Bor 4. Ostashkov 5. Grazovetz Apr. 1940 extermination site of 4,200 officers at Katyn

Sept. 13, 1940, German law on shipping all Polish Jews to ghettos with 110,000 people per sq. km. on 250 calories per person per day; massive smuggling of food sold or donated by Poles interfering with German plan to starve the Jews. Oct. 15, 1941, German law of death penalty for Jews leaving ghettos and for Poles helping them in any manner. By June 1941, Germans causing death of 60,000 and, the Soviets, of 100,000 Jews.

Deportations by the Germans till June 1941: 1,000,000 from annexed areas to the general protectorate; 200,000 children to Germany to be raised as Germans; 1,000,000 Jews to ghettos. 1,000,000 to Nazi camps and slave labor in Germany, 150,000 executed starting in Sept. 1939 in Bydgoszcz with 20,000 killed between ages of 12 to 65 A planned biological extermination of the Polish nation at the same time imposition of Soviet citizenship on 13,200,000 Polish citizens and German citizenship on 5,000,000 Poles to be Germanized and to serve as a cannon fodder for the Nazis.

CONTROLLED BY GERMANY

KILOMETERS

MILES

JUNE 1941 OCCUPIED POLAND
THE MOST TERRORIZED AND DEVASTATED COUNTRY IN EUROPE
Mass murders and deportations by Germans and Soviets before Nazi attack on U.S.S.R. ending the partnership of Hitler and Stalin (a gamble to destroy the Soviets without participation of anti-Communist Russians)

Map: June 1941 Occupied Poland: the Most Terrorized and Devastated Country in Europe.

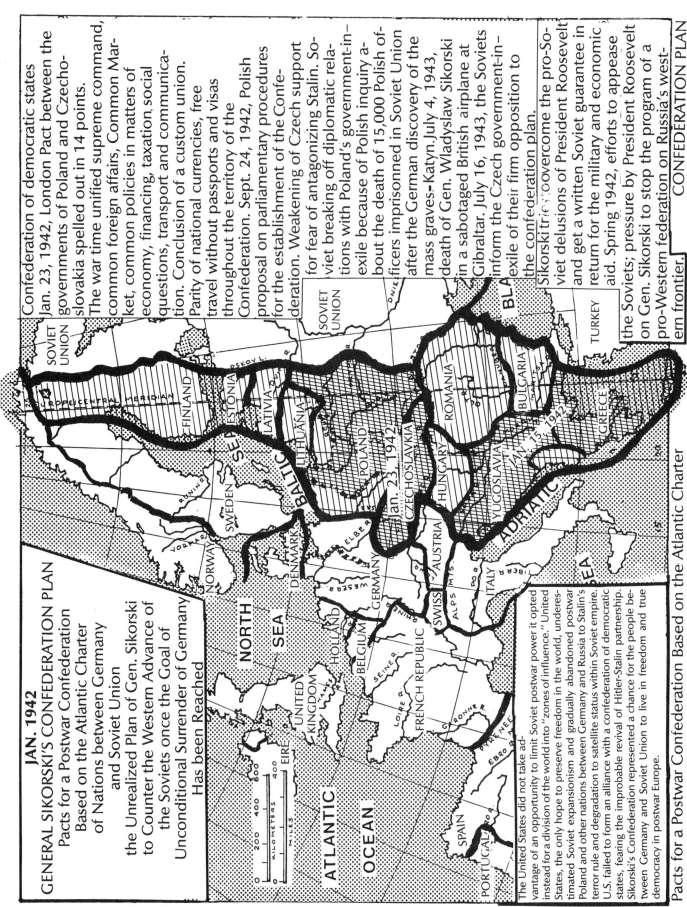

Confederation of democratic states Jan. 23, 1942, London Pact between the governments of Poland and Czechoslovakia spelled out in 14 points. The war time unified supreme command, common foreign affairs, Common Market, common policies in matters of economy, financing, taxation, social questions, transport and communication. Conclusion of a custom union. Parity of national currencies, free travel without passports and visas throughout the territory of the Confederation. Sept. 24, 1942, Polish proposal on parliamentary procedures for the establishment of the Confederation. Weakening of Czech support for fear of antagonizing Stalin. Soviet breaking off diplomatic relations with Poland's government-in-exile because of Polish inquiry about the death of 15,000 Polish officers imprisoned in Soviet Union after the German discovery of the mass graves–Katyn.July 4, 1943, death of Gen. Wladyslaw Sikorski in a sabotaged British airplane at Gibraltar. July 16, 1943, the Soviets inform the Czech government-in-exile of their firm opposition to the confederation plan.

Sikorski tries to overcome the pro-Soviet delusions of President Roosevelt and get a written Soviet guarantee in return for the military and economic aid. Spring 1942, efforts to appease the Soviets; pressure by President Roosevelt on Gen. Sikorski to stop the program of a pro-Western federation on Russia's western frontier. CONFEDERATION PLAN

JAN. 1942
GENERAL SIKORSKI'S CONFEDERATION PLAN
Pacts for a Postwar Confederation Based on the Atlantic Charter of Nations between Germany and Soviet Union the Unrealized Plan of Gen. Sikorski to Counter the Western Advance of the Soviets once the Goal of Unconditional Surrender of Germany Has been Reached

The United States did not take advantage of an opportunity to limit Soviet postwar power it opted instead for a division of the world into "zones of influence." United States, the only hope to preserve freedom in the world, underestimated Soviet expansionism and gradually abandoned postwar Poland and other nations between Germany and Russia to Stalin's terror rule and degradation to satellite status within Soviet empire. U.S. failed to form an alliance with a confederation of democratic states, fearing the improbable revival of Hitler-Stalin partnership. Sikorski's Confederation represented a chance for the people between Germany and Soviet Union to live in freedom and true democracy in postwar Europe.

Pacts for a Postwar Confederation Based on the Atlantic Charter

Map: Jan.1942 Gen.Sikorski's Plan for a Confederation of Nations Between Germany and Soviet Union Based on the Atlantic Charter.

1939-1945 RESISTANCE UNDER GERMAN OCCUPATION

Oct. 27, 1939, Founding of Polish Resistance 500,000 People participated in Polish resistance 1,400 Trains derailed; destroyed were 20,000 railroad cars, and 700 locomotives, 400 German battalions were tied down in Poland

Areas of Armed Struggle of Polish Home Army guerrillas against Soviet-controlled guerrilla executing communist takeover authorized by betrayal of Poland by the West at Teheran in 1943. 1944 beginning of civil war in Poland (1944-47) fought against Soviet domination, imposition of Communist system and inclusion of Poland in the Soviet Empire.

OSTLAND

OCCUPIED BYELORUSSIA

MINSK

KIEV

OCCUPIED UKRAINE

DNIEPER RIVER

1939 Polish Border

Borders of "Great Germany" of Hitler

Northern Bukovina

Bessarabia

ROMANIA

OCCUPIED POLAND

VILNO

LITHUANIA

NOWOGRÓDEK

LACHWA

KILOMETERS

MILES

200

100

100

50

GRODNO

KRYNKI

BIALYSTOK

TREBLINKA

SOBIBOR

BELZEC

LWOW

DISTRICT OF GALICIA

EAST PRUSSIA

GERMANY

STUTTHOF

GDYNIA

BYDGOSZCZ

WARSAW

RADOM

TARNOW

GENERAL PROTECTORATE

BALTIC SEA

STETTIN

BERLIN

GERMANY

POZNAN

VISTULA R.

COLMERHOFF

LODZ

CZESTOCHOWA

BEDZIN

AUSCHWITZ

CRACOW

SLOVAKIA

HUNGARY

GROSS ROSEN

Warsaw Uprising
Aug. 1–Oct. 2, 1944

Mass Extermination Sites

Major Guerrilla Battles

Uprisings of Polish Jews
in German-run Ghettos

Railroad Sabotage

Main Polish

Guerrilla

Soviet
Guerrilla

THE MOST TERRORIZED AND DEVASTATED COUNTRY IN EUROPE

Map: 1939-1945 Resistance under German Occupation; Europe's only Underground State.

1940-1945   CAMPAIGNS OF POLISH ARMED FORCES

1940 Narvik Highland Brigade
Tobruk Carpathian Brigade
1940 France 10th Brigade of Motorized
Cavalry 11th Division of Grenadiers,
2nd Infantry Division
1941 Gr. Britain 1st Corps 1943-45 Italy 2nd Corps
1944 France, Belgium, Holland 1945 Germany
1st Armored Division and Paratrooper Brigade

1940-45 Britain, 14 Air Force Div.
in the Battle of Gr. Britain. Down
15% of German Planes total of 951
plus 190 V-1 Flying Bombs

1939-1945 Gr. Britain Navy in Combat
and Convoy Duty
1944-45 U.S.S.R., Poland, Germany 1st and
2nd Polish "People's" Army 400,000 Men

A.D. 1940-1945

CAMPAIGNS OF POLISH ARMED FORCES

MAY   1945   600,000   POLISH   SOLDERS
ON GERMAN FRONTS, THE 3RD LARGEST
NUMBER   AFTER   U.S.S.R.   AND   U.S.A.
1939-1945   POLISH   GUERRILLAS   UP   TO
300,000;   TYING   DOWN   UP   TO   930,000
GERMAN   FORCES   IN   OCCUPIED   POLAND
Mainly By Armia Krajowa; The Home Army

KILOMETERS

MILES

0   200   400   600
0   200   400

ATLANTIC

OCEAN

NORTH

SEA

BALTIC

SEA

FRANCE
80,000

FALAISE 1944

PARIS

1940

ITALY
1943-1945

MEDITERRANEAN

MONTE
CASSINO

ADRIATIC

1944

TOBRUK

SEA

BLACK SEA

MOSCOW

WARSAW 1944

KIEV

BERLIN

1945

1943

1945

NARVIK

1940

MURMANSK

ARCHANGEL

EUROPE CENTRAL MERIDIAN

U.S.S.R.

CASPIAN

Iran
80,000
Polish
Eastern
Army
1942-43

1940

SYRIA

1942-80,000
Evacuated
From U.S.S.R.

German-Controlled Areas Fall 1942

Neutral Countries
Ireland   Sweden
Switzerland   Portugal

Map: 1940-1945 Campaigns of Polish Forces.

The five component operation Wachlarz or Fanout was conceived by Gen. Stefan Grot-Rowecki (1895-1944) the first commander of the Polish Home Army who believed that Germany cannot win on two fronts. Half of the military appropriations of Poland's underground government was spent on Wachlarz which directed from Warsaw, destroyed over 30 major supply depots and military transports utilizing Poles in thousands of mobile slave labor camps of "Organization Todt" carried on trains, trucks, and above all on horse drawn carts.

JULY 1941–NOV. 1942
OPERATION FANOUT
OR WACHLARZ (vakh-lash)
AN ATTEMPT BY POLAND'S
UNDERGROUND GOVERNMENT
TO WEAKEN AND DISORGANIZE
GERMAN OFFENSIVE AGAINST
SOVIET UNION
AND TO SHIELD A GENERAL
UPRISING IN POLAND
FROM AN AVALANCHE OF
RETREATING GERMAN ARMIES

NOTE: HORSE DRAWN CARTS WERE THE BACKBONE OF GERMAN WAR TRANSPORT

Map: July 1941 - Nov.1942 Operation Fanout or Wachlarz by Poland's Underground Government.

Nov. 1942 Nazi death machine in a full swing. Martyrdom of the Jews

The system of over 8,500 identified German camps composed of the main concentration camps and their branches played the main role in Nazi program of extermination. After introduction of Cyclon "B", gas chambers were installed in major concentration camps. Genocide of European Jews occured in 1942-44 in mass extermination camps. Other camps were punitive-investigative, hard labor, special prison camps for youth and children, transit camps, and ghettos converted into concentration camps. In the prisoner of war camps 3,400,000 Soviet men perished, as did thousands of Italians, Poles, Yugoslavs, Britons, Frenchmen, and others.

13 — Concentration Camp Districts-
Main Camps and Branches: 1. Dachau 2. Buchenwald - Dora 3. Flossenburg 4. Gross Rosen 5. Majdanek 6. Notz Weiler Struthof 7. Neuengamme 8. Auschwitz-Birkenau 9. Ravensbruck 10. Mathausen 11. Sachsenhausen-Oranienburg 12. Stutthof 13. Plaszow
Special Mass Extermination Camps:
1. Dec. 1941-Jan. 1945, Culmhof 360,000
2. Mar. 1942-Apr. 1943, Belzec 600,000
3. Mar. 1942-Oct. 1943, Sobibor 250,000
4. July 1942-Nov. 1943, Treblinka II 750,000 killed by gas Cyclon "B"
5. May 1942-July 1944, Majdanek 200,000
8. Jan. 1942-Nov. 1944, Birkenau-Auschwitz II 3,500,000 killed according to the commission investigating German-Nazi crimes in Poland.

Neuengamme District included Bergen-Belsen.

1939-1945 Poland lost 6,028,000 people or 22% of population, the highest percent of any country in Europe; 644,000 were killed in combat and the rest in prisons, death camps, executions, and annihilation of ghettos; nearly half of the victims were Jews; almost all gypsies were exterminated; 40% of university professors were killed; 27 universities and institutes were destroyed with 50 % of all schools and libraries.

In World War II Poland lost 40% of her gross national wealth.

OCCUPIED POLAND

13 Main Camps

Special Mass Extermination Camps

Nov. 1942 Occupied Poland Nazi death machine in a full swing. Martyrdom of the Jews
System of over 8,500 Nazi camps organized in 13 administrative districts which held during the war 18,000,000 people of which 11,000,000 were killed including 3,500,000 Polish citizens, out of 5,000,000 processed.

World War II was not fought to save the Jews.

Map: Nov.1942 Nazi Death Machine in a Full Swing - Martyrdom of the Jews.

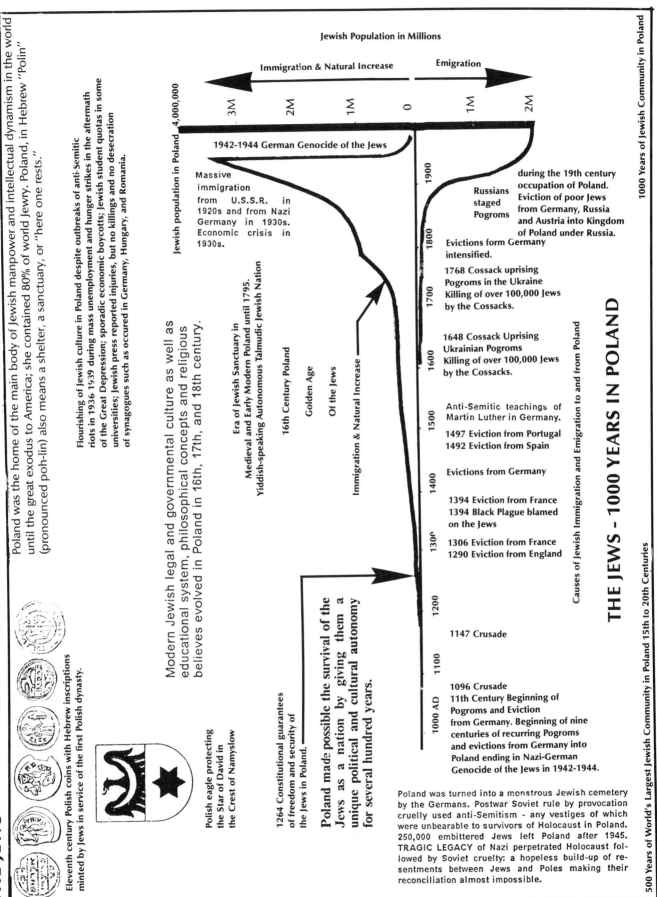

THE JEWS

1000 YEARS IN POLAND

Autonomous Jewish Government in the First Polish Republic

Poland was the home of the main body of Jewish manpower and intellectual dynamism in the world until the great exodus to America; she contained 80% of world Jewry. Poland, in Hebrew "Polin" (pronounced poh-lin) also means a shelter, a sanctuary, or "here one rests."

Eleventh century Polish coins with Hebrew inscriptions minted by Jews in service of the first Polish dynasty.

Polish eagle protecting the Star of David in the Crest of Namyslow

1264 Constitutional guarantees of freedom and security of the Jews in Poland.

Modern Jewish legal and governmental culture as well as educational system, philosophical concepts and religious believes evolved in Poland in 16th, 17th, and 18th century.

Poland made possible the survival of the Jews as a nation by giving them a unique political and cultural autonomy for several hundred years.

Flourishing of Jewish culture in Poland despite outbreaks of anti-Semitic riots in 1936-1939 during mass unemployment and hunger strikes in the aftermath of the Great Depression; sporadic economic boycotts; Jewish student quotas in some universities; Jewish press reported injuries, but no killings and no desecration of synagogues such as occured in Germany, Hungary, and Romania.

Era of Jewish Sanctuary in Medieval and Early Modern Poland until 1795. Yiddish-speaking Autonomous Talmudic Jewish Nation

16th Century Poland
Golden Age
Of the Jews

Immigration & Natural Increase

Massive immigration from U.S.S.R. in 1920s and from Nazi Germany in 1930s. Economic crisis in 1930s.

Jewish population in Poland

Jewish Population in Millions

← Immigration & Natural Increase   Emigration →

4,000,000

3M 2M 1M 0 1M 2M

1942-1944 German Genocide of the Jews

1900

1800

1700

1600

1500

1400

1300

1200

1100

1000 AD

1147 Crusade

1096 Crusade
11th Century Beginning of Pogroms and Eviction from Germany. Beginning of nine centuries of recurring Pogroms and evictions from Germany into Poland ending in Nazi-German Genocide of the Jews in 1942-1944.

Russians staged Pogroms

during the 19th century occupation of Poland. Eviction of poor Jews from Germany, Russia and Austria into Kingdom of Poland under Russia.

Evictions form Germany intensified.

1768 Cossack uprising Pogroms in the Ukraine Killing of over 100,000 Jews by the Cossacks.

1648 Cossack Uprising Ukrainian Pogroms Killing of over 100,000 Jews by the Cossacks.

Anti-Semitic teachings of Martin Luther in Germany.

1497 Eviction from Portugal
1492 Eviction from Spain

Evictions from Germany

1394 Eviction from France
1394 Black Plague blamed on the Jews

1306 Eviction from France
1290 Eviction from England

Poland was turned into a monstrous Jewish cemetery by the Germans. Postwar Soviet rule by provocation cruelly used anti-Semitism - any vestiges of which were unbearable to survivors of Holocaust in Poland. 250,000 embittered Jews left Poland after 1945. TRAGIC LEGACY of Nazi perpetrated Holocaust followed by Soviet cruelty: a hopeless build-up of resentments between Jews and Poles making their reconciliation almost impossible.

THE JEWS - 1000 YEARS IN POLAND

Causes of Jewish Immigration and Emigration to and from Poland

1000 Years of Jewish Community in Poland

500 Years of World's Largest Jewish Community in Poland 15th to 20th Centuries

Diag.: Jews - 1000 Years in Poland: Immigration and Emigration.

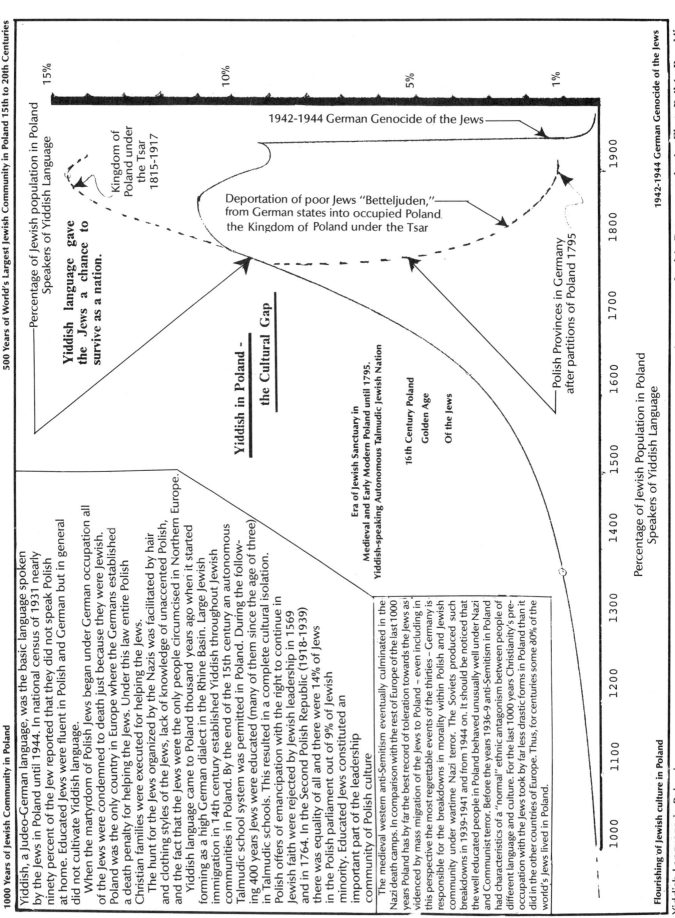

500 Years of World's Largest Jewish Community in Poland 15th to 20th Centuries

Percentage of Jewish population in Poland Speakers of Yiddish Language

15%

10%

5%

1%

1942-1944 German Genocide of the Jews

Kingdom of Poland under the Tsar 1815-1917

Yiddish language gave the Jews a chance to survive as a nation.

Deportation of poor Jews "Betteljuden," from German states into occupied Poland, the Kingdom of Poland under the Tsar

Yiddish in Poland - the Cultural Gap

Polish Provinces in Germany after partitions of Poland 1795

1900

1800

1700

1600

1500

1400

1300

1200

1100

1000

Era of Jewish Sanctuary in Medieval and Early Modern Poland until 1795. Yiddish-speaking Autonomous Talmudic Jewish Nation

16th Century Poland

Golden Age

Of the Jews

Percentage of Jewish Population in Poland Speakers of Yiddish Language

1000 Years of Jewish Community in Poland

Yiddish, a Judeo-German language, was the basic language spoken by the Jews in Poland until 1944. In national census of 1931 nearly ninety percent of the Jew reported that they did not speak Polish at home. Educated Jews were fluent in Polish and German but in general did not cultivate Yiddish language.

When the martyrdom of Polish Jews began under German occupation all of the Jews were condemned to death just because they were Jewish. Poland was the only country in Europe where the Germans established a death penalty for helping the Jews. Under this law entire Polish Christian families were executed for helping the Jews.

The hunt for the Jews organized by the Nazis was facilitated by hair and clothing styles of the Jews, lack of knowledge of unaccented Polish, and the fact that the Jews were the only people circumcised in Northern Europe.

Yiddish language came to Poland thousand years ago when it started forming as a high German dialect in the Rhine Basin. Large Jewish immigration in 14th century established Yiddish throughout Jewish communities in Poland. By the end of the 15th century an autonomous Talmudic school system was permitted in Poland. During the follow-ing 400 years Jews were educated (many of them since the age of three) in Talmudic schools. This resulted in a complete cultural isolation. Polish offers of emancipation with the right to continue in Jewish faith were rejected by Jewish leadership in 1569 and in 1764. In the Second Polish Republic (1918-1939) there was equality of all and there were 14% of Jews in the Polish parliament out of 9% of Jewish minority. Educated Jews constituted an important part of the leadership community of Polish culture.

The medieval western anti-Semitism eventually culminated in the Nazi death camps. In comparison with the rest of Europe of the last 1000 years Poland has by far the best record of toleration towards the Jews as evidenced by mass migration of the Jews to Poland – even including in this perspective the most regrettable events of the thirties – Germany is responsible for the breakdowns in morality within Polish and Jewish community under wartime Nazi terror. The Soviets produced such breakdowns in 1939-1941 and from 1944 on. It should be noticed that the well educated people in Poland behaved unusually well under Nazi and Communist terror. Before the years 1936-9 anti-Semitism in Poland had characteristics of a "normal" ethnic antagonism between people of different language and culture. For the last 1000 years Christianity's pre-occupation with the Jews took by far less drastic forms in Poland than it did in the other countries of Europe. Thus, for centuries some 80% of the world's Jews lived in Poland.

Flourishing of Jewish culture in Poland

Yiddish Language in Poland

1942-1944 German Genocide of the Jews in the First Polish Republic

Autonomous Jewish Government in the First Polish Republic

Diag.: History of Yiddish in Poland - the Cultural Gap.

Nazis imposed German citizenship on 5,000,000 Poles in Silesia, Poznania, Pomerania and Mazuria to use them as cannon fodder in their
ck divisions. The first German paratroops division had a high percent of Poles who when they had a chance volunteered to serve in the Polish
es on the side of Allies.

CAIRO
1669

44TH GERMAN. INF. DIV.
132 GERM. INF. REG.

2ND NEW ZEALAND INF. DIV.

HITLER LINE

CARPATHIAN
LANCERS
REG.

CAIRA

RAPIDO CREEK

945

PASSO CORNO

EAKING OF THE HITLER LINE

MT. CASTELLONE
15TH POZNAN
LANCERS
REG.

771

5TH KRESOWA
INF. DIV.

2ND
POLISH
CORPS

MAY 11-18, 1944

POLISH VICTORY AT MONTECASSINO, ITALY

BATTLE OF MONTE CASSINO

608

PHANTOM RIDGE

706

481

VILLA
SANTA
LUCIA

445

5TH GERM. MT. DIV.

PEDIMONTE
SAN GERMANO

601

SNAKEHEAD RIDGE

175

HITLER LINE

100TH GERM.
MT. REG.

SAN ANGELO

505

ALBAN FARM

444

236

RAPIDO CREEK

CASSINO

ROAD TO ROME Route 6

1ST GERM.
PARA. DIV.

575

516
MONTE
CASSINO

1ST BRIT.
GUARD BRIG.

1 MILE

435

165

3RD GERM.
PARA. REG.

4TH BRIT.
INF. DIV.

KILOMETER

100

CREEK

METERS
ck

13TH BRITISH
CORPS

78TH BRIT. INF. DIV.

MAY 11-18, 1944
OLISH VICTORY AT MONTE CASSINO, ITALY
BATTLE OF MONTE CASSINO
OPENING OF THE ROAD TO ROME
FOR THE ALLIES AT THE COST OF
3783 POLISH CASUALTIES
OF KILLED AND WOUNDED
BREAKING OF THE HITLER LINE

A.M. May 18, 1944, Podole Lancers entering Monte Cassino
May 19, 1944, Last German resistance ends at pick 575 and 505
May 29, 1944, Final Polish breakthrough the Hitler Line
by taking Pedimonte San Germano and fortifications of Villa
Santa Lucia and Passo, Corno. By then Polish casulaties were
4199 including 923 dead.

Positions: Polish
New Zealand

British
German

Polish Infantry Attacks
British Attacks

Polish Tank Attacks

German Retreat

Map: May 11-18, 1944. Polish Victory at Monte Cassino, Italy.

After capitulation, Germans deport the entire population of Warsaw as a reprisal.

MARYMONT

ZOLIBRZ

TARGOWEK

CITADEL

GDANSK
R.R. STA.

STR.
PLANTOWA

WILNO
R.R. STA.

EAST R.R.
STA.

OLD TOWN

PAWIAK
PRISON

RIVERPORT

GROCHOWSKA
AV.

WARSAW CITY CENTER

E. POWERI
PL. 7.

WASHINGTON AV.

WOLA

MAIN R.R.S.

MARSZALKOWSKA AV.

Sept. 15, 1944
Soviet front line
on the east bank
of the Vistula
Sept. 19-21
17-23: 18-29
Attempts to
force the
river.

TO R.R. TUNNEL

JERUSALEM AV.
JEROZOLIMSKIE AV.

POWISLE

UJAZDOWSKI AV.

AGRYKOLA
STR.

VISTULA RIVER

German forces committing
mass murders; using Varsovians
as life-shields on their tanks.

OCHOTA

GROJECKA AV.

PULAWSKA AV.

BATORY AV.

SIELCE

RAKOWIEC

MOKOTOW

**AUG. 1, 1944 - OCT. 2, 1944
WARSAW UPRISING
GERMAN AND SOVIET ROLES**
By Armia Krajowa; The Home Army

CZERNIAKOW

Held by Poles:

Aug. 4, 1944   Oct. 2, 1944

SOBIESKI AV.

Attacks   German   Polish
Beachhead Attempts
by Polish "Peoples" Army
Parachuted Supplies
Losses: Polish: Over 200,000
        German: 26,000

SADYBA

After capitulation, Warsaw 80% destroyed by German army engineers.

Map: Aug.-Oct.1944 Warsaw uprising - German and Soviet roles.

Germans Mass Murdered the Population of Warsaw and the Soviets stood by Across the Vistula

AUG. 1, 1944 - OCT. 2, 1944 WARSAW UPRISING GERMAN AND SOVIET ROLES

Gen. Sosnkowski called by Churchill "The second cross of Lorraine" because his actions were similar to those of Gen. De Gaule.

Sept. 30, 1944, Removal of Commander-in-Chief of Polish Forces Gen. Kazimierz Sosnkowski (1885-1967) under British pressure after his protests against sellout of Poland to the Soviets. He threatened to stop fighting and let the Polish army be intered rather than to accept Soviet domination. Gen. Sosnkowski opposed the staging of the uprising in Warsaw. Questionable nomination of Gen. Tadeusz Bor-Komorowski (1895-1966) as commander-in-chief at the time when he was about to be taken prisoner in the surrender of Warsaw. Gen. Komorowski was the commander of Polish Home Army, one of the largest guerrilla armies in occupied Europe.

German invasion of June 22, 1941, ended Hitler-Stalin partnership in obliteration of Poland. The new phase of Soviet policy towards Poland was formulated by Gen. Aleksander Shcherbakov (1901-45), the political and intelligence head of Soviet armed forces. Poland was to be reshaped into Soviet buffer limiting German potential by territorial shift west, back to the ancient Polish ethnic lands. Soviet controlled Polish "People's" Army was to guarantee the Soviet grip on Poland and when necessary to serve as Polish national government. National symbols and Catholic chaplains were emphasized. The word "Communism" was avoided in line with Stalin's belief that "it is easier to saddle a cow, than to establish Communism in Poland." In Nov. 18-Dec. 1, 1943 in Teheran, secret agreement between Roosevelt, Churchill, and Stalin spelled out the loss of independence of Poland and recognition of the Hitler-Stalin Line on the Bug River as Soviet postwar border. The new and Third Polish Republic was to belong to the Soviet zone of influence enforced by Stalin's terror apparatus. These Western concessions were given in exchange for Soviet promise to enter the war against Japan shortly after the collapse of Germany.

Aug. 8-20, 1944. Crucial victory at Falaise-Chambois made possible liberation of France within a few weeks. Polish First Armored Div. under Maj. Gen Stanislaw Maczek (attached to the 2nd Canadian Corps) closed the Allied's ring around the 8th German Army destroying 344 German tanks, self-propelled guns, and military vehicles and taking 5,000 prisoners.

A.D. 1944
THE AGONY OF
THE SECOND POLISH REPUBLIC

Betrayed by the Western Allies while Germans Mass Murdered the Population of Warsaw and the Soviets stood by Across the Vistula

Map: A.D. 1944 The Agony of the Second Polish Republic.

VII. The Third Polish Republic (1944–)

The Peoples' Poland

WITHIN SOVIET BLOC

Over 2,000,000 men served in Polish armed forces and guerrilla units in World War II.

Apr.-May 1945, 200,000 men in the Polish armed forces in the West. In 1944 the 2nd Corps won the Battle on Monte Cassino and Ancona July 18, 1944; in Apr. 9-21, 1945 Bologna; in France in 1944 the First Armored Div. won at Falaise and in 1945 through Holland, Belgium and Northern Germany, it took the surrender of German Navy Command at Wilhelmshaven. In 1944, Polish paratroopers brigade fought at Arnhem; in 1945 Polish navy had 18 combat ships — during the war it fought in 665 sea engagements and sank or damaged 67 German ships and submarines and 60 aircraft. It travelled in combat a total of 1,213,000 miles.

Soviet mass murders of Polish officers in 1940 facilitated staffing two Polish armies with ranking Soviet officers. These were elite troops with guard rating. Poles were conditioned to fight Germans by the horrors of Nazi occupation. Soviet terror directed against the Polish Home Army of anti-German guerrillas provoked Civil War in Poland and a failure to organize the Third Polish Army which was to join the other two and form a Polish front. The First Polish "People's" Army, after breaking through German defenses in Pomerania, fought its way to Berlin. Once there it hung a Polish flag on the monument "Siegessäule" commemorating defeat of the French in 1870 and proclaiming the short-lived Prussian Empire. Next Polish flag was hanged on the Brandenburg Gate. Poles reached the Elbe River at Kletz. Second Polish "People's" Army and the First Armored Corps broke through the Neisse Line on Apr. 17. On the 18th they were attacked by German Rescue Army heading for Berlin. A double encirclement resulted. The Poles were cut off from their Soviet command and had to use anti-aircraft artillery against three German armored divisions. It was the bloodiest battle of the campaign: Poles lost 11,000 men; the attacking Germans 12,000. In the Berlin operation 185,000 Poles participated with 3,000 guns and mortars, 508 tanks and self-propelled armored guns, and 320 airplanes. Polish losses of 60,000 on the Eastern Front were two and half times greater than those suffered by the Polish soldiers fighting on the Western Front and in Italy.

1932-33, Poles breaking of "Enigma," the German military code system and building of an electromechanical deciphering computer. On July 25, 1939, Poland gave Gr. Britain and France each a copy of the deciphering computer, complete with specifications, perforated cards and updating procedures which were used during the war.

The most important Polish contribution to the Allied victory over Germany was the breaking of German "Enigma."

SOVIET UNION

CASP.

S

CAUCASUS MTS.

KURA R.

SOVIET UNION

BLACK SEA

TURKEY

BULGARIA

ROMANIA

GREECE

ALBANIA

YUGOSLAVIA

HUNGARY

AUSTRIA

CZECHO-SLOVAK.

ADRIATIC

ITALY

POLAND

WARSAW

BERLIN

GERMANY

SWISS

FRANCE

DENMARK

NETH.

BELGIUM

UNITED KINGDOM

NORTH SEA

OCCUPIED NORWAY

NEUTRAL SWEDEN

BALTIC SEA

FINLAND

SOVIET UNION

CENTRAL MERIDIAN

POLAND 1939

ATLANTIC OCEAN

SPAIN

PORTUGAL

TUNISIA

KILOMETERS
0 200 400 600
0   400
MILES

Attacks
Polish
Allied

APRIL - MAY 1945
POLISH SOLDIERS ON THE FRONTS
OF COLLAPSING GERMANY
CIVIL WAR IN POLAND
PROVOKED BY SOVIET TERROR
AND FORCED SOVIETIZATION
1945 NATIONAL BOUNDARIES

Map: Apr.-May 1945 Polish Soldiers on All Fronts of Collapsing Germany;
Civil War in Poland, New National Borders of 1945;
Western betrayal of Poland.

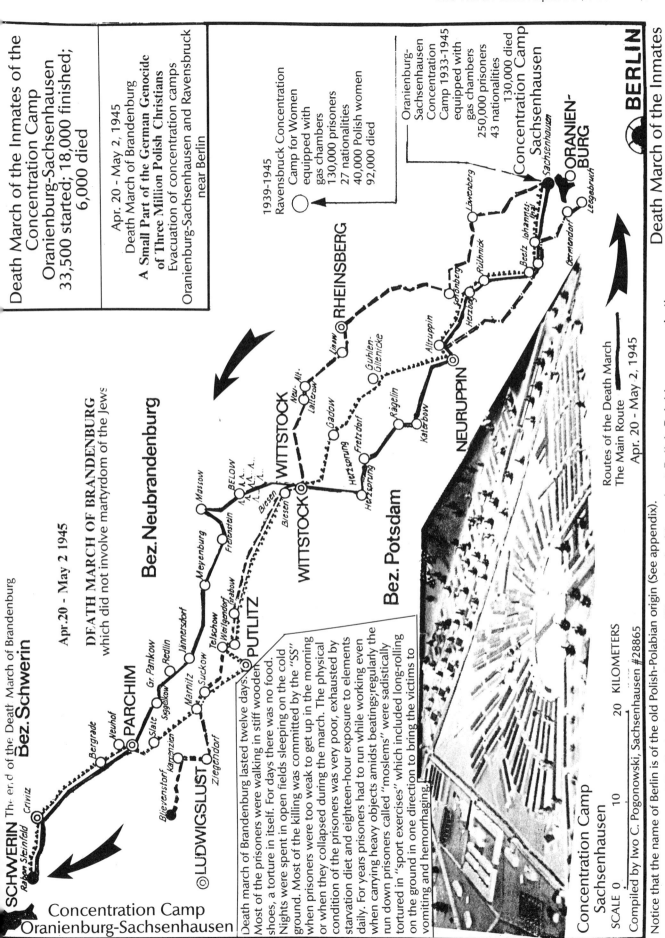

Death March of the Inmates of the Concentration Camp Oranienburg-Sachsenhausen
33,500 started; 18,000 finished; 6,000 died

Apr. 20 - May 2, 1945
Death March of Brandenburg
A Small Part of the German Genocide of Three Million Polish Christians
Evacuation of concentration camps
Oranienburg-Sachsenhausen and Ravensbrück near Berlin

1939-1945
Ravensbrück Concentration
Camp for Women equipped with gas chambers
130,000 prisoners
27 nationalities
40,000 Polish women
92,000 died

Oranienburg-Sachsenhausen Concentration Camp 1933-1945 equipped with gas chambers
250,000 prisoners
43 nationalities
130,000 died
Concentration Camp Sachsenhausen

BERLIN

ORANIEN-BURG

The end of the Death March of Brandenburg
Bez. Schwerin

Apr.20 - May 2 1945

DEATH MARCH OF BRANDENBURG
which did not involve martyrdom of the Jews

Bez. Neubrandenburg

Bez. Potsdam

Death march of Brandenburg lasted twelve days. Most of the prisoners were walking in stiff wooden shoes, a torture in itself. For days there was no food. Nights were spent in open fields sleeping on the cold ground. Most of the killing was committed by the "SS" when prisoners were too weak to get up in the morning or when they collapsed during the march. The physical condition of the prisoners was very poor, exhausted by starvation diet and eighteen-hour exposure to elements daily. For years prisoners had to run while working even when carrying heavy objects amidst beatings; regularly the run down prisoners called "moslems" were sadistically tortured in "sport exercises" which included long-rolling on the ground in one direction to bring the victims to vomiting and hemorrhaging.

Concentration Camp
Sachsenhausen

SCALE 0   10   20 KILOMETERS

Routes of the Death March
The Main Route
Apr. 20 - May 2, 1945

Death March of the Inmates

Compiled by Iwo C. Pogonowski, Sachsenhausen #28865

Notice that the name of Berlin is of the old Polish-Polabian origin (See appendix).
Played out northwest of Berlin in the countryside still marked with ancient Polish-Polabian names in the common language of Polish and Elbe River Slavs. "Polabian" literally means "living on the Elbe (Łaba) River."

Concentration Camp Oranienburg-Sachsenhausen

Map: 1945 Death March in Brandenburg; a Small Part of the German Genocide of Three Million Polish Christians.

Poland becoming the most important Soviet conquest of World War II after Germany destroyed 40% of Poland's national wealth.

4. Departure of Poles from Lvov and Soviet Galicia.
5. Departure of Poles from Vilna, Soviet Lithuania and Byelorussia.
6. Migration of Poles to Silesia.
7. Migration of Poles to West Pomerania.
8. Migration of Poles to Mazuria.
9. Return of Poles from U.S.S.R. immediately after the war.
10. Return of Poles from U.S.S.R. after 1956.
11. Return of Poles from the West France, Germany, etc.
12. Emigration to Germany postwar and later.

THE THIRD POLISH REPUBLIC 1944-present PEOPLE'S POLAND WITHIN SOVIET BLOC

Poland was subjugated to a process of extermination by Hitler-Stalin partnership. Hitler's attack changed Stalin's policy towards Poland from obliteration to conversion into a buffer state limiting German potential. Poland was deprived of sovereignty and became a victim of Soviet exploitation; Sovietization, crippling of Poland's leadership community and paralyzing of private initiative resulted in a low standard of living; Soviet anti-Semitic provocations especially in 1946 and in 1968 were designed to eliminate public support for Poland in the West; these provocations led the Poles to believe that there is an ongoing Soviet propaganda campaign to assassinate Polish national character and to spread in the West the slanderous notion that Poles are "extreme anti-Semites" and therefore that the Polish nation "deserves" the Communist oppression; preoccupation with the slanders resulting from anti-Semitism "Made in Russia" had the unfortunate effect of reducing the alertness of Polish public opinion to actual anti-Semitism of Communist bureaucrats or misguided individuals.

THE AGONY OF THE SECOND POLISH REPUBLIC Betrayed by the Western Allies

World War II deportation and migration involved over 25,000,000 people on the Polish territory.

A.D. 1944-1947 Civil War and Gigantic Deportation shaping the Third Polish Republic The People's Poland within Soviet Bloc

Some 350,000 were killed in the 1944-1947 civil war fought between forces controlled by the Soviets and a guerrilla army resisting Sovietization of Poland.

1. Aug. 2, 1945, Allied decision in Potsdam Oder-Neisse border closed. 5,000,000 German war refugees not allowed to return.
2. Allied decision to transfer 3,500,000 Germans out of Poland, west of the Oder-Neisse border.
3. Return home of Poles deported east out of areas annexed to Germany.

Map: 1944-1947 Civil War and Gigantic Deportations, the People's Poland.

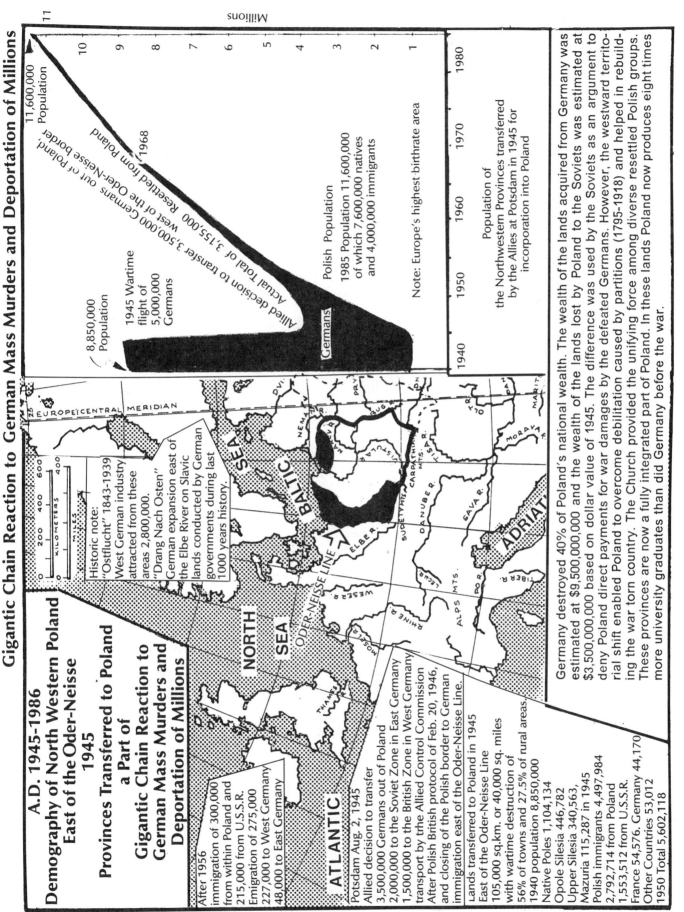

Gigantic Chain Reaction to German Mass Murders and Deportation of Millions

A.D. 1945-1986
Demography of North Western Poland East of the Oder-Neisse 1945

Provinces Transferred to Poland a Part of
Gigantic Chain Reaction to German Mass Murders and Deportation of Millions

Historic note:
"Ostflucht" 1843-1939 West German industry attracted from these areas 2,800,000. "Drang Nach Osten" German expansion east of the Elbe River on Slavic lands conducted by German governments during last 1000 years history.

After 1956 immigration of 300,000 from within Poland and 215,000 from U.S.S.R. Emigration of 275,000 227,000 to West Germany 48,000 to East Germany

Potsdam Aug. 2, 1945
Allied decision to transfer
3,500,000 Germans out of Poland
2,000,000 to the Soviet Zone in East Germany
1,500,000 to the British Zone in West Germany transport by the Allied Control Commission
After Polish British protocol of Feb. 20, 1946, and closing of the Polish border to German immigration east of the Oder-Neisse Line.
Lands transferred to Poland in 1945
East of the Oder-Neisse Line
105,000 sq.km. or 40,000 sq. miles with wartime destruction of 56% of towns and 27.5% of rural areas.
1940 population 8,850,000
Native Poles 1,104,134
Opole Silesia 446,782
Upper Silesia 340,563,
Mazuria 115,287 in 1945
Polish immigrants 4,497,984
2,792,714 from Poland
1,553,512 from U.S.S.R.
France 54,576. Germany 44,170.
Other Countries 53,012
1950 Total 5,602,118

Germany destroyed 40% of Poland's national wealth. The wealth of the lands acquired from Germany was estimated at $9,500,000,000 and the wealth of the lands lost by Poland to the Soviets was estimated at $3,500,000,000 based on dollar value of 1945. The difference was used by the Soviets as an argument to deny Poland direct payments for war damages by the defeated Germans. However, the westward territorial shift enabled Poland to overcome debilitation caused by partitions (1795-1918) and helped in rebuilding the war torn country. The Church provided the unifying force among diverse resettled Polish groups. These provinces are now a fully integrated part of Poland. In these lands Poland now produces eight times more university graduates than did Germany before the war.

Polish Population
1985 Population 11,600,000 of which 7,600,000 natives and 4,000,000 immigrants

Note: Europe's highest-birthrate area

Population of the Northwestern Provinces transferred by the Allies at Potsdam in 1945 for incorporation into Poland

11,600,000 Population

8,850,000 Population

1945 Wartime flight of 5,000,000 Germans

Allied decision to transfer 3,500,000 Germans out of Poland, west of the Oder-Neisse border. Actual Total of 3,155,000 Resettled from Poland

Germans

Millions

1940   1950   1960   1970   1980

Map: 1945-1986 Demography of North-Western Poland, lands East of the Oder-Neisse acquired from Germany in compensation for lands lost to Soviet Union.

Population of Europe	750 Millions
Eur. U.S.S.R. 255M	Hungary 11M
West Germany 63M	Portugal 10M
Italy 58M	Belgium 10M
United Kingdom 57M	Greece 10M
France 56M	Bulgaria 9M
Spain 39M	Sweden 8M
Poland 38M	Austria 7.7M
Yugoslavia 24M	Switzerland 7M
Romania 23M	Finland 5.3M
East Germany 17M	Denmark 5.2M
Czechoslovakia 15M	Ireland 3.5M
Holland 14.5M	Norway 1.2M

Poland and the rest of East-Central Europe is treated by the United States as a peripheral problem. Its surrender by Roosevelt to the Soviets did not buy security for the United States; in fact it escalated U.S. defense expenditures as Soviet Union became a superpower. It is clear that the United States is in no position to challenge militarily the Soviet hegemony over Poland and the rest of Eastern Europe. However the built-in economic inefficiency of Soviet totalitarism permits the United States together with Western Europe and Japan to win the global contest by driving the competition into a race of technology and economy which the Soviets have to lose unless they reform by decentralizing and turning to market economy. This would deny the Soviets the opportunity to continue using economic hardship as one of the means of subjugating people; more immediately the West led by the United States could make conditional the continuous extension of badly needed commercial credits and sales of technology to the Soviets. The condition for these ongoing transactions should be steady progress of the Communists in allowing more freedom in Poland and other countries of east-central Europe.

A.D. 1986

POLISH PEOPLE'S REPUBLIC

WITHIN THE

SOVIET BLOC

Poland Culturally in Western Civilization - Resisting Sovietization

Map: 1986 The Polish People's Republic - within the Soviet Bloc while Culturally a part of Western Civilization - Resisting Sovietization - population numbers.

Map: 1018-1986 The Range of Territorial Changes of the Polish State.

APPENDIX
PREHISTORY AND LANGUAGE EVOLUTION

"Languages are the pedigrees of nations."
Dr. Samuel Johnson (1709–1784)

Introductory Remarks

This appendix presents an abbreviated story of the Indo-European languages in the prehistoric setting which led eventually to the formation of the modern Polish language. It also includes the most important archeological findings and early historic events prior to well-documented history of the Slavs in general and the Poles in particular.

There are a number of theories regarding the length of the process of evolution of the Indo-European languages. The proposed time span of this process ranges from very lengthy to short. This text follows generally the theory of a lengthy evolution in a geographic isolation of the Baltic, Slavic and Germanic languages. This theory is compared to the short evolution theory on the graph on page 000. The short evolution theory proposes a later arrival to Europe of these three branches of the Indo-European family, coming with the last of three waves of immigration from the east.

The long evolution theory accepts the possibility of a much earlier arrival of the Indo-Europeans to central Europe. Both of them accept the possible 4000 year existence of the interphase between the Eastern and Western Indo-European languages in central Europe. Both theories chronicle the end of Slavic prehistory with the detailed descriptions of the Slavic peoples by Byzantine historians some 1500 years ago. The major difference of opinion concerns what happened and when, in the remaining 2500 years.

The historians who favor the short evolution theories ignore the linguistic evidence. Some of these theories actually postulate that the Germanic and Balto-Slavic people all came to Europe as one undifferentiated group, which settled partially on the eastern and partially on the western side of the line dividing Eastern and Western languages of the Indo-European family in central Europe. This is a highly questionable notion because it is not compatible with the long term stability of the East/West division into Satem and Centum.

Study of modern languages gives an indication of language evolution. Correlation of this knowledge with archeological studies of the prehistoric cultures gives information about the remote past before written records. While Mesopotamia in the Middle East saw invention of writing about 2800 B.C., northern Europe had to wait for consistent written records until the sixth century A.D.

The knowledge gained from archeology is indirect and uncertain. The same archeological finds can often be placed differently within the same picture of the past, depending on what kind of correlations and judgments are made. Also, there is nothing certain about the rate of change in a language when the degree and duration of its geographic isolation is not known and the kind of contact it had with other languages is uncertain. The farther back one tries to go into prehistory, the more vague it becomes.

The decision to follow the longer version of the evolution of the Germanic and Balto-Slavic languages was made because the archeologists working in central and eastern Europe generally believe that the archeological findings support a longer period of development. Also, the linguists have gradually been pushing back the estimated time when they believe the Slavic language evolution began.

Study of Greek writings from the second millennium B.C. seems to support the thesis that the Balts and Slavs separated even before the Bronze Age. Early evolutionary stages of all Indo-European languages have been moved by linguists to the beginning of the third millennium B.C. Therefore, major cultural changes within the context of European history are mentioned, especially those which took place on Polish territory. A discussion of the role of the Irano-Sarmatians on the development of the Slavic languages, including Polish, is an important historical and linguistic event, and will be developed in this essay.

Vague Prehistory: About 20,000 B.C.–4500 B.C.

A common and original language that would later become European and South Asiatic is thought to have begun forming its first words some 25,000 years ago on the steppes north of the Caspian Sea. It did not coin an original name for an ocean which meant "a great river" or even for the sea which meant "a lake"; sea in Polish is *morze* (mo-zhe) from archaic *mere* which meant "a pool," "a lake" or "a marsh." This originally landlocked language is called Indo-European because it is related to languages spoken from India to western Europe. Indo-European developed into world's largest family of languages.

The search for the original homeland of this language family led researchers to propose the possibility that the names given to three living things common to all the Indo-European languages, and not necessarily occurring at the location where they are spoken today, might locate the region where the common and original language began its evolution. The three identified living things used were "salmon," "turtle" and "beech tree." These three occur simultaneously only in central Europe in the river basins of the Vistula and Oder in Poland and the Elbe and Rhine in Germany.

Independently it was established that the closest to the original Indo-European were the spoken languages of the Balto-Slavic group, namely modern Lithuanian and the now extinct language of the Prussians. Their location on the lower Vistula places the original Balto-Slavic Prussians in the area identified in the search for the Indo-European homeland.

The preservation of the most archaic Indo-European forms in the languages of the Balts is probably due to the geographic configuration of the Balto-Slavs in which the Slavs were more exposed to foreign influences and invasions and thus shielded the Balts from them.

By 8,500 B.C. northern Europe was the borderland between Paleolithic (paleos—old, litos—stone or chipped stone) and Mesolithic (mesos—middle) Stone Age Cultures and had an unknown population. At that time the waters trapped in the glaciers were receding and exposed a land bridge between the continent and Britain. It was at this time that agriculture was beginning in the Middle East. By 4,500 B.C. the Indo-Europeans were identified in central Europe's Neolithic cultures (neos = new). The idea that they could have been at that time the only speakers of the Indo-European languages may be suggested by the archeological findings which appear to indicate that subsequent expansions of the Indo-Europeans radiated from Central Europe into Western and Northern Europe, into Central Asia, the subcontinent of India, and the Middle East.

Very Remote Prehistory: 4500 B.C.–2000 B.C.

It was the warmest period in the last several tens of thousands of years. Archaeological evidence of the Stone Age indicates an expansion of the Indo-Europeans, reaching the shores of the southwestern, southern, and southeastern Baltic Sea, southern Scandinavia and all of Britain by 2,800 B.C. Meanwhile, in far off Mesopotamia writing was invented, bronze was discovered, and the potter's wheel was first invented and later converted for use in transportation. Ancestor worship was evident in the burial rituals. By 2500 B.C. in Poland, a primitive agriculture was beginning; a primitive hoe was used. A matriarchal society was just starting and, with it, the division of labor. Europe's largest strip chert mine from the end of Neolithic culture is located in Poland. It includes nearly 1000 entrances and 7000 foot-long corridors with ceilings supported on rock pillars. By 2300 B.C. newly arriving tribes were living off animal husbandry, which strengthened the social position of men.

This period seems to end with the gradual formation of an interphase between East and West Indo-Europeans which corresponds to the division into Satem and Centum. Both these words stand for the number "one hundred," a word which was chosen as typically representing the linguistic difference between Eastern and Western Indo-European languages. It appears that the East/West division was located in central Europe for about 4000 years without any major change. The prolonged existence of this interphase carries the conviction of simplicity in favor of the theory of a very lengthy evolution of languages in geographic isolation.

Remote Prehistory: 2000 B.C.–1300 B.C.

The Copper Age was an era of geographic isolation for early Balto-Slavic and Germanic speakers along the south eastern Baltic and in southern Scandinavia. Gradual and separate specification of early Balts and Slavs apparently took place during the Copper Age and the Balto-Slavic original names of rivers were established in the southern and eastern Baltic area.

There is a general acceptance of the location of the Balts in their settlement area at the beginning of this period. The structure of the Balto-Slavic languages implies the contemporary existence of the Slavs in the area immediately to the south of the Balts. Also, there probably was a Baltic influence in the area of the battle-ax cultures to the north and east of them at the beginning of this period.

By 1800 B.C. a patriarchal society started developing on the Polish territory according to anthropological findings. This resulted from the development of animal husbandry. At this time peasant-type agriculture, combining farming and animal husbandry, became common. It has been present in Europe for about 4000 years.

By 1,600 B.C. an expansion of Iranians and Irano-Aryans towards northeast, southwest, and southeast (towards the subcontinent of India) took place. The knowledge of metals was in the beginning stage. There are in Poland rare finds of copper-tin alloy and bronze from this period. Patriarchal clans started to unify themselves into tribes.

Prehistory: 1300 B.C.–400 B.C.

The Bronze Age arrived to the proto-Slavs earlier than to the Baltic and Germanic speakers isolated further north. Geographic isolation and language specification of the Slavic, Baltic and Germanic languages in northern Europe continued as an original linguistic

development—achievable at a very slow rate.

Bronze Age cultures are considered to be the genesis of the Slav peoples. Western Slavic or Lusatian (Lausitz) culture introduced cremation and use of urns for burial of the ashes. The Lusatians apparently hoped to help their loved ones unite with the eternal fire of the sun through the fire of cremation. The resulting cemeteries are known as urnfields. Urnfield cemeteries are seen as an expression of a Slavic ethnic community consciousness expressed in the disposal of its deceased.

A separate Eastern Slavic Bronze Age culture of the middle Dnieper represents the beginning of differentiation of eastern and western branches of the early Slavs primarily by cultural, rather than linguistic differences, since their area of geographic isolation was relatively undisturbed judging by the archeological findings. Further development of animal husbandry was evident and metal tools were used in agriculture. The use of horses changed from meat supply to riding. The Slavs used a solar calendar typical of agrarians and not the lunar calendar usually used by shepherds watching at night over their flocks.

The name "Slavs" comes from slovo, which means "spoken word." The Slavs identified themselves as people who communicated by word of mouth as distinct from people whose languages they could not understand and who were to them dumb or speechless, in Slavic Niemiec (ne-myets). With the passage of time this term became associated exclusively with the name of the Germans and today it is used in this way in all modern Slavic languages.

It is interesting to note that the noun slovo contains the first letter "s" which as a prefix means "together," followed by the root lov (wov) which in turn is associated with hunting, fishing, catching, chasing, retrieving, heeding, understanding, or even deciding what to do. "O" is a typical Slavic noun ending in nouns derived from other words. Slovo in Polish slowo (swo-vo) or the spoken word is related to the noun slawa (swa-va) which at first meant "the fame by a word of mouth" and later simply "fame," "glory," etc.

The names of a number of Indo-European subfamilies originate with the idea of communicating with a common language. Thus, the Germans call themselves Deutsch related to the word deutilch meaning understandable. In antiquity deutlich was tutlich a form which survived in Swiss dialects and is related to "teutonic" which in turn relates to diuten meaning "to understand or to clarify". Also, in the old Germanic, the word for "our people" was theodesko which survived in Italy as the noun describing the Germans. Italy is called Wlochy (vwo-khi) in Polish because of similarity between Italian and Vlach or Walachian languages. Walachian (now called Romanian) is an Illyrian language with Latin and Slavic overlay.

The standard of living and size of the population increased while greater differences in the wealth of the clans became noticeable. Houses started to be built above the ground. However, all the Slavic languages kept the terminology of earlier dwelling constructions dug into the ground.

In Polish, for example, a wall is called sciana (shchana) meaning "a cut ground face," the stairs are schody (skho-di) meaning "steps down," the floor is podloga (pod-wo-ga) meaning "laid under," ceiling is powala (po-va-wa) meaning "thrown over on the ground," and a bath or washroom is called lazienka (wa-zhen-ka) or laznia (wazh-na) meaning a space related to dawdling, loitering, crawling or climbing. The last two meanings might suggest use of ground water for washing in sunken tubs or wells dug below the floor level in dug-out dwellings.

Gradual expansion of urnfield cemeteries into the adjacent area populated by the Celts starting in 1,200 B.C. is shown on the map of 1,000 B.C. The approximate location of the interphase between Eastern and Western Indo-Europeans is also shown. By 830 B.C. amber from the Balto-Slavic coast was reaching Middle Eastern markets. Traders and prospectors were coming to northern Europe from the Mediterranean area.

By 670 B.C. Irano-Scyths came in contact with the Eastern Slavs. The map shows approximately what is also indicated by the linguistic evidence, namely, that the Slavs during their formative period had some contact with other East Indo-Europeans, primarily the Balts, then Irano-Sarmatians who have followed the Irano-Scyths, Illyrians and the Thracians. This map is in agreement with the linguistic evidence of early Slavinic contact with West Indo-Europeans, namely, the Celtic and the Germanic tribes. These early contacts are seen also in the Slavic borrowings present in Germanic languages, such as the word "weather" in German, *Wetter*, coming from the old Slavic word for "wind," the weather maker. In Polish wind is *wiatr* (vyatr). The 670 B.C. map agrees with the linguistic findings indicating the long geographic isolation from which the Slavs were dispersed relatively recently. Some writers prefer to insist on a Slavic homeland about two hundred miles farther east so that they could call the lower Vistula and the entire basin of the Oder River German "ancestral" land. The small area left for the early Slavic people, for most of the next 1000 years is on the foothills of the Eastern Carpathian Mountains. This area is so small that it could not possibly have supported enough people to produce the "Slavic flood" starting in the fourth and lasting to seventh century A.D. It is located too far in the south-eastern direction from the Balts without whom the Balto-Slavic development would not have been possible.

Meanwhile, according to archeologic findings, by 700–500 B.C. the Western Slavs had lived through a period of prosperity of their Lusatian culture. They had been in contact with the Iron Age through the Celts. By 550 B.C. an island fortress of Biskupin was built in north central Poland. It housed about 1200 people. Biskupin is just one of many such fortified towns, which were built since 700 B.C. AND COVERED BETWEEN FIVE TO TWELVE ACRES EACH. WELL PRESERVED REMAINS INDICATE AN ADVANCED WOODEN ARCHITECTURE.

POLISH ARCHEOLOGISTS MADE THE DISCOVERY OF BISKUPIN IN THE 20TH CENTURY. THE TOWN LAYOUT INDICATES AN EQUALITY OF THE INHABITANTS. THERE WAS NO SPECIAL HOUSE FOR A PATRIARCH OR A CHIEFTAIN. A CLAN COMMUNITY CONSTITUTED THE SOCIAL ORDER. RUINS OF TWO SUCH TOWNS INDICATE ATTACKS BY THE IRANO-SCYTHS BY 500 B.C.

By 480 B.C. the Western Slavs introduced designs representing faces of the deceased on their burial urns. These new urn designs at first started spreading in the southeastern direction. This direction, however, does not appear to be the result of a Germanic pressure, as it is sometimes supposed. At the time, technological backwardness of the Germanic area apparently resulted in a quiet Germano-Slav border. A relatively undisturbed evolution of the early Slavic and Germanic languages had a chance to continue.

The location of the East Slavs as shown on the map of 480 B.C. is compatible with the description by Herodotus who called the Slavs "Scythian farmers" in contrast to the nomadic Irano-Scyths. Herodotus located the Slavs in the 5th century B.C. at three day's march from (the mouth of) the Dnieper. Meanwhile the main theater of cultural and political activity continued on the shores of the Mediterranean Sea, well documented in written records. In the west Carthage was a great power, while in the east the great Persian Empire was expanding and threatening the progress of the Greeks. Herodotus' great work is a history of the Greek and Persian wars from 500 to 479 B.C. His systematic treatment and mastery of style have gained for him the title of "Father of History."

Prehistory in Northern Europe: 400 B.C–200 B.C.

During the first part of this period the urnfield culture of Lusatia (Lausitz) ended. The families started to separate themselves and to acquire property. The role of the warriors became more important. However, the isolation of the early Baltic, Slavic and Germanic peoples continued still almost undisturbed. Meanwhile, the small kingdom of Macedon was gaining influence among the Greek states. It reached its maximum strength as the Empire of Alexander in 323 B.C. The Macedonian Empire disintegrated by 301 B.C. into kingdoms of Alexander's generals. By 270 B.C. Carthage reached the peak of its power and Rome had unified most of the Italian peninsula.

The long isolation of the Slavic and Germanic people was coming to an end and so was the undisturbed continuity of evolution of their languages. By 200 B.C. the Germanic pressure on the Gauls and the Irano-Samaritan pressure on the Slavs was just beginning. Apparently the Slavic pressure on the Balts was also beginning at about the same time. West Slavs become known as "Vends" and East Slavs as "Antes." Improved Iron Age technology kept arriving among the West Slavs from the neighboring Celts, who brought the potter's wheel and an improved potter's kiln. Numerous early ironworks from this period are found in southern Poland. The use of iron plowshares began.

Gradual End of Prehistory in the Balto–Slavic Europe; Slavification of Invaders: 200 B.C.–A.D. 650

Amber trade with Rome was well established by 200 B.C. The "amber road" originated in the "amber region" near Gdansk. It followed up the Vistula River to the Moravian Gate through the Carpathians. There it exited from the Polish territory and headed south to Rome. The Roman historian Pliny (A.D. 23–79) called the Vistula River "Vistla" and described the inhabitants as the Venedic Slavs. In connection with the amber trade, Ptolemy, astronomer, mathematician and geographer of Alexandria in the 2nd century A.D., mentioned Karrodunum or Krakow on the Vistula and the amber market in Calixia or Kalisz (ka-leesh.) Ptolemy described the Bay of Gdansk as the Venedic Bay from which maritime trade connected the lower Vistula with the lower Rhine region.

Amber from the Baltic coast was used at the time of Nero (A.D. 54–68) to decorate a large amphitheater and accessories of the gladiators. The largest piece of amber used there weighed 4 kg. (One warehouse found recently in Wroclaw (vrtos-wav), Silesia, contained about 6000 pounds of amber.) Export from the Polish territory to Rome included, besides amber, furs, hides, cattle, horses, and also slaves.

The Roman historian Cornelius Tacitus (A.D. 55?–120?) described the Venedic Slavs. He quoted several names of Slavic tribal chiefs in northern Europe which he called Germania solely because it had a settled population. He did not pay any attention to the languages spoken there. Tacitus contrasted the widespread Slavic practice of carrying weapons by all men with the prohibition to do so in some Germanic tribes. The prohibition was enforced by locking up all weapons overnight under guards loyal to the chieftain.

In the 2nd century B.C., Western or Venedic Slavs formed tribal federations. Then *Antic*, the eastern Slavic name, was apparently derived from the Western Sarmatian Alans known as the *Antae*. Patriarchal society ended and territorial organization began. A form of warriors' democracy is indicated by the widespread presence of weapons in graves. Trade with Rome and an influx of Roman coins continued. Import of iron ores from the south was coming to an end and local ores started to be used.

After the breaking of the power of the Celts by Julius Caesar by the end of the 1st century B.C. the Roman Empire expanded north into Gaul and along the Danube in need of a new supply of slaves. Roman economy was based on slavery. Roman law prohibited the slaves to serve in the army. Meanwhile, the north European barbarians were becoming more experienced and dangerous in warfare. Eventually the Romans started recruiting the Germanic, Slavic, Sarmatian, and other "barbarians" to serve in the legions. In northern Europe, the period at the beginning of the first millennium of the Christian era is marked by invasions and by Slavification of the invaders. Passage through the Slavic settlement area of the nomadic Western Alans of the Irano-Sarmatian language group was followed by the Germanic Goths and Gepids, by the Mongolic Huns, by the Turkic Avars, and Bulgars, and much later by the Ugro–Finnish Magyars or Hungarians. The riches of Rome and her Mediterranean possessions were the main attraction for these invaders. The Slavic territory was of secondary interest to them.

The successive hegemonies of the invaders contributed to the elimination of each other in the Slavic area and left very limited influence on the well formed Slavic language which evolved and crystalized earlier during long geographic isolation. The most noticeable cultural influence was left by the Sarmatians whose property markings, the *Tamgas*, were later used in the designs of a number of Polish coats-of-arms of the 11th to 17th centuries when they became stylized and heraldic.

The most important, however, were the Western Alan Sarmatian tribal names of *Antae*, *Serboi*, *Choroates* and *Aorsi*. These Sarmatian names influenced the naming of a few of the Slavic tribes. Generally, the Slavic tribes named themselves in a descriptive manner in the Slavic language. The name of Poland, for example, means "a country of cultivated fields." However, it is accepted that the names of Lusatian Sorbs and Serbs came from Serboi, the name of Croats came from Choroates; Antae were discussed before.

It is possible that from the name *Aorsi* is derived the word *Rus* (roosh) which describes the territory of the East Slavs. The word *Aorsi* contains the consonants "r" and "s" and the sound "or" easily becomes "ra" or "ru" (roo). These consonants do not occur together in the same order in the Finnish word *Ruotsi* usually proposed by the German writers as the origin of *Rus*. In Finnish the word *Ruotsi* refers to the Scandinavian Germanic people and not to the Balto-Slavic people. The fact that the consonants "ts" can easily change into "s" might have played a lesser role than an ethnocentric German notion. There might be a possibility that name *Rus* came from some Slavic word such as *rosc* (rooshch) meaning "to grow," for example. However, so far there is no proven explanation of the name Rus or Russia.

The linguistic influence of the Western Sarmatian Alans was exerted on both East and West Slavs. As a result it could have been a unifying influence which could have reduced rather than increased the differences between the East and West Slavic languages. At any rate the diversification of the Slavic languages proceeded very slowly. Even today the Slavic languages spoken from central Europe to the Pacific coast of Asia differ among themselves less than do the Germanic dialects on the small area of West Germany. It is possible that this situation resulted from much more extensive early migrations of the Germanic tribes than those of the Slavs.

There is some difficulty with identification of the Irano-Sarmatian words which were absorbed by the Slavs since both language subfamilies are East Indo-European; as Satem languages they have many similar words from the earliest times of their existence. In all Slavic languages, for example, the word for number "four" starts with the identical sound of "ch" which also occurs in both Indic and Sarmato-Iranian languages; in Polish it is *cztery* (chteri). The Polish word *Bog* (book) meaning God is similar to the Indic Bhaga and to the Irano-Sarmatian Baga. In the Old Slavonic Church Language it was Bog. The word *kosz* (kosh) both in Polish and in Sanskrit (written old Indic) means a basket. Pupil, student or apprentice in Sanskrit is *chela;* in Polish it is *czeladnik* (che-la-dneek) to name just a few examples.

Ethnocentric German writers have insisted that the notions of "God" or "Paradise" came to the Slavs very late. Some German writers claim that these were recent borrowings from the Irano-Sarmatians. Contrary to this line of thinking, many ancient Slavic words have philosophic meaning. For example, the Slavic word for a human being, or a man, is a composite of "forehead" or "forefront" and of "age"; combined, they give the meaning of man as the "outcome of an evolution." In Polish it is *czlowiek* (chwo-vyek) and in Russian *chewovyek*.

The indigenous Slavic pagan religion included *Perun* (pe-roon) god of the thunderbolt and war located in the sky. The cult of Perun dominated during wars and migrations. The word *piorun* (pyo-roon) in modern Polish means a thunderbolt. The god of peaceful life, work, and home was *Wolos* (vo-wos). The word *wolos* means hair or furs. It relates to the idea of warmth, protection from the cold etc. In modern Polish *wlos* (vwos) means a hair. *Swarog* (sva-rog) was the god of fire and father of *Dazbog* (dazh-bog) the sun-god. The name *Swarog* contains the root word *war* (var). It means heat or fire. Countless modern Polish words contian this root word; they range from cooking to quarreling and fighting. The name of *Dazhbog* is derived from the verb *dazyc* (da-zhich) which means to give or to provide. Thus the sun-god's name described him as the source of life-giving rays of the sun.

There were also tribal gods such as the other son of *Swarog* the *Swarozyc* (sva-ro-zhits) of the Polabian Veleti. The Rugian Slavs worshiped *Swietowit* (shvan-to-veet), whose statue with four faces was facing four directions of the world. The name "Swietowit" means giving a holy look or blessing the world. It occupied the temple in Arkona. The temple received a head tax from the inhabitants of Ruegen Island, part of their war spoils, and tributes from the arriving merchants, including Christians. Ruegen in Slavic is *Rugia* (roog-ya).

Each family, clan, tribe and region had its own guardian deity. The dead were cremated on a pile of wood and their ashes were buried in urns in the cemeteries. The graves included cremated objects of the deceased so that they could be used in life after death, united through the fire of cremation with the eternal fire of the sun-god Dazbog. The souls of the ancestors were worshiped. Generally statues of the gods were made out of wood; occasionally, also out of stone.

The Roman Empire expanded farthest north by A.D. 230 adding territory up to the limit of intensive agriculture. There the Roman legions could supply themselves well and control the land capable of supporting a relatively high density of population. Meanwhile the Germanic tribes overcrowded the Oder and the southern Vistula region and again started to move south towards the Roman frontiers. The last to depart the Polish territory were the Gepids.

By A.D. 362 the Ostrogoths organized a kingdom on the shores of the Black Sea. It extended its hegemony over most of the Balto-Slavic lands and came in contact on the Dnieper River with the approaching Huns. The Huns defeated them in A.D. 375. Apparently at that time Germanic tribes were near the Roman frontiers and the Slavic Vends became again the sole inhabitants of the Polish territory.

One linguistic relic left by the Gothic transit through the Polish lands could be the word "szlachta" (shlakh-ta). It is a Slavization of the Germanic word "Schlacht" meaning "battle," "killing," etc. In English it survived in the word "slaughter." In Polish-Polabian language at first it described the warriors. Later in Polish it meant the knightly class of gentry or nobility.

After Byzantium became the new capital of the Roman Empire in A.D. 323 the defense of the Empire depended entirely on the mobile army. It grew at the expense of the garrison army which protected the frontier provinces. As the borderlands became depopulated by continuous warfare with the barbarians, their repopulation was achieved by Germanic tribes such as Franks and Burgundians who were earlier defeated and subjugated by the mobile Roman army. They were under a strong pressure to Romanize.

The fall of the Western Roman Empire in A.D. 476 occurred after the Germanic tribes such as the Ostrogoths and Visigoths, fleeing the Huns, broke through the Roman borders. Saxons and Anglos went to England which until then was populated by the Celts. Eventually the Germanic invaders became Latinized in Spain, in France, and to some extent in England. Thus French is a Celto-Germanic language with a Latin overlay, while English is a Germanic language with a French overlay. English went through a "pidgin" stage of linguistic mixture before acquiring its modern form of a "position language" without ending changes in its nouns and adjectives. The Southern Slavs, who settled later in the former Roman Illyria, kept their own languages which did not undergo a Latin overlay. The Illyrians themselves were, however, of the same Eastern Indo-European group as were the Slavs.

By the end of the 4th century A.D. the great Slavic migration began. It was made possible by the warriors democracy which evolved an efficient military organization led by an elective commander called *wojewoda* (vo-ye-vo-da) or a leader of warriors, *czelnik* (chel-neek) or headman—a word derived from the noun *czolo* (cho-wo) meaning a forehead, and *knedz* (knandz). Knedz, in old Slavic "a leader," later evolved into *ksiaze* (kshown-zhe), "a prince" or "a ruler," and into *ksiadz* (kshowndz), meaning at first "a bishop" and in modern Polish "a priest."

The Slavs at first avoided battles in an open field. However, by the middle of the 6th century the Slavs were able to defeat Byzantine armies in open fields and reduce their fortresses by use of siege machines.

The Slavic warriors fought in a loose formation designed to take advantage of the terrain. Slavic formation was effective because of the high degree of motivation of the fighters. At first the Byzantine generals thought that the Slavic loose formation was highly disorderly. It certainly contrasted with the orderly arrangement of the lines of Byzantine soldiers, where the order also helped to apply enough coersion to maintain army discipline.

In A.D. 551 the Slavs routed the Byzantine army at Adrianopolis and after A.D. 558 started to settle in large groups on the land previously invaded and devastated. Slavic invaders usually proceeded to wreck the conquered lands, destroy what they could not carry with them, kill off the men, and take with them women and children. When the Slavs settled on a new land they built fortifications of timber and soil. New land was put to the plough. The Western Slavs pressed Germanic tribes out of the basin of the Elbe River after A.D. 512. They established themselves in Luneburgian, Hanoverian, and Danish Vendenland (named after the Slavic Vends; the name "Hanover" is derived from Slavic locality Hanov to which Germanic ending "er" was added). The Northwestern Slavs became known as the Polish-Polabians. Southwestern Slavs became known as Czechs, Moravians, and Slovaks, and occupied their present territory after A.D. 526. Farther west the Upper Bavarian Slavs were Christianized by Saint Boniface (680?–754) about two centuries later.

The 6th century ecclesiastic and historian Jordanes wrote about A.D. 550 that by the end of the 4th century Ostrogoths defeated King Boz of the Antic Slavs and crucified him and 70 Slavic tribal chiefs. Jordanes wrote that the Slavs were of "one blood" and lived in three groups: Venedic (western), Antic (eastern and southern), and Sklavinian (southern).

Detailed descriptions of the Slavs were given also in the 6th century in the Byzantine handbook on military science *The Tacticon* by Pseudo-Mauritius and history books by Procopius of

Caesarea and Theophilact of Simocatta. According to them the Slavic families lived from agriculture and animal husbandry. These families were united in clans which descended from a common ancestor. They described public meetings where all the favorable and unfavorable matters were discussed as the Slavs governed themselves democratically and did not live under one man's rule. By A.D. 550 the formation of the feudal system began in the Polish territory. The living standards began to fall when a large part of the population emigrated. The commercial contacts with the Mediterranean markets were broken. Metallurgy and pottery declined.

This period ends with the formation of the first Slav state of Samo, A.D. 623–661 (see page 000), which resulted from the overthrowing of the Avar hegemony during a widespread Slavic uprising. Agricultural skills of the Slavs tended to make permanent their acquisitions of new lands. Early invention of the Slavic plough was very important. Thus, for example, its Polish name *plug* (pwook) is a descriptive term for the implement's horizontal cutting function; it gave origin to the English word *plough* and German *Pflug*. By the 8th century Slavic agriculture was based on ploughing with horses. Slavic economy at that time became increasingly self sufficient.

BEGINNING OF THE WRITTEN SLAVIC HISTORY AND CHRISTIANIZATION OF THE SLAVS, A.D. 650–A.D. 1000. DOCUMENTED EVOLUTION OF SLAVIC LANGUAGES

In the 7th century A.D. the "Slavic flood" continued. Slavic eastern tribes headed northeast into the territory of the Balts and Finns to become Great Russians and east to expand as Byelorussian and Ukrainian Ruthenians; both Western and Eastern Slavs migrated into the Balkans to become Slovenes, Croats, Serbs, Macedonians and Bulgarians; the Western Slavs moved west into the entire Elbe River basin and along the Wesser River and north up to the Danish border to become the Polabians, the Lusatian Sorbs and Vends, the Polish Pomeranians and Silesians, and the Czechs, Moravians, and Slovaks.

Remolded by migrations, the old Slavic language was divided into three language groups: the Western or Polish-Polabian and Czecho-Slovak, the Eastern or Ruthenian and Russian, and the Southern or Serbo-Croatian, Macedonian, and Bulgarian.

Population movements tend to bring changes in the language transferred to a new territory. The idea that the western Slavic languages originally evolved in the basins of the Vistula and Odra rivers is supported by the archeological evidence and by the fact that the archaic nasalized vowels "a" (own) and "e" (an) survived only in the Polish language among all the modern Slavic languages.

The nasalized vowels are considered the oldest sounds produced by human speech organs. Linguistic researchers have proven that the vowels have much less staying power and less resistance to change than do the consonants. Among the vowels, the nasalized vowels have the least durability, especially when exposed to relocations and migrations resulting in exposure to foreign languages. Thus, Polish nasalized vowels suggest a long and continuous presence of the Slavs in the area of Poland ever since the long period of geographic isolation during which the Slavic languages were first forming and evolving.

The great civilizing role of Christianity in this period brought the riches of the Mediterranean cultures and civilizations into northern Europe. Christianization moved through Europe from west to east, from more densely to less densely populated lands. The fertile western European river valleys with a more benign climate were able to support denser population than were the central and northeastern rivers valleys. Thus, the march of Christianity marks the reversal of the main direction of migrations in Europe.

The ancient Indo-Europeans are believed to have migrated towards the west before the geographically isolated homelands of language subfamilies were formed. The spread of Christianity coincided with the population pressures that were building up in an eastern direction. Christianization set off a reversal of migratory trends from westwards to eastwards.

The French exerted pressure on the Rhine River valley settled by the Germans. The Germans encroached on the Elbe River Slavs, the Polabians (literally "those living on the Elbe"). This was followed by the German pressure on the Pomeranian and Silesian Poles, on Czechs and on the Balkan Slavs. The Swedes and Russians put the pressure on the Finns.

The entire eastern border of the Frankish Empire was controlled by the Slavs after the final dispersion of Avars in 796. The Slavs also colonized large areas along the upper Main River. Charlemagne's fortifications consisted of the Danish mark in the north, followed the fortified Slavic border known as the *Limes Sorabicus*. It was named after the Lusatian Sorbs. At the southern end of the fortifications was the Mark of Avaria.

The Mark of Avaria overlapped with today's Bavaria. The Latin word *Bavaria* was apparently produced by contamination of the name of Turkic Avars and Germanic Bayuvars.

The German advance against the Slavs is known as the *Drang nach Osten*. It began in the 10th century and produced devastating German defeats in the 15th and 20th centuries. The *Drang nach Osten* ended on the Elbe River, in the same place where it began one thousand years earlier. Its net effect was to weaken the Western Slavs and bring Russian domination all the way to the River Elbe. Together with a large immigration it brought the knowledge of German ways, language and culture to the Balto-Slavic Europe.

The first 500 years of the *Drang nach Osten* culminated in German defeat by the Polish-Lithuanian army in 1410 at Stebark (stan-bark) (Tannenberg) and Grunwald, north of Warsaw. The Polish victory stopped the German advance for nearly 400 years. Eventually the Russo-German alliance against Poland was concluded. In 1795 it obliterated the Polish state.

The second 500 years of the *Drang nach Osten* was ended shortly after a revival of the Russo-German alliance against Poland in 1939. The Hitler-Stalin partnership was broken with the German attack on Russia. Thousand years of German advance against the Slavs culminated in the battle of Stalingrad in 1943. The fall of Berlin in 1945 resulted in Soviet Russian domination over two-thirds of the European continent.

It is interesting to note that in spite of the one thousand years duration of the *Drang nach Osten*, Konrad Adenauer, while serving as a Chancellor of West Germany, felt that the German refugees from the east of the Elbe differed culturally from the West Germans and that the East Germans were in fact Slavs who "forgot" their language.

The wave set in motion by the spread of Christianity also produced a 500-year-long Polonization of the Balts and Ruthenians (Byelorussians and Ukrainians). It started with Christianization of Lithuania in 1386 and dwindled after the Bolshevik expansion in 1917–1946. The Russian drive east through Siberia, Alaska, Northern California and Hawaii could be viewed as the latest wave of the advance of Christianity which ended in the 19th century.

The Germanic encroachment on the Slavs occurred during the formation of the modern German language. It was formed as a transition language between Slavic and Germanic tribes. The Slavic influence brought an increase in the number of words to the German language by making a qualitative change in the language itself through the addition of the augmentative and diminutive forms which facilitated expression of emotional values by word structure. These augmentative and diminutive forms, especially plentiful in Slavic languages, serve to make the meaning of nouns and adjectives precise by broadening and clarifying them. The modern German and Dutch, in contra-distinction to other Germanic languages, make a considerable use of these forms in Slavic style.

The modern German has, besides structural influences, also numerous borrowings from the Slavic languages such as the word *Grenze* which comes from the Polish word *granica* (gra-nee-tsa) meaning a frontier or a border. Near the Dutch border the peasant or farming population is called *Klopleute* from the Slavic word *chlop* (khlop) which means a peasant or a man. Apparently from this word also comes the name of the town of Cloppenburg in northwestern Germany.

The final formation of the national Slav languages took place during and after Christianization of all the Slavic peoples. Western Slavs became members of Western Christianity and adopted the Roman alphabet while Eastern Slavs became members of Eastern Christianity and adopted the Greek alphabet. Thus, the interphase of Greek and Roman alphabet does not follow the East/West interphase of the Indo-European languages.

The Old Slavonic Church language was created by the Brothers of

Solun (so-woon) as Saint Cyril and Methodius from Tessalonika are known among the Slavs. Slavic church vocabulary created by them was very important in limiting the linguistic and therefore political influence of the Germans on the Western Slavs and of the Byzantine Greeks on the Eastern and Southern Slavs.

An anonymous Bavarian geographer described Slavic tribal territories north of Danube and east of the Elbe-Saal line, including the Polish area and the names of the Polish tribes. Apparently this description was prepared in order to orient the first king and founder of Germany, Louis II the German (843–876), in the military potential of the Slavs.

The main Slav states were formed during this period. After the first Slav state of Samo (623–661) followed the Great Moravian Empire (822–907). The Moravians brought Christianity to southern Poland in 866–885. The first Polish dynasty (c. 840–1370) brought Western Christianity to all of Poland in A.D. 966. The Piasts unified the Polish ethnic area in 989–992.

The early Piast period starting in A.D. 840 was very important in the evolution of the Polish identity.

The first crowned Polish king, Boleslaus the Brave was sent the crown in A.D. 1000 by Pope Sylvester II (999–1003) with the support of the Holy Roman Emperor Otto III (983–1002). Boleslaus I was actually crowned in 1025. The delay was caused by the machinations of the last Saxon king of Germany, Henry II (1002–1024).

The Polish Empire of Boleslaus I became a great power from 992 to 1031. At about the same time the Danish Empire of Boleslaus' nephew, Canute the Great, included Denmark, England, Norway and Sweden. In 1018 Boleslaus I conquered Kiev and placed on the Kievian throne his son-in-law Swiatopelk as the Grand Duke of Kiev, the huge state of the East Slavs. These two were historically important, though short-lived, early northern European empires.

After formation of the medieval Polish state, an important expansion of the Polish vocabulary occurred as a result of the immigration of speakers of German, Yiddish, and Dutch languages. They contributed Germanic trade and commerce terms such as *handel* (khan-del), *gwint* (gveent) from Gewinde or screw thread, *gielda* (gew-da) from Gilde (old Scandinavian gildi) or exchange, clearing house, or stock market; and *zegar* (ze-gar) from Zeiger meaning the big hand of the clock, or a clock. Early Polish literary language was influenced by Latin.

Medieval and early modern Poland became a sanctuary for the world's largest Jewish community which was allowed to cultivate faithfully its Judeo-Germanic roots and use, almost exclusively, the Yiddish language. This led at the beginning of the 20th century an English writer to state that in Poland "once a Jew, always a German." This oversimplification emphasizes the profound cultural gap which resulted from early Polish toleration and divided the masses of Polish and Yiddish-speaking people. The population census of 1931 indicated that nearly 90 percent of the Polish Jews did not speak Polish at home. They used almost exclusively the Yiddish language, and very few spoke Polish without a foreign accent. However, Yiddish does have a large number of borrowings from the Polish.

Only limited diversification of the Slav languages occurred during the extensive territorial expansion west to Weser River, south into Greece, and east into Ugro-Finnish territory, upper Volga, upper Don, and the full length of the Dnieper, to the shores of the Black Sea. The agricultural character of the Slavic settlers continued to make permanent their acquisitions, especially where the land was suitable for ploughing. The Slavs were on their way to becoming the largest branch of the Indo-European language family in Europe and eventually to occupy two thirds of the European landmass and vast areas of northern and central Asia.

The early achievements of the Greek and Italic peoples on the shores of the Mediterranean enriched the vocabularies of all modern European languages with a large number of Greek and Latin words in literature, sciences, and law. Christianity spread throughout Slavic Europe from the end of the 6th to the end of 13th centuries. It brought there, as it did to the rest of the world, the great legacy of the Mediterranean cultures of antiquity.

The Old Church Slavonic language was created in the 9th century by Saints Cyril and Methodius on the basis of the Slavic south Macedonian. It was the oldest literary Slavic language. It included the archaic Slavic nasalized vowels. In the 9th century it was used throughout the Balkans and in the Great Moravia. It was used by the East Slavs and in Romania in the 10th century. In the twelfth century the Old Church Slavonic language was changed into East Slavic, Bulgarian, Serbian, and Croatian literary languages. Highlights of the relative progress of the Slavic languages are indicated on the graph.

During the Medieval period in Poland and in the rest of the countries within Western Christianity, the Church organized the education and schools. There the Poles had to struggle with Latin grammatical forms. Polish language became increasingly more pliable. Polish became the languge of the royal court. The first writing in Polish occurred in the 13th century. The earliest Polish poem is the battle hymn *Bogurodzica* (bo-goo-ro-dzhee-tsa). It asks St. Mary's intercession for good life on earth and for paradise after death.

The maps showing the peoples of Europe at A.D. 1000 and at present indicate the stability of the interphase between the East and West Indo-European languages. It is compatible with the estimates of 2000 B.C. and 1000 B.C. Even the simultaneous expansion of the Roman Empire by the beginning of the Christian era, and the great shift towards the Roman frontiers of the Germanic tribes, originally from Scandinavia, had little effect on the location on the East/West interphase. Thus the Indo-European division into Satem and Centum could be 4000 years old or even older, and therefore it is an important historic reference line helpful in correlation of prehistoric archeological findings.

The tiny duchy of Brandenburg dragged the name of Balto-Slavic Prussia across the East/West interphase in 1701 in order to exploit the troubles of the Polish Republic with the Tsar of Russia; it renamed itself Kingdom of Prussia and eventually built the warlike Prussian Empire (1871–1918). Brandenburg, as a junior partner of Russia, precipitated the partitions of Poland. By 1795 over 60 percent of the population of the new Prussia was Polish speaking and under 40 percent were German speaking. In order to acquire a solid German majority, the Berlin government embarked on the "blood and iron" unification program to control the 350 independent duchies and principalities in the territory of Germany.

The short-lived Prussian Empire founded in the 1870s was destroyed in 1918. Then, with the rebirth of Poland and Czechoslovakia the East/West Indo-European interphase started moving back towards its long established location along the Oder and upper Elbe rivers. The defeat of Germany in World War II resulted in re-establishing the linguistic interphase along its long lasting location—to which the western frontiers of Poland, Czechoslovakia and Yugoslavia of today conform.

The interphase between East and West Indo-Europeans is consistent with the prehistoric and historic evidence. It allows for the long geographic isolation necessary for the formation and evolution of Germanic and Balto-Slavic languages, eventually leading to the formation of the Polish language. The long duration of the interphase between East and West Indo-European languages carries the conviction of simplicity.

LANGUAGE FORMATION IN GEOGRAPHIC ISOLATION

FOREIGN INVASIONS AND
SLAVIFICATION OF INVADERS

FORMATION OF SLAVIC STATES AND
EARLY CHRISTIANIZATION

PREHISTORY AND HISTORY OF THE INDO EUROPEAN LANGUAGES LEADING TO THE MODERN POLISH

PREHISTORY
THE RANGE OF THEORIES ON EVOLUTION OF INDO-EUROPEAN LANGUAGES

A COMPARISON

Indo-Europeans First Identified In Europe	4500 BC	1st Wave of Old Europeans or Proto-Thracians (Satem?)
Indo-Europeans in the Neolithic Cultures From England to Caspian and Aral Seas	3000 BC First Writing	Funnel Beaker & Rope Print Pottery Culture
Distinction Betwen Indo-Europeans In Europe (Centum & Satem). In Asia Minor Hittites (Centum) and in Eurasia Irano-Aryans (Satem)		Battle-Axe Cultures
West Indo-Europeans Celto-Ligurians, Italics, Greeks, Germa Centum East Indo-Europeans Illyrians Thraco-Cimmerians, Balto-Slavs: Satem	2000 BC	2nd Wave Thraco-Illyric; Satem Battle Axe Cultures
Differentiation of Slavs and Balts Lusatian Slavic Urnfield Cemeteries Differentation of East and West Slavs Slow Evolution in Geographic Isolation	1000 BC	Distinction Between Indo-European Groups Satem and Centum Introduction of Urnfield Cemeteries 3rd Wave Undifferentiated Balto-Slavic and Germanic
Herodotus Describes Slavs as Scyth Farmers Cremation Fire to Help the Deceased To Join the Fire of Eternal Life of the Sun		Differentiation of Germanic and Balto-Slavic
Venedic Slavs Described by Tacitus Invasions and Slavicisation of the Invaders Remolding of Slavic Languages by Migrations	0.0 BC The End of Slavic Prehistory	Differentiation of Slavs and Balts, Venedic or West, Antic or East and Sklavinian or South Slavic
Great Migrations Slavic Flood Old Church Slavonic Literary Language	AD 1000	Christiantization of West, South and East Slavs Formation of Slavic National Languages Formation of Slavic Literary Languages
Polish Language of the Royal Court Polish Language of Civility and Elegance in Multinational Commonwealth from the Baltic To the Black Sea Modern Polish Recent Polish	AD 1985 AD 2000	Czech Literature First Among The Slavs Polish Literature First Among the Slavs Russian Literature First Among the Slavs Contribution of Russian Prison Theme To the World Literature

HISTORY OF FAMILY OF INDO-EUROPEAN LANGUAGES
SLAVIC SUBFAMILY

**Diag. The Range of the Theories on Language and European Migrations.
Prehistory and History of the Indo-European Languages Leading to Modern Polish.**

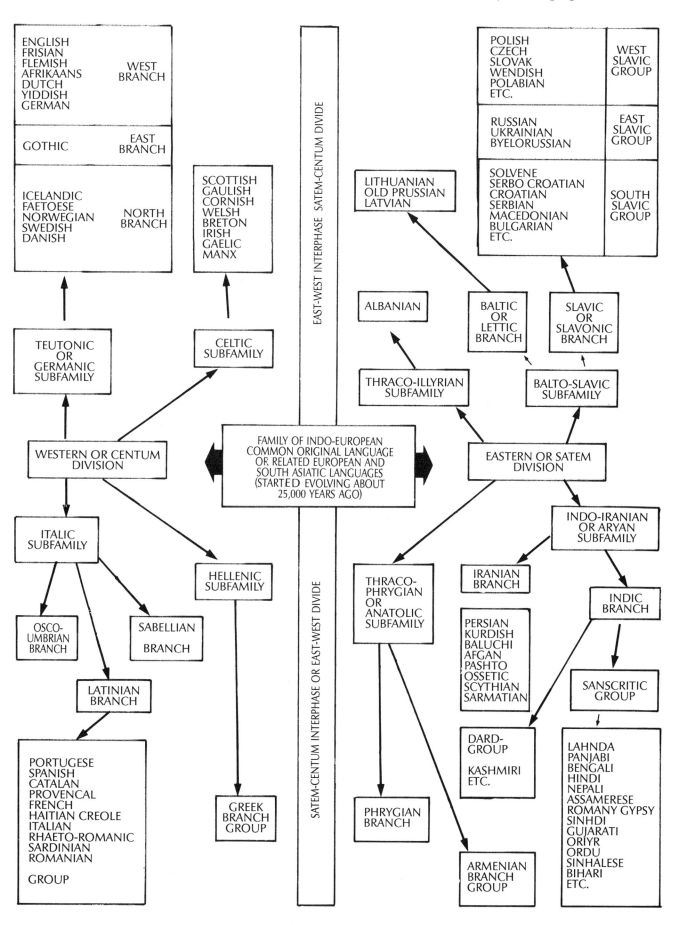

FAMILY OF INDO-EUROPEAN LANGUAGES
Diag. The Indo-European Language Family and the Satem-Centum Divide.

EVOLUTION OF SLAVIC LANGUAGES
WITHIN THE INDO-EUROPEAN FAMILY

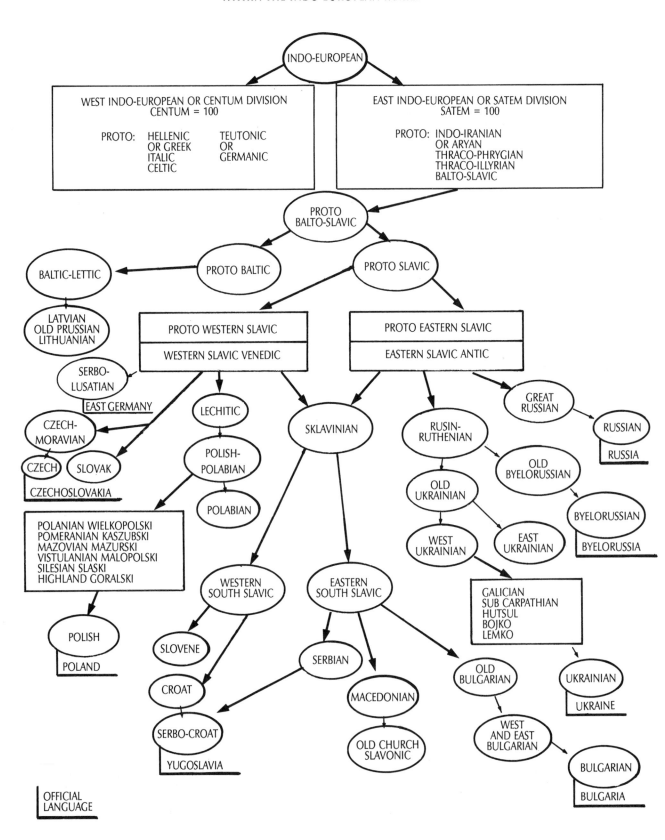

SLAVIC LANGUAGES
COUNTRIES OF ORIGIN AND USE AS OFFICIAL LANGUAGES
Diag.The Slavs among Indo-Europeans.

Diag. Arrival of the Indo-Europeans.

Map: 8500 BC. Beginning of Agriculture.

Map: 4500 BC. First Indo-Europeans in the Neolithic Europe.

Map: 2800 BC. Indo-European Expansion within Neolithic Cultures.

Map: 1600 BC. Bronze Age Indo-European East/West Interphase.

Map: 1300 BC. Lusatian and Dnieper Bronze Age Cultures the Genesis of the Slav Peoples.

Map: 1200 BC. West Slavic Urnfield Burials Spread to the Celts.

Map: 1000 BC. Expansion of the Western Slavs and Illyrians.

Map: 700 BC. Migration: Irano-Scyths the Nomadic Horsemen.

Map: 550 BC. Beginning of the Iron Age of the Slavs.

BISKUPIN

Biskupin causeway built to expose the unshielded right side of intruders to arrows shot from the fortress (the shields were carried on the left arm). By 450 B.C. rising lake waters made the island fortress uninhabitable, but preserved the foundations until today.

UGRO-FINNS

APPROXIMATE EAST/WEST SATEM/CENTUM INTERPHASE

EUROPE CENTRAL MERIDIAN

CASPIAN S.

IRANO-SARMATIANS

UGRO-FINNS

IRANO-SCYTHS

IRANIANS

PERSIAN EMPIRE

IRANIANS

BLACK SEA

GREEKS

BALTS

EASTERN SLAVS

IRANO-SCYTHS

THRACIANS

BALTIC SEA

WESTERN SLAVS

NEW URNFIELDS

GERMANIC TEUTONS

ILLYRIANS

ADRIATIC

GREEKS

NORTH SEA

HALLSTATT CELTS

CELTS

ITALIC

MASSILIAN GREEKS

CARTHAGE

SEA

CELTS

CELTS

IBERIANS

HALLSTATT CELTS

CARTHAGE

CARTHAGE

MEDITERRANEAN

ATLANTIC OCEAN

BERBERS

470 B.C.
BISKUPIN
ISLAND FORTRESS
(550–450 B.C.)
CONTINUING GEOGRAPHIC
ISOLATION OF
BALTO-SLAVIC
AND GERMANIC PEOPLES

Map: 470 BC. Biskupin Island Fortress: 550-450 B.C.

Map: 190 BC. Migration of Irano-Sarmatians the Nomadic Horsemen.

Map: 90 BC. Gothic and Irano-Sarmatian Pressure on the Slavs.

Map: Rome A.D. 20 Roman Expansion after Breaking the Power of the Celts.

Map: 250 Advance of Germanic tribes towards the Roman Frontiers.

**A.D. 360
SHORT LIVED
OSTROGOTHIC
HEGEMONY OVER
THE BALTO-SLAVS -
ADVANCE
OF THE HUNS**

Northern Roman Borderlands were settled with the defeated and subjugated Germanic tribes who were under a strong Romanization pressure. Formation of the French language.

Formation of the French Language.

Northern Roman Borderlands settled with the defeated Germanic tribes

**Map: 360 Short Lived Ostrogothic Hegemony over the Balto-Slavs -
Advance of the Huns.**

Map: 400 Advance of the Huns and Flight of the Germanic Tribes.
Huns defeat the Ostrogoths and drive the Germanic tribes into Rome.

Map: 450 Hegemony of the Huns.

Map: 476 Fall of Rome.

Map: 540 Slavization of Sarmatian Antes, Serboi, and Choroates.

A.D. 540

SLAVIZATION OF
SARMATIAN ANTES,
SERBOI AND CHOROATES.
SARMATIAN MIGRATIONS
400 B.C. – A.D. 540

SARMATIAN "TAMGA":
Signs, property markings and cattle brands, (1st to 7th century), showing some Greek influence. These Tamgas appear in heraldic designs of a number of Polish coats of arms from the 11th to To 17th century, (The Lower Row).

Map: 570 Avar Advance, Hegemony, and Alliances with the Slavs.

**Map: 623-658 The first Slav State of Samon -
defeat of the Avars.**

Map: 740 Success of Slavic Military Democracies.

After the final dispersion of the Avars in A.D. 796 the Slavs controlled the entire eastern border of the Frankish Carolingian Empire. Frankish defences were anchored in the Danish mark in the north and in the Avarian mark in the south. Between them streached the fortifications of the Slavic Frontier known as "Limes Sorabicus" and "Limes Saxoniae"; continuous line of Slavic settlements streaching from the North Sea to the Adriatic remained unbroken even after the breakup of the Frankish Empire in A.D. 843 and until the arrival of the Hungarian Magyars in A.D. 896.

Fortified Lines:
"Limes Sorabicus"
"Limes Saxoniae"

A.D. 880
AREA
SETTLED
BY
THE SLAVS

Map: 880 Area Settled by the Slavs.

Map: 20-570-880 Expansion of Slavic settlements.

One, two, and three fields crop systems. The efficiency of use of arable acreage crop system:

One Field 30% Called: UGOR (oo-goor)
Two Fields 50% OZIMINA (o-zhee-mee-na)
Three Fields 70% JARZYNA (ya-zhi-na)

SOCHA (so-kha) PRIMITIVE WOODEN PLOUGH

PLOUGH WITH METAL SHARES

A.D. 880
THE USE OF PLOUGH
WITH METAL SHARES

NOTE: Three field crop system used first by the Dnieper Slavs in Roman times.

Map: 880 The use of the plow with metal shares.

Map: *A.D. 1000* **Languages of Europe - Slavization of the Bulgars. Arrival of the Hungarian Magyars and Illyrian Vlachs into the central Balkans - the Vlachs later founded Romania.**

A.D. 600-1500
ADVANCE OF
CHRISTIANITY
BY CENTURIES
AND ISLAM
UNTIL 1200 ⎯⎯
& 1500 ×—×—×

Universities

⬡ Universities founded up to the end of 15th century.

ARMED MONASTIC ORDERS

☐ Spanish Brethren
◨ German Brethren "The Black Crusaders"-Teutonic Knights
⊠ German Monastic state:

13th Century genocide of the Prussian people; extinction of the Prussian language; conducting predatory wars against Poland, Lithuania, Livonia, and Russia. Plundering and committing mass murders. Defeated in one of the largest medieval battles, north of Warsaw in 1410. Secularized in 1525. Transformed into a Polish fief of Prussia.

Map: 600-1500 Advance of Christianity by Centuries
(and Islam at 1200 and 1500).

Map: 1986 The Legacy of Eastern and Western Christianity - Roman and Greek Alphabets

BIBLIOGRAPHY OF RECOMMENDED READINGS ON POLAND

Recently published works which together with standard encyclopedias and atlases were helpful in preparation of *Poland: A Historical Atlas.*

Ascherson, Neal. *The Polish August: The Self-Limiting Revolution.* New York: The Viking Press, 1982.

Bertrand, Gustave. *Enigma, ou la Plus Grande Enigme de la Guerre 1939–1945 (Enigma: The Greatest Enigma of the War of 1939–1945).* Paris: Librerie Plon, 1973.

Bliss-Lane Arthur. *I Saw Poland Betrayed.* New York, 1948.

Brumberg, Abraham, ed. *Poland: Genesis of a Revolution.* New York: Vintage Books, 1983.

Brzezinski, Zbigniew. *Game Plan: A Geostrategic Framework for the Conduct of the U.S.-Soviet Contest.* Boston-New York: Atlantic Monthly Press, 1986.

Checinski, Michael. *Poland: Communism, Nationalism, Anti-Semitism.* New York: Karz-Cohl Publishing, 1982.

Czaplinski, Wladyslaw, ed. *The Polish Parliament at the Summit of Its Development: 16th–17th Centuries.* Wroclaw, Warsaw, Cracow, Lodz: Ossolineum, 1985.

Cynk, Jerzy B. *History of the Polish Air Force, 1918–1968.* London: Osprey Publishing Ltd., 1972.

Davies, Norman. *God's Playground: A History of Poland.* New York: Columbia University Press, 1982.

Davies, Norman. *Heart of Europe: A Short History of Poland.* Oxford: Clarendon Press, 1984.

Davies, Norman. *White Eagle, Red Star: The Polish-Soviet War, 1919–1920.* London: Macdonald & Co. Ltd, 1972.

Gieysztor, Aleksander, et al. *History of Poland.* Warsaw: P.W.N., 1979.

Iranek-Osmecki, Kazimierz. *He Who Saves One Life.* New York: Crown Publishers, Inc., 1971.

Jedruch, Jacek. *Constitutions, Elections, and Legislatures of Poland, 1493–1977: A Guide to Their History.* Washington, D.C.: University Press of America, Inc., 1982.

Jedzejewicz, Waclaw. *Pilsudski: A Life for Poland.* New York: Hippocrene Books, 1982.

Karski, Jan. *The Great Powers & Poland: 1919–1945, From Versailles to Yalta.* Lanham, MD.: University Press of America, TM Inc., 1985.

Kielar, Wieslaw. *Anus Mundi: 1500 Days in Auschwitz/Birkenau.* New York: The New York Times Book Co., Inc., 1980.

Korbonski, Stefan. *The Polish Underground State: A Guide to the Underground 1939–1945.* New York, Hippocrene Books, 1978, 1981.

Kozaczuk, Wladyslaw. *Enigma: How the German Machine Cipher Was Broken, and How It was Read by the Allies in World War Two.* University Publications of America, Inc., 1984.

Kruszewski Z. Anthony. *The Oder-Neisse Boundary and Poland's Modernization. The Socioeconomic and Political Impact.* New York: Praeger Publishers, 1972.

Lukas, Richard C. *Forgotten Holocaust: The Poles Under German Occupation 1939–1944.* Lexington, KY.: The University Press of Kentucky, 1986.

Majdany, Fred. *The Battle of Cassion.* New York: Balantine Books, 1957.

Manning, Clarence A. *Soldier of Liberty; Casimir Pulaski.* New York: Philosophical Library, 1945.

Massie, Robert K. *Peter the Great: His Life and World.* New York: Ballantine Books, 1981.

Milosz, Czeslaw. *History of Polish Literature.* London: Macmillan Company, 1969.

Milosz, Czeslaw. *Native Realm.* New York: Doubleday & Company, Inc., 1968.

Moczarski, Kazimierz. *Conversations With an Executioner: An Incredible 255-day Long Interview With the Man Who Destroyed the Warsaw Ghetto.* Englewood Cliffs, N.J. Prentice-Hall, Inc., 1981.

Niezabitowska, Malgorzata. *Remnants: The Last Jews of Poland*. Friendly Press, 1986.

Nowak, Jan. *Courier from Warsaw*. Detroit: Wayne State University Press, 1982.

Olszer Krystyna M. *For Your Freedom and Ours: Polish Progressive Spirit, From the 14th Century to the Present*. New York: Frederic Ungar Publishing Co., 1981.

Piekalkiewicz, Janusz. *Secret Agents, Spies, and Saboteurs: Famous Undercover Missions of World War II*. London: William Morrow & Company Inc., 1973.

Pilsudski, Jozef. *Year 1920: Its Climax—Battle of Warsaw*. London-New York: Pilsudski Institute of America, 1972.

Rejewski, Marian. *An Application of the Theory of Permutations in Breaking the Enigma Cipher*. Warsaw: Applications Mathematicae, vol. 16, no. 4, 1980.

Revel, Jean F. *How Democracies Perish*. Garden City, New York: Doubleday & Company, Inc., 1983.

Stankiewicz W. J., ed. *The Tradition of Polish Ideals*. London: Orbis Books Ltd., 1981.

Steven, Stewart. *The Poles*. New York: Macmillan Publishing Co., Inc. 1982.

Tec, Nechama. *When Light Pierced the Darkness: Righteous Christians and the Polish Jews*. New York, Oxford University Press, 1986.

Watt, Richard M. *Bitter Glory: Poland and Its Fate*. New York: Simon and Schuster, 1979.

Weschler, Lawrence. *Solidarity: Poland in the Season of Its Passion*. New York: Simon and Schuster, 1982.

Wirth, Andrzej. *The Stroop Report: The Jewish Quarter of Warsaw Is No More!"* New York: Pantheon Books, 1979.

Wytrwal, Joseph A. *Poles in American History and Tradition*. Detroit: Endurance Press, 1969.

Zaloga, Steven. *The Polish Campaign 1939*. New York: Hippocrene Books, Inc., 1985.

Zawodny, J. K. *Death in the Forest: The Story of the Katyn Forest Massacre, 1940*. University of Notre Dame Press, 1962.

COATS OF ARMS OF POLISH TOWNS

ampling of 144 coats of arms of Polish towns appears in color on the end leafs of *Poland: A Historical Atlas*. They
e selected from more than 1000 town coats of arms in existence today. In order to help the reader more fully
reciate them, below is an identification key with a guide to abbreviation of names and pronunciation of regions.

Abbreviation of Names and Pronunciation of Regions:

Bialystok—BK (bya-wi-stok)
Bydgoszcz—BZ (bid-goshch)
Gdansk—GK (gdansk)
Katowice—KA (ka-to-vee-tse)
Kielce—KE (kel-tse)
Koszalin—KN (ko-sha-leen)
Krakow—KW (kra-koof) Cracow
Lodz—LZ (woodz)
Lublin—LN (loob-leen)
Olsztyn—ON (olsh-tin)
Opole—OE (o-po-le)
Poznan—PN (poz-nan)
Rzeszow—RW (zhe-shoof)
Szczecin—SN (shche-cheen)
Warszawa—WA (var-sha-va) Warsaw
Wroclaw—WW (vrots-wav)
Zielona Gora—ZA (zhe-lo-na goo-ra)

Coats of Arms

1. Adamow (a-da-moof), LN
2. Aleksandrow Kujawski (a-le-ksan-droof koo-yas-kee), BZ
3. Andrychow (an-dri-khoof), KW
4. Annopol (an-no-pol), LN
5. Augustow (aw-goos-toof), BK
6. Banie (ba-ne), SN
7. Barlinek (bar-lee-k-nek), SN
8. Bartoszyce (bar-to-shi-tse), ON
9. Belchatow (bew-kha-toof), LZ
10. Bialystok (bya-wi-stok), BK
11. Bierun Stary (bye-roon sta-ri), KA
12. Biskupiec (bees-koo-pyets), LN
13. Bnin (bneen), PN
14. Bodzentyn (bo-dzan-tin), KE
15. Bogoria (bo-gor-ya), KE
16. Bransk (bransk), BK
17. Bydgoszcz (bid-goshch), BZ
18. Cedynia (tse-di-na), SN
19. Chociwel (kho-chee-vel), SN
20. Chodecz (kho-dech), BZ
21. Cieszyn (che-shin), KA
22. Czestochowa (chan-sto-kho-va), KA
23. Daleszyce (ba-le-shi-tse), KE
24. Debica (dan-bee-tsa), RW
25. Debno (dan-bno), KE
26. Dobre (dob-re), WA

27. Dobrodzien (do-bro-dzen), KA
28. Elblag (el-blowng), GK
29. Elk (ewk), BK
30. Filipow (fee-lee-poof), BK
31. Firlej (feer-ley), LN
32. Fordon (for-don), BZ
33. Frampol (fram-pol), LN
34. Frombork (from-bork), ON
35. Garwolin (gar-vo-leen), WA
36. Gdansk (gdansk), GK
37. Gdynia (gdi-na), GK
38. Gliwice (glee-vee-tse), KA
39. Glogow (gwo-goof), ZA
40. Glowno (gwov-no), LZ
41. Gniezno (gnez-no), PN
42. Goleniow (go-le-noof), SN
43. Goldap (gow-dap), BK
44. Goniadz (go-nowndz), BK
45. Gozdnica (dozd-nee-tsa), ZA
46. Grabow Nad Prosna (gro-boof nad pros-nown), PN
47. Grodzisk Wielkopolski (gro-dzeesk vyel-ko-pol-skee), PN
48. Gryfow Slaski (gri-foof slown-ski), WW
49. Hel (khel), GK
50. Horodlo (kho-ro-dwo), LN
51. Horodyszcze (kho-ro-dish-che), LN
52. Hrubieszow (khboo-bye-shoof), LN
53. Ilawa (ee-wa-va), ON
54. Ilza (eew-zha), KE
55. Imielin (ee-mye-leen), KA
56. Inowroclaw (ee-no-vro-tswav), BZ
57. Iwaniska (ee-va-nees-ka), KE
58. Jablonowo (yab-wo-no-vo), BZ
59. Janowiec Wielkopolski (ya-no-vyets vyel-ko-pol-skee), BZ
60. Janow (ya-noof), BK
61. Jastrzab (yas-tzhownb), KE
62. Jaworzno (ya-vazh-no), KW
63. Jedlinsk (yed-leensk), KE
64. Jordanow (yor-da-noof), KW
65. Katowice (ka-to-vee-tse), KA
66. Katy Wroclawskie (kown-ti vrotz-wav-ske) WW
67. Kielce (kel-tse), KE
68. Knurow (knoo-roof), KA
69. Koszalin (ko-sha-leen), KN
70. Kowary (ko-va-ri), WW
71. Kozie Glowy (ko-zhe gwo-vi), KA
72. Krakow (kra-koof), KW
73. Labedy (wa-ban-di), KA
74. Laziska Gorne (wa-zhis-ka goor-ne), KA

75. Legnica (leg-nee-tsa), WW
76. Leszno (lesh-no), PN
77. Lodz (woodz), LZ
78. Luban (loo-ban), WW
79. Lublin (loob-leen), LN
80. Miechow (mye-khoof), KW
81. Mielec (mye-lets), RW
82. Mikolow (mee-ko-woof), KA
83. Mordy (mor-di), WA
84. Mosina (no-shee-na), PN
85. Myslowice (mi-swo-vee-tse), KA
86. Naleczow (na-wan-choof), LN
87. Nasielsk (na-shelsk), WA
88. Nidzica (nee-dzee-tsa), ON
89. Niedobczyce (ne-dob-chee-tse), KA
90. Niemcza (nem-cha), WW
91. Olsztyn (olsh-tin), ON
92. Opalenica (o-pa-le-nee-tsa), PN
93. Opole (o-po-le), OE
94. Osiek (o-shek), KE
95. Ostrow Wielkopolski (ost-roof vyel-ko-pol-skee), PN
96. Ozarow (o-zha-roof), KE
97. Pacanow (pa-tsa-noof), KE
98. Piekary Slaskie (pye-ka-ri sown-ske), KE
99. Piotrkow Trybunalski (pyotr-koof tri-boo-nal-skee), LZ
100. Poznan (poz-nan), PN
101. Prusice (proo-shee-tse), WW
102. Przow (pshoof), KA
103. Pultusk (poow-toosk), WA
104. Radlin (rad-leen), KA
105. Radom (ra-dom), KE
106. Radymno (ra-dim-no), RW
107. Rybnik (rib-neek), KA
108. Rzeszow (zhe-shoof), RW
109. Sandomierz (san-do-myesh), KE
110. Slupsk (swoopsk), KN
111. Sosnowiec (sos-no-vyets), KA
112. Stary Sacz (sta-ri sownch), KW
113. Stawiszyn (sta-vee-shin), PN
114. Strumien (sroo-myen), KA
115. Swidnica (shveed-nee-tsa), WW
116. Szczecin (shche-cheen), SN
117. Tarczyn (tar-chin), WA
118. Tarnowskie Gory (tar-nov-ske goo-ri), KA
119. Torun (to-roon), BZ
120. Trzcinsko Zdroj (tshcheen-sko zdrooy), SN
121. Trzebiatow (tshe-bya-toof), SN
122. Turek (too-rek), PN
123. Ujazd (oo-yazd), LZ
124. Ujscie (ooysh-che), PN
125. Ulanow (oo-la-noof), RW
126. Uniejow (oo-ne-yoof), LZ
127. Ustron (oo-stron), KA
128. Wadowice (va-do-vee-tse), KA
129. Warszawa (var-sha-va), WA
130. Warta (var-ta), LZ
131. Wejcherowo (vey-khe-ro-vo), GK
132. Wieliczka (vye-leech-ka), KW
133. Wiliamowice (vee-la-mo-vee-tse), KW
134. Wisla (vee-swa), KA
135. Wisnicz Nowy (vish-neech no-vi), KW
136. Wodzislaw Slaski (vo-dzees-wav shlown-skee), KA
137. Wolbrom (vol-brom), KW
138. Wroclaw (vrots-wav), WW
139. Zabrze (zab-że), KA
140. Zakopane (za-ko-pa-ne), KW
141. Zielona Gora (zhe-lo-na goo-ra), ZA
142. Zmigrod (zhmee-groot), WW
143. Zory (zho-ri), KA
144. Zywiec (zhi-vyets), KR

MULTILINGUAL GLOSSARY OF PLACE NAMES

aid the reader in recognition of place names used in *Poland: A Historical Atlas*, this multilingual glossary provides
t the place name in Polish (or the original language) followed by one or more versions in other languages identified
the abbreviations as noted.

abic **A**
elorussian **B**
zech **C**
iglish **E**
tonian **Es**
ench **F**
eorgian **Geo**
erman **G**
reek **Gr**
ungarian **H**
alian **I**
tin **L**
tvian **Lat**
thuanian **Lit**
lish **P**
omanian **Ro**
ussian **R**
erbohorvatian **Se**
ovak **S**
ovene **Sl**
rbian **So**
rkish **T**
krainian **U**

drianopol, Adrianople (**E**), Edirne (**T**)
kerman, Belgorod (**R**), Bilhorod (**U**)
lgier, Algiers (**F**), El Djezair (**A**)
ltmark (**G**), Stary Targ (**P**)
ndruszow, Andrusovo (**R**)
ncona (**I**)
rkona (**P**), (**G**)
usterlitz (**G**), Slavkov (**C**)
zow, Azov (**R**)

ajonna, Bayonne (**F**)
edzin, Bendin (**R**)
erdyczow, Berdichev (**R**), Berdichiv (**U**)
eresteczko, Berestechko (**U**)
iala Cerkiew, Bila Tserkva (**U**), Belaya Tserkov (**R**)
ialystok, Belostok (**R**)
ielawa, Langen-Bielau (**G**)
obrujsk, Bobruysk (**R/B**)
ogumin, Bohumin (**C**)
olkow, Bolkenheim (**G**)
oryslaw, Borislav (**U**)
raclaw, Bratslav (**R/U**)
randenburg, Brenna (**P**)
raniewo, Brunsberg (**G**)
ratyslawa, Bratislava (**C/S**), Pozsony (**H**), Pressburg (**G**)

Brest, (**R**), Brzesc (**P**)
Brenna, (**P**), Brandenburg (**G**)
Briansk, Bryansk (**R**)
Buczacz, Buchach (**U**)
Budapeszt, Budapest (**H**)
Brzeg, Brieg (**G**)
Brzesc, Brest/Brest-Litovsk (**R**)
Budziszyn, Bautzen (**G**), Budysin (**So**)
Byczyna, Pitschen (**G**)
Bydgoszcz, Bromberg (**G**)
Bytom, Beuthen (**G**)

Carycyn, Tsaritsin (**R**), Stalingrad (**R**), Volgograd (**R**)
Cecora, Tutora (**Ro**)
Cedynia, Zehden (**G**)
Charkow, Kharkov (**R**), Kharkiv (**U**)
Chelm, Kholm (**U**), (**R**)
Chelmno, Kulm (**G**)
Chojnice, Konitz (**G**)
Chorzow, Koenigshutte (**G**)
Cieszyn, Tesen (**C**), Teschen (**G**)
Cracow (**E**), Krakow (**P**), Krakau (**G**)
Czarnobyl, Chernobyl (**R**), Charnobil (**U**)
Czernichow, Chernigov (**R**), Chernihiv (**U**)
Czerniowce, Chernivtsi (**U**), Chernovtsy (**R**), Cernauti (**R**)
Czerwien, Cherven (**U**)
Czestochowa, Tschenstochau (**G**), Tschenstochov (**R**)
Czortkow, Chortkiv (**U**)

Darlowo, Ruegenwalde (**G**)
Dabrowa Gornicza, Dombrova (**R**)
Dorpat (**P**), (**G**), (**R**), Tartu (**Est**)
Drezno, Dresden (**G**)
Dymin, Demmin (**G**)
Dyneburg (**P**), (**G**), Dvinsk (**R**), Daugavpils (**Lat**)
Dzialdowo, Soldau (**G**)

Elblag, Elbing (**G**)
Elk, Luck (**G**)

Florencja, Florence (**E**), Firenze (**I**)
Friedland (**G**), Korfantow (**P**)

Gdansk, Danzig (**G**)
Gdynia, Gdingen (**G**)
Genua, Genoa (**I**)
Gizycko, Loetzen (**G**)
Glogow, Glogau (**G**)
Gniezno, Gnesen (**G**)

Gniew, Mewe (G)
Gorzow, Landsberg (G)
Grodno, Hrodno (B)
Grodek Jagiellonski, Horodok (U), Gorodok (U)
Grudziadz, Graudenz (U)
Grunwald (P/G)
Gubin, Guben (G)

Hadziacz, Hadiach (U)
Halicz, Halych (U), Galich (R)
Hel, Hela (G)
Homel (P/B), Gomel (R)
Hrubieszow, Hrubeshiv   (U)
Human, Uman (U)

Ilawa, D. Eylau (G)
Inowroclaw, Hohensalza (G)
Iwano Frankovsk (U), Stanislawow (P), Stanislaviv

Jampol, Yampil (U)
Jam Zapolski, Yam Zapolye (R)

Kaliningrad (R), Koenigsberg (G), Krolewiec (P)
Kamieniec Podolski, Kamyanets Podilskyy (U), Kamanets Podolskiy (R)
Kamionka Strumilowa, Kominka Struylova (U), Kamenka Bugskaya (R)
Kaniow, Kaniv (U), Kaniov (R)
Katowice, Katowitz (G)
Ketrzyn, Rastenburg (G)
Kies, Wenden (G), Cesis (Lat)
Kiev (E), Kyiv (U), Kijow (P)
Kirchholm (P/G), Salspils (Lat)
Kiszyniow, Kishinev (R), Chisimau (Ro)
Knipawa, Kneiphof (G)
Kluczbork, Krenzburg (G)
Kluszyn, Klushino (R)
Kolobrzeg, Kolberg (G)
Komarno (P/S/C), Komaron (H)
Konstantynopol, Stambul (P), Constantinople (E), Istanbul (T)
Kopanica, Koepenick (G)
Kopenhaga, Copenhagen (E)
Korfantow, Friedland (G)
Koszyce, Kosice (S/C), Kassa (H)
Kowel, Kovel (U/R)
Kowno, Kaunas (Lit)
Krakow, Cracow (E), Krakau (G)
Krewo, Kreve (Lit)
Krolewiec, Koenigsberg (G), Kaliningrad (R)
Krosno, Krossen (G)
Krzyz, Krenz (G)
Kudak, Kodak (U)
Kujawy, Cuiavia (L)
Kwidzyn, Marienwerder (G)

Legnica, Liegnitz (G)
Lidzbark, Heilsberg (G)
Lipsk, Leipzig (G)
Ludwigowo, Ludwigsdorf (G)
Londyn, London (E)
Lubeka, Luebeck (G)
Lublana, Ljubjana (SC)
Lubusz, Leubus (G)
Luck, Lutsk (U)
Lwow, Lviv (U), Lvov (R), Lemberg (G)

Malbork, Marienburg (G)
Mazowsze, Mazovia (E), Masovia (L)
Misnia, Meissen (G)
Mohacs (H), Mochacz (P)
Moskwa, Moskva (R), Moscow (E)
Mozajsk, Mozhaysk (R)

Namyslow, Namslau (G)
Nidzica, Neidenburg (G)
Niemcza, Nimptch (G)
Nieswiez, Nesvizh (R/B)
Nowe, Neuenburg (G)
Nowogrodek, Novogrodok (R/B)

Nowogrod, Novogrudok (R/B), Naugardukas (Lit)
Nysa, Neisse (G)

Oczakow, Ochakiv (U), Ochakov (R)
Opole, Oppeln (G)
Orawa, Orava (C)
Olomuniec, Olomouc (C), Olmetz (G)
Olsztyn, Allenstein (G)
Olsztynek, Hohenstein (G)
Orneta, Wormditt (G)
Orsza, Orsha (R), Hohenstein (G)
Ostrzyhom, Esztergom (H)
Oswiecim, Auschwitz (G)

Parkany, Parkanyi (H)
Paryz, Paris (E/F)
Peszt, Pest (H)
Pila, Schneidemuehl (G)
Pilawa, Pilan (G)
Pisz, Johannisburg (G)
Poczdam, Potsdam (G)
Podhajce, Pidhaytsi (U)
Podole, Podolia (L), Podilia (U)
Polanow, Polanovo (R)
Polock, Polotsk (R)
Poltawa, Poltava (U/R)
Pomorze, Pomerania (E/L)
Poznan, Posen (G)
Prabuty, Riesenburg   (G)
Praga, Prague (E), Praha (C)
Preszow, Presov (S/C)
Pruska Ilawa, Preussisch Eylau (G)
Psie Pole, Hundspeld G)

Ragneta, Ragnit (G)
Rarancza, Rarancha (U)
Riazan, Ryazan (R)
Rowne, Rivne (U), Rovno (R)
Roztoka, Rostock (G)
Ryga, Riga (Lat/R)
Rzym, Roma (I), Rome (E)

Saloniki, Salonika (E), Thessaloniki (Gr)
Sandomierz, Sandomir (L)
Santok, Zantoch (G)

Saratow, Saratov (R)
Sicz, Sich (U/R)
Sluck, Slutsk (U/R)
Slupsk, Stolp (G)
Sopot, Zoppot (G)
Stalingrad see Carycyn
Stambul, see Konstantynopol
Stebark, Tannenberg (G)
Stryj, Stryy (U)
Swidnica, Schweidnitz (G)
Szczecin, Stettin (G)
Szczytno, Ortelsburg (G)
Sztum, Stuhm (G)
Sztumska Wies Stumsdorf (G)

Tannenberg, Stenbark (P)
Targowica, Torgovyca (U)
Tarnopol, Ternopil (U), Ternopol (R)
Tarnowskie Gory, Tarnovitz (G)
Tczew, Dirschau (G)
Torun, Thorn (G)
Trembowla, Terebovyla (U)
Tuchola, Tuchel (G)
Turso, Elblag (P)
Twer, Tver (R)
Tyflis, Tblisi (Geo), Tiflis (R)
Tylza, Tilsit (G)

Ujazd, Ujest (G)
Upita, Upyte (Lit)
Ustka, Stolpmuende (G)
Uznam, Usedom (G)
Uzhorod, Uzhhorod (U), Uzhgorod (R)

Vienna, *see* Wieden

Walbrzych, Waldenburg (**G**)
Warna, Varna (**E**)
Warszawa, Warsaw (**E**)
Warta, Warthe (**G**)
Welawa, Wehlan (**G**)
Wenden, *see* Kies
Wiatka, Vyatka-Kirov (**R**)
Wieden, Vienna (**E**), Wien (**G**)
Wielen, Filehne (**G**)
Wielkie Luki, Vyelikye Luki (**R**)
Wilno, Vilna (**G/R**), Vilnius (**Lit**)
Wisla, Vistula (**E/L**), Weichsel (**G**)
Witebsk, Vitebsk (**B/R**)
Wlodzimierz, Vladimir (**R**), Volodymyr (**U**)

Wroclaw, Breslau (**G**), Vratislavia (**L**)
Wrzesnia, Wreschen (**G**)

Zabrze, Hindenburg (**G**)
Zagrzeb, Zagreb (**S-C**)
Zaleszczyki, Zalishchyky (**U**)
Zbaraz, Zbarazh (**U**)
Zgorzelec, Goerlitz (**G**)
Zielona Gora, Gruenberg (**G**)
Zloczow, Zolochiv (**U**)
Zlotoryja, Goldberg (**G**)

Zagan, Sagan (**G**)
Zolkiew, Zhovkva (**U**), Nestrov (**R**)
Zurawno, Zhuravno (**U**)
Zytomierz, Zhytomyr (**U**), Zhitomir (**R**)

POLES AND THEIR ANCESTORS IN WORLD PANORAMA
OF THE INDOEUROPEAN FAMILY OF LANGUAGES

AN APPROXIMATE CHRONOLOGY

25,000 years ago: Beginning of the evolution of the original common language of related European and south Asiatic languages of the Indoeuropean family.

6,500 years ago: Indoeuropeans present in the Neolithic central Europe; possible beginning of the east-west or Satem-Centum division.

THE FIRST GREAT INDOEUROPEAN EXPANSION

4,000 years ago: Balto-Slavic and Germanic languages forming subfamilies while the first Greeks enter Greece.

3,900 years ago: Balto-Slavic and Germanic early language evolution established in the geographic isolation between the Baltic and the Carpathians and in southern Scandinavia respectively; Celto-Ligurians advance into western Europe; Pre-Romans move towards Italy; Irano-Aryan Hittites move south of the Black Sea.

3,700 years ago: Irano-Aryan Mittrani arrive in Persia.

3,600 years ago: Gradual separation of the Balto-Slavic language into early Baltic (Lettic) and early Slavic (Slavonic) branches; Irano-Aryans advance west into Asia Minor.

3,500 years ago: Irano-Aryans advance east, collide with the Chinese and turn south into subcontinent of India.

3,300 years ago: Early Baltic and Slavic languages forming - the genesis of the Slav peoples during bronze cultures; western early Slavic initiating urnfields of Lusatian culture and eastern early Slavs initiating the Upper Dnieper culture (p.237).

3,200 years ago: Early Slavic urnfield culture spreads west to Celts; Pre-Romans are established in Italy; Irano-Aryans advance towards the Gulf of Persia.

3,000 years ago: Expansion of early western Lusatian culture.

2,400 years ago: The end of early western Slavic Lusatian urnfield culture; spreading of Western Slavic fortified settlements (in evidence in Poland).

2,200 years ago: The end of Slavic geographic isolation; beginning of foreign invasions and Slavification of invaders.

1,300 years ago: Success of Slavic tribal military democracies; the "Slavic Flood," beginning of formation of Slavic states in contact with Christianity; remolding of the old eastern and western Slavic languages during the great Slav expansion; Slavs inventing the plough and, first in Europe, using horses for ploughing.

1,150 years ago: Founding of the first Polish-Polablan dynasty of the Polanian Piasts; beginning of the evolution of the Polish language.

1,000 years ago: The unfication of ethnic Poland; Polish language evolving out of the Polanian, Vistulanian, Silesian, Mazovian, Pomeranian and Highland dialects. German evolving as a borderland language influenced in structure and vocabulary by the Slavic Lechitic or Polish-Polabian as well as Lusatian Sorbic.

Maturing of the Polish Monarchy as a Western Christian nation, a part of the Republica Christiana; Poland recognized as equal with Italy, France and Germany by the Holy Roman Emperor Otto III. After Arab expansion into the Mediterranean basin, the center of Christianity shifting north into western and central Europe; the concept of "Respublica Christiana" being born there - eventually including Czechs, Poles, Hungarians, Ruthenians and Scandinavians.

750 years ago: The Mongol invasion during feudal fragmentation of Europe spreading terror and destruction; subjugating the Russians for 250 years and depriving them of the fertile southern lands. Mongols introducing in Russia the tradition of servility towards state authorities and giving the role model for building of a despotic empire.

600 years ago: The Grand Duchy of Lithuania accepted Christianity from Poland. Beginning of development of the Polish indigenous democratic process.

THE SECOND GREAT INDOEUROPEAN EXPANSION

CHRISTIANITY AS A STATE IDEOLOGY
THE COLONIAL EMPIRES

500 years ago: Christianization of Europe completed. In 1492 Columbus discovers America. In 1493 the Polish Parliament the Seym, first in Europe, becoming bicameral, and Poland becoming a constitutional monarchy. The coming of the age of discovery and exploration followed by European maritime colonization of the New World. Founding of Tobolsk in 1587 - the Russians starting to build their empire through northern and central Asia all the way to the Pacific which they reached before 1650, filling the power vacuum left after the collapse of the Mongol Empire in the 15th century.

TWO POLISH CHALLENGES FOR LEADERSHIP OF THE GREAT EXPANSION EAST

The first Polish challenge for leadership of the great Slavic expansion east coming shortly after the founding in 1569 of the First Polish Citizen-Soldiers Republic in the Kingdom of Poland and Grand Duchy of Lithuania. The Republic included Europe's largest political nation of free citizens. The Polish Republic was the eastern bastion of Western Christianity. In 1582 it won a war against Orthodox Russia, who had proclaimed itself the third and last "Rome." With the support of Pope Sixtus V, Poland preparing for the campaign to unite with Russia after again defeating Ivan the Terrible. Poland trying to unify and lead all the Slavs after freeing the Balkans from the Moslems. Polish King Stefan I Bathory accepting to be the supreme commander of the Christian forces. His death ending the mobilization for the planned Slavic unification campaign and a decisive crusade to rid the Balkans of the Moslem yoke.

The second Polish challenge for leadership of the great Slavic expansion east coming in 1610 after surrender of Moscow to the Poles. There Polish Defense Minister Stanislaw Zolkiewski proposing reconciliation and union of Russia with the Polish Republic - Russian Boyars being for the union with Poland in return for their full citizenship in the Nobles' Republic. Papal pressure for an immediate conversion of Russia to Western Christianity ruining the agreement. Thus ending the second Polish chance to lead in the great eastern expansion and to introduce to Russia the Polish democratic process, civil liberties and respect for an independent position of the church. (Later Peter the Great in 1721 finalizing the subjugation of the Russian Orthodox Church to the State.)

In 1667 Polish political expansion east ending and Russian expansion west beginning. The Polish Republic exhausted by Cossak revolution, Swedish invasion, and by fighting on the two main fronts, namely against Turkey and Russia while her forces were being sapped by parasitic activities of tiny Saxony and Brandenburg of Germany (which remain fragmented into over 300 self-governing states). Polish Republic beginning her decline into a landlocked middle ground between the two great Indoeuropean colonial expansions. The western expansion created Neo-Europes out of both Americas, Australia and New Zealand. The eastern expansion towards the Pacific building the huge and despotic Russian Empire shaped by the earlier influence of the Byzantine and Mongol Empires.

The nations in the landlocked middle ground between the two great expansions suffering decline, intensification of serfdom, stagnant agricultural economies, political conservatism, partitions, and a lack of independence. Amid hopelessly overlapping multitudes of quarelling ethnic groups, the Polish struggle for independence becoming, by the end of nineteenth century, a role model in east central Europe.

GERMAN COLONIAL FERVOR

German colonial fervor being directed mostly towards the Poles and Balts. The Berlin government even adopting for Germany the Balto-Slavic name of "Prussia" in order to legitimize its colonial aspirations.

The short lived unification of Germany (1871-1945) resulting from international pillage known as the Partitions of Poland in 1772-95 and finalizing after the defeat and plunder of France in 1871, allowed by Russia because of the earlier Franco-British invasion of Crimea. Growing in strength Germany provoking two devastating world wars in 1914 and in 1939, the first leading to Russian revolution and the second leading to the victory of Soviet-Russian empire, which in 1947, together with the United States and Great Britain, formally abolished the German-run colonial state of Prussia.

1917 RUSSIAN REVOLUTION
ABOLISHING OF CHRISTIAN IDEOLOGY
ESTABLISHING OF A TOTALITARIAN STATE
BASED ON COMMUNIST-LENINIST IDEOLOGY

Soviet totalitarian state taking totalitarian control, by methods of organized crime, over the population and means of production. Land collectivization campaigns and Communist industrial "gigantomania" being conducted at a devastating human cost - in many instances resulting in an ecological catastrophe. The Soviet Empire creating an archipelago of slave labor camps. Russian economy being crippled by substitution of "power motive" for the "profit motive."

POLISH VICTORIES IN WAR OF 1919-20
DELAYING SOVIET ADVANCE
INTO CENTRAL EUROPE
FOR A QUARTER OF A CENTURY

In 1920 Poland playing a major role on the interphase between Western democracies and the revolutionary Russian empire. In life and death struggle Poland defeating the invading Soviet armies. The Polish plan of a democratic federation of nations between Germany and Russia could have become a reality. It depended on the transfer to Poland of German arsenals surrendered in 1918 to the victorious Western Allies. The British opposing the Polish plan, underestimating the Soviet potential and worrying that France would have a strong ally in the Polish-led federation. This British decision contributing to the outbreak of World War II and disintegration of the British and other western colonial empires. The 1945 surrender of east-central Europe, and western betrayal of Poland in particular, giving the Soviets a chance to become a superpower reaching for world domination.

International atomic balance of terror benefiting the Soviet empire. Hampering the Soviet empire are: the current information revolution, computerization, backward economy, paralyzed by Communist bureaucracy and relatively high increase of non-Russian Moslem population. Soviet Union being the last great colonial empire surviving in the twentieth century.

Outline

of Polish History

Map Titles and Annotations

(page numbers)

Historians call Poland the heart of Europe. The history of Poland reveals the struggle for democracy in advance of the rest of modern Europe. The millennium of Poland (966-1986) includes centuries of great power status as well as long periods of crisis.

Basic democratic ideals were crystallized in the 15th and 16th century Poland, during the rise of east-central Europe under Polish leadership. These ideals were: the social contract between government and the citizens, the principle of government by consent, personal freedom and civil rights of the individual, freedom of religion, the value of self-reliance, general elections and prevention of authoritarian power of the state.

Democracies are vulnerable, and their price of freedom carries the seeds of their own self-destruction. This is evident in the confrontation of Polish democratic process with absolute monarchies in the 17th and 18th century, in the Polish struggle for independence in the 19th century, and in Poland's disastrous confrontation with the totalitarian onslaught of Nazi Germany and Soviet Russia in the 20th century.

The precarious geographic position of Poland made the Polish quest for representative government more difficult to achieve in comparison with the relative safety of the British Isles and the inaccessibility of the Swiss Alps; the latter countries also sought early to establish democratic governments.

CONTENTS

The area between Germany and Russia ranging from Finland to Greece is now called "Eastern Europe" or "East-Central Europe." In this part of the world Poland is the largest country. There a vital part of the Western Civilization was born. East-Central Europe remains vital for continuation and survival of Western Civilization.

Christianity came to Poland from two sources. The southern or Lesser Poland of the Vistulanians with capital at Cracow, received Christianity from Great Moravia, shortly after the 863 arrival of the Apostles of the Slavs, Saints Cyril and Methodius. The northern or Greater Poland of the Polanians, with capital at Poznan, received Christianity from Bohemia, in 966 by decision of Mieszko I, of the first Polish dynasty (c.840-1370).

German genocide of the Jews in 1942-1944, eviction of the Germans and mass resettlement of the Poles, resulted in the loss of multinational character of Poland's towns for the first time in history. Territorial shift to the western frontier, on the Oder-Neisse, enabled Poland to overcome economic debilitation caused by partitions, 1795-1918.

In the early 1970's Poland became one of the ten world's largest industrial states. By 1987, the Sovietization and Communist mismanagement of economy and ecology, brought about a crisis of catastrophic proportions. It threatens to degrade Poland, to a level of an under developed country as the industrial production fell below 40 percent of capacity.

At the beginning of 1987, the Communists still keep on crippling private farming, the mainstay of Polish agriculture. In 1986, they finally rejected the Catholic Foundation for Aid to the Private Farmers in Poland, which was initiated by Pope John Paul II. Potentially the Foundation could have brought important foreign aid for badly needed modernization of Polish farms.

A.D. 1000 - Pilgrimage to Poland by the Holy Roman Emperor Otto III, to recognize Poland as politically equal of Italy, France, and Germany, and to create an independent Polish See of Gniezno, and formally agree to the crowning Boleslaus I as King of Poland; also to conduct negotiations for succession of Boleslaus I as a Holy Roman Emperor after Otto III.

Polish language used at the royal court. Battle hymn "Bogurodzica" (bo-goo-ro-dzee-tsa) asked St. Mary's intercession for good life on earth and for paradise after death. (The origins of this oldest known Polish religious song is estimated to be in the 11th, 12th or 13th century.)

The 1228 Act of Cienia, limited the power of the throne, by the promise to observe "just and noble laws according to the council of the bishops and the barons." It followed the 1180 Act of Leczyca, which first limited the power of the throne in favor of the Church, and 1220 Act of Cracow on mining rights. 1291 Act of Lutomysl guaranteed that no new taxes would be imposed by the decree of the throne.

The 1374 Act of Koszyce, started Poland on its way to become the main scene of development of civil liberties in Europe; especially, when England drifted in the direction of absolutism, and Magna Carta Libertatum of 1215 became ineffectual for several centuries. At that time, a unique Polish civilization was born. It was based on the nascent democracy of citizen-soldiers. These unusually high numbers of Polish nobility formed Europe's largest political nation of free citizens, for the next four hundred years ending in 1795.

German Brethren, known as Teutonic Knights, committed (1233-1283) a genocide, of the original Balto-Slavic population of Prussia (east of Gdansk and north of Warsaw), and brought eventual extinction of the Prussian language.

1364 University founded in Cracow (or Krakow), colleges of liberal arts, medicine and law (before founding of the University of Vienna in 1365, and the University of Heidelberg in 1385, the oldest in German ethnic area). Latin influenced legal and scientific vocabulary. Czech literary language influenced Polish. German and Yiddish, were spoken in enclaves. Borrowed German terms were used in trade.

Protection was extended to the Jews, against persecution by their fellow immigrants from Germany. Germans often formed the patriciate of Polish towns and were seeking political power. "Statut Kaliski of 1264," exceptional in Europe, became the basis of Jewish autonomy until 1795.

Chapter 2

TRANSITION TO CONSTITUTIONAL MONARCHY
1370-1493
Multinational Commonwealth Europe's Largest Territory.

German and Mongol empires were in decline. The Monastic State of the Teutonic Order of German Brethren became a deadly menace along the Baltic coast, as it threatened a massive invasion, under the guise of a "noble crusade." The brethren were mobilizing a large number of western European knighthood.

Forces were gathered for the "Battle of the Century" at Tannenberg. There the German "fake crusade," against Poland and Lithuania, suffered a defeat. 3-Phase Diagram of the Battle for Prussia at Tannenberg-Grunwald-Ulnowo, is shown as it was fought on the battlefield north of Warsaw.

Victory at Tannenberg-Grunwald-Ulnowo was also seen as a culmination of 500 years of recurring German aggression against the Slavs. It began on the Elbe River, and was called by the Germans "Drang nach Osten," or a push to the east.

Victory was followed, in 1413, by the "Union of Horodlo" of Poland and Lithuania. Its preamble states the noble ideas which are echoed throughout the documents of the evolving democracy of the citizen-soldiers of Poland-Lithuania "...its foundation upon Love. For Love alone diminishes not, but shines with its own light, makes an end of discord, softens the fires of hate, restores peace to the world, brings together the sundered, redresses wrongs, aids all and injures none... For by Love, laws are made, kingdoms governed, cities ordered, and the state of the commonweal is brought to its proper goal..."

Polish families extended the use and privileges of their coats-of-arms to Lithuanian and Ruthenian clans.

The Union Act of 1413 redefined the office of wojewoda (vo-ye-vo-da), as a provincial governor and commander. This established a model for provincial administration and defense, in central and eastern Europe.

1425 Act of Brzesc, a fundamental law, it was equivalent to the English Act of Habeas Corpus of 1679 and preceded it by 254 years. Its title: "Neminem Captivabimus Nisi Iure Victim" (no one will be imprisoned without a legal decision by a proper court).

C.1449 "Song of Wycliffe" (in a poetic style) by Jedrzej Galka of Dobczyn (c.1395-c.1455), dean of the liberal arts college at the university of Krakow. He advocated a national church. The "Song of Wycliffe" is the first known manuscript of Polish Reformation, which was inspired by the teachings of John Wycliffe (c.1320-1384) and Jan Hus (c.1369-1415).

National parliament, the Seym, and regional parliaments called Seymiki, became catalysts of social and cultural life in Poland; a role played in the rest of Europe by the royal court and the town. Seym became a forum for competition of talents. A new book market in Polish was developed. Change from Gothic to Roman type letters, made print easier to read.

Polish became the official language of the state. Political writings in Latin, promoted development of a republican government in Poland. Jan Ostrorog (1436-1501) published "Pro Republicae Ordinatione." He demanded a legal equality of all, codification of Polish laws, use of Polish language in all courts, and a greater control over the immigrant German burgers and clergy.

Muscovy won victory over Novgorod; maturity of Russian political expansionism was evident in systematic mass deportations of Novgorodians to the Urals; it was the beginning of 500-year tradition of empire building by coercion, deportation and despotism. (German migration to Poland and eastern Baltic ended.)

Massive expulsions of the Jews from Western Europe to Poland.

Jews prospered in the freedom of Poland, as nowhere else in the medieval and early modern world. They were allowed to form an autonomous Yiddish-speaking nation of free men. Jewish parliamentary democracy, followed the evolution of the democracy of the masses of Polish nobility. It was based on an electorate of 25 percent of Jewish population - relatively the highest of any, then contemporary, European society.

Jewish parliamentary self-government in Poland, was unique in history between Sanhedrin of antiquity, and Knesset of the State of Israel. The Jews became a community of craftsmen, traders and financiers, living under protection of Polish nobility.

Demographic studies indicate that from the end of the 14th century, until 1772, Jewish population in the Polish Commonwealth grew about seventy five times, while Polish population grew five times. By the end of the 18th century, the number of Jews reached one million and equaled the number of noble citizens in the First Polish Republic. For half a millennium a vast majority of world's Jews lived in the historic Polish lands. This ended in the 20th century, with exodus to America which was followed in 1942-44, by Nazi German genocide of European Jews, mostly citizens of Poland.

1505 - passing of the first Polish constitution "Nihil Novi" or "Nothing new about us, without us..." - Polish Parliament, called the Seym, proclaimed itself the supreme power in the Commonwealth, and was recognized as such by the King.

Nicolas Copernicus, doctor of philosophy, law and medicine, founder of modern astronomy by establishing the theory that, earth rotates daily on its axis, and that planets revolve in orbits around the sun. The accurate Copernican calendar gave Christians their first chance to date reliably, the resurrection of Christ and Easter holidays.

Nicolas Copernicus, the Chancellor of Warmia and Commanding Officer in the Mazurian fortress of Olsztyn, was beleaguered by the Germans in 1519-1521. During the siege, he successfully combated an epidemic, by designing and conducting the world's first prospective epidemiological study which found that bread was the vector.

Copernicus ordered that all loaves of bread be coated with butter at bakeries, so that foreign matter, accumulated during delivery, could be readily detected and discarded. The plague was checked. This event is known in the history of medicine, as the Inception of Bread-Buttering by Nicolas Copernicus.

Recurring counterfeit schemes by the Hohenzollerns, minting of debased Polish currency, and tampering with the Vistula grain trade. Nicolas Copernicus, combatting fraudulent schemes of the Hohenzollerns, while serving on the legislative committee for the reform of Polish currency, (1517-1519) for the first time in history wrote the economic principle that "bad money drives good money out of circulation". This Copernican principle was later, in England, attributed to Thomas Gresham (1519-79).

Hohenzollern actions against Poland had the support of the Muscovites, who from 1512 on, for three years, at the siege of Smolensk, suffered ten thousand dead each season. Their bloodiest losses of 30,000 dead, including 1500 boyars occurred at the battle of Orsha on September 8, 1514 when Polish victory was secured by a skillful use of artillery. The Hohenzollern homage took place at the time when the support for them by Muscovites weakened.

Map: 1526 Disaster at Mohacz; death of Louis II, the second Jagiellonian king killed in battle against Moslems; Polish Jagiellonian Realm under pressure from Turks, Russians, and Austrians.
.... *p.99*

Suleiman the Magnificient, led the Turks to take in 1521, Belgrade; in 1522, Rhodes; in 1526, Buda; in 1529 he besieged Vienna. Central Europe was thrown into turmoil. The Jagiellonian Realm was diminished.

1562 - European School of Rationalist Philosophy founded by the Polish Brethren in advance of the intellectual currents of Europe. It was summarized in 1665, in the monumental Biblioteca Fratrum Polonorum published in Amsterdam. It become the basis of philosophy of Benedict Spinosa (1632-77), and of John Locke (1632-1704), whose teachings were fundamental in formulation of the American Declaration of Independence.

Printing was done on a large scale. Gradual Polonization of the leadership community of Lithuania, Latvia, Byelorussia and Ukraine progressed. Polish became the language of civility and elegance, in the multinational commonwealth led by Poles. The number of schools increased. New academies and universities were founded. p.Progress was made in geography and cartography. 1526 map of Poland was prepared by Bernard Wapowski (c.1450-1535) using scale of 1:1,000,000. Waclaw Grodecki (Grodziecki, Godreccius)(c.1535-1591) published a map of Poland in 1558; it was included in the Atlas of Ortelius.

Printing houses were opened in provincial areas. Widespread polemics on religious questions, often resounded all over Europe. Protestants contributed to wider use of the Polish language. Mikolaj Rey (1505-1569), was called the father of Polish literature.

Polish literature was flowering - it was leading among the Slavs. High quality poetry was created by Jan Kochanowski (1530-1584), and literary prose by Lukasz Gornicki (1527-1603). Republican political writings in Latin were continued.

Andrzej Frycz Modrzewski, published "De Republica Emendada" on reforms, republican in character, against the oppression of the peasant serfs, and inadequate laws to protect them, and for legal equality of all. He advocated a strong central government, strictly controlled by laws; an efficient administration, and an independent court system capable to guarantee social justice, and a high quality education independent from the Church. He is one of the pioneers of European science of government and laws. His works were translated into German, Spanish, French and Russian.

Wawrzyniec Goslicki (1530-1607) published, in 1568 "De Optimo Senatore," his program for the Polish republican system, based on a pluralistic society, with perfect equilibrium between power and liberty. His work was published in 1568 in English, as "The Counsellor Exactly Portraited." It was immediately confiscated, but secretly, it became popular. It was analyzed and highly praised 150 years later by Sir Robert Walpole (1676-1745). Even earlier, Willian Shakespeare (1564-1616), commemorated Goslicki by giving the name of "Polonius" or "a Pole," to the chief advisor of Hamlet.

Renaissance architecture blossomed. Calvinism spread among gentry and Lutheranism among burgers. Perfecting of Latin poetry continued as a long tradition in Poland. Plebean humanist comedy about soldiers, beggars etc. was popular. A unifying "low brow" Sarmatian myth claimed that all the people of the Polish Commonwealth descended from Sarmatians, the legendary invaders of Slavic lands in antiquity.

Map: 1514 Battle of Orsha; 1531 Battle of Obertyn

Chapter 4

THE FIRST POLISH REPUBLIC 1569-1795

Polish Nobles' Republic of One Million Citizens, of Kingdom of Poland and Grand Duchy of Lithuania.
.... *p.101*

When Poland was facing Turkish and Russian Empires, tiny Saxony and Brandenburg, acting as international parasites, gradually caused the destruction of the Polish State in 1795. This event led to unification of Germany, fragmented for centuries, into 350 self-governing states. In 1871, Germany was unified under the "Blood and Iron" hegemony of the Berlin government.

Diagram of Government Structure of the Republic.

Table of General Elections.

Poland was the world's only major country to be a republic, until the founding of the United States of America. At the founding of the Polish Republic in 1569 she had a larger number of voting citizens then did the American Republic, (two hundred years later), at the time of her declaration of independence in 1776. Poland-Lithuania was the largest and strongest state in east-central and eastern Europe. Polish republican system was formed at the height of internal prosperity, when external threat was still small.

Diagram of Autonomous Jewish Government in the Polish Republic.

Map: 1569 Founding Of The First Polish Republic Amidst Absolutist Europe.

"The Republic of Good Will...Free Men with Free. Equals with Equal..."

Pride in Polish citizenship throughout the Republic.

The Seym (the Parliament of Poland) established the Social Contract of the Polish Republic and an Impeachment Procedure, as well as General Elections called "Viritim," to elect the King and the Chief Executive of Polish Nobles' Republic, in one person.

The Seym failed to pass a restrictive law limiting the elections to native candidates only; despite the political campaign by Chancellor Jan Zamoyski, who was warning against foreign interference in the internal affairs of the Republic, if foreign candidates were admitted. The candidates were screened and qualified by the Seym.

The General Election Law was accompanied by judicial reform. Elected judges were independent of the executive branch. Courts of appeal were established. The Seym was elected on a two year schedule.

A law was passed abolishing nobility titles, and giving equal rights to all the nobles, including the large numbers of Polish citizen-soldiers, who lived in fortified villages called "zascianki" (za-shchan-kee). Every Polish noble, no matter how small his landholdings, was proclaimed politically equal to a provincial governor. "Szlachcic na zagrodzie rowny wojewodzie" (shlakh-tseets na za-gro-dzhe roov-ni vo-ye-vo-dzhe).

Map: 1569 Lands of the First Polish Republic.

Map: 1569 Political Situation during the founding of the Republic of Poland-Lithuania.

Map: 1576-1582 Poland's Victorious Campaign in War with Muscovy-Russian Empire over Livonia (Latvia).

Tsar Ivan IV "Grozny" or "Threatening," known in English as " The Terrible," was defeated by Poland. He staged an official campaign in the general elections of 1573, as a candidate for the office of King of Poland and Chief Executive of the Republic of Poland-Lithuania. No one in Poland took his candidacy seriously. Ivan IV earned his nickname because of his reaction to the news of founding of the Republic of Poland-Lithuania. In 1569 in Novgorod, the most civilized city of Russia, he ordered the torture of suspected sympathizers of the Polish Republic, and then systematically had them killed daily in batches of 500 to 1000 men for five weeks. Ivan's atrocities engulfed also hundreds of Muscovites, for the same reason.

Map: 1585-1586 Unrealized Plan to Unify All the Slavs, Free the Balkans, and Evict the Moslems from Europe - the Proposed Campaign.

Map: 1594-1596 Nalevayko's Uprising for Civil Rights of Ukrainian Cossacks.

Map: 1600 Jan Zamoyski's Defense Line on the Danube River.

Map: 1605 Victory over the Swedes at Riga-Kirchholm, and 1610 Victory over the Russians near Moscow at Klushino; occupation of Moscow (battle diagrams).

Spectacular Polish victories were accomplished by very small numbers of well equipped elite cavalry, riding on unusually well trained horses. Brilliant battlefield generalship of hetmans loyal to the Republic, was made possible by the broad freedom of action given to them.

The preoccupation to prevent growth of authoritarian power of the state, was already evident in the perennial problem of passing of sufficient appropriations for the regular army of the Republic, especially, when absolutist tendencies were shown by the king, who was elected to be the chief executive.

Recurring power struggle, between the central government and the parliament, weakened the defense establishment. This problem eventually produced the main avenue of subversion, for domestic and foreign enemies of the Polish Republic. It was aggravated by the self-confidence of Polish nobility, which represented the largest number of citizen-soldiers anywhere in Europe.

The huge Polish noble host or "pospolite ruszenie" (pos-po-lee-te roo-she-ne) became antiquated at the time when professional armies were becoming increasingly more important.

Map: 1606-1609 Civil War to Uphold the Constitution and Social Contract of the Republic Led by Zebrzydowski.

Map: 1609-1618 Victory in War with Russia; 1619-1621 Inconclusive War with Turkey.

Map: 1618 Republic of Poland-Lithuania The Bastion of Western Christianity (population numbers of European countries).

"Polish eyes on Paris; Polish hearts on Rome; Polish sabers on Russia." Height of Poland's superiority over Russia. Formation of an unreasonable contempt for everything Russian in Poland, and a suspicion for everything Polish in Russia.

High standard of nonconformist education was achieved in private colleges. Cultural life was decentralized. Publication of books, dictionaries, grammars, etc. increased. The influence of Polish language and culture spread in Lithuania, Latvia, Prussia, Byelorussia and Ukraine. Historiography and philosophy of history was developed; Jan Brozek (1585-1652) developed the theory of learning.

Map: 1618 Grain Export - Waterways and Trade - The Index of Polish Economy.

1604-1619 - The last period of booming economy in Poland and relatively high efficiency in agriculture of the First Polish Republic.

Map: 1618 - The First Republic within International Trade Routes.

Agricultural efficiency table presents the effects of climatic changes, and a critical temperature lowering in 1600-1860. Also unusually frequent droughts at critical times for agriculture resulted in difficulties to rebuild from war destruction, and convert from serf labor to monetary rents; eventually this contributed to a catastrophic decline of Polish towns.

Map: 1618 - Fortresses and Defense Castles of the Republic.

Map: 1618 - Languages of the Multinational Republic.

Map: 1644-47 An Unrealized Plan to Eliminate Tartar Terrorism, (the "Hornets' Nest" of Crimea) and to Free the Balkans from the Moslem Yoke.

Map: 1648-1651 Cossack Uprising - The End of Great Power Status of the Polish Nobles' Republic.

Map: 1648-1651 Cossack Uprising - Battles and Pacts.

Poles in Lwow beleaguered by Cossack armies in 1648 and 1655. Each time they rejected Bohdan Khmyelnitskyy's demands, to hand over to him all Jewish inhabitants as a price of lifting the siege. Mass murders of Catholics and Jews exceeded 100,000 of each, during the 1648-1656 Cossack wars against the Polish Republic.

Multinational city of Lwow, was one of major centers of Polish culture for 600 years. Its thriving pluralistic society included, besides the Polish majority, Ukrainians, Armenians, Jews, Wallachians, Hungarians, and Germans. As late as the end of nineteenth and early twentieth century, Lwow was producing the largest numbers of Polish scientists and literary figures. Lwow (Lvov or Lviv) became a part of the Russian state, for the first time in history after World War II.

Kazimierz Siemienowicz, an officer of Engineers of the Polish Army and Deputy Commander of Artillery, published in 1650 in Amsterdam, a standard textbook on rocketry: "Artis Magnae Artilleriae Pars Prima," including multistage rockets for the first time in world's literature. Siemionowicz wrote design and production specifications for military rockets, as well as firing and steering characteristics including for the first time the stabilizing fins rather than an iron ball hanging on a chain, to prevent the rocket from flipping in flight.

Kazimierz Siemienowicz described a number of his inventions. For more than a century his text served as a handbook on military rocketry, and was translated into French (1651), German (1676) and English (1729).

1652 Creation of disastrous precedent by illegal admission, of an absentee protest vote or the "Liberum Veto," which disrupted the parliamentary session. The speaker, Andrzej M. Fredro was the author of "Philosophy of Anarchy." He ruled that an absentee vote of an illegally departed deputy, was in fact legal and valid. This extremely harmful precedent was followed, despite constant objections, for about one hundred years, long enough to be one of the main causes of critical weakening of the First Republic.

The Army of the Republic never lost a battle with the Russians and just recently it occupied the Kremlin of Moscow. It was superior to the Muscovites, and could have evicted them from the eastern Ukraine and Byelorussia. This would have made the Republic of the Three Nations of Poland, Lithuania and Ruthenia (Ukraine) a stable reality.

The Army of the Republic was ready to march east, when it was thrown into a fratricidal civil war by the conservative hetman, Jerzy Lubomirski, who opposed necessary constitutional reforms. Civil war in Poland, and the resulting default of the Republic, permitted the Muscovites to control permanently Kiev, and the crucial lands of the eastern Ukraine and Byelorussia.

Vasa leadership in Poland came to a bitter end. The Republic was seriously weakened by the losses on the east bank of the Dnieper, and by the earlier loss in 1657 of the Polish fief of Prussia, to the Hohenzollerns of Berlin. Between 1634 and 1667 the Republic lost several million people and some 260,000 square kilometers, of strategically crucial territory.

Protestants won a victory in Sweden against Polish Catholic Vasas. This destroyed the plan "Pax Baltica" of Jan Zamoyski, for a union in freedom, of the Polish Republic with Sweden, (which had population only one fifth the size of the Republic). The Swedes presented Russia with an opportunity to break piecemeal, the Polish and Swedish power.

Polish Vasas failed, as chief executives of the Polish Nobles' Republic, by not preventing the growth of political machines of huge landowners. They failed to rebuild the alliance of the throne with the "Respect for the Law" or "Execution of the Law" movement, of the multitudes of the middle and lower nobility, which was basic for the vitality of the Republic.

The Vasas failed to provide leadership, to pass by the parliament, of necessary constitutional reforms, for strengthening of the executive branch of Republic's government, and the defense establishment. They did not prevent critical territorial losses, which were the foundation for growth of strength of Brandenburgian Hohenzollerns, and allowed Russia to increase greatly, her margin of survivable error while dangerously decreasing that of Poland.

1667 - The end of Polish expansion eastward, and the beginning of Russian expansion westward - Poland still could regain the upper hand. However, the exhausting war with Turkey, drove Poland to give critical territorial concessions to Russia in 1686, in the Eternal Peace of Moscow in return for "alliance" against the Turks and Tartars, and foreign aid of 146,000 rubles.

Economic and political crises in the midst of religious strife, ended with triumph of Counter-Reformation. Poland's Orthodox minority, was placed under the Metropolitan of Kiev, a Muscovite state official, at the time when religion was the state ideology. All this led to the retreat of Polish Latin Christianity amid ruined economy, loss of territory to Russia, corrupt political machines of the aristocrats; victorious battles leading to lost wars, victorious wars leading to a lost peace.

Participation of foreign candidates in the general elections led to forming of political parties sponsored by France, Austria, etc., all of whom worried about the effect of Polish elections, on the European balance of power and on their own countries. General elections for kings, responsible to the parliament, and sworn to act as chief executives of the Polish Nobles Republic, disturbed European rulers striving for absolute power.

Contradictory trends developed: rationalism of the Polish Brethren vs. Sarmatian irrationalism. The once unifying Sarmatian myth, was reshaped by exclusion of the lower classes, from the ancient Sarmatian links, as a justification of social injustices. Architecture was in style of the Polish Sarmatian Baroque. Censorship of books forbidden by the Church, hampered cultural communications and cultural standards. It brought a utilitarian approach to learning.

Advances in astronomy were made by Jan Hevelius (1611-1687). Jan Chrisostom Pasek (1636-1701) wrote memoirs in style of a historical novel. Warsaw court opera (1637-1746) flourished. 1661 Merkuriusz Polski was published as the first Polish language journal. Large volume of sophisticated private correspondence in Polish, was written by King Jan Sobieski. High quality public speaking in the Seym and in provincial legislatures was cultivated.

Map: 1683 - Poland Facing Turkish and Russian Empires; Turkish Empire at the Zenith of Territorial Expansion, while the Russian Empire gradually filled the Power Vacuum left after the Collapse of the Mongol Empire.
.... *p.131*

Map: 1683 - Aug.-Sept. Sobieski's Victorious Campaign Against Turkey.
.... *p.132*

Map: 1683 - Sept.12: 5a.m.-2p.m. Sobieski's Victory at Vienna.
.... *p.133*

Map: 1683 - Sept.12: 2p.m.-4p.m. Sobieski's Victory at Vienna.
.... *p.134*

Map: 1683 - Sept.12: 4p.m.-10p.m. Sobieski's Victory at Vienna.
.... *p.135*

The crushing victory over the Turks by King John III Sobieski, brought the end of Turkish expansion into Europe, and the beginning of lifting of the Turkish yoke in Southern Europe. It strengthened the struggle for national independence of the Balkan Christians; mainly Slavs.

Map: 1697 - Rape of the Polish Election.
.................:... *p.136*

The paradox of the largest number of citizen-soldiers of Europe unable to defend their Polish homeland. It was a prelude to the crisis of sovereignty and political paralysis. In 1697-1717, the Saxons, critically weakened the defense establishment. A century of economic stagnation made impossible, the recovery from the deluge of invasions and later wars.

Saxons submitted to Russian control, in exchange for the privilege to conduct exploitation of Poland. The Republic, with her pool of military manpower unequalled in Europe, was disarmed by skillful subversion. Regular army of the Republic dwindled to 1/28 in relation to Russia; to 1/17 in relation to Austria; and to 1/11 in relation to Prussia.

Map: 1697 - Poland Succumbing to the Saxon Night of Degradation, Plunder of Polish Resources, and Nearly a Century of Economic Stagnation, Preventing Recovery from War Destruction.
.... *p.137*

1697-1763: Personal union with tiny Saxony, when Saxons were controlled by the Russians; an absentee government ruled from Dresden; Saxony's economic exploitation of Poland, and demoralization brought dismal lowering of educational standards, spread obscurantism, anarchist "golden freedom," megalomania and chauvinism. The plunder of Poland is still evident in the museums and art collections of Dresden, Saxony, in Leningrad's Hermitage and in many other Russian and Swedish locations.

The Saxons wasted the opportunity to form a strong union in freedom, of tiny Saxony, with the much larger Polish Nobles' Republic. To be a great power the union had to be based on respect for Polish republican institutions. Its policies had to be made in Warsaw and not by an absentee court in Dresden.

The delicate balance of power between the king elected to act as the chief executive, and the citizens was vulnerable. The head of state could lead if he was loyal to the republican institutions of Poland. He had to be intelligent and needed good judgement to achieve consensus. Unfortunately, the Saxons did not have any of these qualities. By their behavior they nurtured the natural weaknesses within Polish democratic process, which they opened to Russian and Prussian subversion.

Great and successful leaders of Poland, achieved as much power as they needed through personal skill and understanding of the workings of the Republic. It is clear that the task of governing, planning and execution of the foreign policy of the despotic rulers, was far simpler than it was for the parliamentary government of Poland. Under Saxon administration, the naturally unstable democratic process could not defend itself against subversion, by despotic regimes which surrounded the Republic. Their stability was based on a well organized coercion.

Swedish-Russian war and the anarchy brought to Poland by the Saxons, gave the opportunity to the Hohenzollerns of Berlin, to proclaim a new "Kingdom of Prussia" in Brandenburg with capital in Berlin. It was a new use for the name "Prussia." It indicated a hope of revival of the "Drang nach Osten," by recalling the conquest and the genocide of the Balto-Slavic Prussians, committed in the 13th century by the German Brethren of the Teutonic Order who were defeated in 1410 and disbanded in 1525, after secularization of Prussia. (Germans caused the extinction of the Prussian language.)

The Hohenzollerns hoped to take further advantage of the troubles, that the Polish Republic had with the Russian Empire, and at the same time to form a political entity, independent from the fragmented Holy Roman Empire, which was for them a bothersome legal fiction. They gambled and only narrowly escaped destruction, after their conquest of Silesia in 1740.

The Hohenzollerns of Berlin, built the cradle of modern German militarism, on land wrestled from the Slavs east of the Elbe River. There, over centuries, German colonists established themselves, but a majority of population remained of Slavic descent. It was gradually Germanized especially after the 1732 colonization program when the Berlin government resettled Protestant refugees from Salzburg, in East Prussia, and additional 300,000 Germans in Silesia and Pomerania.

Poland, the Slavic Athens, Wavering before the Russian Empire, Formed into a Sparta, by Peter the Great.

Collegium Nobilium founded in 1740, was the first to use teaching aides, globes, maps, experiments in physics etc. In 1747, opened in Warsaw, the first public library in Europe. It was a 400,000 volume library and 10,000 manuscript collection donated to the Republic by the Zaluski brothers (Andrzej, the bishop of Krakow, and Jozef, the bishop of Kiev). It was followed by the development of library science and bibliography.

In a new wave of political reformist publications, Stanislaw Konarski (1700-1773) published "On Effective Counsels" in 1760. It dealt with ways to overcome the decline of the Republic, and the anarchy fostered by Prussia and Russia, with the help of rebellious magnates often accepting foreign bribes, general corruption, mania of law suits and spread of lawlessness.

Hohenzollerns conquest of Silesia was made possible by severe taxing of Brandenburg and East Prussia, illegal tapping of the Polish Vistula grain trade, and by flooding Poland with counterfeit money.

The Kingdom of Brandenburg-Prussia was saved from destruction, by Polish rejection of the exchange of fertile southern lands, for the Mazurian lakeland, and the rest of East Prussia, (as the Germans renamed the original land of the Balto-Slavic Prussians.)

The Russian plan included a possibility of recovery of Silesia by Poland, in exchange for parts of Byelorussia. Silesia was originally an ethnic Polish province. It would have been a land bridge from Poland to Saxony; thus, improving the power position of Polish-Saxon union, a development difficult to achieve as Russia wanted to dominate, the Polish Republic.

Poles did not want to accept the Russian plan, because it would have strengthened the enforcement of Russia's protectorate over the Republic. Polish resistance against Russia not only saved the Hohenzollerns of Berlin from destruction, but actually gave them an opportunity to improve their position in fragmented Germany, and permitted them to return to the plans for destruction of the Polish Republic. The first step, was to separate Saxony from Poland, and then to provoke a series of Polish-Russian wars; each war giving a chance for robbery of Polish land by annexation.

The separation of Saxony from Poland was accomplished when a "Piast," (a native candidate) was elected to the Polish throne in 1764 as head of state, and chief executive of Polish Nobles' Republic. Stanislaw August Poniatowski was a patriot and a dedicated reformer, but not a soldier. He tried to avoid war with Russia and thought that a limited Russian domination over Poland was, for the moment, a lesser evil than a military defeat. He thought that with time an opportunity will present itself to regain full independence, once Poland's government and economy is strengthened.

During the seven year war (1756-63), Berlin was twice occupied by conquering armies; by Austrians in 1757 and by Russians in 1760. Peace treaty of 1763 stabilized the position of the new Kingdom of Prussia, and gave it a chance to return to anti-Polish activities. The bankrupt treasury in Berlin was restocked, by imposition of forced contribution on the northern Polish provinces, and again by flooding them with worthless counterfeits of the Polish currency.

The initiatives of the Berlin government were facilitated, by the wounded pride of the Poles, who felt that any degree of Russian domination, was a national disgrace. No democratic process could cope with the situation of Poland.

The Polish Republic could not compete with the absolute monarchies, which were surrounding and subverting her. No democracy can survive when confronted with absolute or totalitarian regimes determined to destroy it, once they achieve a critical level of subversion. Everywhere on earth, crooks can be found to betray their country to the enemies.

Berlin insidiously paralyzed the efforts of progressive and patriotic Polish leaders, and managed to provoke the wars of the three partitions of Poland (1768-1794).

The foreign subversion of Poland used five "eternal and invariable" principles to keep the Republic paralyzed. They were: 1. General elections by a rally of all voters, (usually near Warsaw) rather than voting by precincts; also participation of foreign candidates, and of foreign sponsored political parties, in the process of general elections, for the head of state and chief executive. 2. Permanence of the "Liberum Veto." 3. The right to renounce allegiance to the elected head of state. 4. Noble citizens' exclusive right to own land and hold state offices. 5. The control of the landowners over the peasant serfs (rather than rent paying tenant farmers).

Map: 1768-1772: War of The First Partition, Fought by the Confederacy Established in Bar, on the River Rov (Feb. 22, 1768). The Birth of Modern Polish Nationalism (the first in Europe).

Russian diversion encouraged a simultaneous outbreak of the rebellion "Kolishchizna," by Ukrainian Cossacks and peasants, known as "Haydamaks," against Catholic landowners and Jews. It was a protest against shift work or "koley," economic exploitation, and pressure to convert from Orthodox to Uniate Church. The mass killing of Catholics, Jews and Ukrainians culminated in the slaughter at Human, where thousands of Catholics and Jews, were murdered.

Total losses exceeded 200,000 people killed. Russia at first supported the Haydamak uprising, then fearing spread of it to the eastern Ukraine, switched to extremely bloody pacification against the Ukrainians. That campaign was jointly conducted by Russian and Polish troops, controlled by the Tsar.

Map: 1772 The First Partition of Poland During National Rebirth.

Map: 1773 The School System under the First Ministry of Education in Europe.

May 3, 1791 Constitution: the first modern and formal constitution in Europe, including for the first time, a voluntary extension of civil rights to towns people and in a more diluted form, to the peasantry; soon recognized as "more moderate than the French and more progressive than the Engilsh." (Edmund Burke, 1729-1797.)

A minister of the Berlin government, Ewald F. Hertzberg (1725-1795) reported on the Constitution of May 3. He called it the "Polish coupe de grace" to the Hohenzollern monarchy in Prussia.

Map: 1792-1793 - War of the Second Partition.

Map: 1793 - The Second Partition of Poland.

Despite their reforming zeal and patriotism, the Poles lost an uneven struggle. Their forces were sapped by protracted parasitic abuse by Saxony and Brandenburg, followed by provocations by the Berlin government. Subversion by the neighboring absolutist regimes, of the open parliamentary government of Poland and blocking of the passage of defense appropriations, were the main causes of defeat.

The abrupt fall of Polish civilization threw the Poles into a dark age of tyranny. Polish traditional government-from-below, controlled by provincial parliaments, was replaced by an oppressive rule from above by foreign governments. Thus, ended four centuries of a pioneering effort of the Poles to make a representative government work in the pluralistic society of the Commonwealth (1374-1569) and the Republic (1569-1795).

In a paradox of history the exponents of Enlightment, ignorant of the Polish history and values, became apologists for the crime of partitions, Voltaire was especially servile towards the despotic courts of Prussia and Russia. Poland, once the most tolerant of the great powers of Europe, became in her moment of crisis, a scapegoat for all the enemies of the Catholic Church, as well as for all flatterers and propagandists of the despots of Berlin, Moscow and Vienna.

The legacy of the First Polish Republic is a lasting contribution to development of representative government in Europe and in America.

Partitions of Poland did not have to happen. They were caused by parasitic growth at Poland's expense, of the Hohenzollerns of Berlin, who were the initiators of the crime of partitions. Without their initiative and provocations, Poland would have survived undivided, under Russian domination, until the Napoleonic campaigns. Then, in 1807 or in 1812, Poland could have declared in favor of France in war against Russia and thus, regain Polish independence.

Annihilation of Poland, had no precedent in modern European history. She was the only major European state which was a republic in an era of absolutism. Foreign subversion obstructed all attempts of reform. The immediate cause of the destruction of Poland, was not the anarchy but the struggle against it, and passage of reforms which could have rebuild the power position of Poland.

Anti-Polish conspiracy of Prussia and Russia, initiated by Berlin, took full advantage of the seeds of self-destruction present in all democracies. The love of liberty in Poland-Lithuania was exploited by Prussia and Russia, to bring the destruction of the Republic. This event robbed Poland of a normal progress during the 19th century.

Polish traditional ideals formulated in 15th and 16th century were shared by 18th century Americans. They were: the social contract between government and the citizens, the principle of government by consent, personal freedom and civil rights of the individual, freedom of religion, the value of self-reliance, general elections and prevention of authoritarian power of the state.

Chapter 5

CENTURY OF PARTITIONS 1795-1918
The Struggle for Independence.

Reopening of the Polish University of Wilno and College of Kamieniec. Polish educational levels were by far the highest within the Russian Empire.

1806 - Publication of a huge dictionary of the Polish language, which remained the most advanced among the Slavs, and was as developed as the German. Development of indigenous Polish scientific vocabulary in philosophy, mathematics, biology etc., especially by the Sniadecki brothers (Jan 1756-1830, Jedrzej 1768-1838).

Polish Legions in Italy, join the French revolutionary forces(1797-1803), in the "struggle for the rights of man," actually used to put down Italian revolts and losing 6,000 men in putting down a Negro revolt in Haiti 1802-3. Program for Polish national liberation by Jozef Pawlikowski, confiscated by the French police, immediately after publication in 1800. Legions' battle hymn, later become Poland's national anthem.

Exploitation by Napoleon of the Polish struggle for independence. Formation of an unfortunate Polish notion, that a decisive help for Poland would come from the West.

Poland's Napoleonic epic drew hundreds of thousands into the struggle for independence, and the heroism of Polish soldiers, partly redeemed the disgrace of the partitions. Napoleon's limited support and Polish military successes, restored confidence in efforts to regain national independence.

Russian victory brought confiscation of over 5400 manors (1 in 10) in Poland and Lithuania - 80,000 Poles were condemned to deportation - 254 political and military leaders were condemned to death - 10,000 Poles left the country forming the core of "The Great Emigration" - 2,000,000 rubles were collected in punitive taxes. Holy Alliance was strengthened and in 1832 the Pope condemned the uprising. The British did not protest against treatment of the Poles, in order to be consistent with their denial of the home rule in Ireland.

Poles participated in the Belgian revolution; called "Polish Knights of Liberty." General Jan Skrzynecki (1787-1860) was nominated Commander-in-Chief of the Belgian army. In 1836 Polish artillery men participated in the battle for Texas at San Jacinto.

The "organic work" spread as a legal activity in defense of Polish national culture and land ownership. Poles worked for eradication of illiteracy and for an increase of national consciousness, especially, in the Grand Duchy of Poznan, Silesia, Pomerania, Mazuria, and Warmia. Also in the Kingdom of Poland under Russia, and in Lesser Poland (Galicia) under Austria.

"Spring of the Nations" in Europe, brought demands for liberation from the German and Turkish yoke of western and southern Slavs. Poles demanded to convert the 1848 Slavic Congress of Prague into a "Slavic Parliament," in order to defend the Slavs against German expansion and subjugation, by governments of Berlin and Vienna.

The Poles protested against German aggressive policies, advocated by extremists in the parliament in Frankfurt, which was dealing with the plans for unification of Germany, after centuries of fragmentation. There, the ominous concept of German "Lebensraum" in the East, became a new version of the "Drang nach Osten." (It eventually was embraced by Hitler and caused World War II.)

Poles planned unification of the southern Slavs and Greeks, in a large Balkan federation of peoples freed from the Turkish and Austrian empires. The idea of a union of the southern Slavs and Greeks reappeared during World War II, as a part of General Sikorski's Confederation Plan, based on the Atlantic Charter, of nations between Germany and Soviet Union.

Positivist response to the failure of 1863-1864 uprising, brought organic work for social progress, through democratization, full emancipation of women and Jews, (whose situation seriously deteriorated after abolition of Jewish autonomy in 1795), educational reforms, and progress through science and technology. The culture for the masses was widely propagated in publications and literature.

1872 - Pact of Three Emperors or "Dreikaiserbund," was initiated by the Prussian Empire founded in 1871. It included Russia and Austria. The pact commemorated the centennial of successful beginning of the robbery of Polish territory in 1772-1795, and recommitted the participants to purge Polish presence from the cultural and political history of Europe. The Berlin government was hopeful that the common cause of subjugating the Poles, might continue to cement the weakening alliance of Prussia, Austria and Russia.

Germans were frightened that Russia was getting ready to play the "Slavic Card." The conglomerate Austrian Empire was particularly vulnerable having Slavs as a vast majority of its population. The Berlin government worried about its own Slavic population of the Sorbs or Vends of Lusatia, and above all of the Poles in Silesia, West and East Pomerania with Gdansk, Warmia, Mazuria and the entire Greater Poland centered on Poznania.

The short life of the German-Prussian Empire was to end in 1918, despite the high hopes that the annexation of one million square kilometers of the lands of the old Polish Republic would make the alliance of Austria, Russia and Prussia last "for ever."

1872 - "Kulturkampf" political program against Catholics, mainly Poles, was launched on the centennial of the partitions of Poland (1772-1795). The awareness that the unification of Germany was made possible by international pillage and obliteration of Poland, a major historical European state, and insecurity bred by long centuries of fragmentation, resulted in development of national megalomania in the new German-Prussian empire. This was strengthened by the traditional German fear of the Slavs and the memory of recent defeats by Napoleon.

Field Marshal Helmut von Moltke said "Prussia will be Polish or German, but it can not be both." The "Kulturkampf" propaganda and anti-Polish colonization programs, helped to prepare the ground for the eventual rise of Hitlerism.

Between 1797 and 1910, Polish provinces of Prussia underwent a reduction of Jewish population from 10 to 1.3 percent as the Berlin government kept on evicting the poor Jews (the "Betteljuden"), to central or "Russian" Poland, while permitting emancipation of the wealthy Jews (the "Schutzjuden"), especially, after 1883.

The assimilated wealthy Jewish minority was touched by the spirit of German megalomania, and soon developed a contempt for eastern Jews (the "Ostjuden"), living in the historic Polish lands within Russian Empire. The trickle of less affluent Jewish immigrants from the east, was made aware of this attitude, especially because they spoke the Yiddish version of German.

The Berlin government committed 995,000,000 marks to the program of German Colonization Commission in Polish provinces, for the purpose of expropriation of the Poles. German machinations were defeated by Polish solidarity, in cooperative economic action of self-defense.

Poles won the struggle for the land, and emerged with a net increase of their landholdings by the beginning of World War I. This was one of the causes of the "Ostflucht," or German flight from the Polish lands in the Prussian Empire. The "Ostflucht" was also caused by the growth of west German industry, financed by the plunder of France in the war of 1870-71, and the resulting demand for labor.

Greman anti-Polish excesses included, in 1901, public flogging, in Wrzesna, of school children for praying in Polish, rather than in German; protesting parents were jailed, up to two years. German "muzzle law" of 1908, forbade the use of the Polish language, in public programs and meetings. It caused widespread protests, including all Slavic deputies to the Austrian parliament, (Poles, Czechs, Ukrainians, Slovaks and Slovenes).

Chapter 6

THE SECOND POLISH REPUBLIC
Rebuilding of the Nation.

Poland's victory over the Soviets in 1920, during the revolution in Germany, delayed Communist advance into central Europe for a quarter of a century.

A chance to stabilize Europe, and prevent another world war failed, because of shortsightedness of Great Britain's underestimating the Soviet threat, and worry that France would have a strong ally in Poland.

Ignorance of the history of East-Central Europe, and traditional fear of France, led the British government under Lloyd George (1863-1945), to make pro-German and pro-Soviet decisions, which made World War II inevitable, and with it the disintegration of the British Empire.

Lloyd George never understood the facts and ramifications of the life and death struggle between the Soviets and the Poles. Ignorance and confusion in the Western capitals prevailed, concerning the situation on the Soviet-Polish front.

The Allies kept on destroying the stocks of German weapons, instead of turning them over to Poland, which in artillery alone was outgunned by the Soviets 3:1. The British had a notion "to kill Communism with kindness," and proclaimed a policy of "hands off Russia."

By 1920, Soviet army strength approached three million men - four times larger than that of the Polish forces. Hard-fought battles in Poland prevented the Soviets from continuing the grand march to the west, and bringing a decisive support to the German Communists in Berlin.

April 5, 1919 - Controversial execution of 34 Jews in Pinsk, as allegedly Soviet guerrillas, who killed one Polish soldier and severely wounded another. Strong criticism by Jews, especially Zionists; stating that Bolshevism is incompatible with Jewish national aspirations, and that the Polish soldiers over-reacted on the frontline at Pinsk. May 24, 1921 Polish Parliament passed a resolution number 1856, which called on the government to refer this matter to the military courts and to pay compensation to the families affected.

September 3, 1919: the Soviets formed the "Bureau of Illegal Acivities" for subversion, sabotage and disinformation behind Polish lines, using appeals of coerced Polish prisoners of war. The word "disinformation," entered Russian vocabulary some fifty years earlier then the English.

The concept of disinformation as an effective tool of subversion, matured in Russia during the successful efforts to subdue the First Polish Republic in the 18th century. Disinformation remains one of the basic tactics of Soviet Russia. (For example, in 1986 Soviet controlled press accused the United States of having produced the AIDS virus as a part of American biological arsenal.)

Soviet Strike Forces of 800,000 vs. 700,000 Poles.

Soviet Order of July 4, 1920 signed by Leon Trotsky: "To the West over the corpse of Poland on the road to worldwide conflagration."

Ukrainian aspirations for national independence were frustrated. They resulted in the killing in the Ukraine of some 70,000 Jews during the Russian revolution, and war against Poland. Widespread pogroms in the Ukraine occurred amid anti-Semitic slogans that "all Jews are Bolsheviks." Ukraine was the most important state in Pilsudski's federation plan. Unfortunately she lacked unity.

The Ukrainians gave only a weak support to the government of Semen Petlura (1877-1926), who was for the democratic federation with Poland. The horrible human losses in Soviet Collectivization Campaign and in the Terror Famine, could have been avoided, some ten years later, had the Ukrainians fully supported Hetman Petlura. They could have helped to make Pilsudski's federation a reality.

In the plebiscite in Mazuria, Warmia, and Powisle thirty counties voted for incorporation into Poland. Military control under the Allied Conference of Ambassadors, dominated by the government of Great Britain, permitted incorporation into Poland of only eight counties, while the other twenty two were assigned to Germany.

Lloyd George wanted Poland to be a weak ally of France. He did not understand the full implication of the Polish Soviet set up by Feliks Dzierzynski in Bialystok, with an obvious intent to move it to Warsaw and to convert all of Poland into a Soviet republic.

Lloyd George, with his narrow vision of Europe, could not perceive the magnitude of Soviet threat and instead he indulged in publicly insulting Polish envoys who were bringing to him the facts on the Communist march to the west.

Lloyd George was set on an anti-French and anti-Polish course and relied on advisers of similar orientation. Lord Curzon said that Lloyd George was "a bit of a Bolshevik himself." He managed to press the French to terminate their military credits for Poland.

July 10, 1920 Spa Conference of Allied Ambassadors proposed a demarcation line to serve as Polish-Soviet border - later known as the "Curzon Line." It included the entire region of Lwow (Lvov,Lviv) as a part of Poland.

On July 11 the decision of Spa was falsified in the office of Lloyd George. The proposed border line was redrawn to include Lwow in the Soviet Union. The proposal of the Allies was sent to Moscow from London in the falsified form.

Hitler-Stalin line of partition of Poland in 1939 was similar to the line used by Lloyd George in 1920. In 1945 it was convenient, for all parties who intended to recognize the Hitler-Stalin Line (also known as Molotov-Ribbentrop Line) to call it the "Curzon Line." Thus, the anti-Polish machinations by Lloyd George, were instrumental in acquisition

of Lwow by the Russian state for the first time in history. Lwow was for 600 years an important center of Polish culture. It was lost by Poland in 1945.

The road to Moscow was opened by the Polish Army. Lenin was suing for peace. Had the British turned over to the Poles, German arsenals, instead of destroying them, Pilsudski's federation would have been a reality. The probability of another world war would have diminished. Polish led federation of democratic states would have stretched from Finland to Armenia.

Pilsudski's federation would have included the industrial basins of coal and steel from Silesia, through Krivoy Rog, with one of the world's richest ore fields, to Donbas. It would have included the Ukrainian granary, the most valuable in Europe. It would have had enough strength to stabilize Europe. The western civilization would have been extended in freedom, in the Polish-Jagiellonian tradition, of a voluntary union of nations for peaceful cooperation and security.

The Poles had enough engineers and scientists to cooperate with the western capital and develop these assets as they did in Silesia. Polish military men have shown that they were capable to control the lands of the proposed federation if they had enough weapons.

Lloyd George stubbornly insisted to preserve Soviet and German strength as a part of his "balance of power." Blindly, he made World War II inevitable. When the French were not able to keep the British from turning the delta of the Vistula, (the main Polish river,) into a German dominated "free city of Danzig-Gdansk," the French marshal Ferdinand Foch (1851-1929) pointed to Gdansk and said that there will start the next world war. Unfortunately his was right.

The hope of George Clemenceau (1841-1929) that Poland be "a barrier against Russia and a check on Germany" was destroyed by Lloyd George, whose lame excuse was that he would "rather see Russia Bolshevik, than Britain bankrupt." He could not see that he was preparing the ground for World War II and the disintegration of the British Empire.

March 17, 1921 - The Constitution guaranteed general, equal, direct, secret, and proportional voting rights to everyone over 21 years of age including women (by election ordinance of November 26, 1918 - two years earlier than in the United States of America).

May (12-14, 1926) Coup d'etat by Marshal Jozef Pilsudski against corruption and for a stronger executive branch of the government, resulted in an authoritarian rule, which was formalized in the constitution of March 23, 1935 - an unsuccessful effort to follow the American Constitution, as a model in the precarious situation of Poland.

Meanwhile in the neighboring Ukraine, millions were killed by the Soviet military and police forces in the Collectivization Campaign (1928-1932), soon to be followed by the Terror Famine (1932-1933), in which even more millions were starved to death, as the Communist used hunger as a weapon to subjugate the Ukrainians, limit their number to a size manageable within U.S.S.R., and forestall the dream of an independent Ukraine.

Requests by Polish government to ship food to starving Ukraine were denied by the Soviets. Ukrainian representatives in the Polish Seym fought in vain, to help their starving brothers on the Soviet side of the border.

The Great Depression: Lack of investment capital brought rural unemployment to a near crisis level of 8,000,000 people, causing hunger strikes and outbursts of anti-Semitism. Seventy percent of Polish population was rural and thirty percent was urban. This ratio was reversed some 40 years later, after relocation of Poland west to the Oder-Neisse frontier, followed by a massive recon-

struction and industrialization which made Poland, in the early seventies, one of the ten most industrialized countries of the world.

1932-33: Breaking of the German "Enigma" code system by the Polish Intelligence. Developing of an electromechanical deciphering computer by linguists, mathematicians and engineers of the University of Poznan. The Polish built computer was successfully operating in 1938 and thus, it was the world's first.

Oct. 29, 1938 German police driving at gun point 13,000 Jews, who were Polish citizens, into the no man's land, between Germany and Poland. They survived the elements and hunger, thanks to food and shelter donated to them, by 6,000 Polish inhabitants of the town of Zbaszyn.

Total of 20,000 Polish citizens, mainly Jews, were evicted at gun point from Germany, after confiscation of all their property. It was a prelude to the "Kristallnacht" wave of massive pogroms in Germany, burning of synagogues, looting of stores, and severe beatings and mistreatment of thousands of Jews.

July 25, 1939. Poland gave England and France each a copy of the deciphering electromechanical computer, complete with specifications, perforated cards and updating procedures for reading German military code "Enigma." The solving of German "Enigma," eventually became the most important Polish contribution to the victory over Germany in World War II; it made possible the British "Ultra".

Poles were among the pioneers of computer science. They introduced the "Polish Notation" and "Reversed Polish Notation," now in common use in the computer industry. The Slavic word "robot" used for a mechanical man or brain - not always in a complementary sense - is accepted internationally. It was also introduced in a title of a Czech stage play. It is derived from the original Slavic word "robota" meaning "work."

The map includes signatures of Stalin, Molotov and Ribbentrop. It served as a basic document in delineation of the Hitler-Stalin Line to complete the German-Soviet pact of friendship and cooperation. The conclusion of Hitler-Stalin pact on Aug. 23, 1939 precipitated the attack on Poland and the beginning of World War II.

Deportations to Soviet Union included about 50 percent ethnic Poles, 30 percent Jews, while Ukrainian nationalists represented most of the remaining 20 percent. Of the 1,700,000 deported, 900,000 were dead by October 1942, including 15,000 Polish army and police officers mass murdered by the Soviets in April 1940.

Germans uncovered 4,200 of the executed Polish officers in the graves of Katyn. Today, Soviet statistics still show the effects of 1939-41 deportations; for example, they indicate the presence of some 50,000 Poles in Kazakhstan, which before the war did not have any Polish population.

1941 - Polish intelligence thwarted the German invasion of Sweden.

The United States not taking advantage of an opportunity to limit Soviet postwar power, opted instead for a division of the world, into "zones of influence." The United States, the only hope to preserve freedom in the world, underestimated Soviet expansionism; gradually abandoned postwar Poland and other nations lying between Germany and Russia, to Stalin's terror rule and degradation, to satellite status within the Soviet empire.

U.S. failed to form an alliance with a Confederation of democratic states, fearing the improbable revival of Hitler-Stalin partnership. Sikorski's Confederation represented a chance for the people located between Germany and Soviet Union, to live in freedom and true democracy in postwar Europe.

Dec. 10, 1942 A formal appeal to the United Nations, was made from London, by the Polish Government-in-Exile. It demanded "...effective and certain means of preventing the Germans from continuing...to mass murder (and)...systematically destroy the whole Jewish population in Poland, together with thousands of Jews transported into Poland from East and Central Europe as well as from the German Reich."

In 1942, the Polish government informed in detail, the governments of all civilized countries about the gas-chamber method, and all other means of extermination of the Jews, used by German authorities in occupied Poland.

The Polish Home Army organized several secret battalions among the inmates of Auschwitz for a joint action with allied's bombing, and/or paratrooper attack, which Poles requested in order to interrupt the mass killing of Polish Jewry.

The Jews represented some 90 percent of the two and half million people, sent directly to the gas chambers without entering the camp. But of the 340,000 who died in Auschwitz-Birkenau out of total of 404,000 inmates of many nationalities, a vast majority were Polish Christians.

World War II was not fought to save the Jews. Intelligence obtained for the United States by Allen Dulles in Switzerland, confirmed Polish reports on German genocide of the Jews, but the Western Allies decided to suppress them. They feared that these reports and focus on the enormity of Jewish tragedy, would actually help Nazi anti-Semitic propaganda in the West and weaken public resolve to fight the war. (The demographers estimated at 50 million the number of people killed in World War II, which was precipitated by the Hitler-Stalin partnership; the total Jewish losses were estimated at about six million.)

When the Nazis found a Jewish child in a Danish home, a monetary fine was imposed on the occupants; a similar event in Poland, resulted in the killing of the entire Polish family. When in Poland, Denmark, or anywhere in occupied Europe, a Jew was identified, he was murdered by the Nazis.

Nazis declared sub-human, Poland's Christians and Jews, and actually killed about the same number of each. However, if a Jewish baby had been taken by a Polish foster mother, it had an incalculably higher chance of survival, than if it stayed with its Jewish mother.

Thousands of Jewish children survived Holocaust with Polish families. When Jewish parents survived the war, sometimes they had to go to court to regain their children from adoptive parents, who wanted to keep them; many times the children wanted to stay with their adoptive parents, the only parents they knew. The postwar courts in Poland returned the children to their natural parents.

Nearly a quarter of a million small Polish Christian children were deported to Germany to be brought up as Germans. At the end of the war only 20 percent of them were recovered by their parents in Poland. Thus, there are today some 200,000 Germans, who do not know that they are Polish and possibly thousands of Poles who were not told that they were adopted Jews.

Robbery of Polish children was committed by the Nazis, in order to offset the effects of negative population growth in Germany. Decline of German population, threatened Hitler's expansion plans.

Diagram: Jews - 1000 Years in Poland: Immigration and Emigration.

Poland provided a sanctuary to the Jews in medieval and early modern Europe when they were threatened with extinction. Poland made possible the survival of the Jews as a nation, by giving them unique political and cultural autonomy for several hundred years.

Modern Jewish legal and governmental culture as well as educational system, philosophical concepts and religious beliefs, evolved in Poland in the 167h, 17th and 18th century. All this is overshadowed today by the tragic legacy of Nazi perpetrated genocide of the Jews (1942-1944), and the cruel Soviet rule using anti-Semitic provocations. The trauma has resulted in the extraordinary divorce of Polish and Jewish memory of last seventy years.

In a typical human reaction under extreme terror and cruelty, the victims often resent each other more than they do their common oppressors. Thus, the build-up of mutual resentments between Jews and Poles, makes their reconciliation almost impossible to achieve.

Few seem to realize that the offenses and transgressions across the ethnic boundary between Jews and Poles, are out of any proportion to the genocides and terror committed by the Nazis and the Soviets. Now, good will and dedicated effort are needed to remove this legacy of Nazi terror and Soviet cruelty, to overcome the resulting ethnocentric blight, and accept an honest common history of Poles and Jews.

Diag.: History of Yiddish in Poland - the Cultural Gap.

The medieval western anti-Semitism eventually culminated in the Nazi death camps. In comparison with the rest of Europe of the last 1000 years, Poland has by far the best record of toleration towards the Jews, as evidenced by mass migration of the Jews to Poland; even including in this perspective the most regrettable events of the thirties.

Germany is responsible for the breakdowns in morality within Polish and Jewish community under wartime Nazi terror. The Soviets produced such breakdowns in 1918-20, 1939-41 and from 1944 on. It should be noticed that many people in Poland behaved unusually well under Nazi and Communist terror.

Vast majority of the world's Jews lived in Polish lands for centuries. Generally, anti-Semitism in Poland had characteristics of a "normal" ethnic antagonism between people of different language and culture. For the last 1000 years Christianity's preoccupation with the Jews had far less drastic forms in Poland, than it did in other countries of Europe.

Political anti-clericalism of the democracy of Polish nobility virtually prevented the excesses of the Holy Inquisition. In 1552, 1562 and in 1565, the Seym passed laws which banned it from Poland. (In the 17th century alone, the Holy Inquisition in western Europe caused killing of about one million women accused of witchcraft.)

Map: May 11-18, 1944. Polish Victory at Monte Cassino, Italy.

Map: Aug.-Oct.1944 - Warsaw uprising - German and Soviet roles.

Deadly struggle between Germans and Soviets did not prevent them from joining hands against the Poles.

German atrocities in Warsaw were committed under the specter of oncoming total defeat. Historians see the battle of Stalingrad in 1943 as the culminating point in the 1000 years of German "Drang nach Osten," or push to the east against the Slavs, mainly Poles.

German defeat at Stalingrad, was engineered by Polish born Soviet marshal Konstanty Rokossowski (1896-1968). Stalin later groomed him to serve as Soviet viceroy in Poland. Stalin felt that years in prison of the Soviet secret police was a lesson which assured Rokossowski's reliability. (During the thirties, he was a victim in a massive purge of Soviet officers and of Polish Communists.)

Map: A.D. 1944 - The Agony of the Second Polish Republic.

Poland became the most important Soviet conquest of World War II, after Germany destroyed 40 percent of Poland's national wealth.

Western "benign neglect" of Poland, is reflected in the fate of all four wartime commanders-in-chief of the armed forces of the Second Polish Republic.

Marshal Edward Rydz-Smigly died in Warsaw in 1941, as one of the resistance leaders; after Great Britain and France did not fire a shot to help Poland during the 1939 campaign.

General Wladyslaw Sikorski, was killed in a sabotaged British airplane in 1943, while proposing a confederation of states between Germany and Russia, and demanding Red Cross investigation of mass murders of Polish officers in Soviet Union.

General Kazimierz Sosnkowski, was deposed under British pressure, in 1944 because of his protests against the sellout of Poland to the Soviets in 1943 at Teheran.

General Tadeusz Bor-Komorowski was made the last Commander-In-Chief of Polish Armed Forces of the Second Republic when becoming German prisoner of war. He could not protest in the West against Sovietization of Poland from his P.O.W. camp in Germany.

Chapter 7

THE THIRD POLISH REPUBLIC 1944-present
PEOPLE'S POLAND WITHIN SOVIET BLOC

Map: Apr.-May 1945: Polish Soldiers on All Fronts of Collapsing Germany; Civil War in Poland, New National Borders of 1945; Western betrayal of Poland.

The Soviet Union became de facto, the sole guarantor, of Poland's western frontier on the Oder-Neisse Rivers; the Polish border with Germany was reduced from 1200 to 287 miles.

Soviet commitment to make permanent the Oder-Neisse border, is based on a policy to prevent any expansion of German territory, unification of Germany, and formation of an anti-Soviet alliance of Germany and China. All this does not prevent the Soviets, from bluffing the Poles with a possible giveaway of Stettin to East Germany, while in reality the Soviets are constantly expanding their own advanced marine and air bases, in the delta of the Oder River and on nearby Ruegen Island.

Soviet leverage over Poland, is enhanced by German opposition to the Oder-Neisse border, such as the postwar anti-Polish propaganda program called "Heimatsrecht," which contained many overtones of the earlier "Kuturkampf" and "Lebensraum." The Poles perceive them as continuation of German "Drang nach Osten," which began 1,000 years ago, culminated in the battle of Stalingrad, and set off new waves of German "Ostflucht," or fight from the Slavic east.

The Polish-German reconciliation made some progress during the thirty five years after the war, amid efforts of Christian churches. Massive sending by private people in West Germany of food and medical supplies to Polish families occurred in the early eighties after breaking of Solidarity in Poland. Recent government statistics indicated that there are some 2,000,000 in West Germany, who are fluent in Polish as primary or secondary language. The very presence of these new people, influenced West German attitude towards Poland.

Map: 1945 - Death March in Brandenburg; a Small Part of the German Genocide of Three Million Polish Christians.

Death March in Brandenburg was conducted northwest of Berlin in the countryside still marked with ancient Polish-Polabian names in the common language of Polish and Elbe River Slavs. "Polabian" literally means the language of the Slavs who live on the Elbe River, where 1000 years ago began German "Drang Nach Osten," against the Slavs.

In 1945 the "Drang Nach Osten" ended on the Elbe River in the same area where it began. Its net effect was to weaken the Western Slavs and bring the domination by the Eastern Slavs all the way to the Elbe River. German dream of Hitlerian "Thousand Year Reich," or German expansion east for the next 1000 years, was coming to a bitter end.

German defeat generated history's largest "Ostflucht," or flight of the Germans from the historic Slavic lands. Some 5,000,000 Germans escaped accross the line of Oder-Neisse Rivers, which was becoming Poland's western frontier. They were running in front of the advancing Red Army, including two Polish "People's" Armies.

Evictions of Germans from eastern and central Europe followed, as was authorized, by Allied Control Commission (3,155,000 from Poland alone). Over three million Germans escaped west from East Germany, to seek freedom under American protection. Thus, well over ten million Germans were displaced across the Elbe River, in a gigantic chain reaction to German-Nazi mass murders and deportation of millions. It was the history's largest "Ostflucht," or German flight away from the historic Slavic lands.

Map: 1944-1947: Civil War and Gigantic Deportations, the People's Poland.
.... *p.216*

Poland was subjugated to a process of extermination by Hitler-Stalin partnership. Following Hitler's attack, Stalin changed his policy towards Poland from obliteration to conversion into a buffer state limiting German potential. Poland was deprived of sovereignty, and became a victim of Soviet exploitation and Sovietization process; crippling of Poland's leadership community and paralyzing of private initiative, which resulted in a low standard of living.

Soviet anti-Semitic provocations, especially in 1946 and in 1968, were designed to eliminate public support for Poland in the West; these provocations led the Poles to believe that there is an ongoing Soviet propaganda campaign, to assassinate Polish national character, and to spread in the West the notion that Poles are "extreme anti-Semites," and therefore that the Polish nation "deserves" the Communist oppression.

Preoccupation with the slanders against the Polish people, which resulted from anti-Semitism "Made in Russia," had the unfortunate effect of reducing the sensitivity of Polish public opinion to the actual anti-Semitism of Communist bureaucrats, or misguided individuals.

Map: 1945-1986: Demography of North-Western Poland, lands East of the Oder-Neisse acquired from Germany in compensation for lands lost to Soviet Union.
.... *p.217*

Germany destroyed 40 percent of Poland's national wealth. The wealth of the lands acquired from Germany was estimated at $9,500,000,000, and the wealth of the lands lost by Poland to the Soviets was estimated at $3,500,000,000, based on the dollar's value in 1945. The difference was used by the Soviets as an argument, to deny Poland direct payments for war damages by the defeated Germans

Territorial shift westward, enabled Poland to overcome debilitation caused by partitions (1795-1918), and helped in rebuilding the war torn country. The Church provided the unifying force among diverse resettled Polish groups. These provinces are now a fully integrated part of Poland.

The full extent of the integration into Poland of the lands acquired from Germany, is well documented by the fact that in 1980 Solidarity was born there. This extraordinary massive labor and patriotic social movement spread throughout Poland, with phenomenal speed and included fourteen million people; ten million in urban and industrial areas and four million in rural areas, (or nearly 40 percent of the population in 1980).

The nonviolent Solidarity was committed to ease the totalitarian grip of the regime controlled by the Soviets, and to rebuild the economy and ecology brought to catastrophic conditions by the Communists.

Martial law imposed in December 1981, together with delegalization and persecution of Solidarity by the Soviet-controlled regime brought further economic decline.

An ineffectual economic reform was passed by the Seym in January 1982. It ruled that all enterprises would operate on the basis of self-management, independence and self-financing. Soon, it was followed by some 12,000 ministerial and parliamentary decrees, which paralyzed it.

In 1986, Poland's industrial production fell below 40 percent of capacity; the inflation was estimated at 20 percent. Frequent and sudden price rises exasperated the public, and bred suspicion that the Soviets are ordering them, in order to derail the political activity of the opposition.

The private farmers provided the only bright spot as the most productive segment of Poland's economy. Their achievements, resulted primarily from plentiful harvests rather than from any helpful government policy. Severe winter of 1986/87 threatens to end the spell of good harvests.

Cancellation of the planned Foundation for Aid to Private Farmers in Poland, was ordered in 1986 by the Soviets. This further hurts the prospects of Polish agriculture. The proposed foundation was a form of foreign aid. It was to be conducted by the Catholic Church and was initiated by Pope John Paul II.

The government of General Wojciech Jaruzelski is trying to follow Gorbachev's "glasnost" or openness, in Polish "jawnosc" (yav-noshch). However, the ruling neo-feudal elite, the corrupt Nomenclatura of several hundred thousands, long known as the "new class of exploiters," defends its privileges and opposes the needed reforms. Further catastrophic decline of the economy, threatens to degrade Poland into an under-developed country.

Poland's situation in winter 1986/87, became so desperate that the government quit hiding the facts of the economic disaster, and might have to quit persecuting the opposition. In December 1986 almost all political prisoners were released. The Poles wondered when they will be re-arrested, as happened after previous "amnesties." It is just possible, that extent the of economic crisis might drive the Communists to allow for some degree of opposition, in order to rebuild the economy of Poland.

General Jaruzelski, is considered by an increasing number of Poles, including leaders of Solidarity, to be more intelligent, better educated and better informed than the previous Soviet viceroys in postwar Poland, (their usual title was a "secretary" or guardian of of Communist Party secrets). He assembled the best team of experts. However, while he is consolidating his political power and has Gorbaczev's support, the corruption and an underground economy is spreading.

The ecology crisis deepened. Poland's air is among the most polluted in the world. One third of the population lives under an impending ecologic disaster (covering some ten percent of Poland's area). Water is toxic, to the point of affecting the health of the entire population.

Life expectancy, especially among men, dropped in 1986 to the lowest level in Europe, and the natural population growth dropped to 7 per 1,000 which is the lowest in postwar Poland. Infectious diseases, especially among children, are on a steep increase. The number of narcotic addicts is growing alarmingly. Alcohol and tobacco consumption is at a very high level, contributing to the general decline of health of Polish population.

It is clear that in 1980, Solidarity was a reaction to the deepening crisis. It opposed Sovietization of Poland, and the crippling subjugation to Communist dictatorship, of the so called "three way masters" who are striving to impose total control, (1) over people's world-view and creeds, (2) over all political activity and (3) over the entire economic life of the country.

Solidarity exposed the illegality of Communist government, its actions "above the law" and enforcement of Sovietization by methods of organized crime. Solidarity exposed the sham of Communist party's claim that it is "a servant of the working class." In reality it was its oppressor, ready at any moment, to enforce its dictatorship by using the brutal "Zomo" police forces. These forces included many criminals, for whom serving of prison sentences were substituted, with the service in the "Zomo" riot police.

Solidarity stood for the respect of human dignity and for loyalty to Poland's democratic ideals.

Map: 1986 - The Polish People's Republic - within the Soviet Bloc, while Culturally a part of Western Civilization; Resisting Sovietization (population numbers of European countries).
.... *p.218*

Poland and the rest of East-Central Europe is treated by the United States as a peripheral problem. Its surrender by Roosevelt, to the Soviets did not buy security for the United States; in fact it escalated U.S. defense expenditures, as the Soviet Union became a superpower. It is clear that the United States is in no position to challenge militarily the Soviet hegemony over Poland, and most of Eastern Europe.

The built-in economic inefficiency of Soviet totalitarianism permits the United States together with Western Europe and Japan, to win the global contest, by driving the competition into a race of technology and economy which the Soviets have to lose, unless they reform by decentralizing and turning to a market economy. This would slow down Soviet expansionism and prevent their use of economic hardship, as one of the means of subjugating people.

The West, led by the United States, could make conditional the continuous extension of badly needed commercial credits, and sales of technology to the Soviets. The condition for these ongoing transactions, should be a steady progress of the Communists, in allowing more freedom in Poland and other countries of East-Central Europe.

In 1986, the dynamic equilibrium of the economic strength in the world turned precarious as the United States government debt exceeded $2,100,000,000,000 and the consumer debt reached $580,000,000,000; while the noncommercial consumer mortgages were at $1,500,000,000,000. The international debt of about $1,000,000,000,000 (mostly held by the U.S.) is mainly owed by the third world countries, many of them unable even to pay the interest charges.

In 1986, in proportion to the gross national product of $4,200,000,000,000, the indebtness of the United States was not yet critical. However, the unstable economic equilibrium is evident when the effects of the negative balance in the international trade, are considered together, with the eventually inevitable increase in the rates of interest. The U.S. is the world's largest debtor nation, and the center of world's financial strength is shifting towards Japan.

In some aspects of technology of the Strategic Defense Initiative, the Soviets maybe ahead of the United States. This brings to mind, an old Polish military maxim, which states that "a projectile is superior to an armor," (or "pocisk ma przewage nad pancerzem," po-cheesk ma pshe-va-gan nad pan-tze-zhem). This means that effective offensive weapons, are soon available, once the defense is known. Generally, offensive weapons cost less, than does the corresponding defense.

The great value of the S. D. I., for the United States, is in the fact, that the very existence of such

defense, seriously reduces the chances of Soviet first strike, aimed at the elimination of American retaliatory forces.

Soviet expertise in subversion of democracies should be recognized; it is based on Russia's long experience in dealing with Polish democratic process, beginning with the First Republic (1569-1795). The Soviets are using the same methods, with ever greater skill, to eliminate democracies. The continuity of Russian imperial policies is evident; even today in the Soviet Union the archives of tsarist foreign service are guarded as state secrets.

Map: 1018-1987: The Range of Territorial Change of the Polish State in the Second Millenium A.D.

.... *p.219*

TABLE OF INTERNATIONAL DEBTS ILLUSTRATING FINANCIAL SITUATION OF POLAND							
Global debt in millions of dollars in 1984		Per capita debt in dollars in 1984		Ratio of debt to Gross National Product in 1983		Ratio of debt to export in 1983	
Poland	26,799	Poland	722	Poland	36.6%	Poland	4.41
Brazil	105,390	Israel	5014	Israel	94.4%	Egypt	8.24
Mexico	94,692	Chile	1757	Chile	89.9%	Morocco	5.54
S.Korea	44,382	Venezuela	1657	Egypt	85.7%	Argentina	5.24
Argentina	44,347	Greece	1590	Morocco	72.3%	Brazil	4.49
Indonesia	32,735	Argentina	1494	Peru	69.2%	Mexico	4.43
Venezuela	28,681	Portugal	1396	Argentina	67.0%	Peru	4.27
Egypt	28,199	Mexico	1262	Mexico	55.5%	Israel	4.00
India	26,575	S.Korea	1109	S.Korea	53.6%	Colombia	3.81
Turkey	24,091	Malaysia	1107	Malaysia	50.6%	Turkey	3.73
S.Africa	22,700	Hungary	993	Venezuela	47.1%	Greece	3.38

The international debt of Poland is on the increase, as the unpaid interest charges augment it each year. It reached $32,000,000,000, at the beginning of 1987. At the same time Poland's indebtness to the Soviets, is equivalent to eight billion dollars, making a total of $40 billion of Polish foreign debt. The Soviets use their political leverage to press Poland harder than they do the other satellites, and of course much harder than the western creditors. Thus, the pact signed in Moscow on May 4, 1984 spells out virtual absorption of Poland economy by Soviet Union, by the year 2000.

"Brain drain" to U.S.S.R. is formalized in direct Soviet agreements with 96 Polish institutions of higher learning concluded by an "intergovernmental commission." These agreements work through joint projects - jointly financed but shifting an increasing number of Polish engineers and scientists to the Soviet payroll. On January 4, 1987 a pact was signed in Moscow, by political rather than cultural representatives. It spells out

the terms of cultural and scientific exploitation of Poland, through "cooperation."

Soviet cultural invasion of Poland is on the increase. Early 1987 press reports indicated that one third to one half of prime time television viewing in Poland, (6 pm to 10 pm daily), will be soon in original version in Russian. The Soviets will see to it that their programs are more attractive than those locally transmitted. They will show a better quality of films, sports, theater, opera and ballet than will be shown on the Polish channels at the same time.

Sovietization of Poland goes on by political, economic and cultural penetration and with it the enforcement of Soviet-style neo-colonialism. Nomenclatura or the neo-feudal ruling elite, is paid with privileges, for enforcing Soviet domination of Poland. This domination goes on "without ever technically breaking" Roosevelt's executive agreements. Admiral Leahy predicted this during the surrender of Poland to the Soviets at Yalta in 1945.

APPENDIX
PREHISTORY AND LANGUAGE EVOLUTION
"Languages are the pedigrees of nations."
Dr. Samuel Johnson, (1709-1784)

LANGUAGE FORMATION
IN GEOGRAPHIC ISOLATION

Diagram: The Range of the Theories on Language and European Migrations.

Prehistory and History of the Indo-European Languages Leading to Modern Polish.

Diagram: The Indo-European Language Family and the Satem-Centum Divide.

Linguists believe, that the beginning of the evolution of Indo-European languages, occurred some 25,000 years ago, in a landlocked area, north of the Caspian Sea.

Indo-Europeans were present in Neolithic central Europe some 6,500 years ago. Indo-European language families originated during this period; agriculture developed and animals were domesticated. The division of the Indo-European language family into Eastern or Satem and Western or Centum, apparently originated in Neolithic period. This resulted in a linguistic division, which today is shown in every major dictionary.

Irano-Arian conquest of the subcontinent of India, brought the Indo-European languages to southern Asia in the second millennium B.C., but did not replace completely the local cultures. Such replacement occurred some 3,000 years later, when the so-called "Neo-Europes" were created.

In the second millennium A.D., the Europeans conquered both Americas, Australia and New Zealand and replaced local cultures and languages with their own. It was an environmental invasion involving transplantation of European plants, insects, animals, as well as germs and parasites causing infectious diseases. The initial conquest by force of arms, was followed by biological assault of epidemics on a "virgin soil" which led to decimation and even eradication of native populations.

Today the Indo-European language family is the world's largest as a result of the two waves of conquest some 3,000 years apart.

Diagram: The Slavs among Indo-Europeans.

Diagram: Arrival of the Indo-Europeans - The Migration Resulting in an East/West or Satem/Centum Interphase.

Apparently the East/West or Satem/Centum interphase stayed in about the same location in Europe for more than 4,000 years.

Map: 8500 BC. Beginning of Agriculture.

Map: 4500 BC. First Indo-Europeans in Neolithic Europe.

Map: 2800 BC. Indo-European Expansion within Neolithic Cultures.

Map: 1900 BC. Geographic Isolation of Language Sub-families. East/West Interphase of language subfamilies Balto-Slavic, Germanic etc. (Copper Age)

Map: 1600 BC. Bronze Age Indo-European East/West Interphase.

Map: 1300 BC. Lusatian and Dnieper Bronze Age Cultures the Genesis of the Slav Peoples.

First European urnfield cemeteries by the Western Slavs in Luzyce (woo-zhi-tse) (Luzyce = Lusatia = Lausitz).

Indigenous ancient Western Slavic belief that the fire of cremation insures the union with eternal fire of the sun, and gives the deceased life after death.

Map: 1200 BC. West Slavic Urnfield Burials Spread to the Celts.

Map: 1000 BC. Expansion of the Western Slavs and Illyrians.

Map: 700 BC. Migration: Irano-Scyths the Nomadic Horsemen.

Map: 550 BC. Beginning of the Iron Age of the Slavs.

Map: 470 BC. Biskupin Island Fortress: 550-450 B.C.

Continuing of geographic isolation of the Balto-Slavic and Germanic Peoples. Slavic-Germanic border on the central Elbe River and near Oder Delta; arrival of Irano-Sarmatians.

FOREIGN INVASIONS AND SLAVIZATION OF THE INVADERS

Slavic staying power: well formed language and agricultural techniques; evolution of Slavic military democracies.

Roman army defeated and subjugated the Germanic tribes. Forced settling of Germanic tribes in Gaul, and forced Romanization of Germanic tribes in Gaul, resulted in the beginning of French language.

The name of East Goths was changed, while in transit through the Slavic territory, from Germanic "Ostar" to the Slavic word "Ostro," hence "Ostrogoths," which has a connotation of aggression. In all Slavic languages the word for a German or "Niemiec" (ne-myets) means "speechless" or "dumb." This reflects the difficulty of language communication between Slavs and Germans. A Slav, on the other hand, is called "Slowianin" (swov-ya-neen) which means a "master of words" or a "master of speech" - a person communicating by means of a spoken language (see text for discussion of the ethnocentric character of names of peoples.)

Sarmatian Migrations: 400 B.C.-A.D. 540; Sarmatian "Tamga" signs later used in heraldic designs in a number of Polish coats-of-arms.

FORMATION OF THE SLAVIC STATES AND EARLY CHRISTIANIZATION

Poland in the middle ground formed by language and alphabet interphase.

Index of Poland: a Historical Atlas

POLAND IN EAST-CENTRAL EUROPE - GROWTH DESPITE ADVERSITY

EAST-CENTRAL EUROPE - A HISTORIC IDENTITY

East-central Europe consists of the region east of Germany to the furthest limits of the influence of western Christianity, east of which the Russian Orthodox domain extends, characterized by cultural retardation, conservatism and servility towards state authorities.

Poland provided the main organizational basis for the history of east-central Europe - a pluralistic unity between Romano-German and Greco-Slavic worlds.

Polish historian Oskar Halecki, formulated the historic perspective of Europe in terms of western, west-central, east-central and eastern European regions. He felt that the Mediterranean epoc ended with the Arab expansion. It was followed by the north-western European period also known as the Respublica Christiana. Culturally, Poland was a part of the medieval Respublica Christiana. Halecki defined Europe as a continent of great diversity, enriched by the civilizing role of Christianity, which brought to it the cultural legacy of Greece and Rome of antiquity.

East-central Europe felt the Byzantine influence until the formation of Polish-Lithuanian Commonwealth in the north and the Turkish Empire in the south. After Poland and Turkey exhausted each other in the seventeenth century, Russia became the next dominant power center. The conglomerate Austrian state played a transitional and much less important role.

PRECARIOUS GEOGRAPHY

The short period of German unification and leading technological achievement (1871-1945) brought to east-central Europe the catastrophy of both World Wars and the conversion of the Great Russian Empire into a new and dominant center, namely the Soviet superpower.

Ethnic cultures appear to be indestructible everywhere in Europe, and especially in east-central Europe. There, in the middle ground between the great colonial expansion, bounded on the west by the maritime empires and on the east by the Eurasian continental Russian empire, the overlapping ethnic groups grew in conflicts stimulated by imperial policies of "divide and rule." A climate of adversity was stimulated during the last one hundred years by the growth of modern nationalisms.

The adversities faced by the Polish people reflect Poland's geography and her commitment to the western civilization. The precarious situation of Poland could not be ameliorated despite common defense alliances or the obvious common interests in freedom and in the representative form of government. This situation lasted ever since the Napoleonic wars.

ALLIANCES IN A BAD FAITH

Recently, in 1920, Poland single-handedly (with more hindrance than help from the West) delayed for a quarter of a century the expansion of Soviet Communism into eastern and central Europe. The common defense alliance with Great Britain and France led to bitter fighting in the Polish campaign of 1939 while western allies did not fire a shot in defense of Poland; instead they acted as if their purpose was to produce a direct physical contact between Germany and Soviet Union, over the dead body of Poland, with a hope that a war of mutual attrition between Hitler and Stalin would result.

The opportunity for an alliance with a Polish led federation of east-central Europe was wasted when the Soviets were weak and under German attack. In 1943 in Teheran, secret agreements between Roosevelt, Churchill and Stalin spelled out the loss of independence of Poland and most of east-central Europe as well as the recognition of the Hitler-Stalin Line on the Bug River as Soviet western border. Postwar Poland and most of east-central Europe was to belong to the Soviet zone of influence enforced by Stalin's terror apparatus. Later in Yalta and Potsdam the Teheran agreement was implemented.

SOLIDARITY

Poland's growth despite adversity is evident in the demographic record and in the fact that in the early 1970's Poland became one of the world's ten largest industrial states. In 1980 the rise of the Solidarity mass movement in Poland was an important contribution to the cause of freedom everywhere. Solidarity exposed to the world the sham of the claim that Soviet-Communist parties are "servants of the working class."

Solidarity was committed to ease the totalitarian grip of the regime controlled by the Soviets, and to rebuild Poland's economy and ecology, brought to catastrophic conditions by the Communists. In 1981 the Soviets ordered military take over and enforcement of a "state of war" in Poland in order to break the Solidarity movement. The West responded by imposing economic sanctions.

The sanctions were directed primarily against Poland and had practically no effect on the Soviets, who ordered the break up of Solidarity. The Polish economy, already bogged down with international debts, suffered a fall of industrial production to less than 40% of capacity and faced a decline to a level of an underdeveloped country. In the aftermath of sanctions, the Soviet Bloc was weakened slightly. The Polish people paid for this weakening with an economic catastrophe and exhaustion.

Solidarity not only exposed the truth of the Soviet version of socialism, it also accelerated Soviet moves towards reforms. The Polish people had to pay dearly for their struggle for freedom and human dignity. The waste of the Polish renaissance in the form of Solidarity left Polish people tired, depressed and hemorrhaging with massive emigration and brain drain.

SOVIET "NATIONAL COMMUNISM"

The Soviet Union is in another wave of modernization under the leadership of Gorbachav and national-communists who intend to continue using the Soviet system as a vehicle of Russian imperialism. To be a reliable Russian one has to have at least one Russian parent. There are many candidates for inclusion into the Great Russian nation. In the state-wide Soviet military establishment the Slavs represent 90% of the officers of higher rank. Most of the non-commissioned officer are Ukrainians.

In the Ukraine a recent meeting of 200 leaders of the Young Communist League produced 97% of speeches in Russian and only 3% in Ukrainian. This reflects the proportion of Russian and Ukrainian languages used in schools in the Ukraine today. However, the Russian population is not growing fast enough to keep up with the on-going expansion into the cold reaches of the Soviet north-east and also to procede efficiently with the Russification program.

The Soviets tolerate some Polish cultural life in Lithuania and Byelorussia as an irritant to the local nationalism to act as a decoy for the Sovietization program. In the Soviet Union the Polish ethnic minority of about one and half million is discriminated against because of their traditional Roman Catholic affiliation with the western civilization and their strong pro-western orientation.

Poland, the most important Soviet conquest in World War II, has a special place in the plans of the national-Communists. It is the only nation which has enough stamina to grow in the adverse conditions of the Soviet satelliteempire. With the shortage of Russians to satisfy their program within the Soviet Union, Soviet national-communists view Poland and her growing population as a future junior partner in the west, on the German border, the principal front of the East-West confrontation.

"FINLANDIZATION" OF GERMANY

There is no room for an independent Poland in Soviet plans - only a reduction of coercion in exchange for usefulness in the world's main strategic area of Poland and Germany. Soviet commitment to make permanent the Polish-German border on the Oder-Neisse Line is based on a policy to prevent any expansion of German territory, unification of Germany, and formation of an anti-Soviet alliance of Germany and China.

The Soviets view West Germany as a willing candidate for "Finlandization," ready to keep supplying money and technology and devoid of any will for confrontation with the Soviet Union. German attitude towards Poland's Solidarity seems to substantiate this Soviet view. Even more important is the German view that an atomic exchange in the European theater would be 80% in both Germanies and 20% in Poland, Czechoslovakia, Denmark, etc. Amid German demographic decline the neutralist feelings are fed by fear of "extermination without representation."

"FUNCTIONALITY" OF POLAND

Ever since Hitler invaded Russia the notion of functionality of Poland in the Soviet scheme led to varying degrees of Communist toleration of the Polish Catholic Church. The Soviets would like to exploit the Church's attitude on peace, birth control, social justice and charity as well as its objections to capitalism. They noticed that the great Cardinal Wyszynski said that Poland could in the future support a population of 70 million people.

Legalization of political opposition in Poland and other satellites could be demanded by the West as a price for stopping the arms race. In recognition of the fact that the West is technologically and economically the stronger party, such legalization would guarantee reduction of Soviet pressure on NATO. Instead, the West acts as the weaker party. So far, the Soviet Union is the main beneficiary of the arms control negociations. The discontinuity of policies, the often subverted peace movement and disunity weaken western bargaining positions.

The birth rates in most of Europe are declining. Poland, however, continues to have the stamina to grow in population despite, or because of, the adversities which surround her.